TOKYO MEW MEW

MIA IKUMI & REIKO YOSHIDA

VOLUME FIVE

TOKYOPOP®

LOS ANGELES • TOKYO • LONDON

ALSO AVAILABLE FROM ◎ TOKYOPOP®

**For more
information visit
www.TOKYOPOP.com**

10103

MANGA

.HACK//LEGEND OF THE TWILIGHT
@LARGE
A.I. LOVE YOU February 2004
AI YORI AOSHI January 2004
ANGELIC LAYER
BABY BIRTH
BATTLE ROYALE
BATTLE VIXENS April 2004
BIRTH May 2004
BRAIN POWERED
BRIGADOON
B'TX January 2004
CARDCAPTOR SAKURA
CARDCAPTOR SAKURA: MASTER OF THE CLOW
CARDCAPTOR SAKURA: BOXED SET COLLECTION 1
CARDCAPTOR SAKURA: BOXED SET COLLECTION 2
  March 2004
CHOBITS
CHRONICLES OF THE CURSED SWORD
CLAMP SCHOOL DETECTIVES
CLOVER
COMIC PARTY June 2004
CONFIDENTIAL CONFESSIONS
CORRECTOR YUI
COWBOY BEBOP: BOXED SET THE COMPLETE
  COLLECTION
CRESCENT MOON May 2004
CREST OF THE STARS June 2004
CYBORG 009
DEMON DIARY
DIGIMON
DIGIMON SERIES 3 April 2004
DIGIMON ZERO TWO February 2004
DNANGEL April 2004
DOLL May 2004
DRAGON HUNTER
DRAGON KNIGHTS
DUKLYON: CLAMP SCHOOL DEFENDERS
DV June 2004
ERICA SAKURAZAWA
FAERIES' LANDING January 2004
FAKE
FLCL
FORBIDDEN DANCE
FRUITS BASKET February 2004
G GUNDAM
GATEKEEPERS
GETBACKERS February 2004
GHOST! March 2004
GIRL GOT GAME January 2004
GRAVITATION
GTO

GUNDAM WING
GUNDAM WING: BATTLEFIELD OF PACIFISTS
GUNDAM WING: ENDLESS WALTZ
GUNDAM WING: THE LAST OUTPOST
HAPPY MANIA
HARLEM BEAT
I.N.V.U.
INITIAL D
ISLAND
JING: KING OF BANDITS
JULINE
JUROR 13 March 2004
KARE KANO
KILL ME, KISS ME February 2004
KINDAICHI CASE FILES, THE
KING OF HELL
KODOCHA: SANA'S STAGE
LAMENT OF THE LAMB May 2004
LES BIJOUX February 2004
LIZZIE MCGUIRE
LOVE HINA
LUPIN III
LUPIN III SERIES 2
MAGIC KNIGHT RAYEARTH I
MAGIC KNIGHT RAYEARTH II February 2004
MAHOROMATIC: AUTOMATIC MAIDEN May 2004
MAN OF MANY FACES
MARMALADE BOY
MARS
METEOR METHUSELA June 2004
.METROID June 2004
MINK April 2004
MIRACLE GIRLS
MIYUKI-CHAN IN WONDERLAND
MODEL May 2004
NELLY MUSIC MANGA April 2004
ONE April 2004
PARADISE KISS
PARASYTE
PEACH GIRL
PEACH GIRL CHANGE OF HEART
PEACH GIRL RELAUNCH BOX SET
PET SHOP OF HORRORS
PITA-TEN January 2004
PLANET LADDER February 2004
PLANETES
PRIEST
PRINCESS AI April 2004
PSYCHIC ACADEMY March 2004
RAGNAROK
RAGNAROK: BOXED SET COLLECTION 1
RAVE MASTER
RAVE MASTER: BOXED SET March 2004

10103

Translator - Ikoi Hiroe
English Adaptation - Stuart Hazelton
Contributing Editors - Bryce Coleman and Nora Wong
Retouch and Lettering - Norine Lukaczyk
Cover Layout - Patrick Hook

Senior Editor - Julie Taylor
Managing Editor - Jill Freshney
Production Coordinator - Antonio DePietro
Production Manager - Jennifer Miller, Mutsumi Miyazaki
Art Director - Matthew Alford
Director of Editorial - Jeremy Ross
VP of Production & Manufacturing - Ron Klamert
President & C.O.O. - John Parker
Publisher & C.E.O. - Stuart Levy

Email: editor@TOKYOPOP.com
Come visit us online at www.TOKYOPOP.com

A ⊙ **TOKYOPOP**® Manga

TOKYOPOP Inc.
5900 Wilshire Blvd. Suite 2000
Los Angeles, CA 90036

Tokyo Mew Mew Vol. 5

ISBN: 1-59182-548-2

First TOKYOPOP® printing: January 2004

10 9 8 7 6 5 4 3 2 1
Printed in the USA

TOKYO MEW MEW

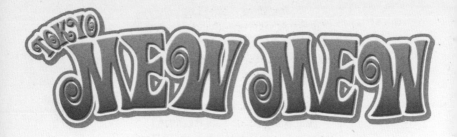

TABLE OF CONTENTS

About this story

Ichigo Momomiya was a normal junior high school student until a freak accident turned her into superhero Mew Mew! Ichigo and her partners are working hard to save the world!

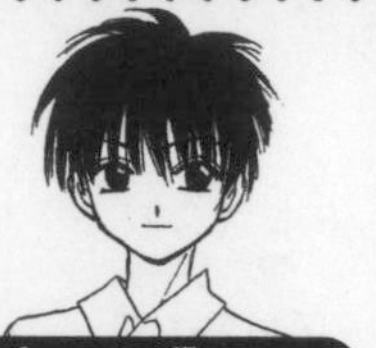

Masaya Aoyama

He's cute, smart and popular! Even better, he's on the kendo team!

CAFE MEW MEW

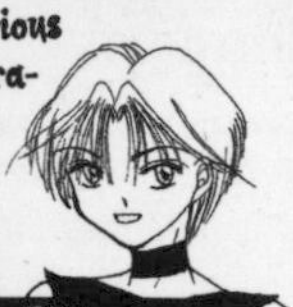

A mysterious and ultra-wealthy high school student.

Ryou Shirogane

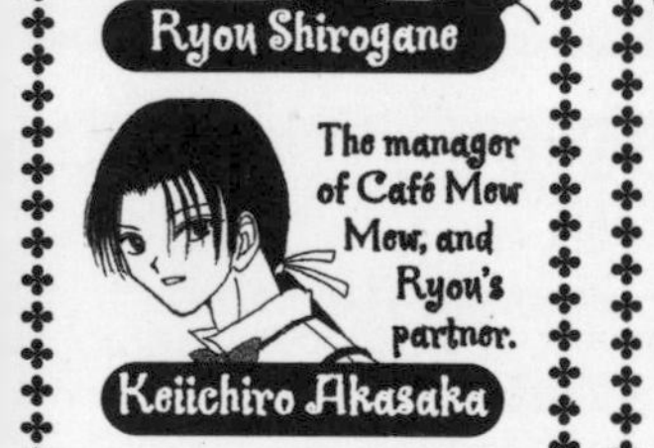

The manager of Café Mew Mew, and Ryou's partner.

Keiichiro Akasaka

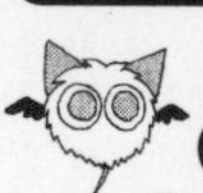

Masha

Ryou's pet robot.

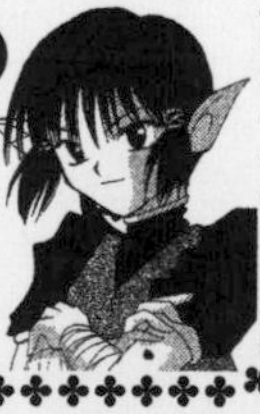

Kish

One of the aliens attacking Earth.

TOKYO MEW MEW

◀ pre-transformation ▼ post-transformation

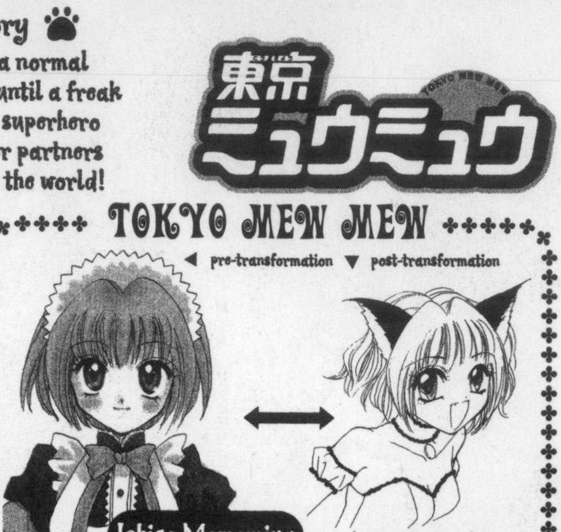

Ichigo Momomiya (Mew Ichigo)

I have a huge crush on Masaya, and I'm in seventh grade. I've been fused with the genes of an Iriomote Cat.

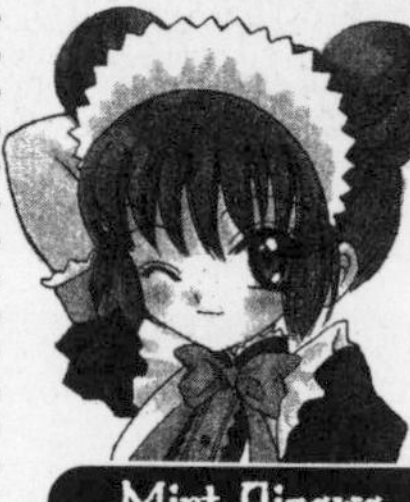

Mint Aizawa (Mew Mint)

A wealthy girl with a totally sarcastic personality.

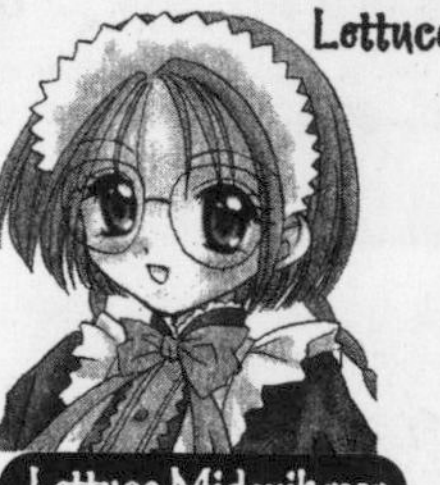

Lettuce Midorikawa (Mew Lettuce)

A sweet and gentle girl, though she's a tad shy.

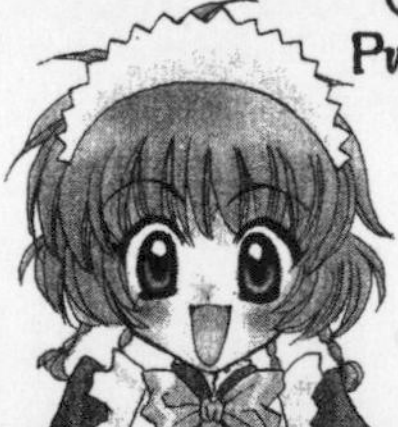

Pudding Fong (Mew Pudding)

She's acrobatic, loves to perform and make money.

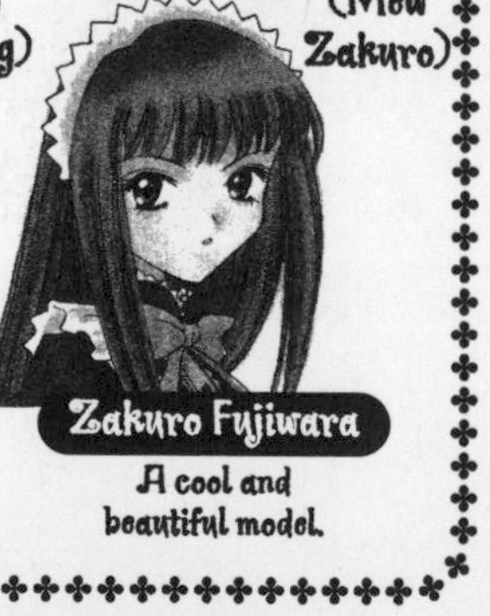

Zakuro Fujiwara (Mew Zakuro)

A cool and beautiful model.

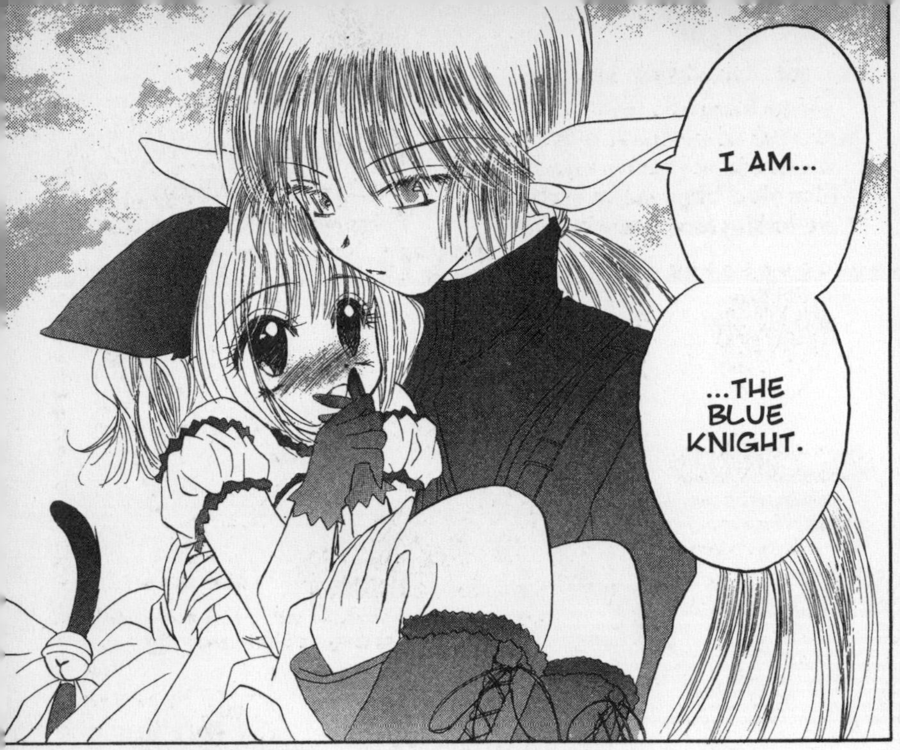
I AM...
...THE BLUE KNIGHT.
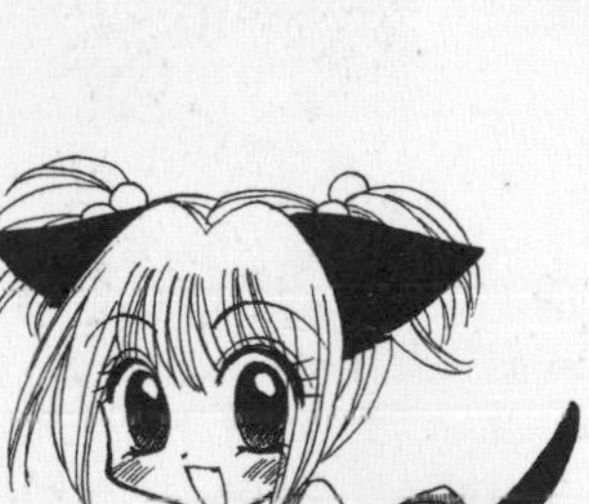

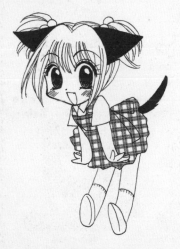

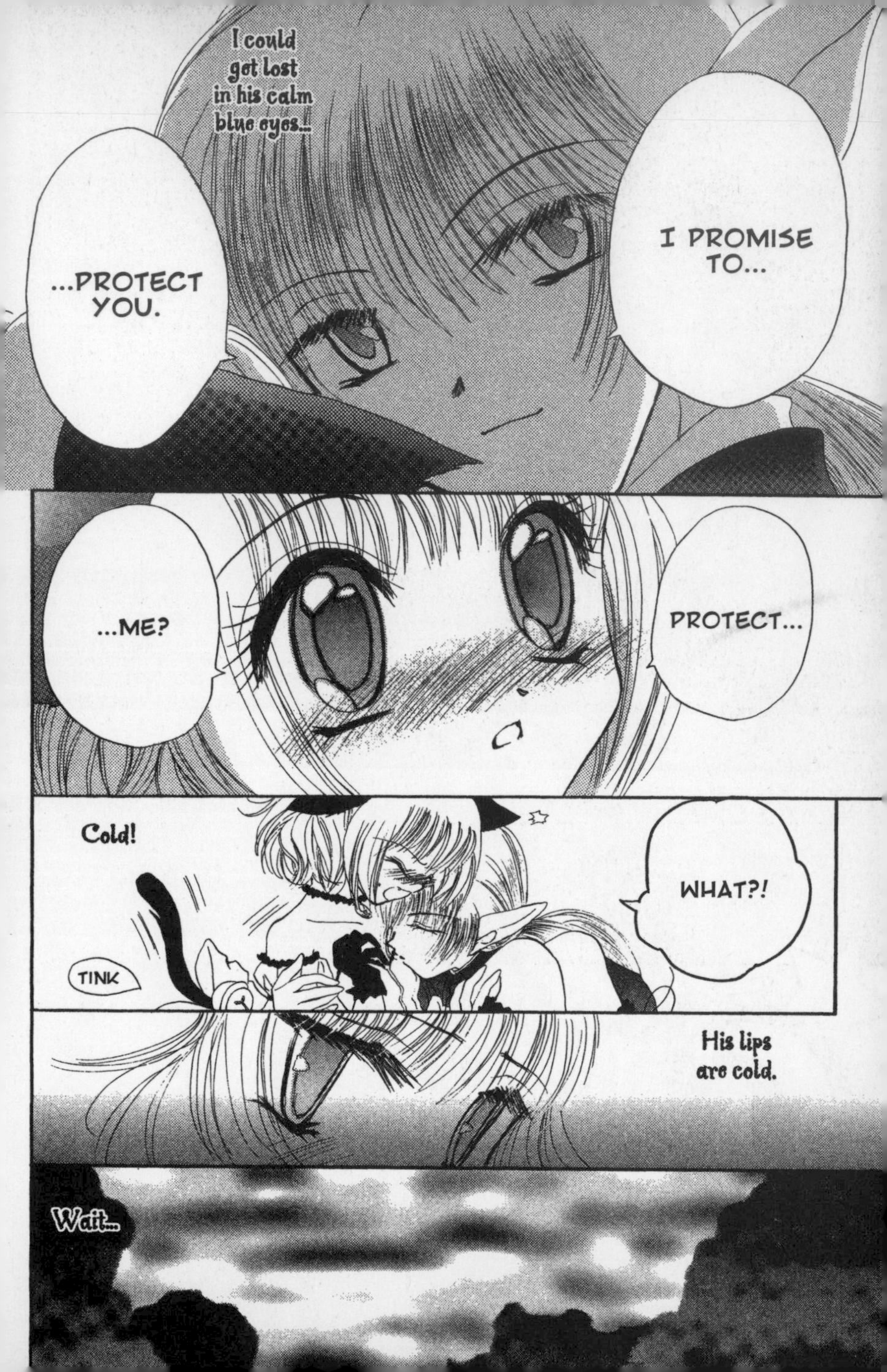
I could get lost in his calm blue eyes...
I PROMISE TO...
...PROTECT YOU.
PROTECT...
...ME?
WHAT?!
Cold!
TINK
His lips are cold.
Wait...

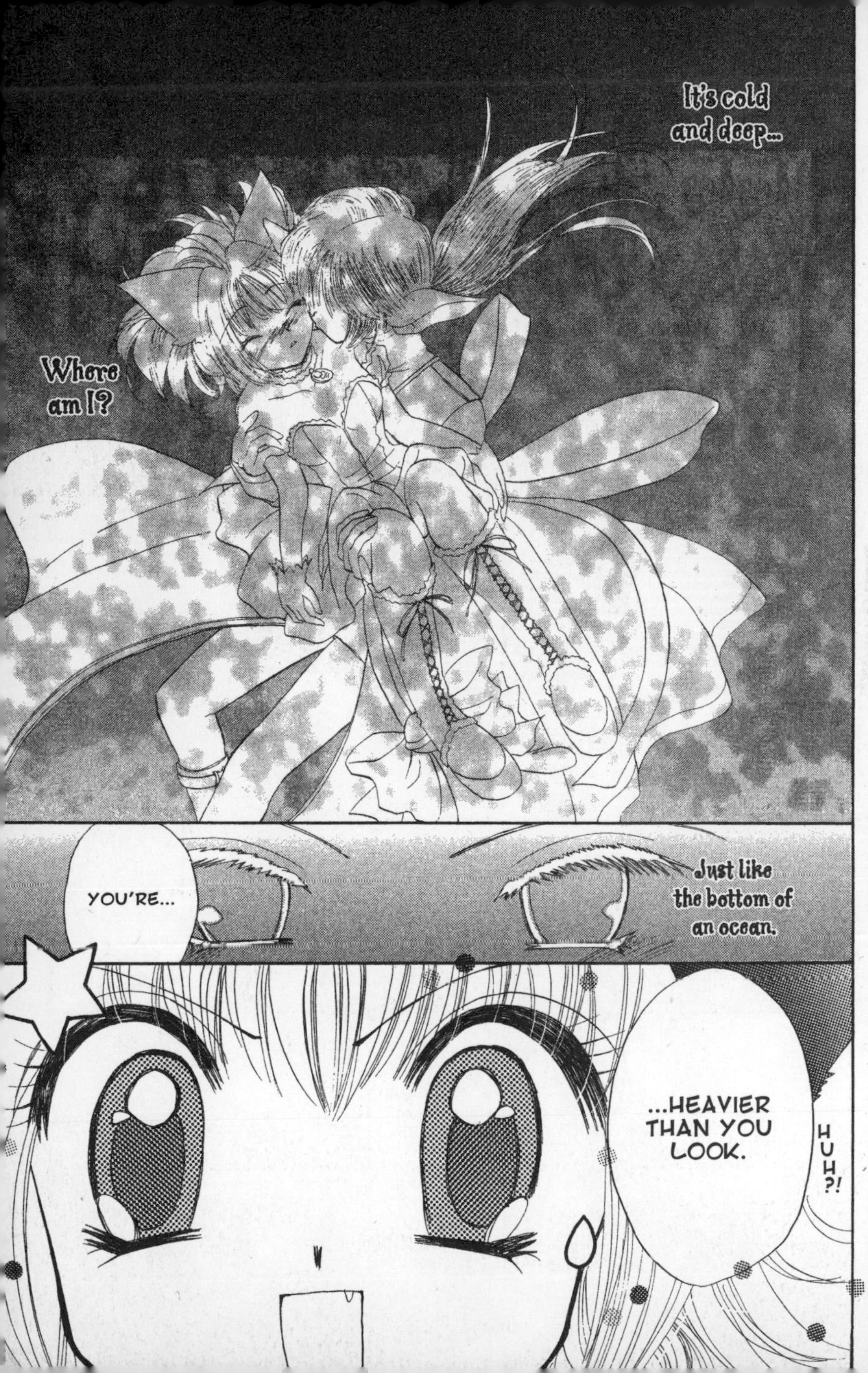
It's cold and deep...
Where am I?
Just like the bottom of an ocean.
YOU'RE...
HUH?!
...HEAVIER THAN YOU LOOK.

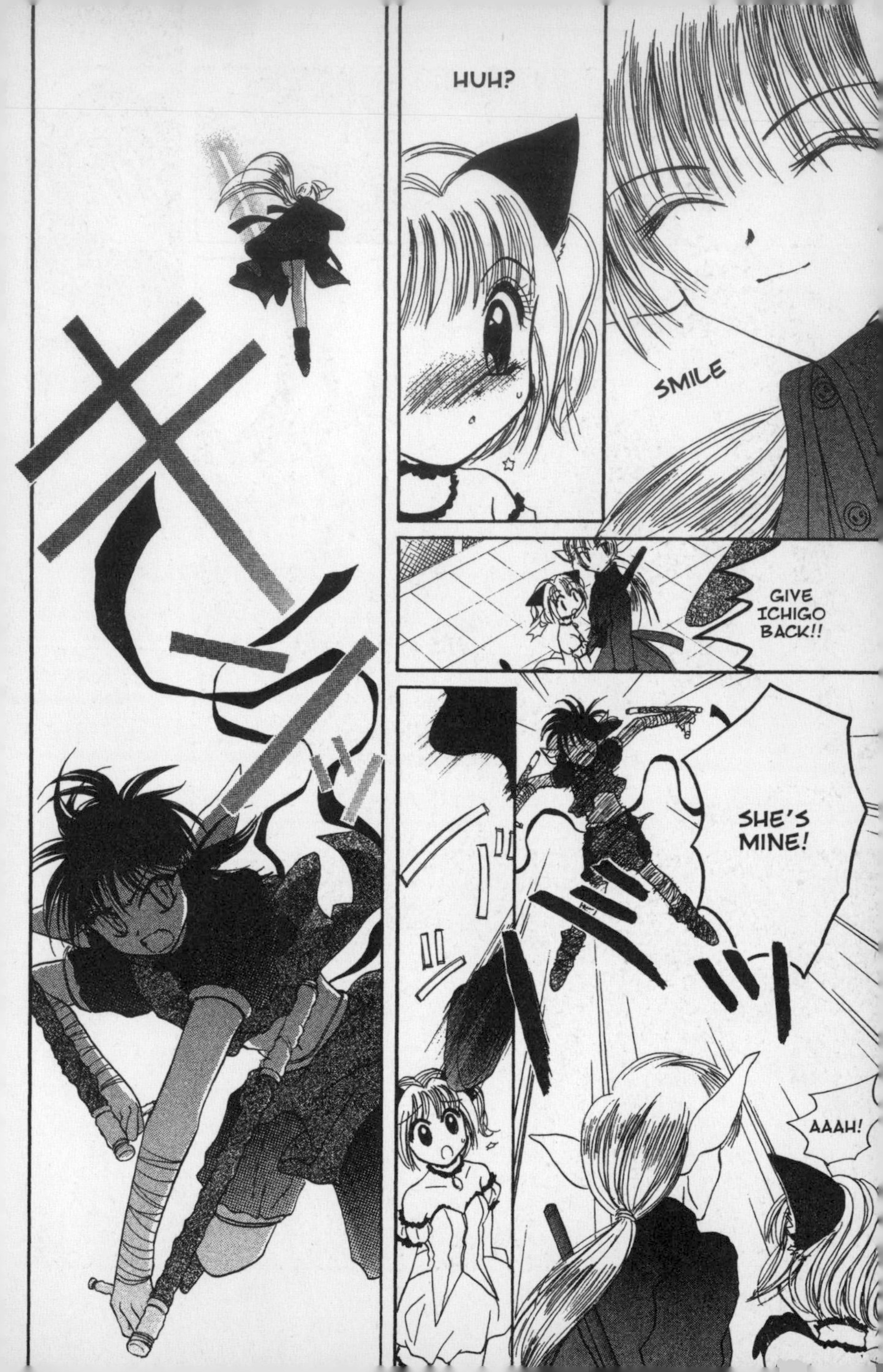
SMILE
HUH?
GIVE ICHIGO BACK!!
SHE'S MINE!
AAAH!

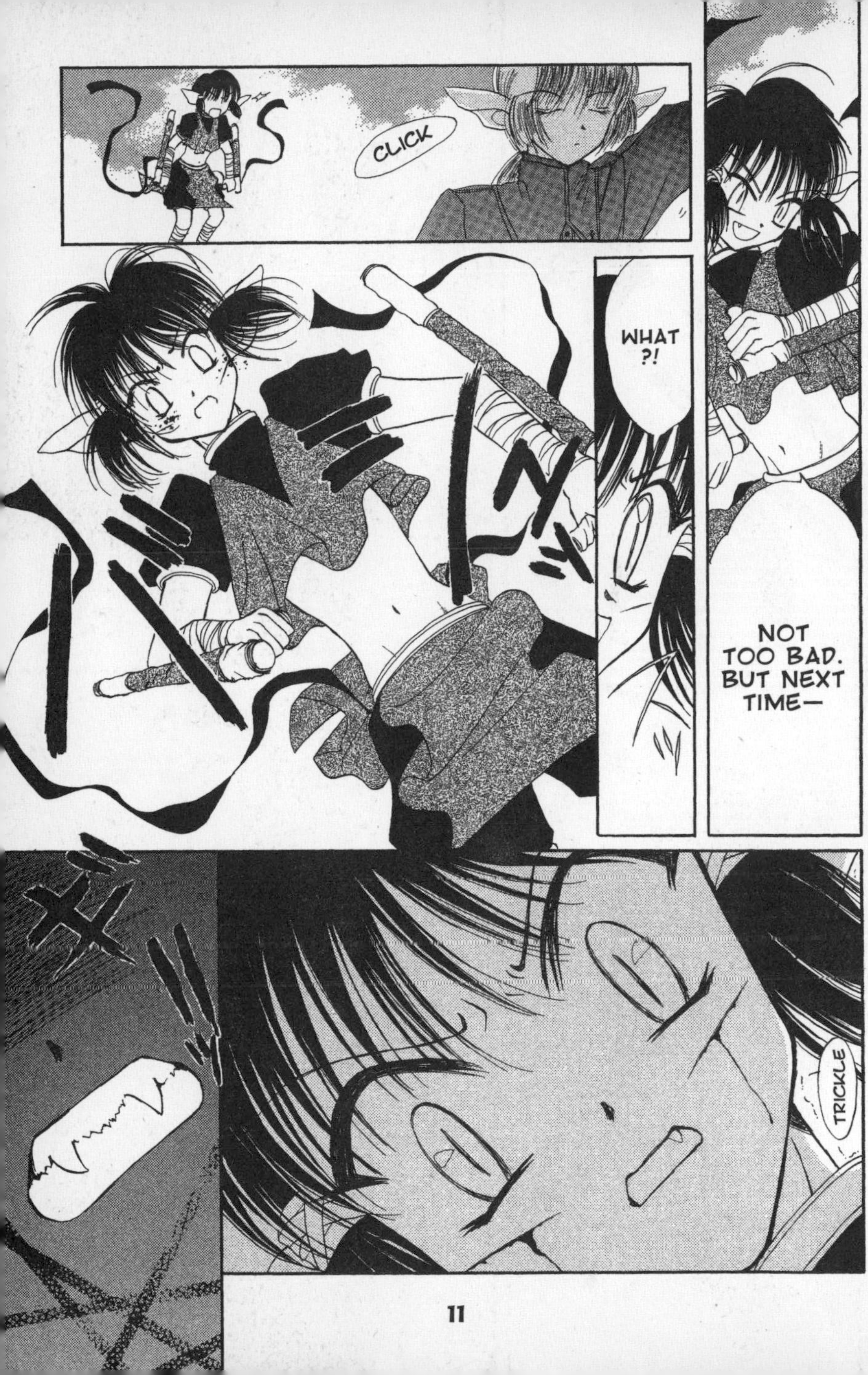
NOT TOO BAD. BUT NEXT TIME—
CLICK
WHAT ?!
TRICKLE

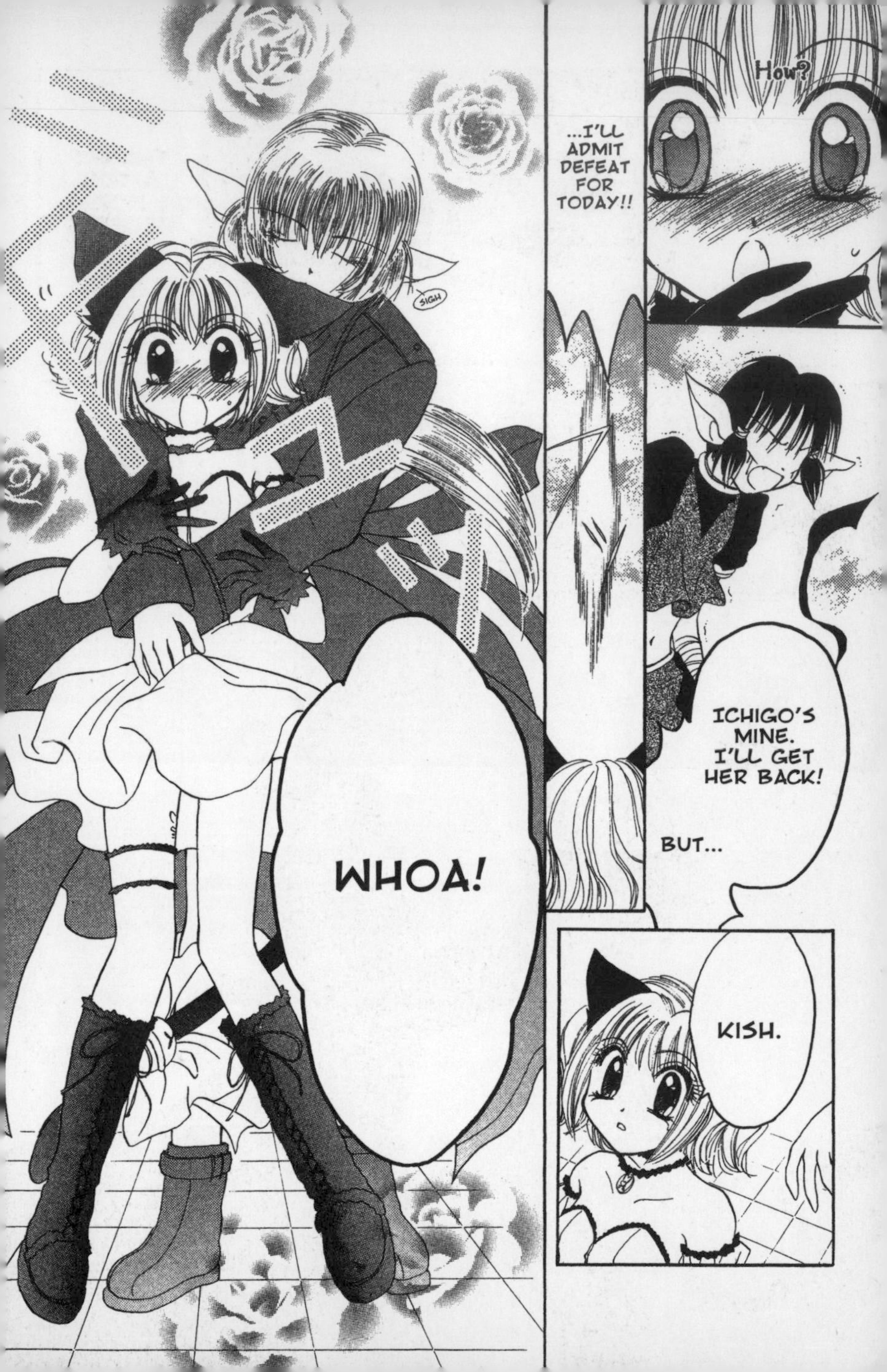
How?
...I'LL ADMIT DEFEAT FOR TODAY!!
ICHIGO'S MINE. I'LL GET HER BACK!
BUT...
KISH.
SIGH
WHOA!

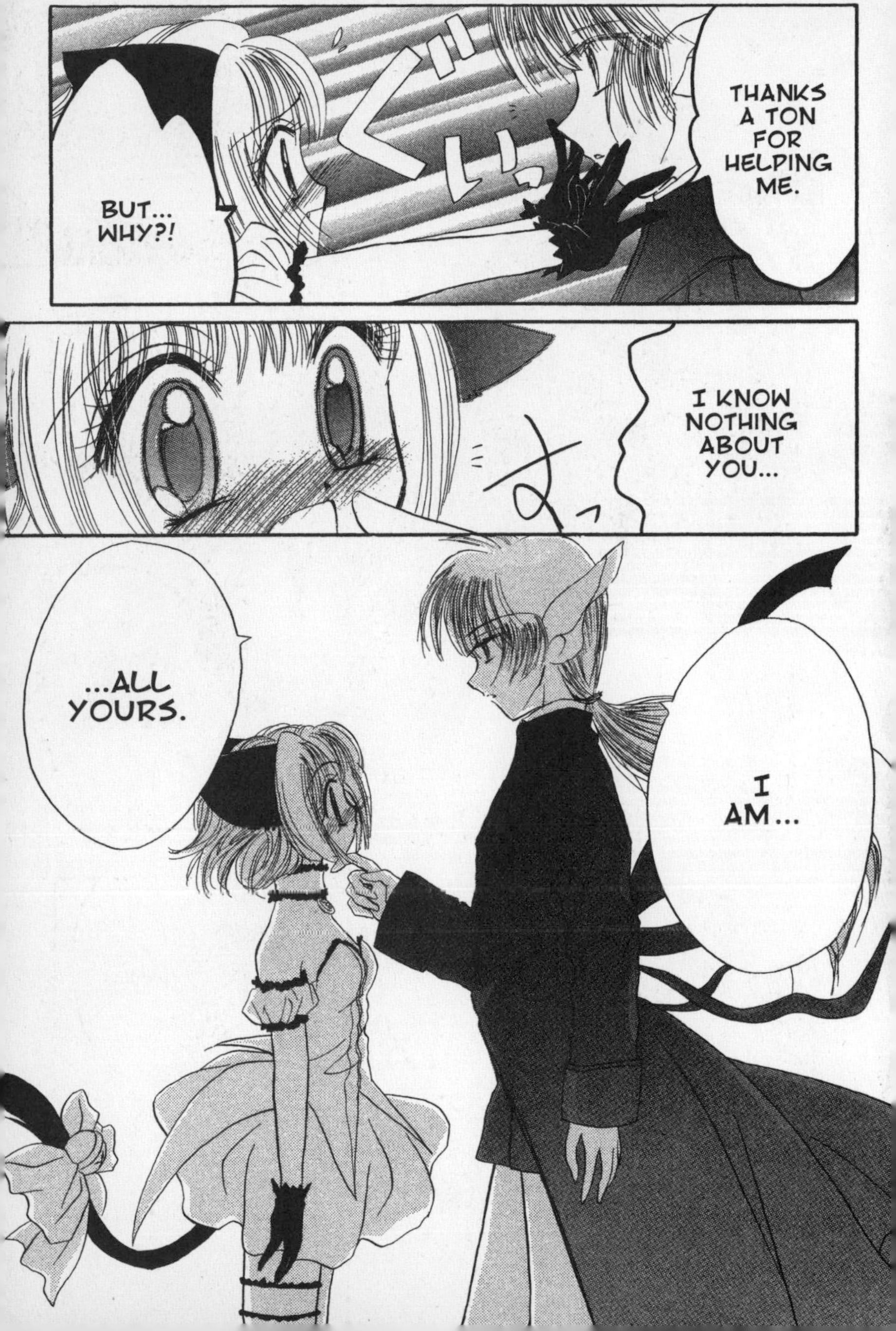
THANKS A TON FOR HELPING ME.
ぐいっ
BUT... WHY?!
I KNOW NOTHING ABOUT YOU...
すっ
I AM...
...ALL YOURS.

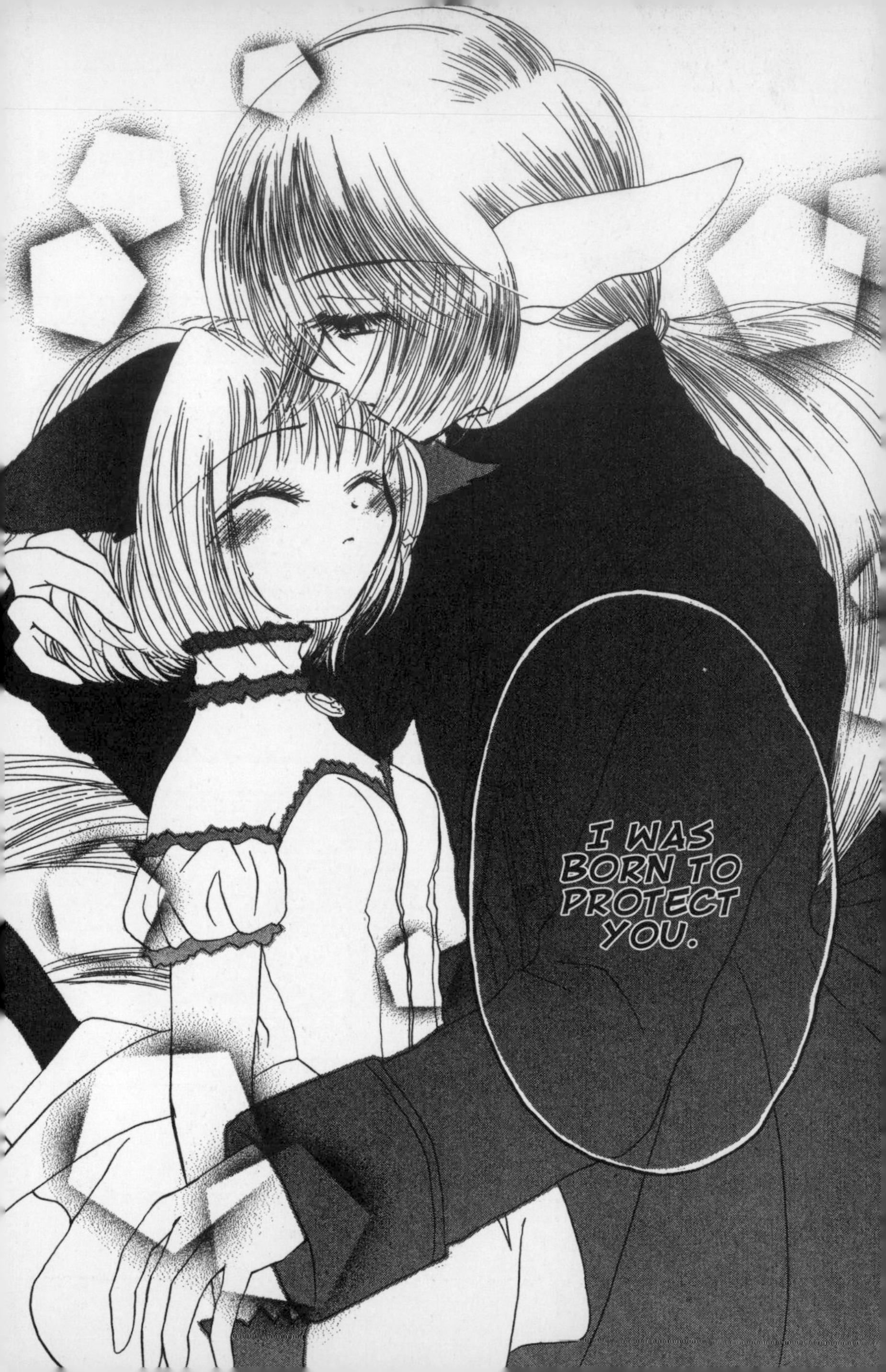
I WAS BORN TO PROTECT YOU.

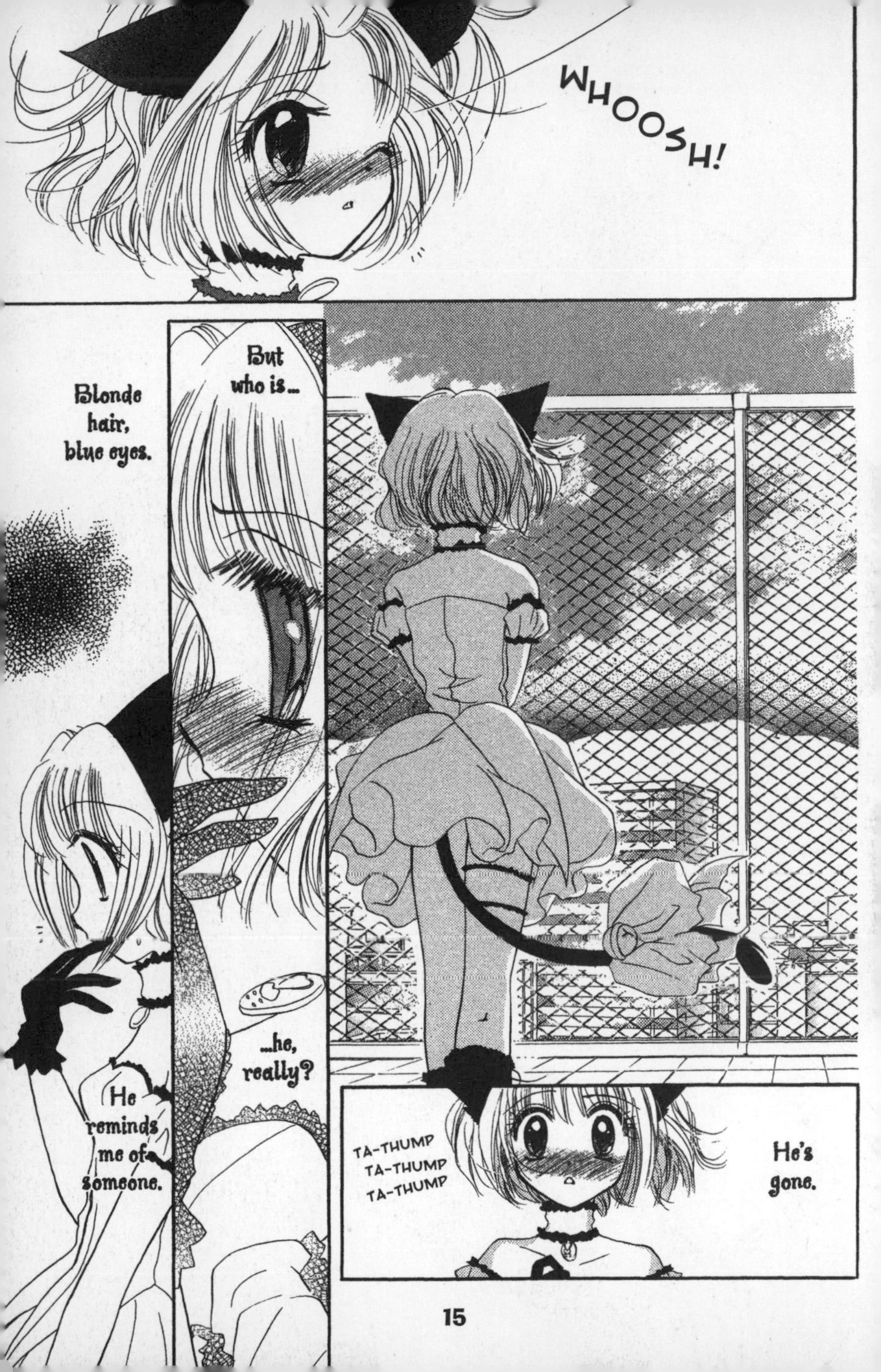
WHOOSH!
He's gone.
TA-THUMP TA-THUMP TA-THUMP
But who is...
...he, really?
Blonde hair, blue eyes.
He reminds me of someone.

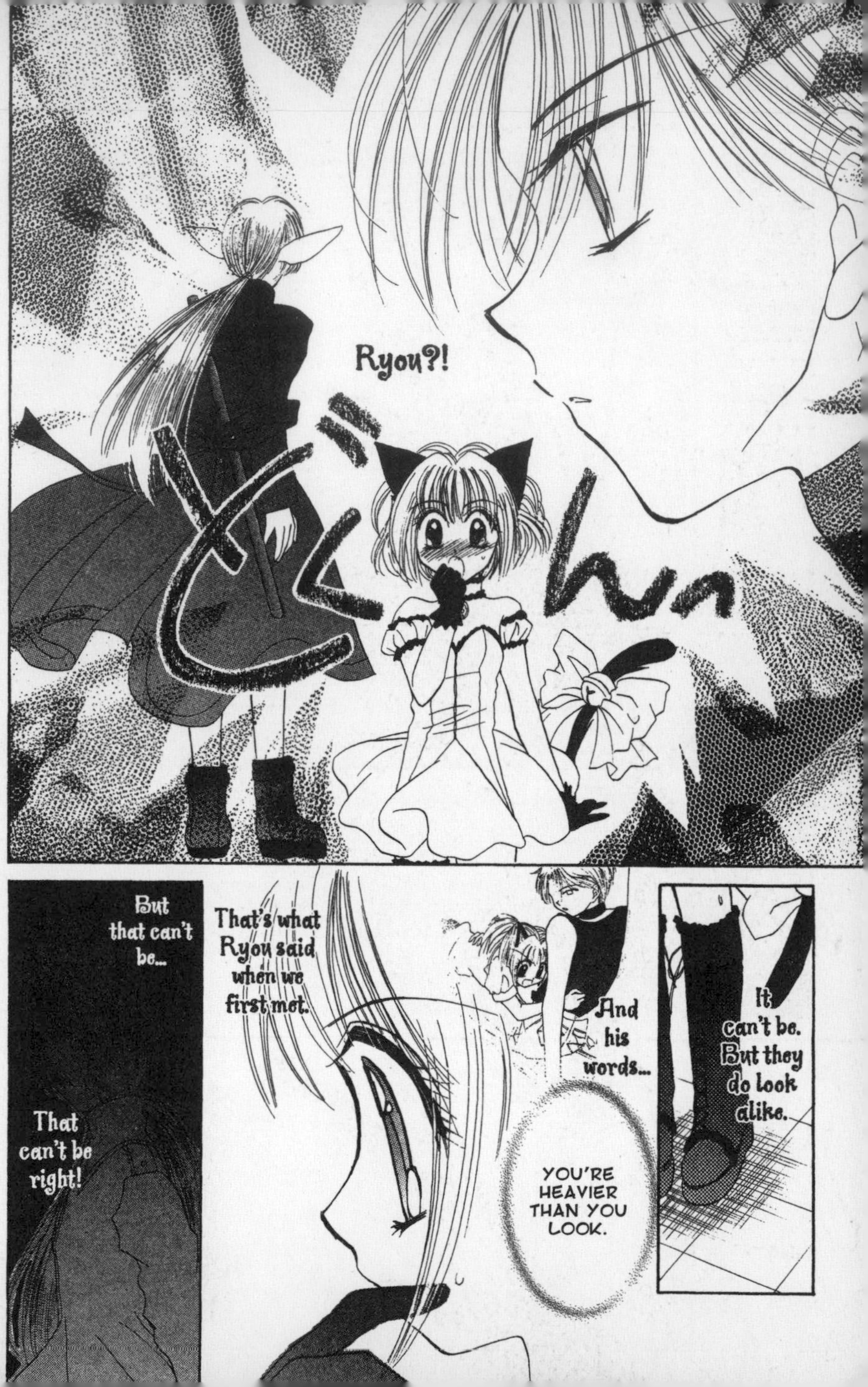
Ryou?!
It can't be. But they do look alike.
And his words...
YOU'RE HEAVIER THAN YOU LOOK.
That's what Ryou said when we first met.
But that can't be...
That can't be right!

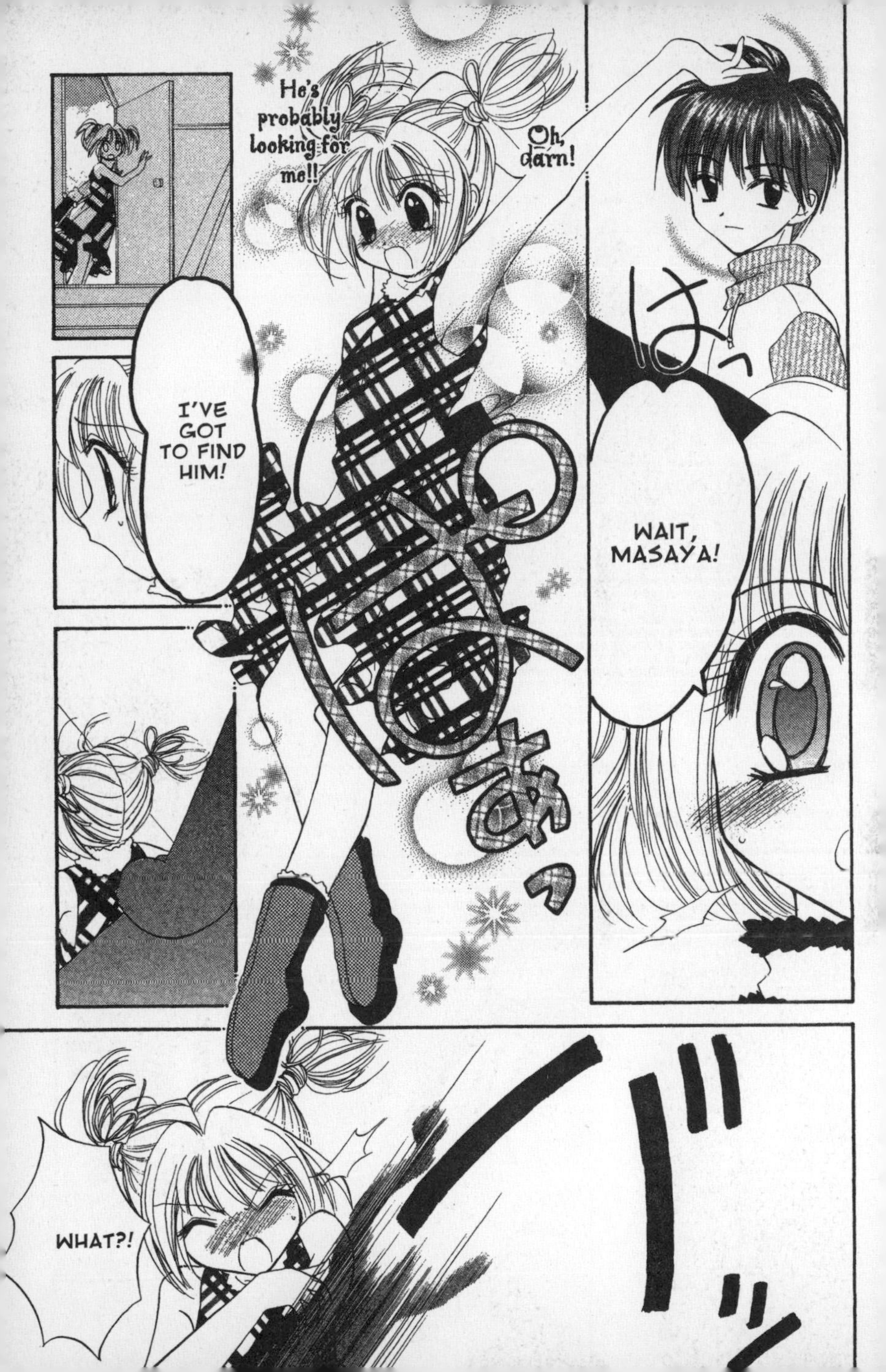
はっ
WAIT, MASAYA!
Oh, darn!
He's probably looking for me!!
I'VE GOT TO FIND HIM!
WHAT?!

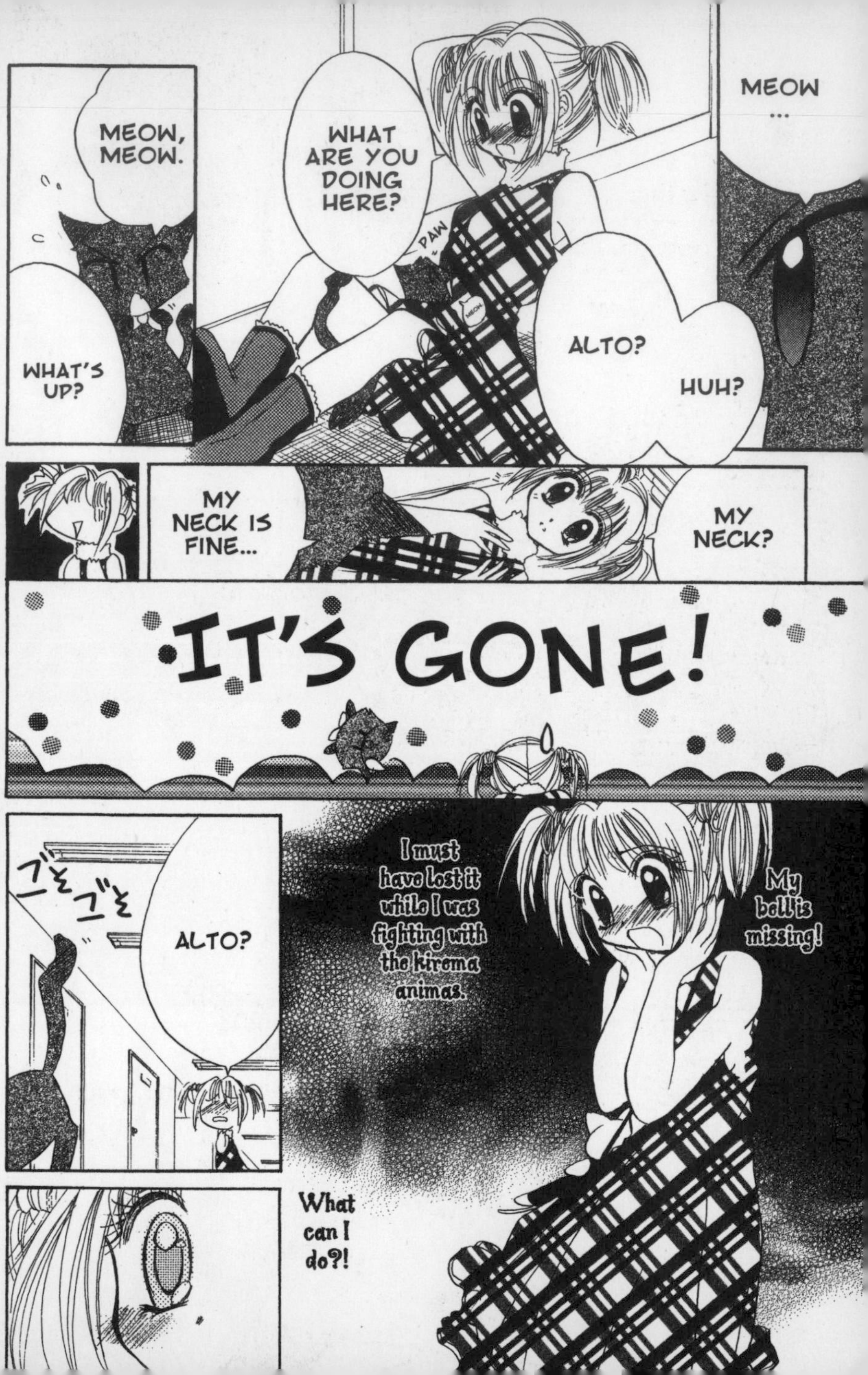
MEOW ...
WHAT ARE YOU DOING HERE?
PAW ~
MEOW
HUH?
ALTO?
MEOW, MEOW.
WHAT'S UP?
MY NECK?
MY NECK IS FINE...
IT'S GONE!
My bell is missing!
I must have lost it while I was fighting with the kirema animas.
What can I do?!
ALTO?
ゴそゴそ

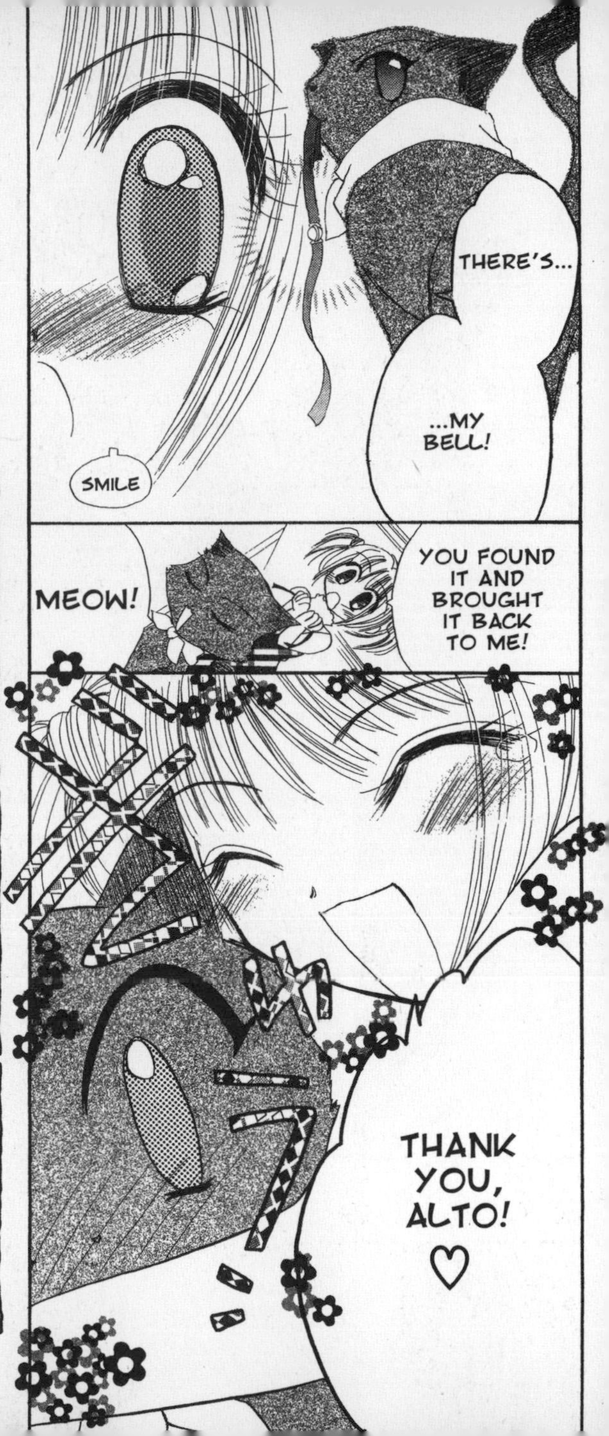
THERE'S...
...MY BELL!
SMILE
YOU FOUND IT AND BROUGHT IT BACK TO ME!
MEOW!
THANK YOU, ALTO! ♡

Ikumi's Day

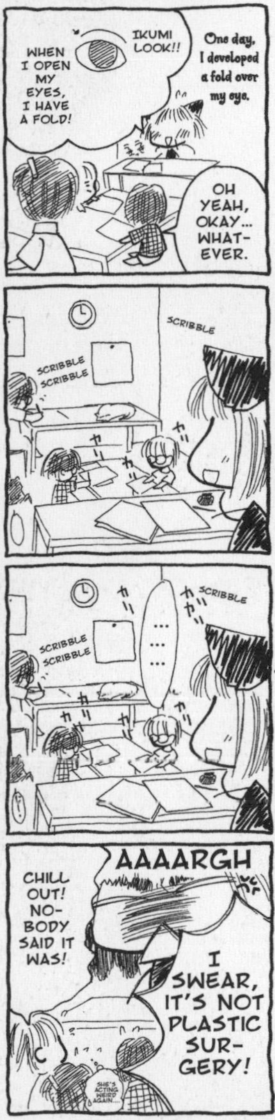
One day, I developed a fold over my eye.
IKUMI LOOK!!
WHEN I OPEN MY EYES, I HAVE A FOLD!
OH YEAH, OKAY... WHAT-EVER.
SCRIBBLE
SCRIBBLE SCRIBBLE
SCRIBBLE
... ...
SCRIBBLE SCRIBBLE
AAAARGH
I SWEAR, IT'S NOT PLASTIC SUR-GERY!
CHILL OUT! NO-BODY SAID IT WAS!
SHE'S ACTING WEIRD AGAIN...

↗ She was super upset nobody paid any attention.

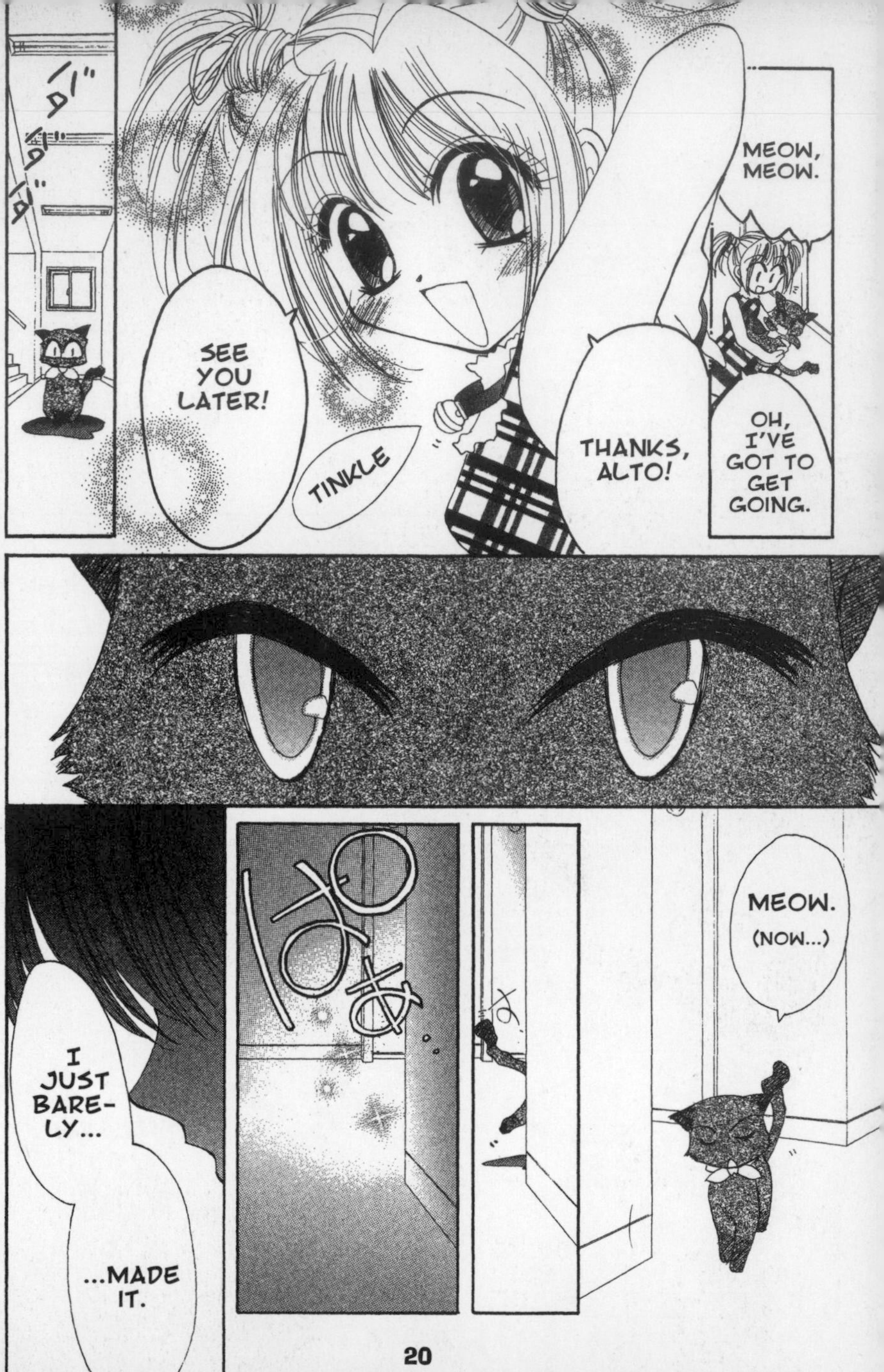
MEOW, MEOW.
OH, I'VE GOT TO GET GOING.
THANKS, ALTO!
TINKLE
SEE YOU LATER!
MEOW.
(NOW...)
I JUST BARE-LY...
...MADE IT.

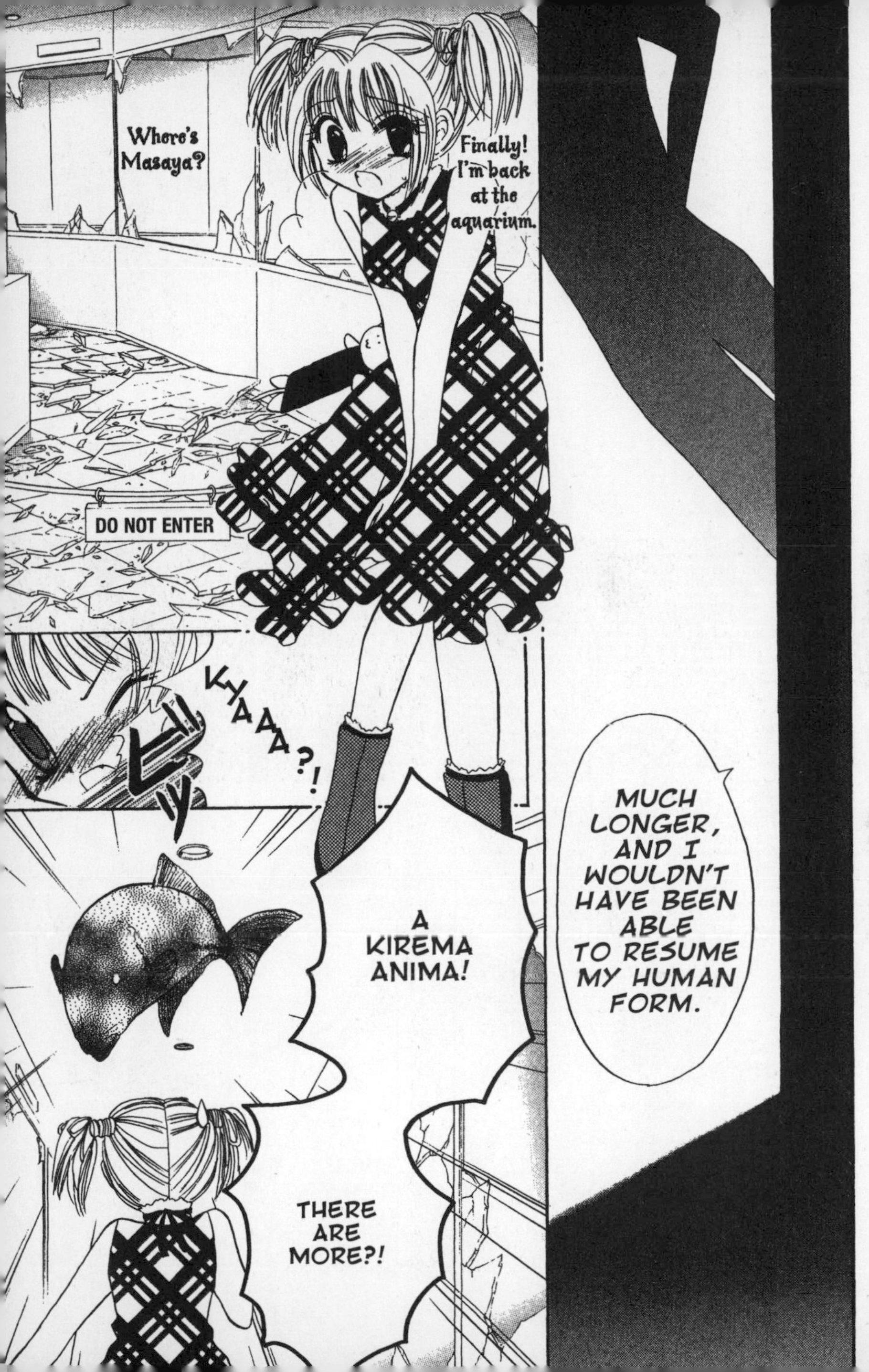
MUCH LONGER, AND I WOULDN'T HAVE BEEN ABLE TO RESUME MY HUMAN FORM.
Finally! I'm back at the aquarium.
Where's Masaya?
DO NOT ENTER
KYAAAA?!
A KIREMA ANIMA!
THERE ARE MORE?!

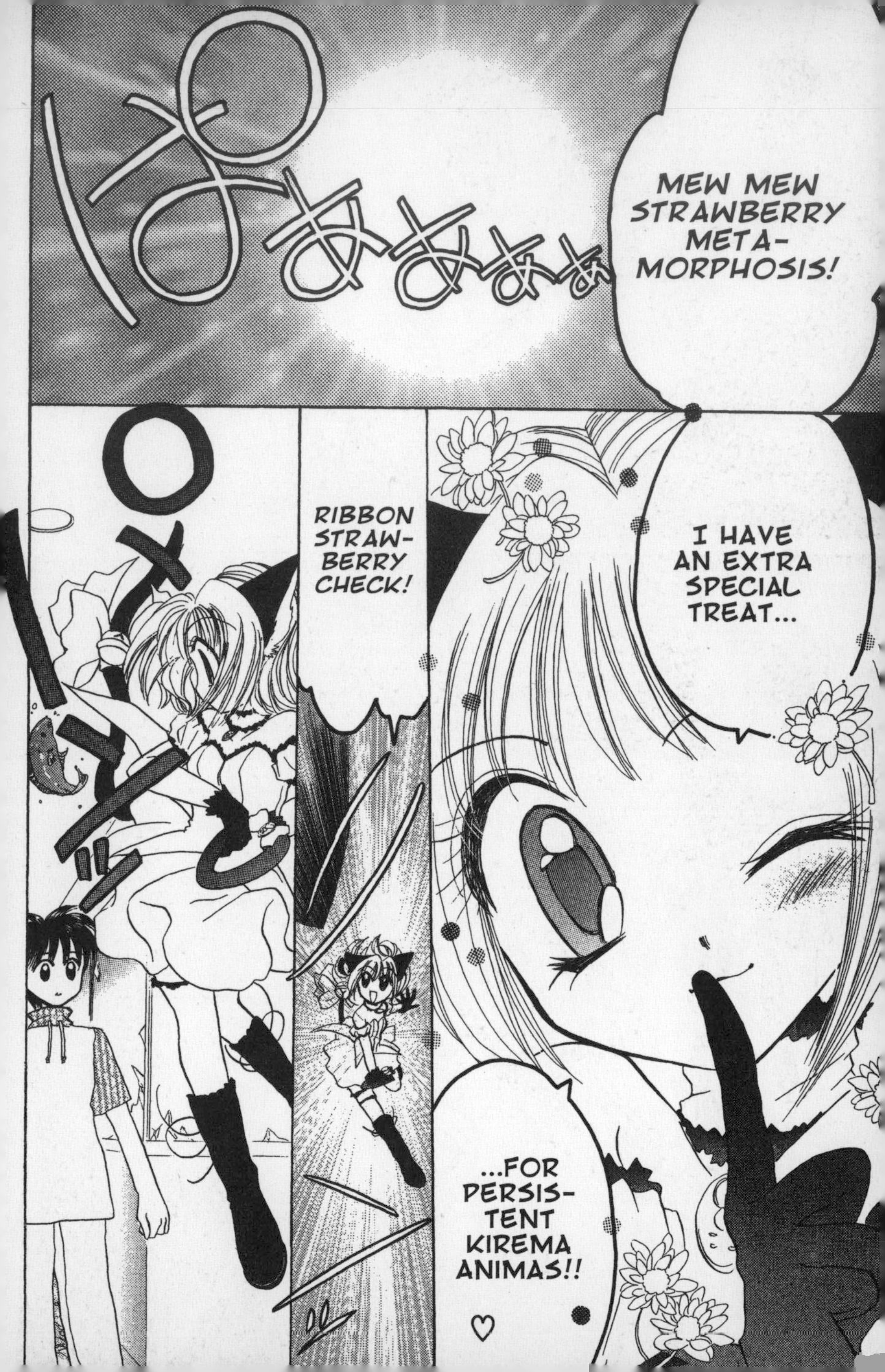
MEW MEW STRAWBERRY META-MORPHOSIS!
ぱあああぁ
I HAVE AN EXTRA SPECIAL TREAT...
...FOR PERSIS-TENT KIREMA ANIMAS!! ♡
RIBBON STRAW-BERRY CHECK!

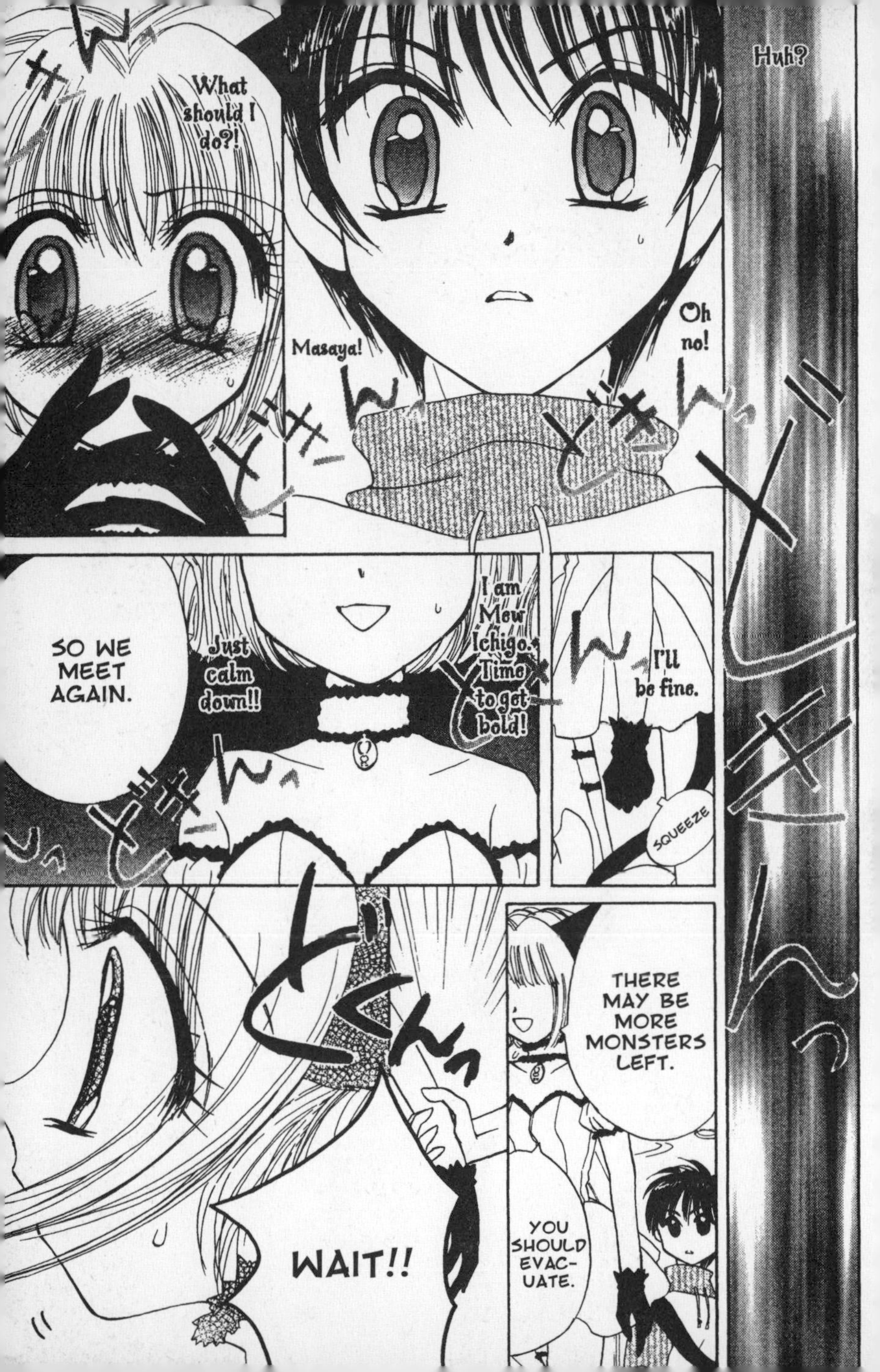
Huh?
Oh no!
Masaya!
What should I do?!
I'll be fine.
SQUEEZE
I am Mew Ichigo. Time to get bold!
Just calm down!!
SO WE MEET AGAIN.
THERE MAY BE MORE MONSTERS LEFT.
YOU SHOULD EVACUATE.
WAIT!!

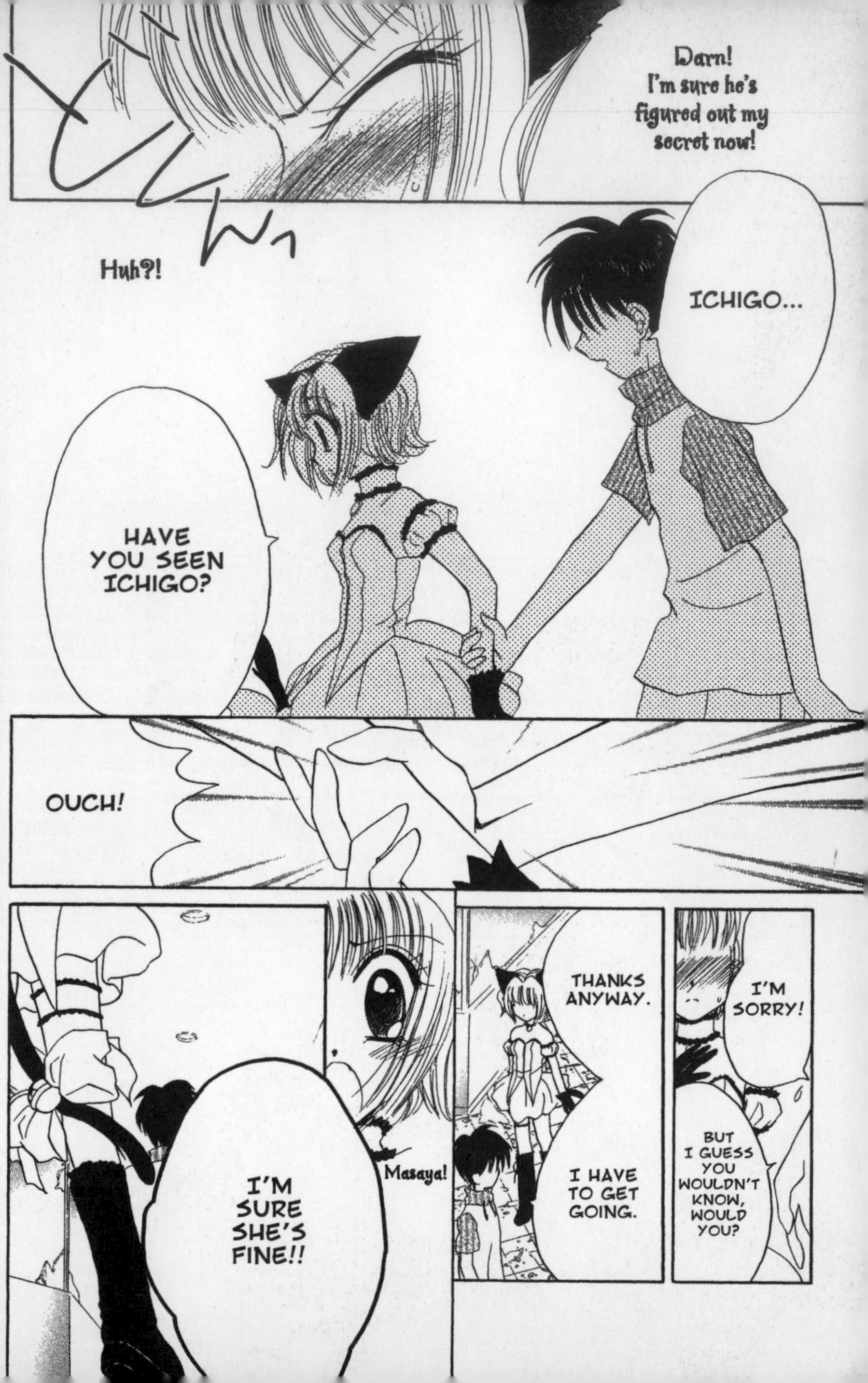
Darn! I'm sure he's figured out my secret now!
ICHIGO...
Huh?!
HAVE YOU SEEN ICHIGO?
OUCH!
I'M SORRY!
BUT I GUESS YOU WOULDN'T KNOW, WOULD YOU?
THANKS ANYWAY.
I HAVE TO GET GOING.
Masaya!
I'M SURE SHE'S FINE!!

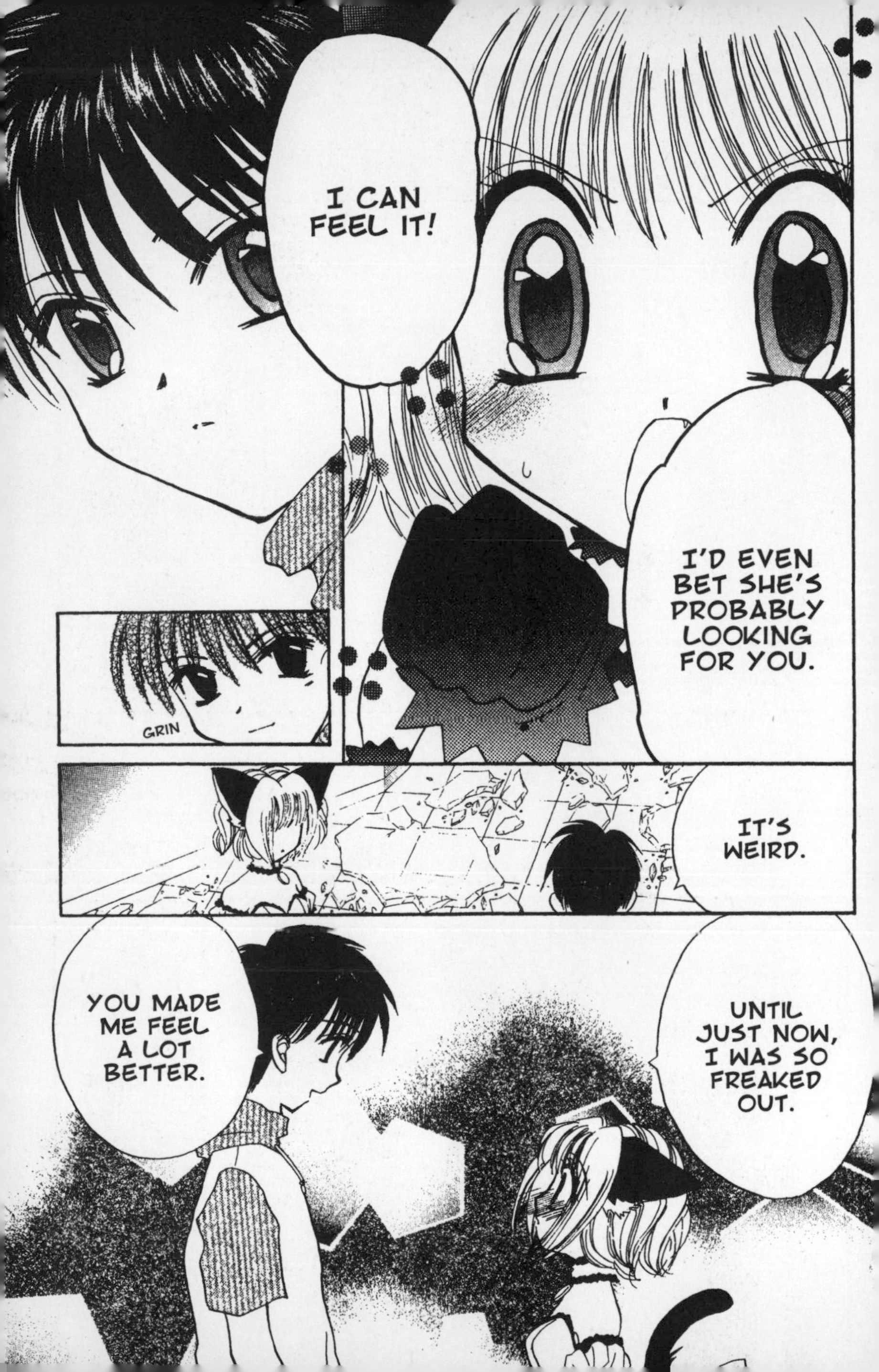
I CAN FEEL IT!
I'D EVEN BET SHE'S PROBABLY LOOKING FOR YOU.
GRIN
IT'S WEIRD.
UNTIL JUST NOW, I WAS SO FREAKED OUT.
YOU MADE ME FEEL A LOT BETTER.

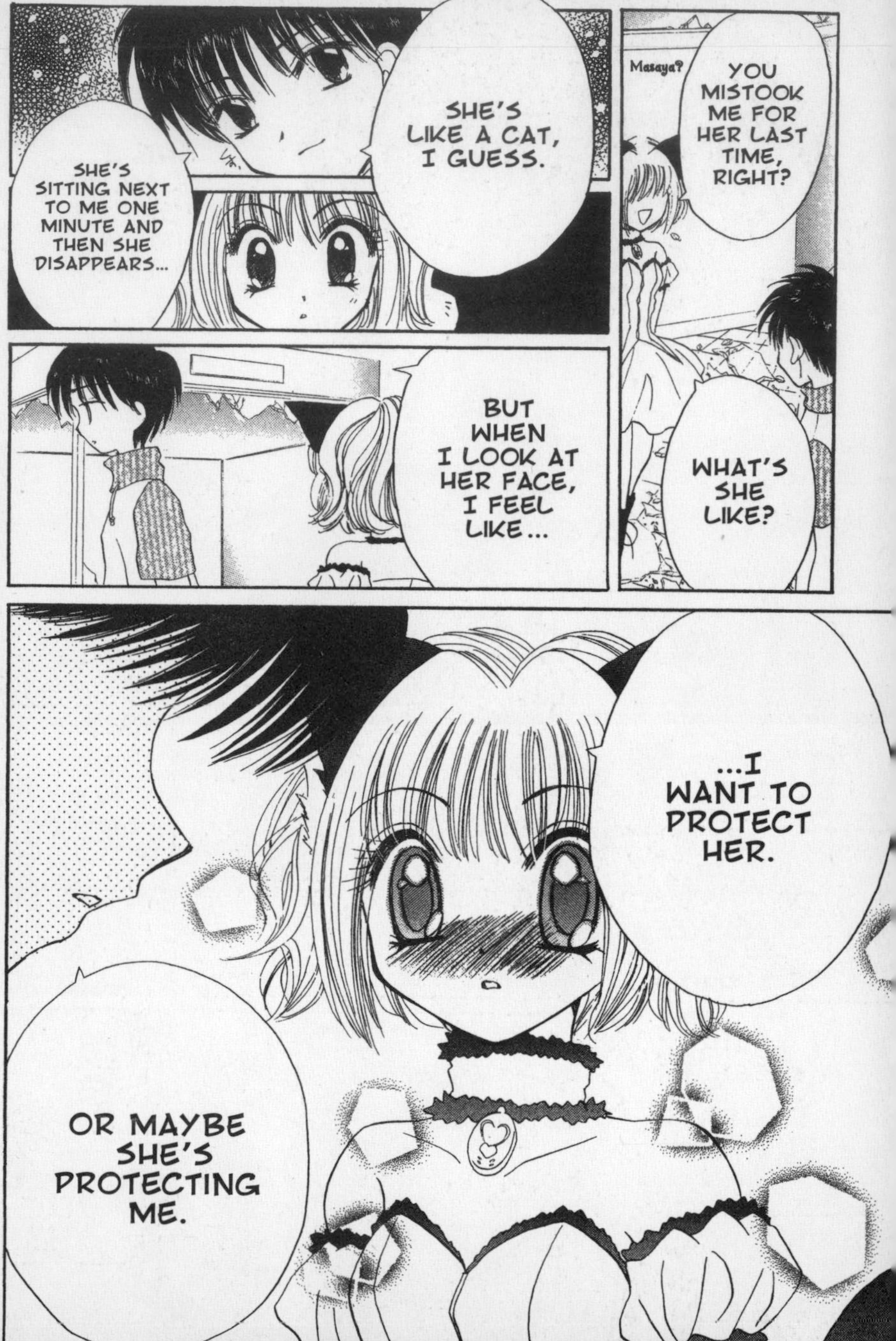
YOU MISTOOK ME FOR HER LAST TIME, RIGHT?
Masaya?
WHAT'S SHE LIKE?
SHE'S LIKE A CAT, I GUESS.
SHE'S SITTING NEXT TO ME ONE MINUTE AND THEN SHE DISAPPEARS...
BUT WHEN I LOOK AT HER FACE, I FEEL LIKE...
...I WANT TO PROTECT HER.
OR MAYBE SHE'S PROTECTING ME.

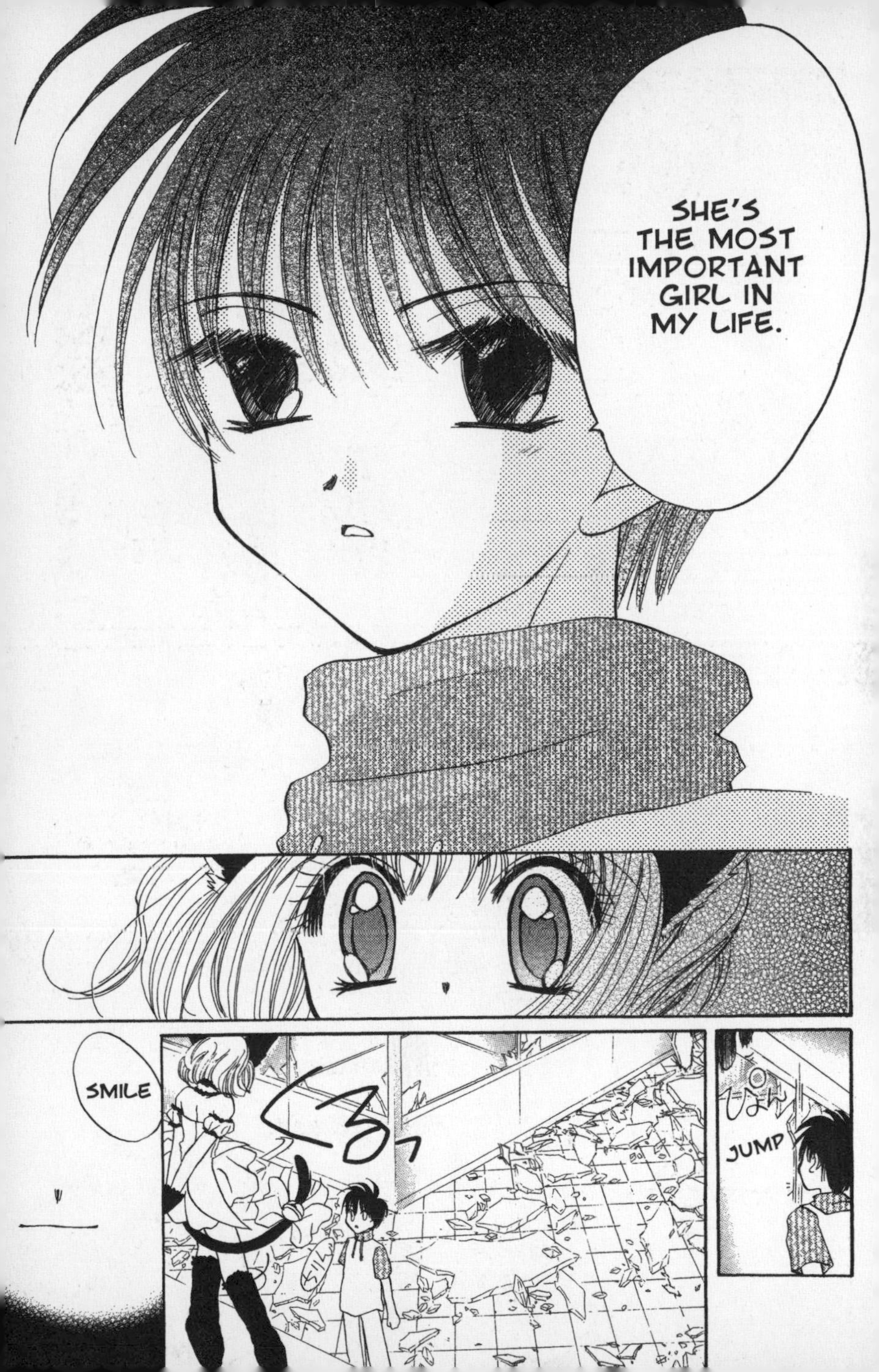
SHE'S THE MOST IMPORTANT GIRL IN MY LIFE.
ぴょん
JUMP
SMILE
くるっ

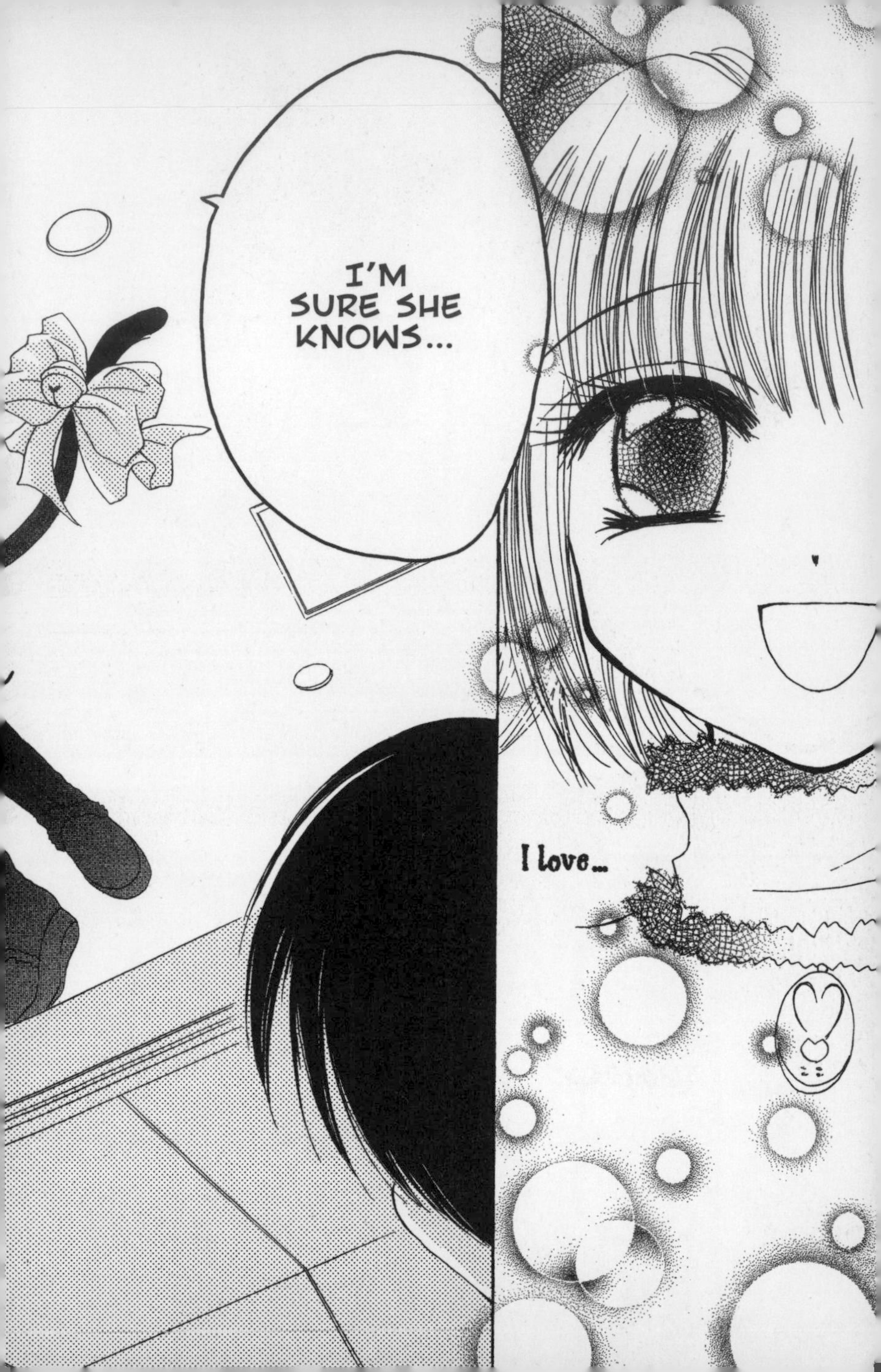
I love...
I'M SURE SHE KNOWS...

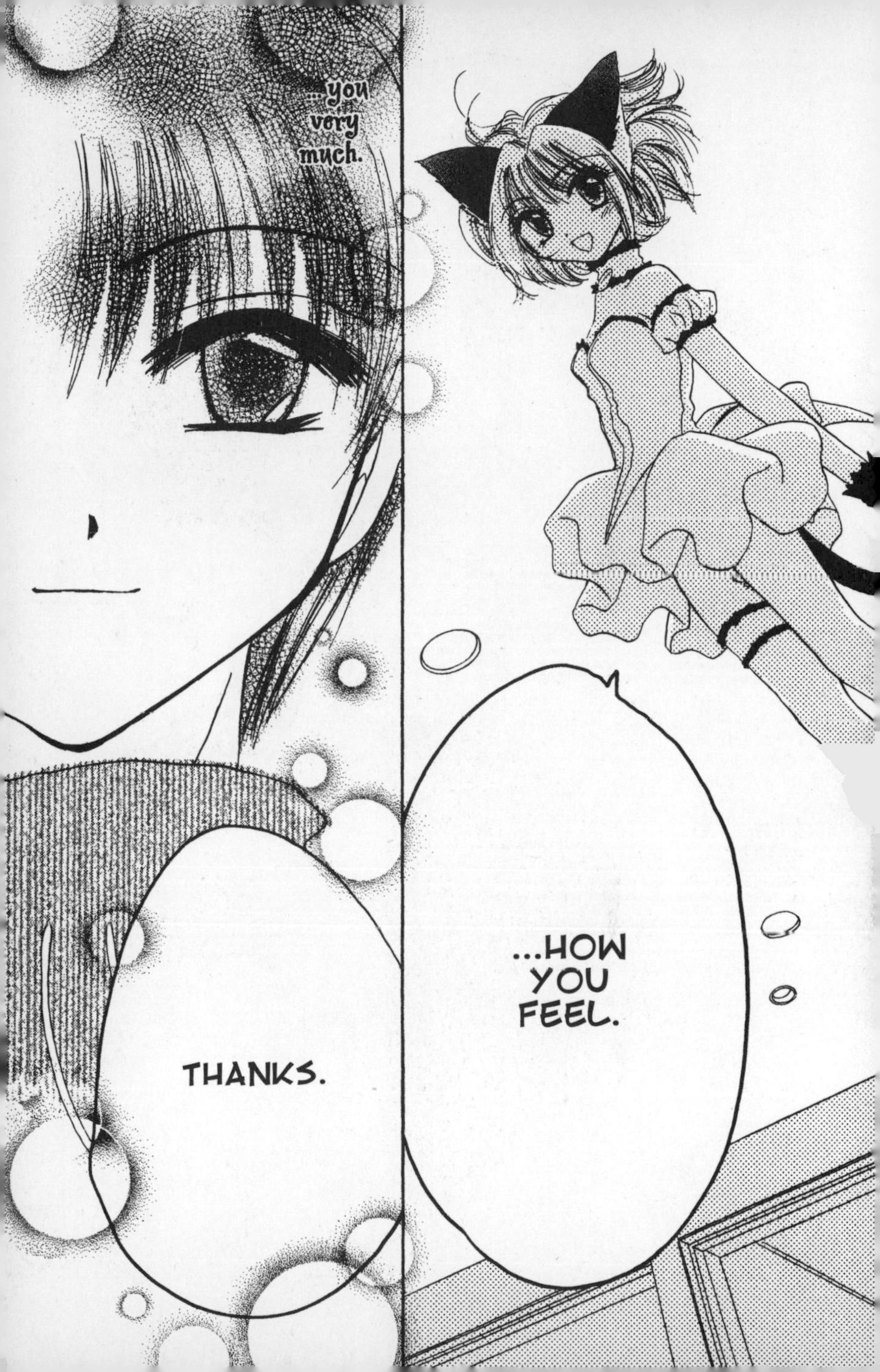
...HOW YOU FEEL.
...you very much.
THANKS.

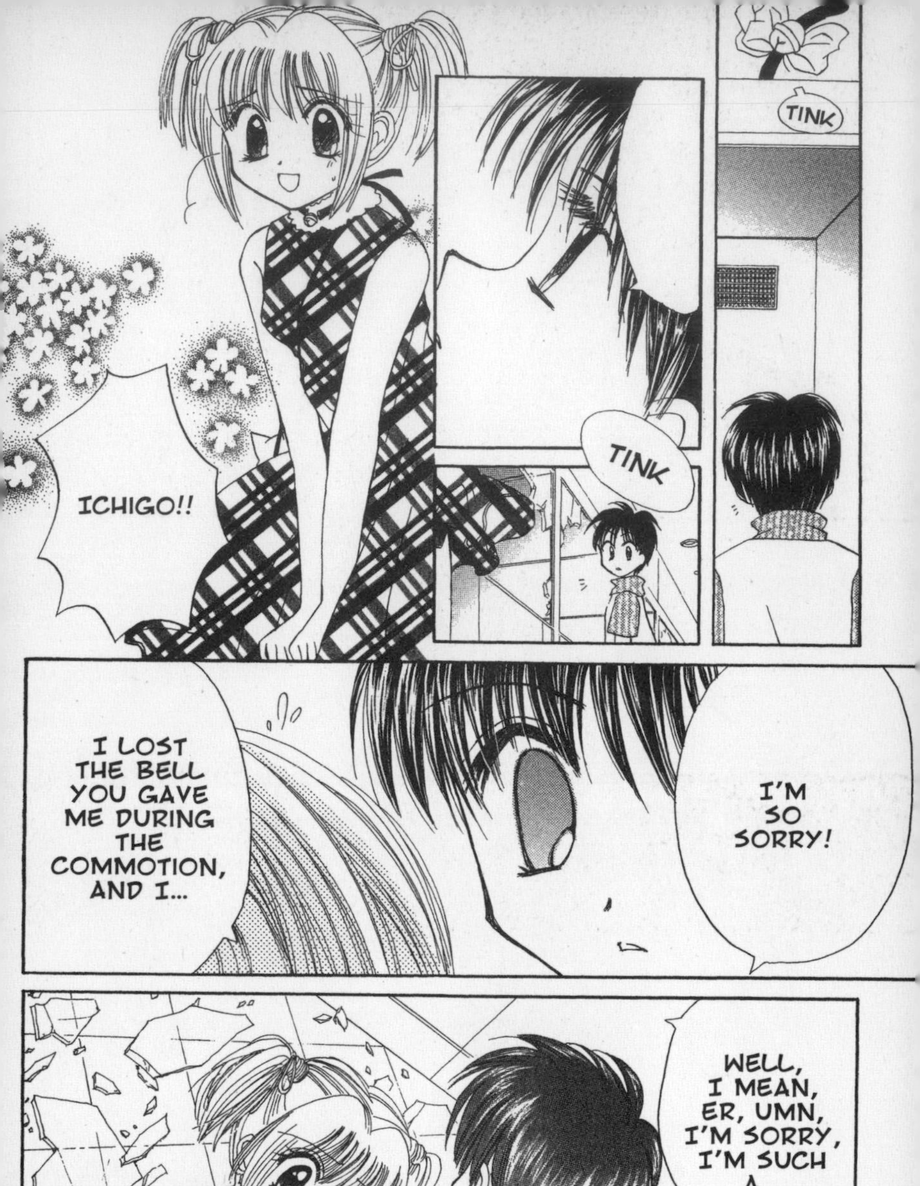
TINK
TINK
ICHIGO!!
I'M SO SORRY!
I LOST THE BELL YOU GAVE ME DURING THE COMMOTION, AND I...
WELL, I MEAN, ER, UMN, I'M SORRY, I'M SUCH A...

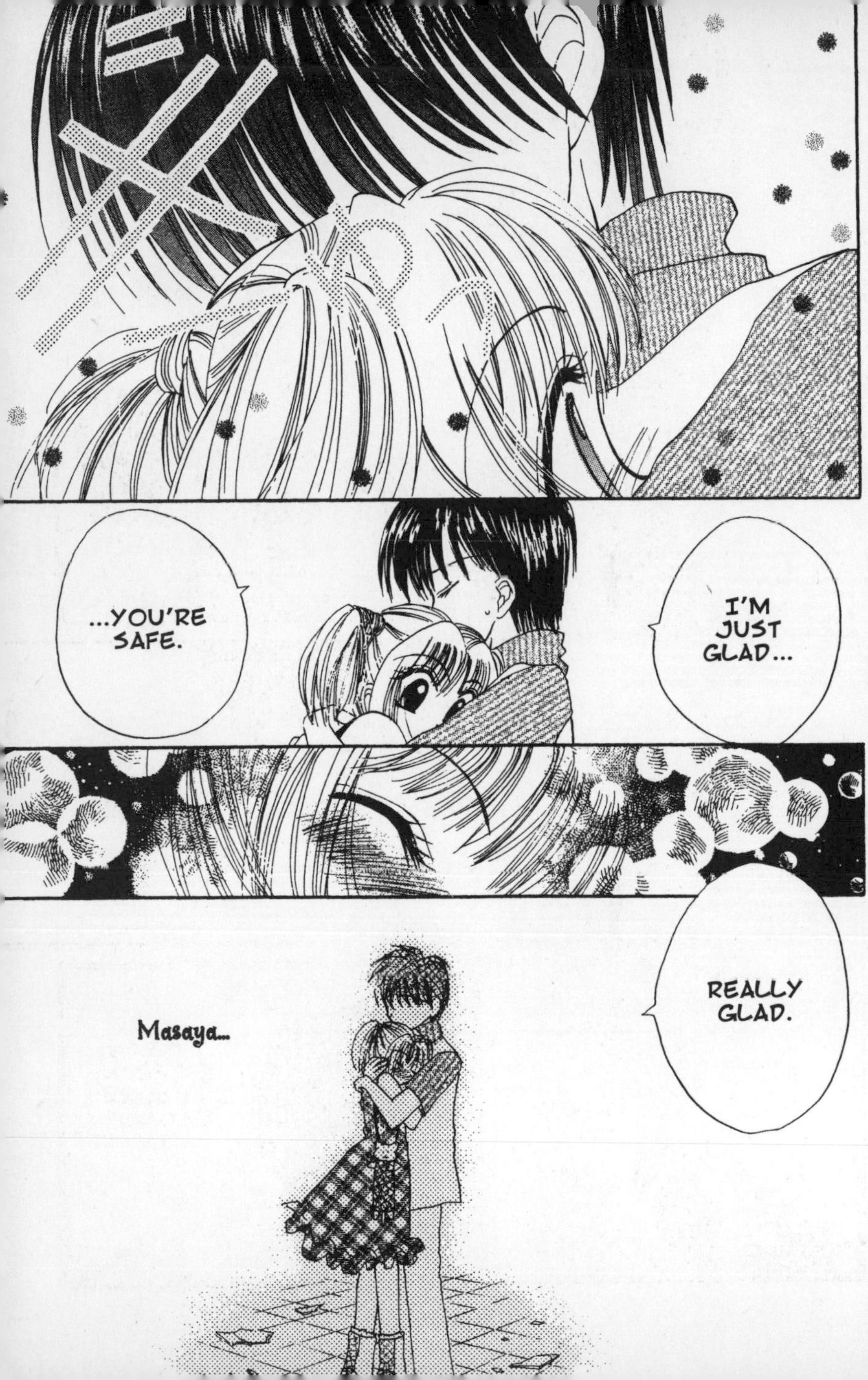
I'M JUST GLAD...
...YOU'RE SAFE.
REALLY GLAD.
Masaya...

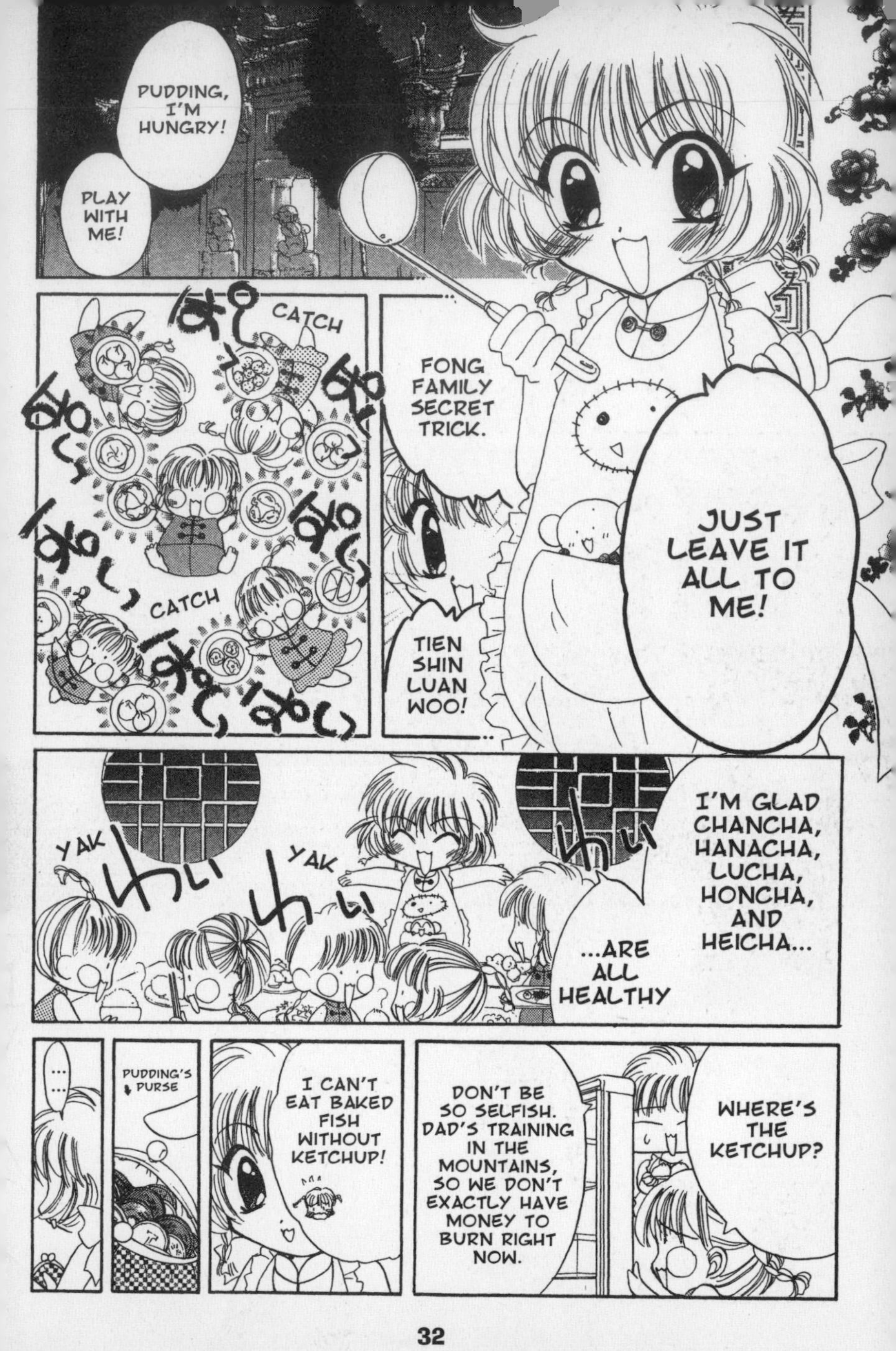
PUDDING, I'M HUNGRY!
PLAY WITH ME!
JUST LEAVE IT ALL TO ME!
FONG FAMILY SECRET TRICK.
TIEN SHIN LUAN WOO!
CATCH
CATCH
I'M GLAD CHANCHA, HANACHA, LUCHA, HONCHA, AND HEICHA...
...ARE ALL HEALTHY
YAK
YAK
WHERE'S THE KETCHUP?
DON'T BE SO SELFISH. DAD'S TRAINING IN THE MOUNTAINS, SO WE DON'T EXACTLY HAVE MONEY TO BURN RIGHT NOW.
I CAN'T EAT BAKED FISH WITHOUT KETCHUP!
PUDDING'S PURSE
......

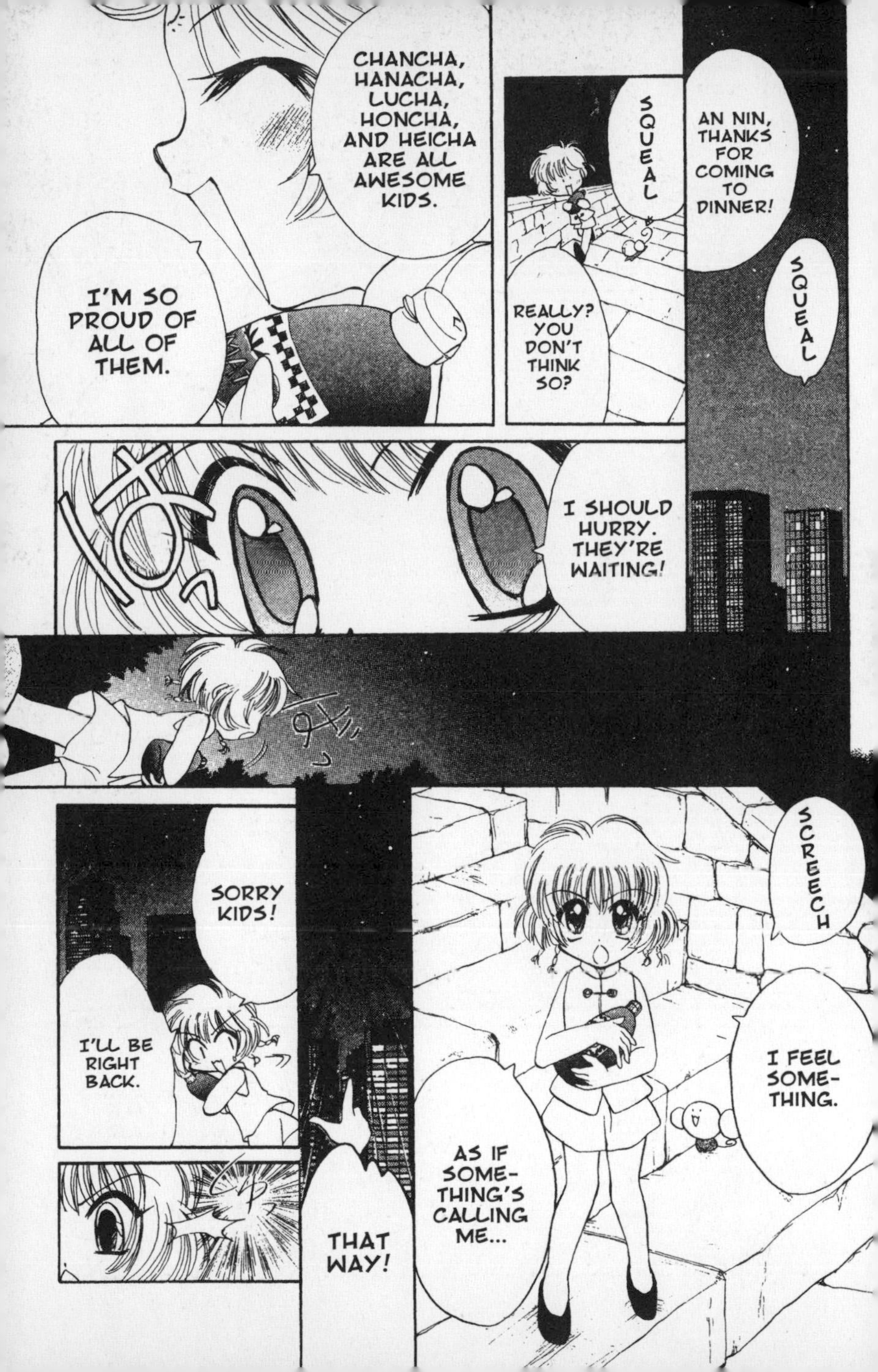
AN NIN, THANKS FOR COMING TO DINNER!
SQUEAL
SQUEAL
REALLY? YOU DON'T THINK SO?
CHANCHA, HANACHA, LUCHA, HONCHA, AND HEICHA ARE ALL AWESOME KIDS.
I'M SO PROUD OF ALL OF THEM.
I SHOULD HURRY. THEY'RE WAITING!
SCREECH
I FEEL SOME-THING.
AS IF SOME-THING'S CALLING ME...
THAT WAY!
SORRY KIDS!
I'LL BE RIGHT BACK.

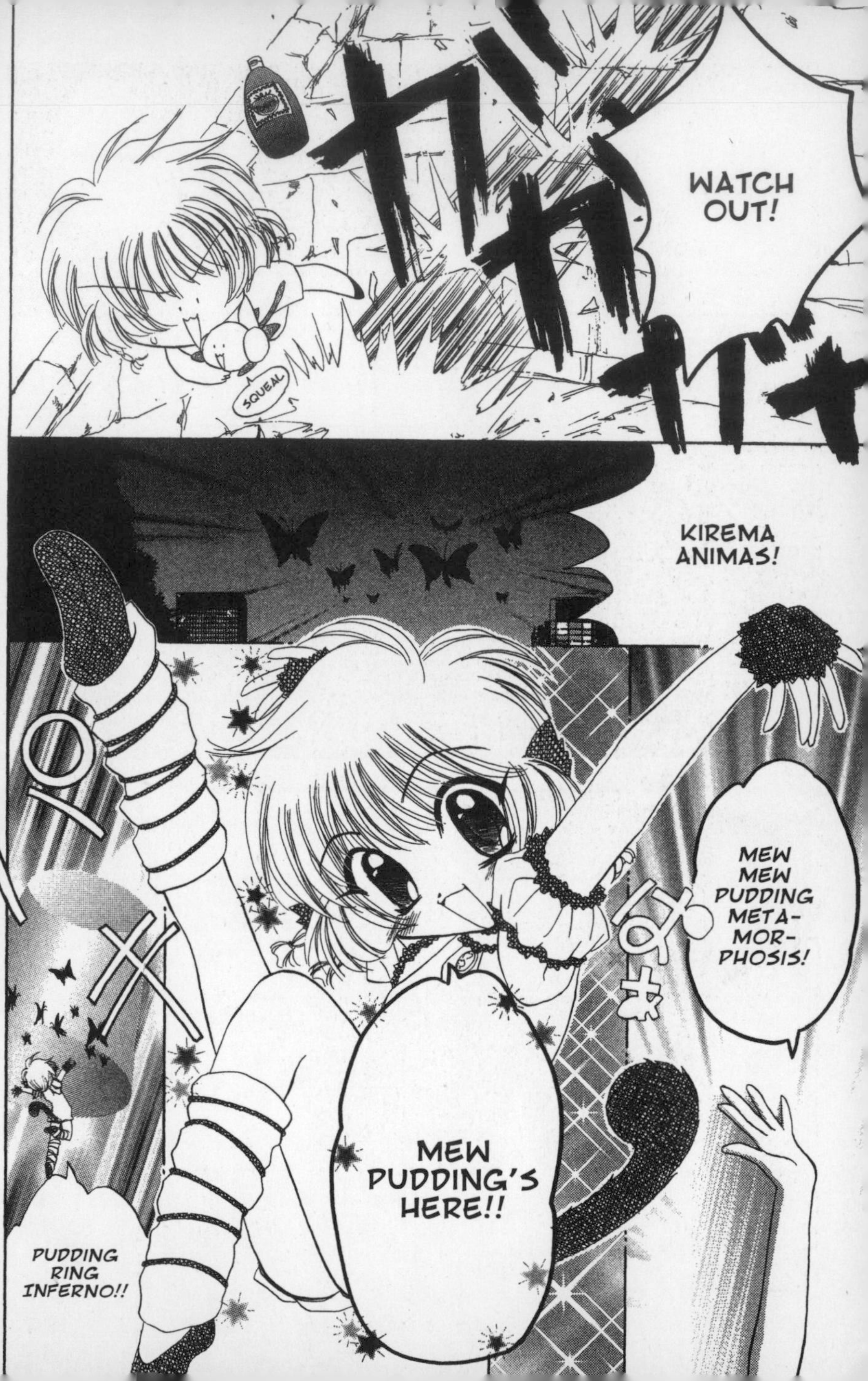
WATCH OUT!
SQUEAL
KIREMA ANIMAS!
MEW MEW PUDDING METAMORPHOSIS!
MEW PUDDING'S HERE!!
PUDDING RING INFERNO!!

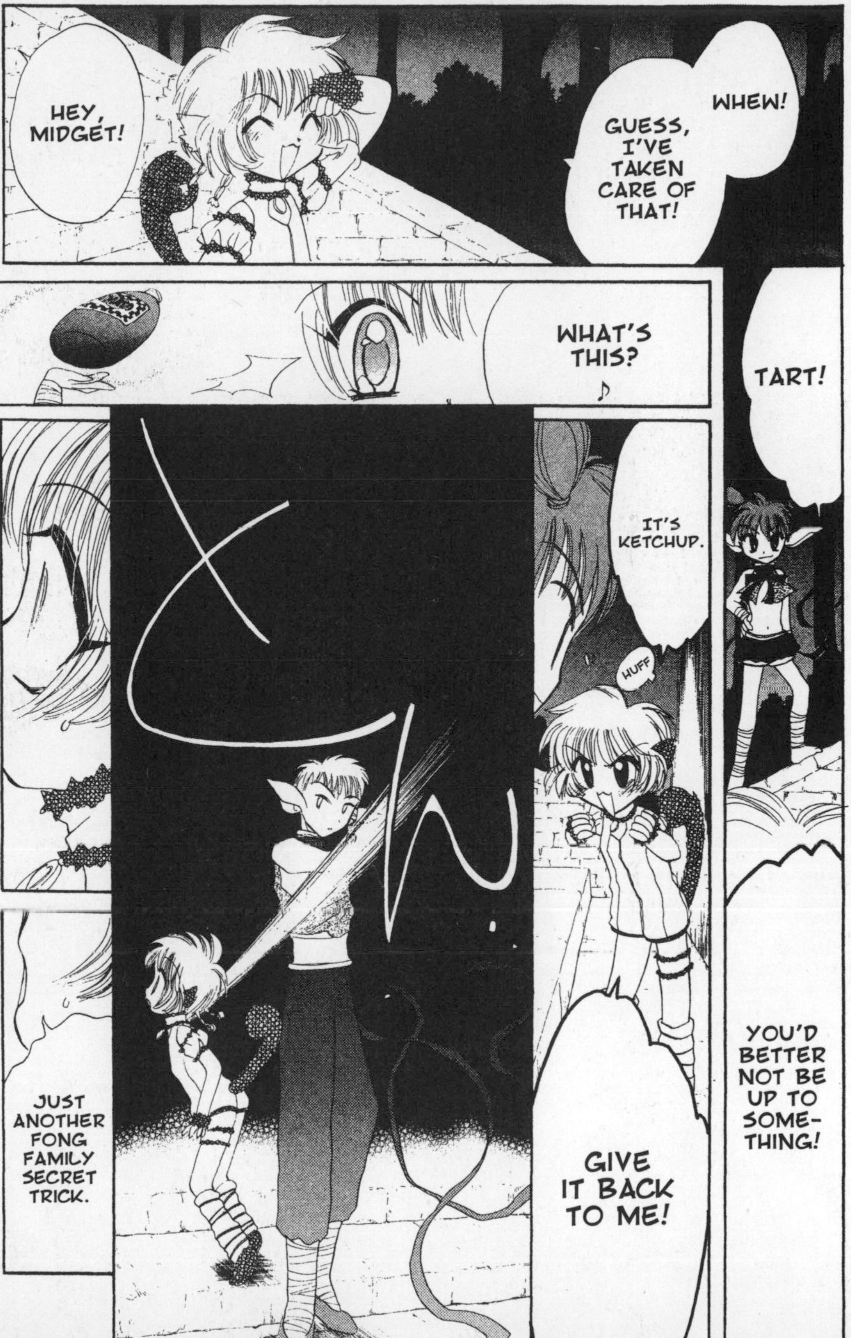
WHEW!
GUESS, I'VE TAKEN CARE OF THAT!
HEY, MIDGET!
TART!
YOU'D BETTER NOT BE UP TO SOME-THING!
WHAT'S THIS? ♪
IT'S KETCHUP.
HUFF
GIVE IT BACK TO ME!
JUST ANOTHER FONG FAMILY SECRET TRICK.

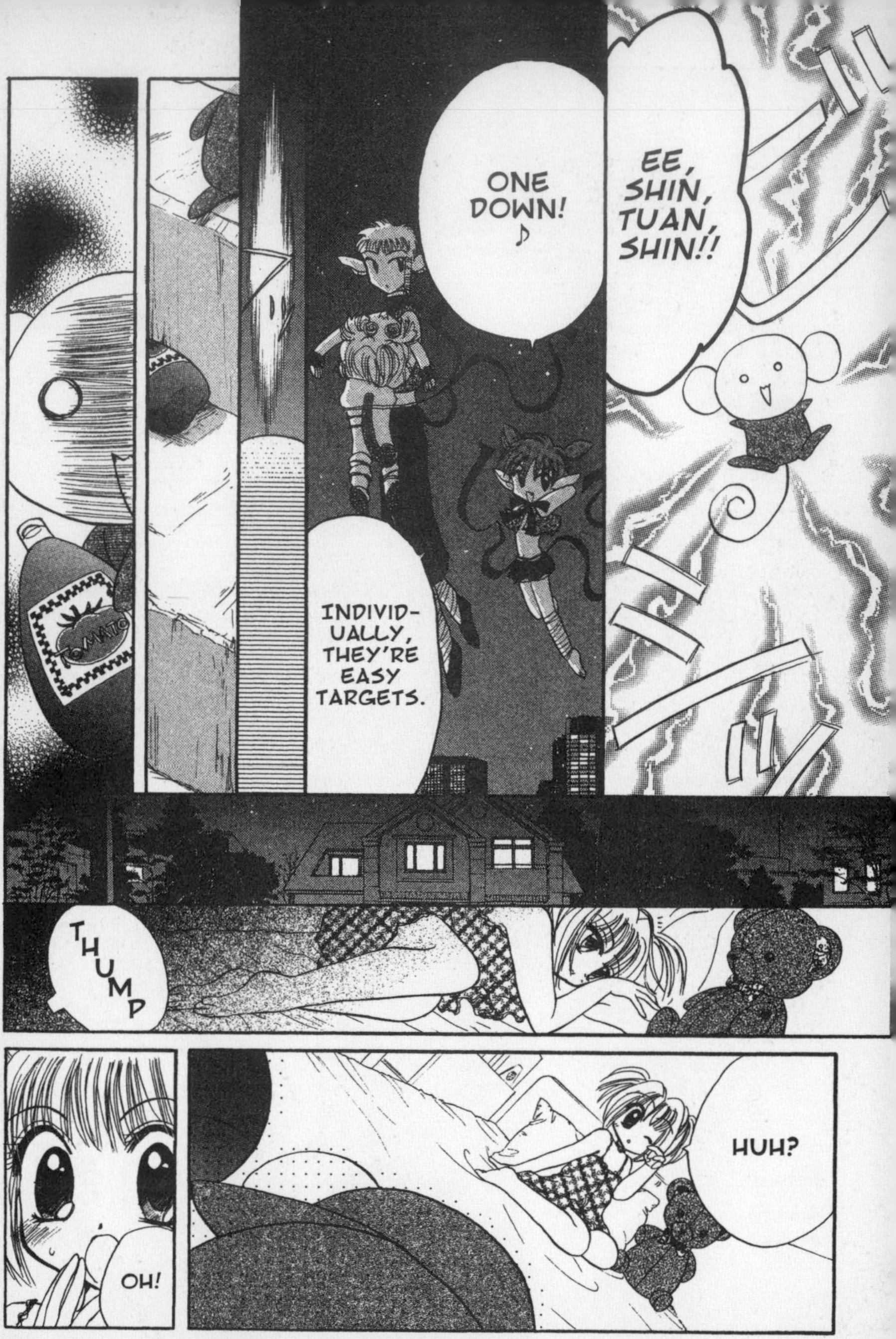
EE, SHIN, TUAN, SHIN!!
ONE DOWN! ♪
INDIVID-UALLY, THEY'RE EASY TARGETS.
THUMP
HUH?
OH!

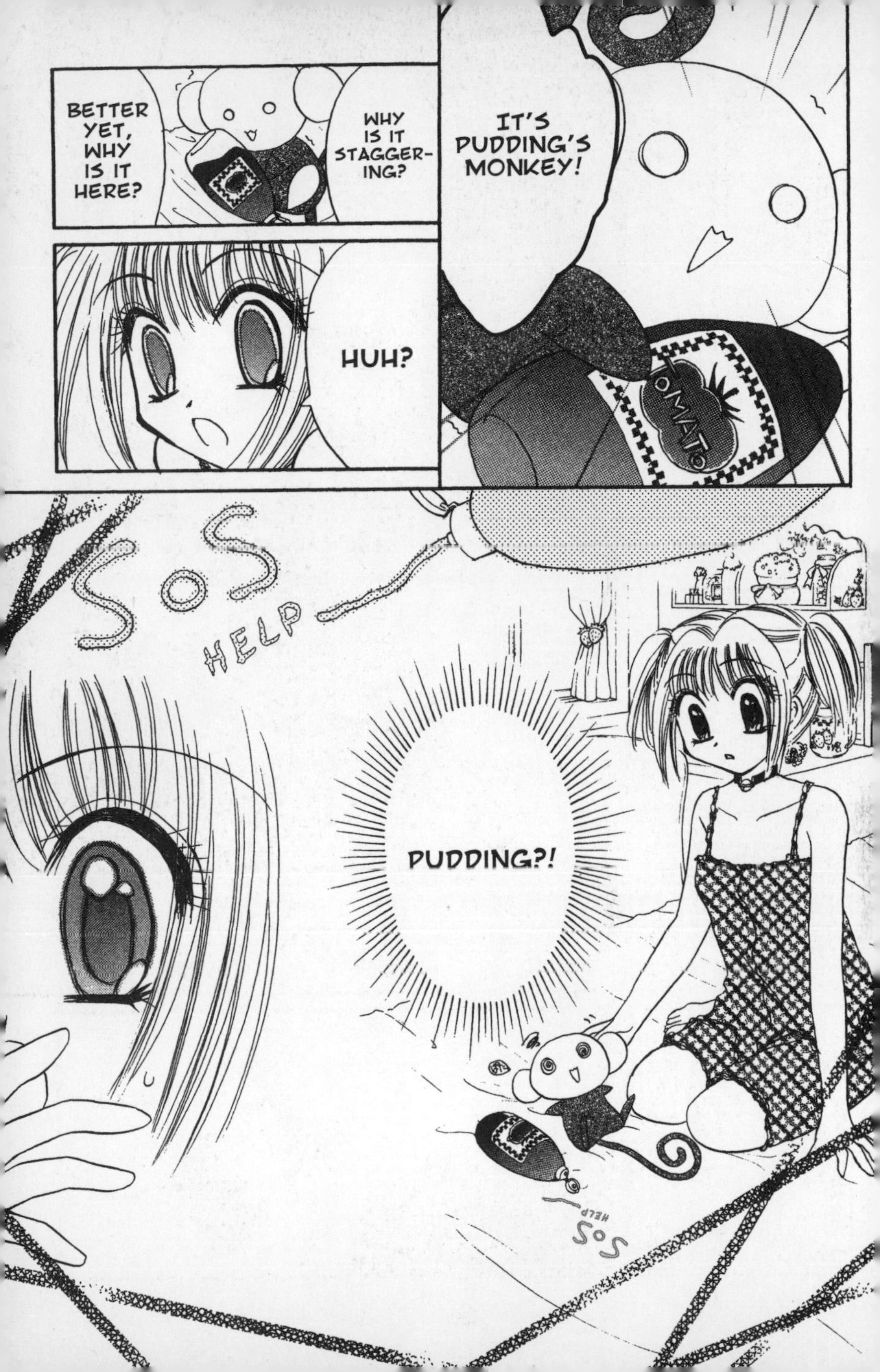
IT'S PUDDING'S MONKEY!
TOMATO
WHY IS IT STAGGER-ING?
BETTER YET, WHY IS IT HERE?
HUH?
SOS
HELP
PUDDING?!
SOS
HELP

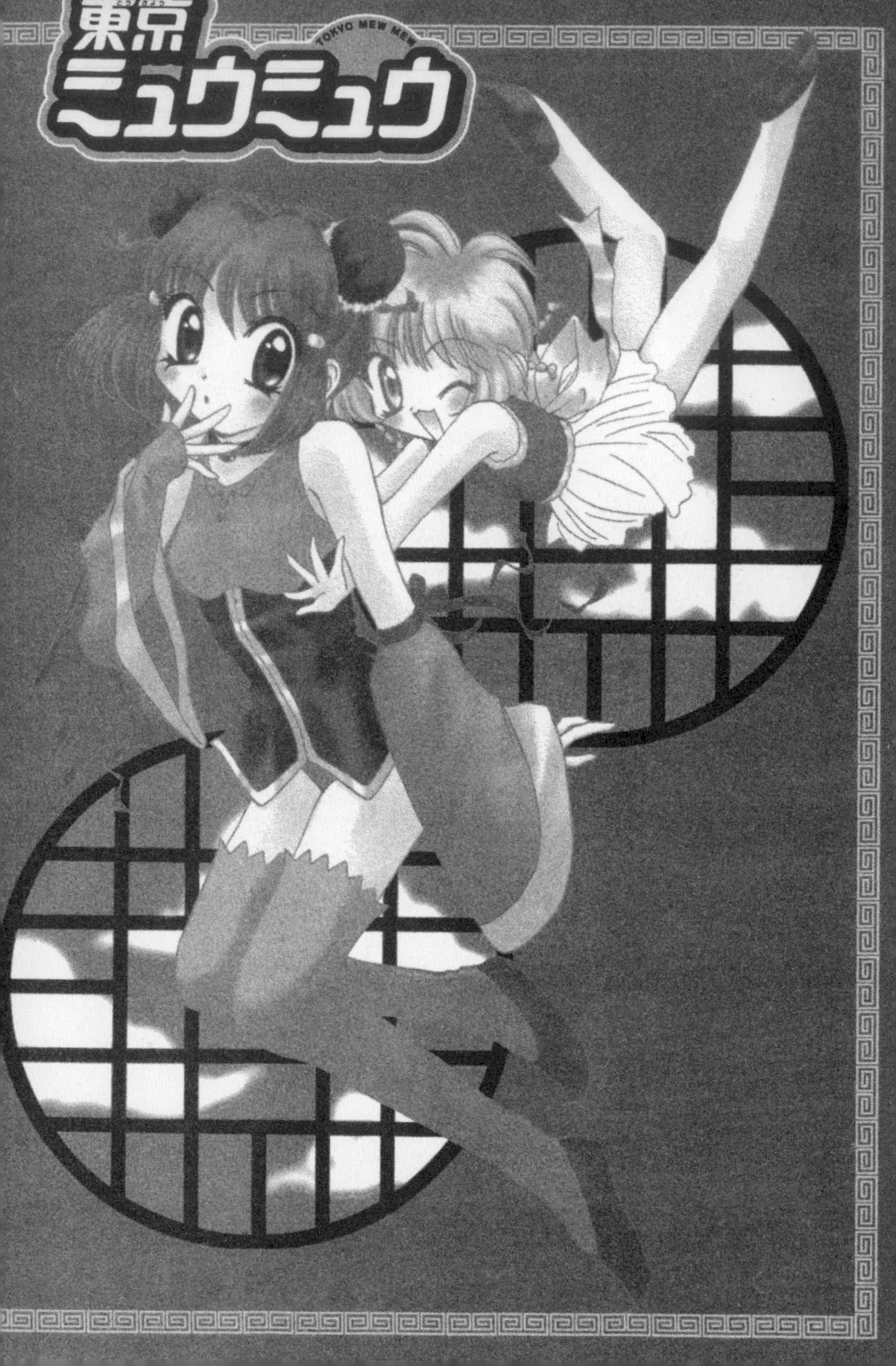
東京ミュウミュウ
TOKYO MEW MEW

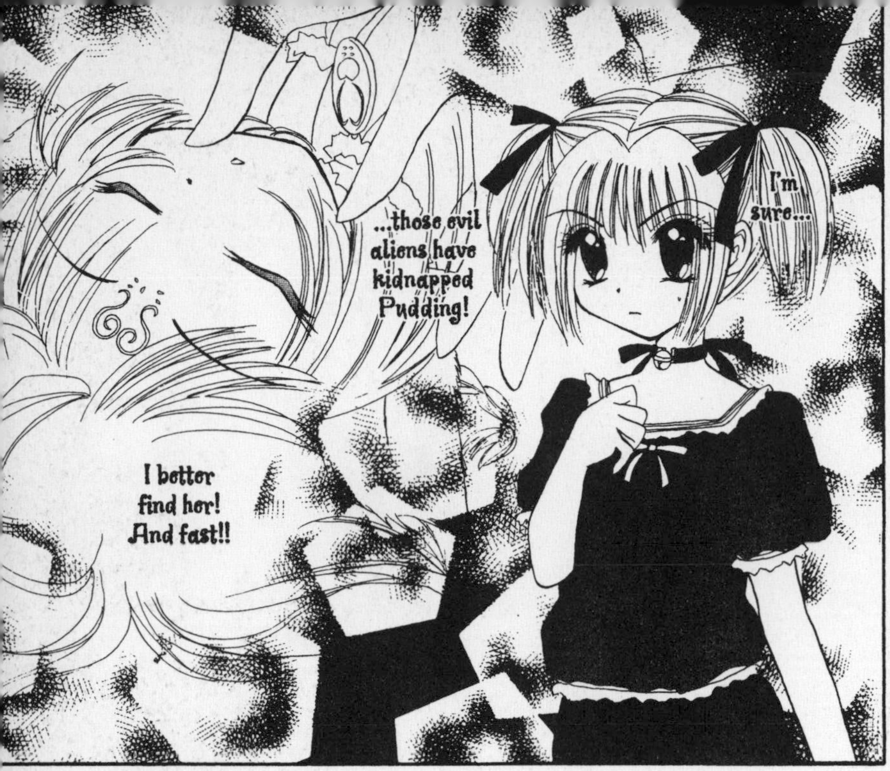
I'm sure...
...those evil aliens have kidnapped Pudding!
I better find her! And fast!!

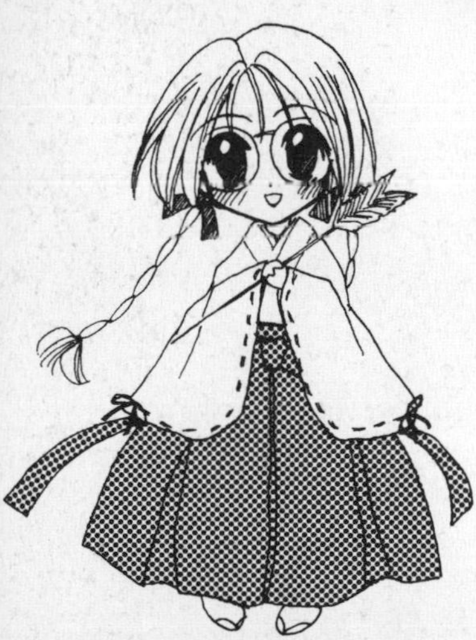

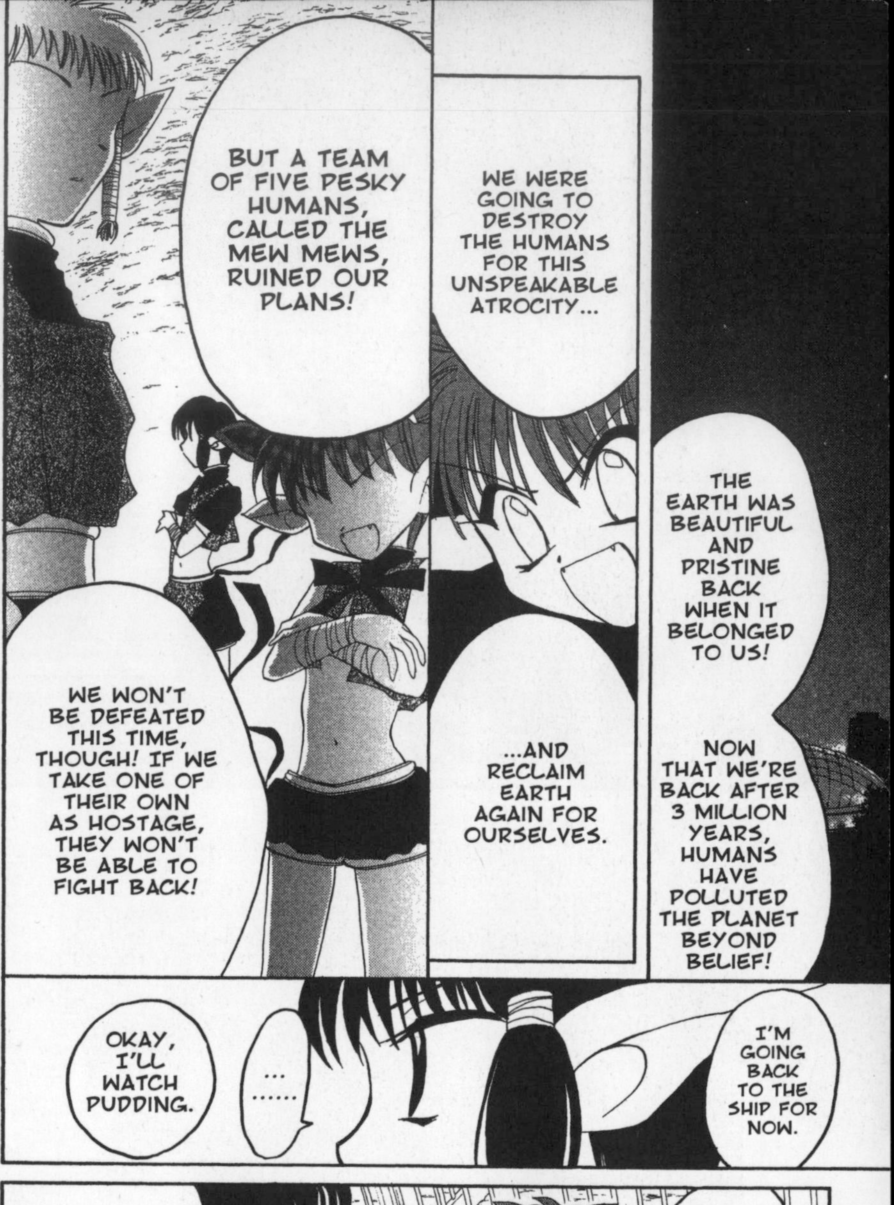
THE EARTH WAS BEAUTIFUL AND PRISTINE BACK WHEN IT BELONGED TO US!
NOW THAT WE'RE BACK AFTER 3 MILLION YEARS, HUMANS HAVE POLLUTED THE PLANET BEYOND BELIEF!
WE WERE GOING TO DESTROY THE HUMANS FOR THIS UNSPEAKABLE ATROCITY...
...AND RECLAIM EARTH AGAIN FOR OURSELVES.
BUT A TEAM OF FIVE PESKY HUMANS, CALLED THE MEW MEWS, RUINED OUR PLANS!
WE WON'T BE DEFEATED THIS TIME, THOUGH! IF WE TAKE ONE OF THEIR OWN AS HOSTAGE, THEY WON'T BE ABLE TO FIGHT BACK!
I'M GOING BACK TO THE SHIP FOR NOW.
... .
OKAY, I'LL WATCH PUDDING.
KISH?!
YEAH?

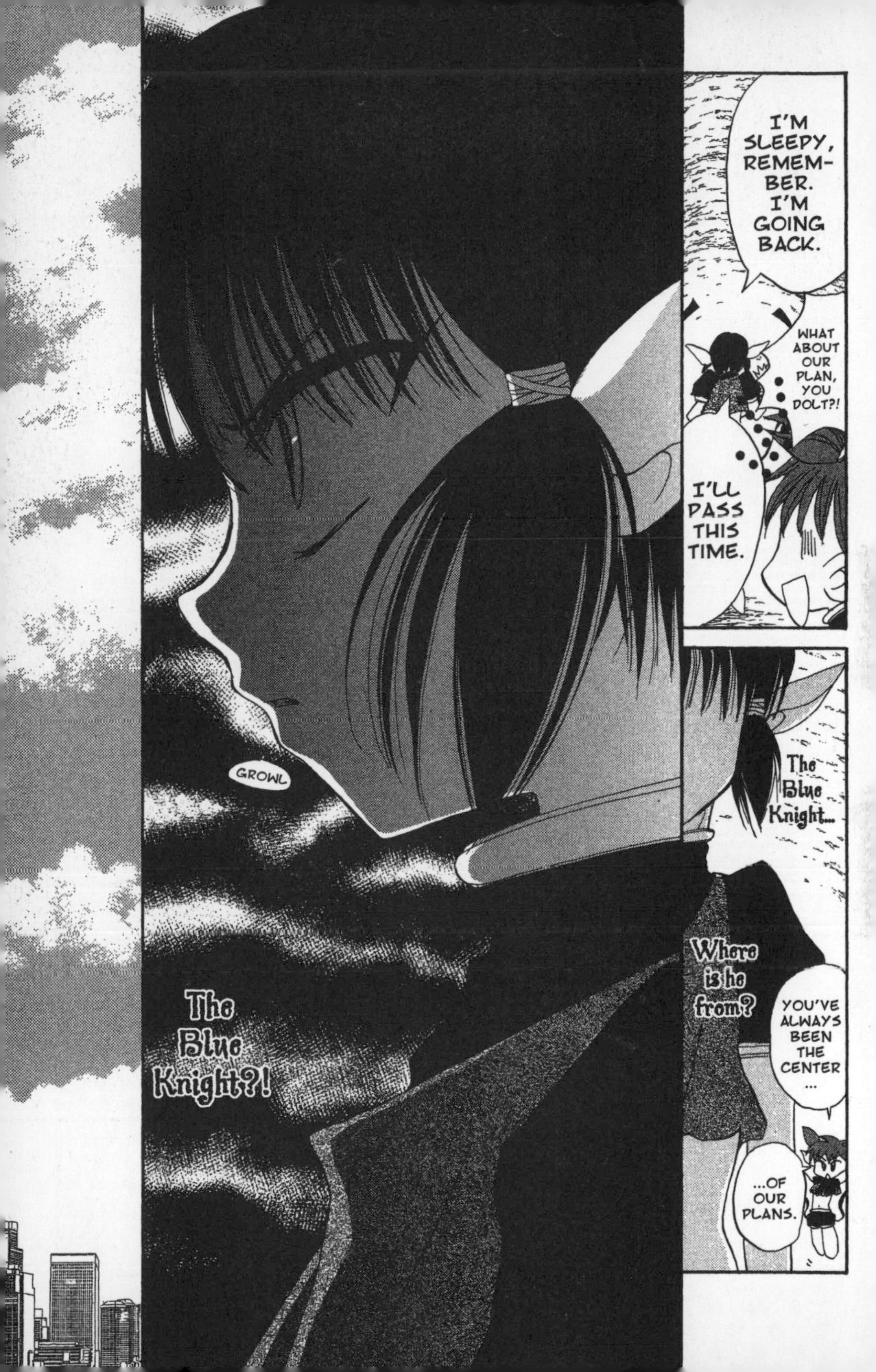
I'M SLEEPY, REMEMBER. I'M GOING BACK.
WHAT ABOUT OUR PLAN, YOU DOLT?!
I'LL PASS THIS TIME.
The Blue Knight...
Where is he from?
YOU'VE ALWAYS BEEN THE CENTER...
...OF OUR PLANS.
GROWL
The Blue Knight?!

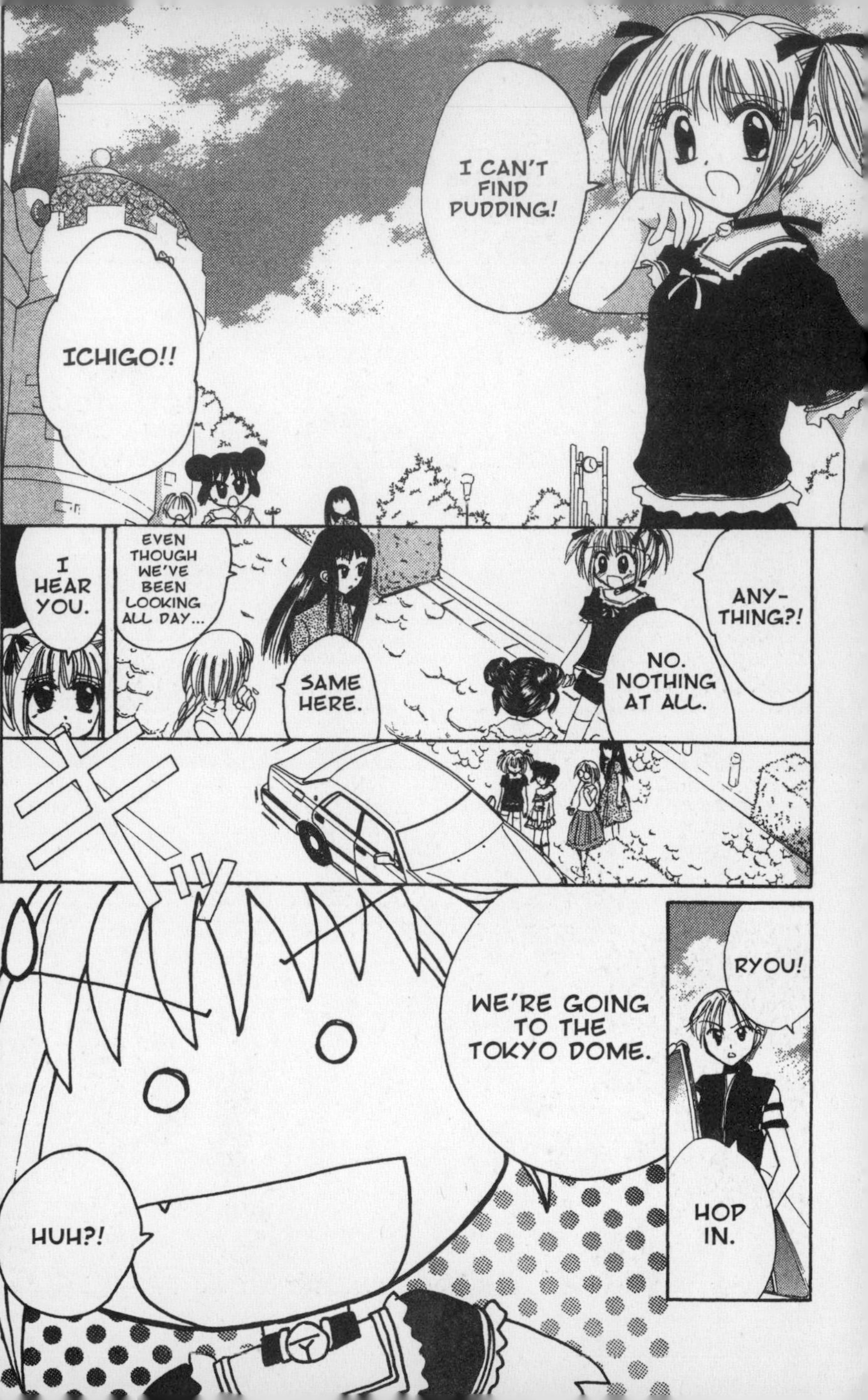
I CAN'T FIND PUDDING!
ICHIGO!!
ANY-THING?!
NO. NOTHING AT ALL.
SAME HERE.
EVEN THOUGH WE'VE BEEN LOOKING ALL DAY...
I HEAR YOU.
RYOU!
HOP IN.
WE'RE GOING TO THE TOKYO DOME.
HUH?!

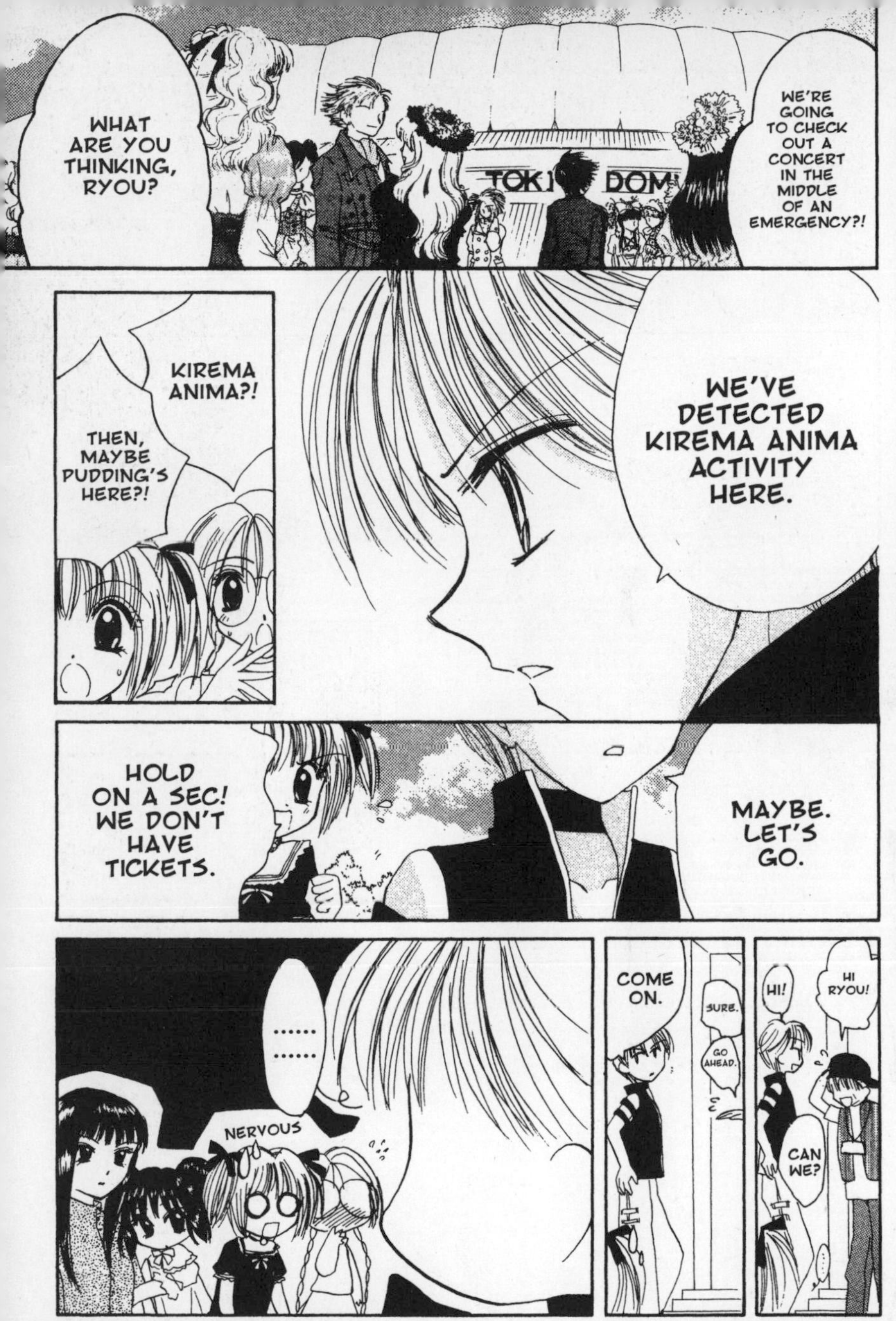
WE'RE GOING TO CHECK OUT A CONCERT IN THE MIDDLE OF AN EMERGENCY?!
WHAT ARE YOU THINKING, RYOU?
WE'VE DETECTED KIREMA ANIMA ACTIVITY HERE.
KIREMA ANIMA?!
THEN, MAYBE PUDDING'S HERE?!
MAYBE. LET'S GO.
HOLD ON A SEC! WE DON'T HAVE TICKETS.
HI RYOU!
HI!
CAN WE?
...
SURE.
GO AHEAD.
COME ON.
......
......
NERVOUS

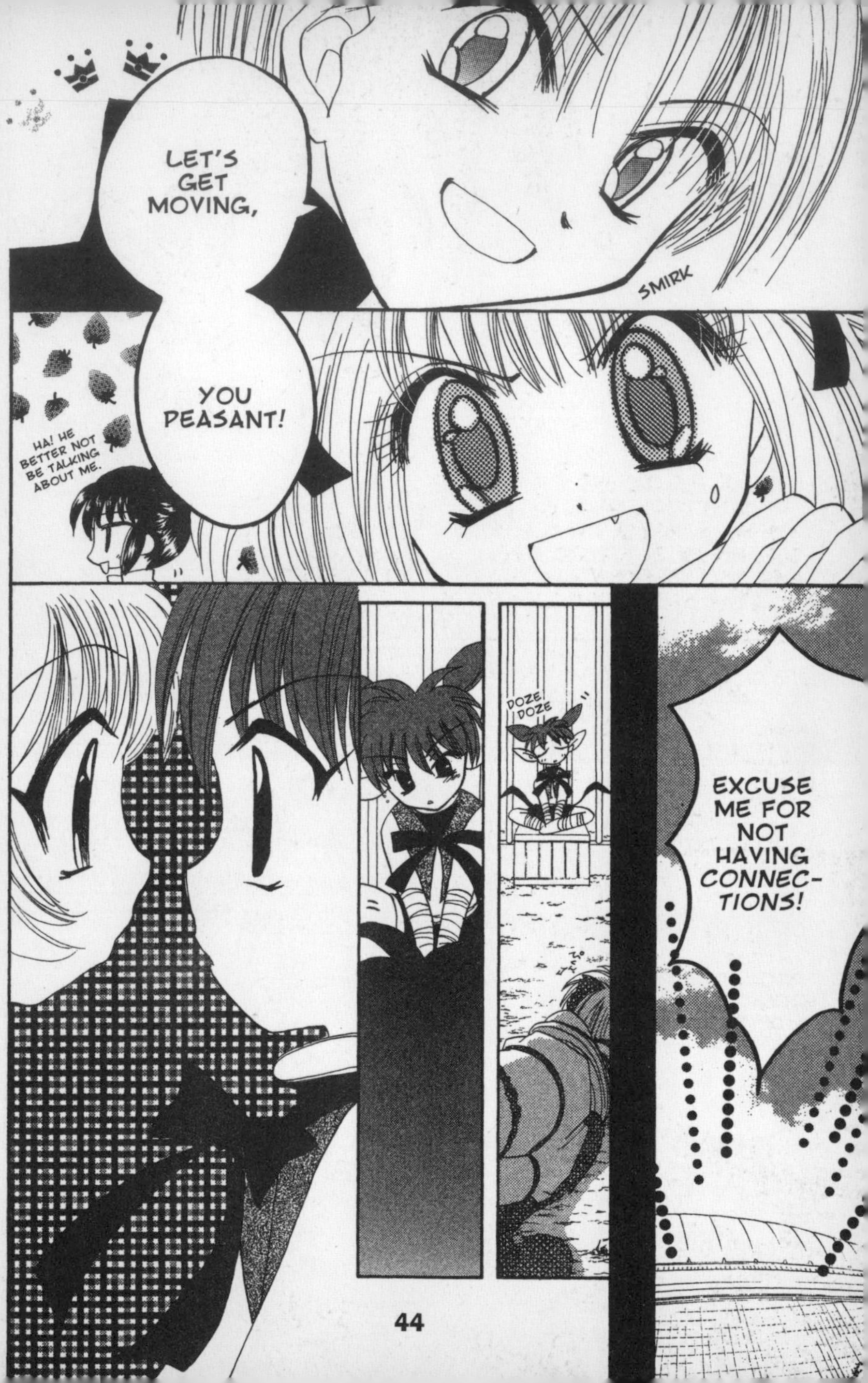
LET'S GET MOVING,
SMIRK
YOU PEASANT!
HA! HE BETTER NOT BE TALKING ABOUT ME.
EXCUSE ME FOR NOT HAVING CONNEC-TIONS!
DOZE DOZE

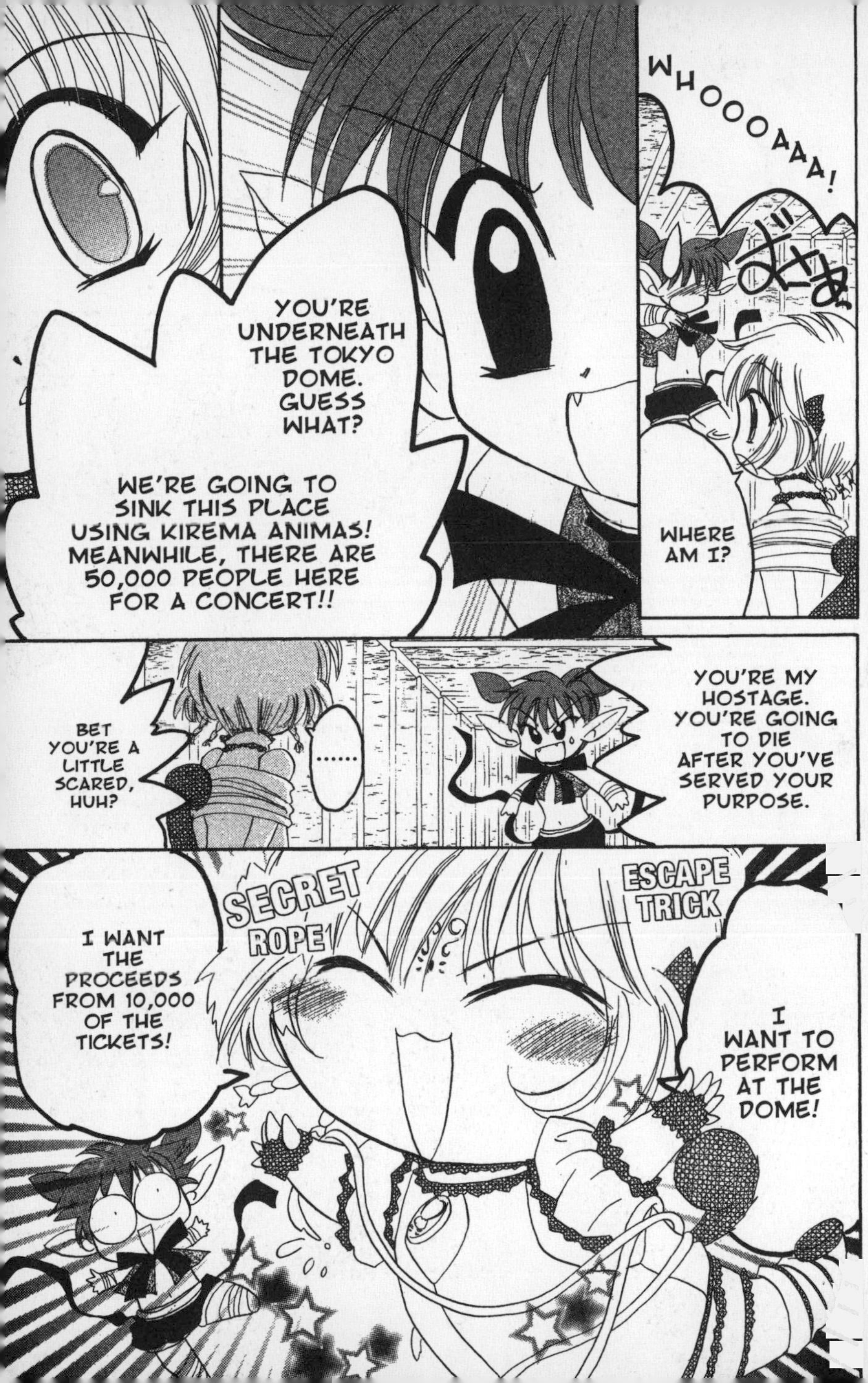
WHOOOAAAA!
WHERE AM I?
YOU'RE UNDERNEATH THE TOKYO DOME. GUESS WHAT?
WE'RE GOING TO SINK THIS PLACE USING KIREMA ANIMAS! MEANWHILE, THERE ARE 50,000 PEOPLE HERE FOR A CONCERT!!
YOU'RE MY HOSTAGE. YOU'RE GOING TO DIE AFTER YOU'VE SERVED YOUR PURPOSE.
......
BET YOU'RE A LITTLE SCARED, HUH?
ESCAPE TRICK
I WANT TO PERFORM AT THE DOME!
SECRET ROPE
I WANT THE PROCEEDS FROM 10,000 OF THE TICKETS!

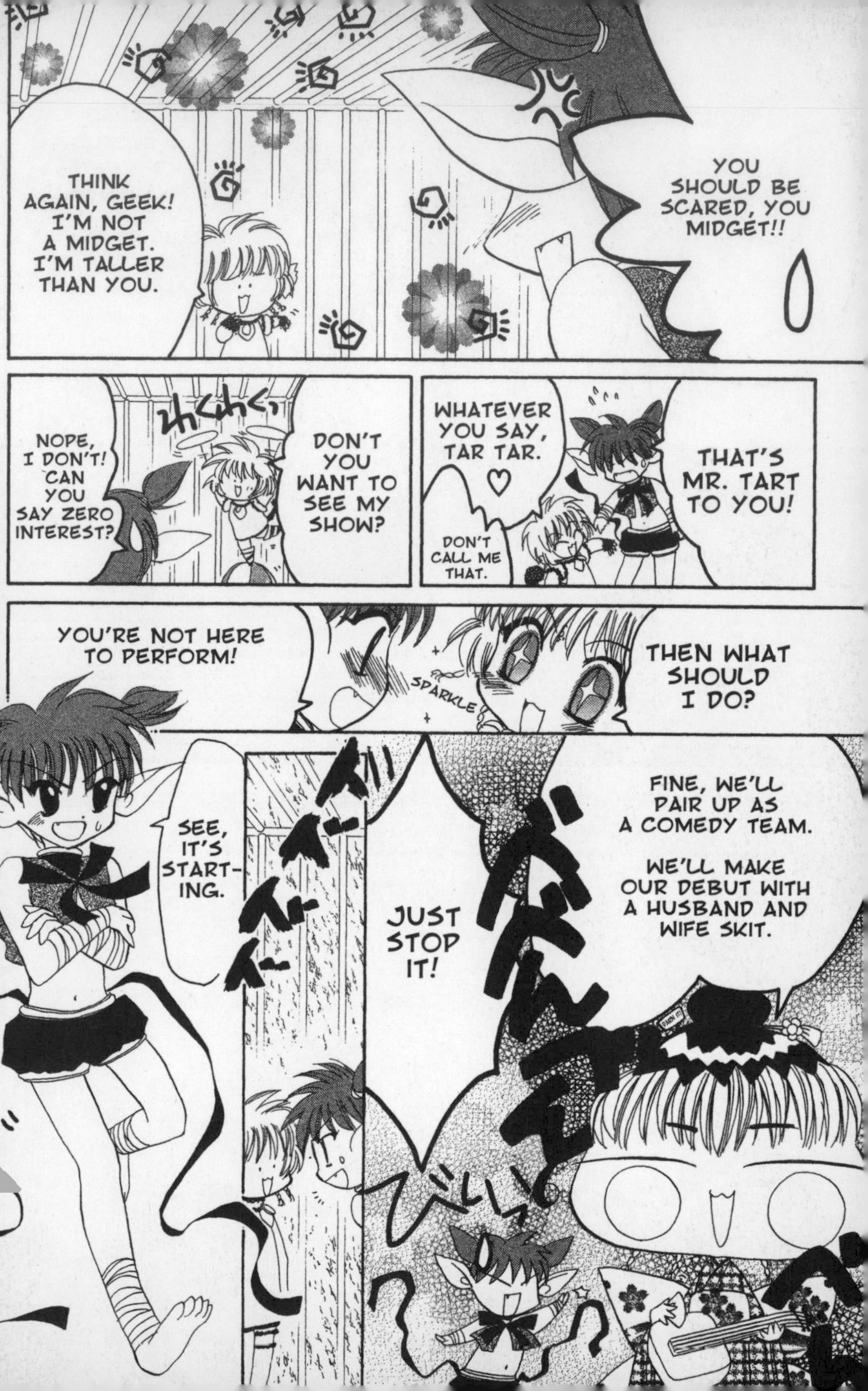
YOU SHOULD BE SCARED, YOU MIDGET!!
THINK AGAIN, GEEK! I'M NOT A MIDGET. I'M TALLER THAN YOU.
THAT'S MR. TART TO YOU!
WHATEVER YOU SAY, TAR TAR. ♡
DON'T CALL ME THAT.
DON'T YOU WANT TO SEE MY SHOW?
NOPE, I DON'T! CAN YOU SAY ZERO INTEREST?
THEN WHAT SHOULD I DO?
SPARKLE
YOU'RE NOT HERE TO PERFORM!
FINE, WE'LL PAIR UP AS A COMEDY TEAM.
WE'LL MAKE OUR DEBUT WITH A HUSBAND AND WIFE SKIT.
JUST STOP IT!
SEE, IT'S START-ING.

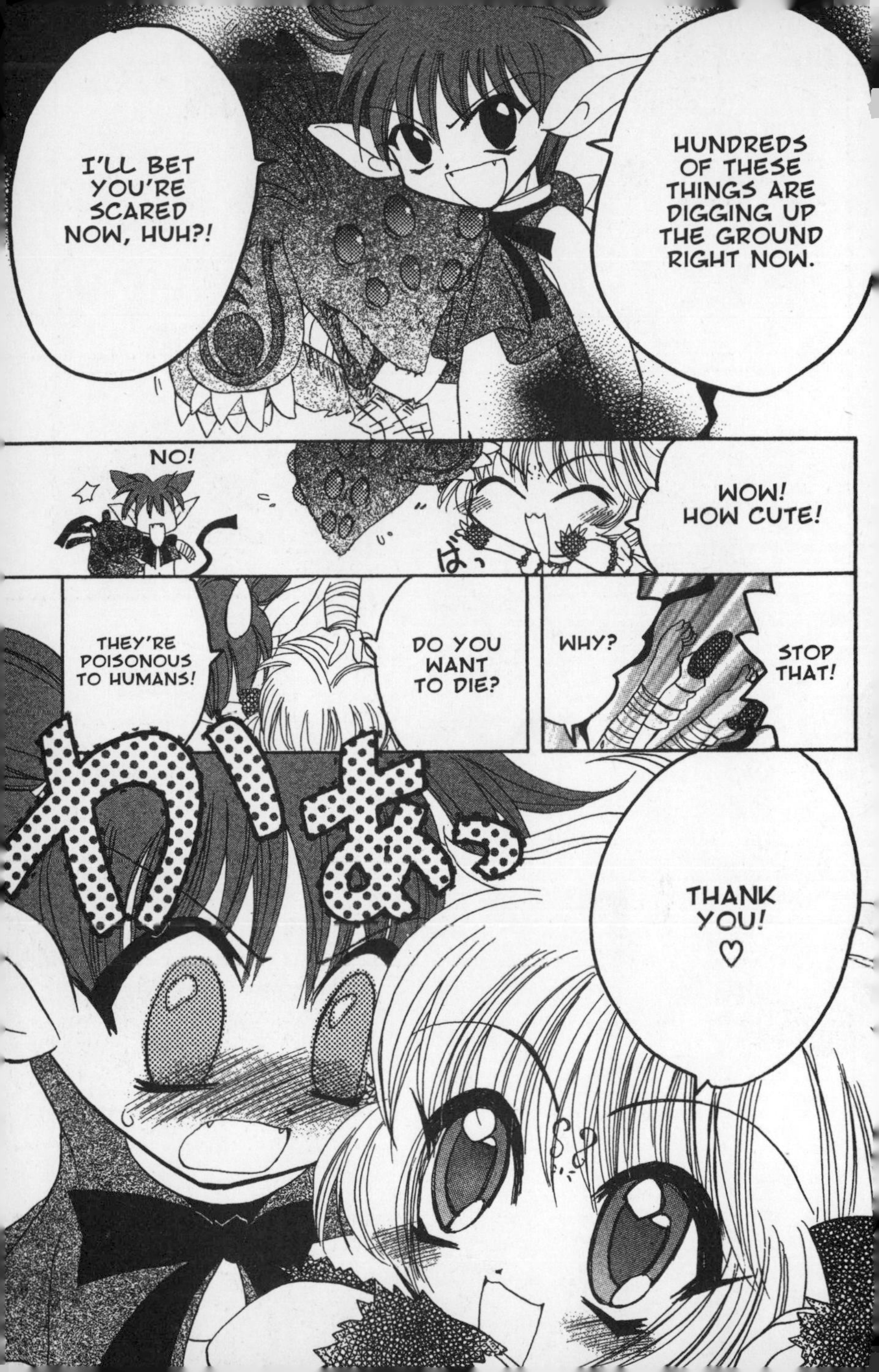
HUNDREDS OF THESE THINGS ARE DIGGING UP THE GROUND RIGHT NOW.
I'LL BET YOU'RE SCARED NOW, HUH?!
WOW! HOW CUTE!
ばっ
NO!
STOP THAT!
WHY?
DO YOU WANT TO DIE?
THEY'RE POISONOUS TO HUMANS!
THANK YOU! ♡

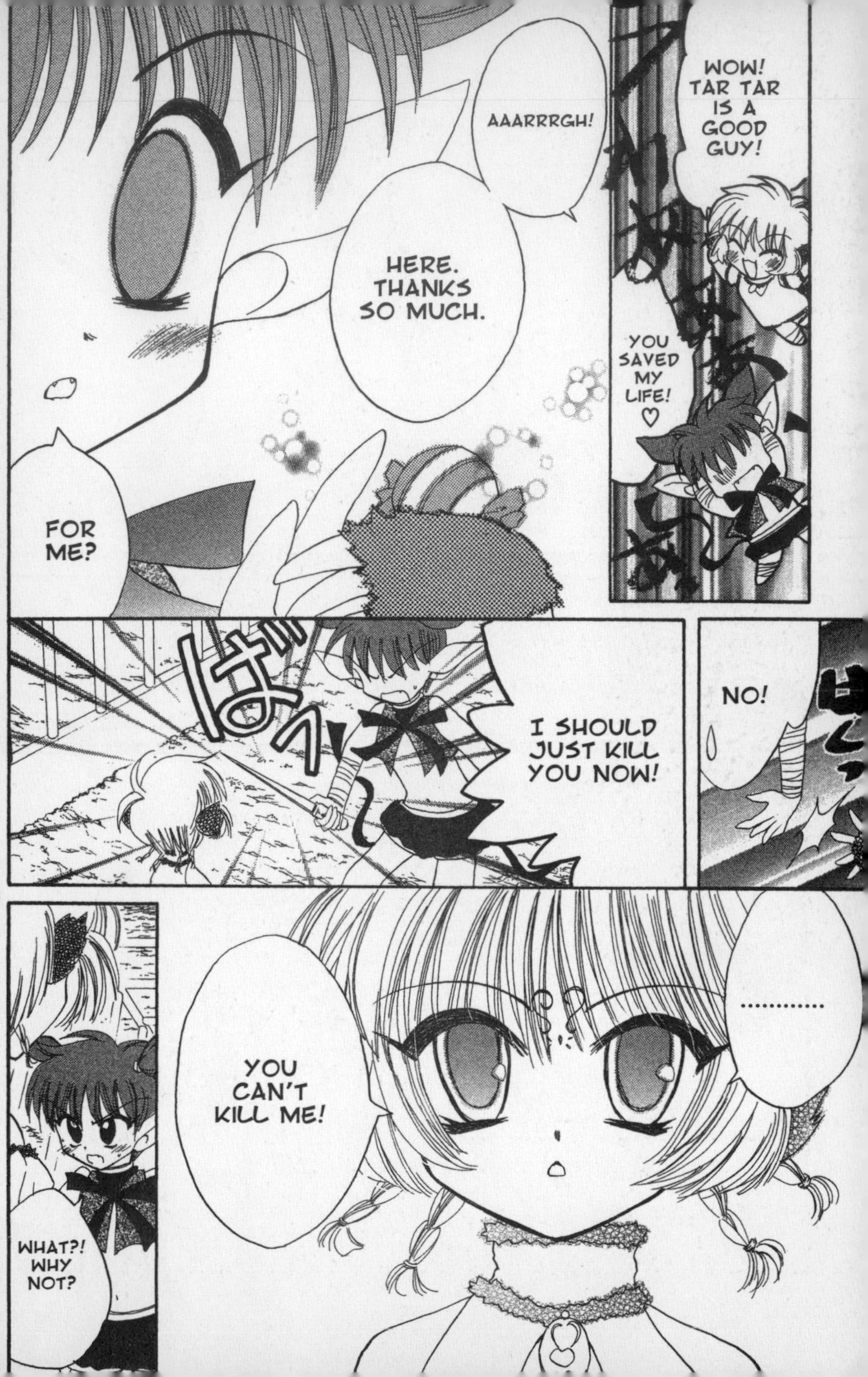
WOW! TAR TAR IS A GOOD GUY!
YOU SAVED MY LIFE! ♡
AAARRRGH!
HERE. THANKS SO MUCH.
FOR ME?
NO!
I SHOULD JUST KILL YOU NOW!
....
YOU CAN'T KILL ME!
WHAT?! WHY NOT?

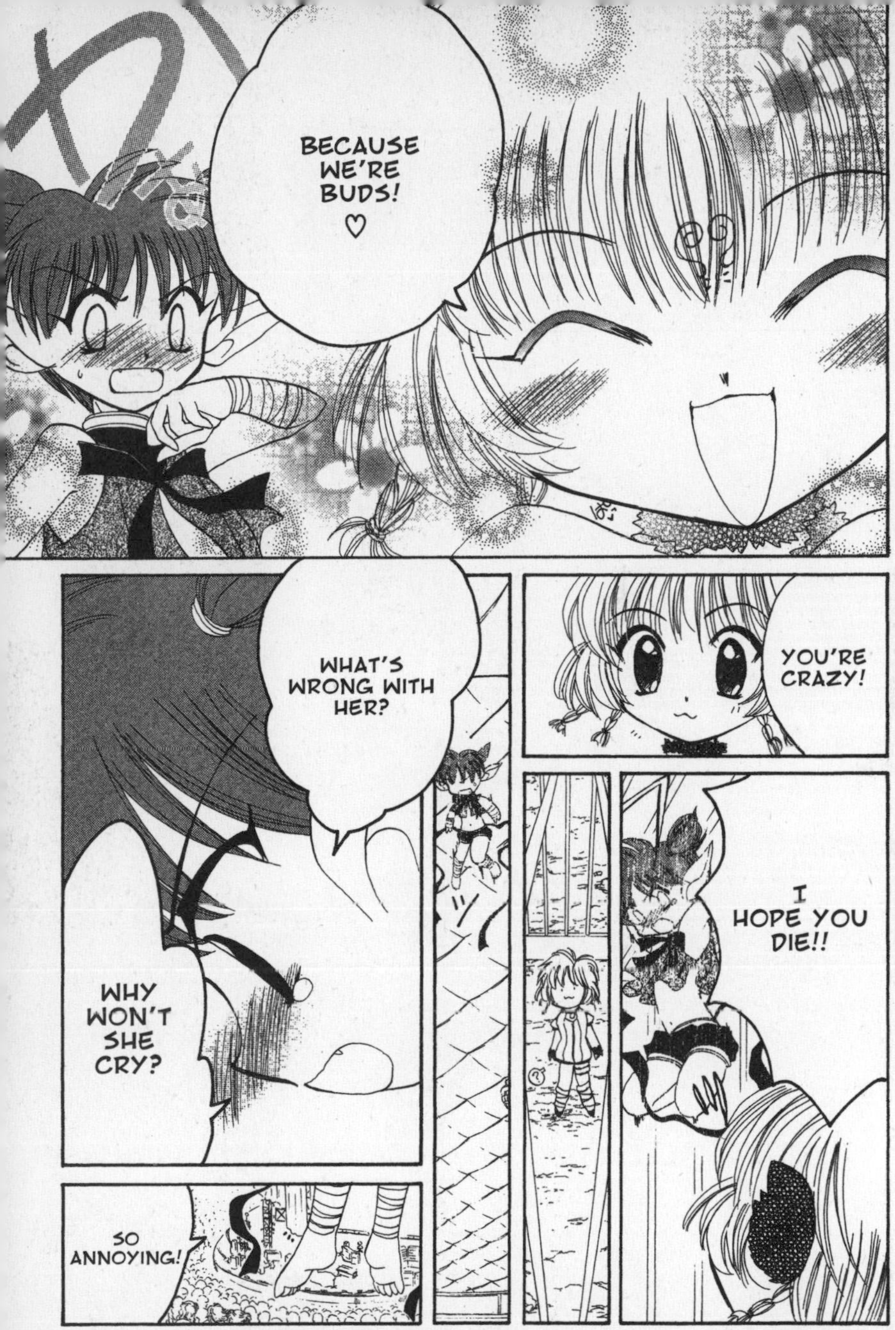
BECAUSE WE'RE BUDS! ♡
YOU'RE CRAZY!
I HOPE YOU DIE!!
WHAT'S WRONG WITH HER?
WHY WON'T SHE CRY?
SO ANNOYING!

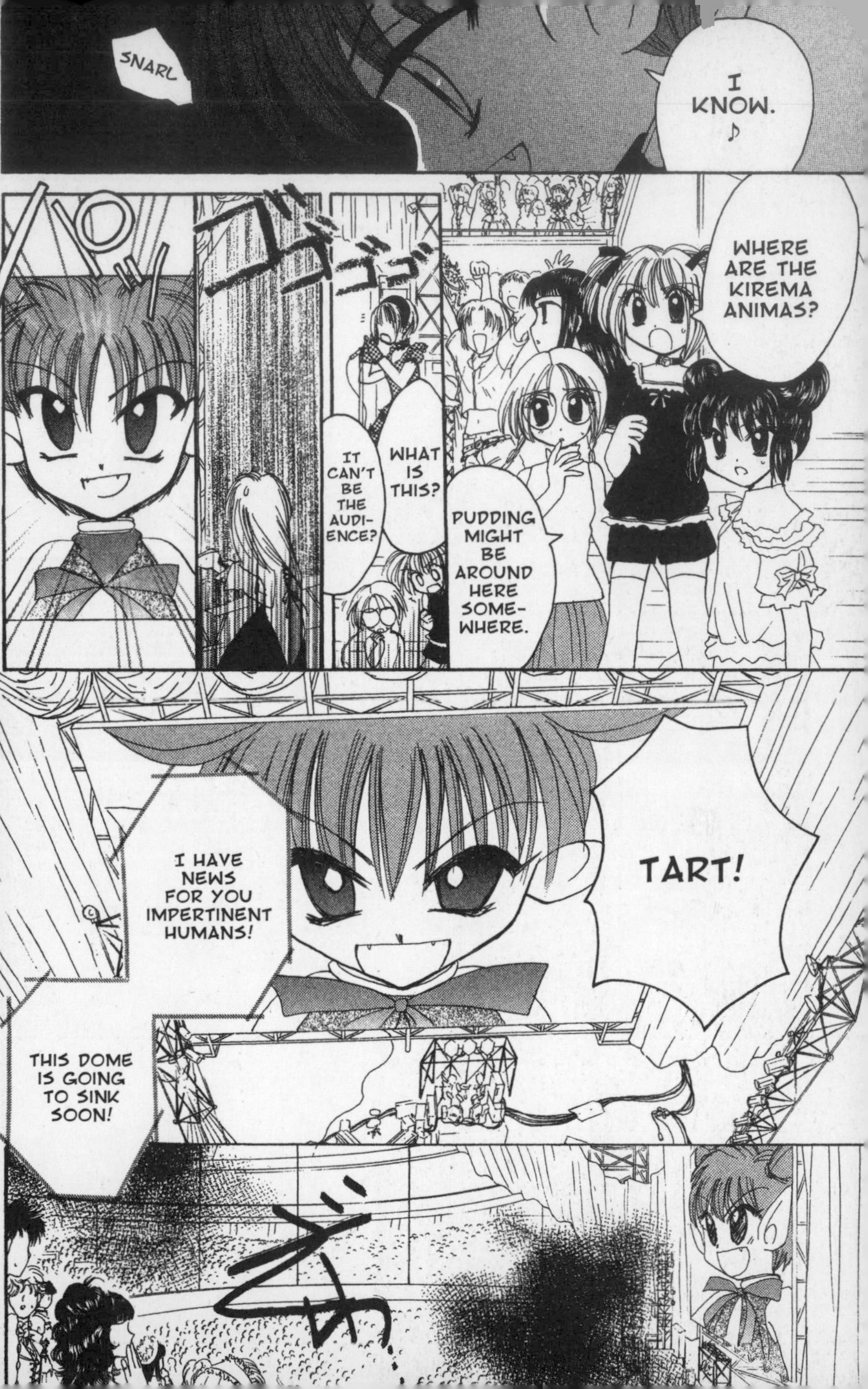
I KNOW. ♪
SNARL
WHERE ARE THE KIREMA ANIMAS?
PUDDING MIGHT BE AROUND HERE SOME-WHERE.
WHAT IS THIS?
IT CAN'T BE THE AUDI-ENCE?
TART!
I HAVE NEWS FOR YOU IMPERTINENT HUMANS!
THIS DOME IS GOING TO SINK SOON!

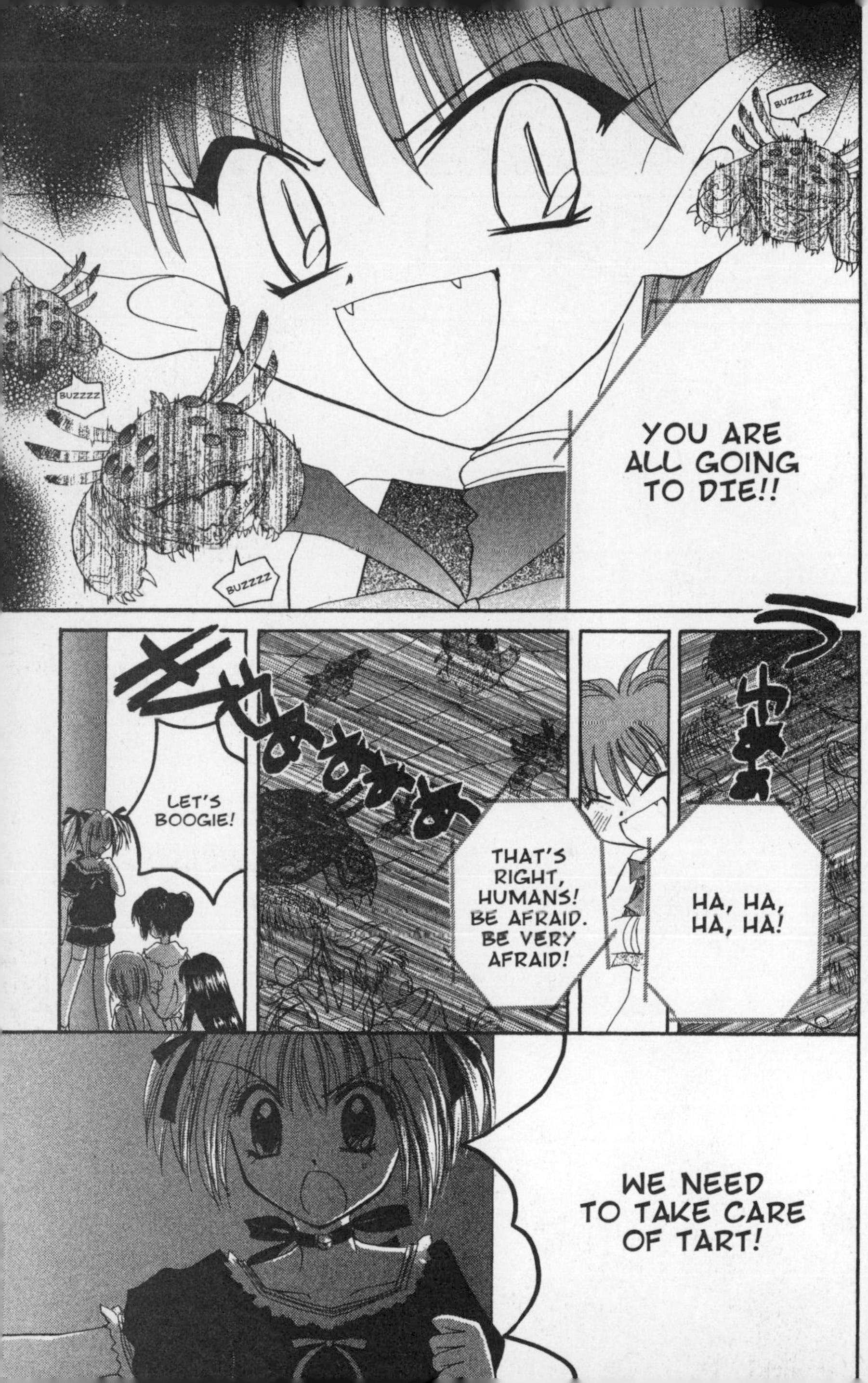
BUZZZZ
YOU ARE ALL GOING TO DIE!!
BUZZZZ
BUZZZZ
HA, HA, HA, HA!
THAT'S RIGHT, HUMANS! BE AFRAID. BE VERY AFRAID!
LET'S BOOGIE!
WE NEED TO TAKE CARE OF TART!

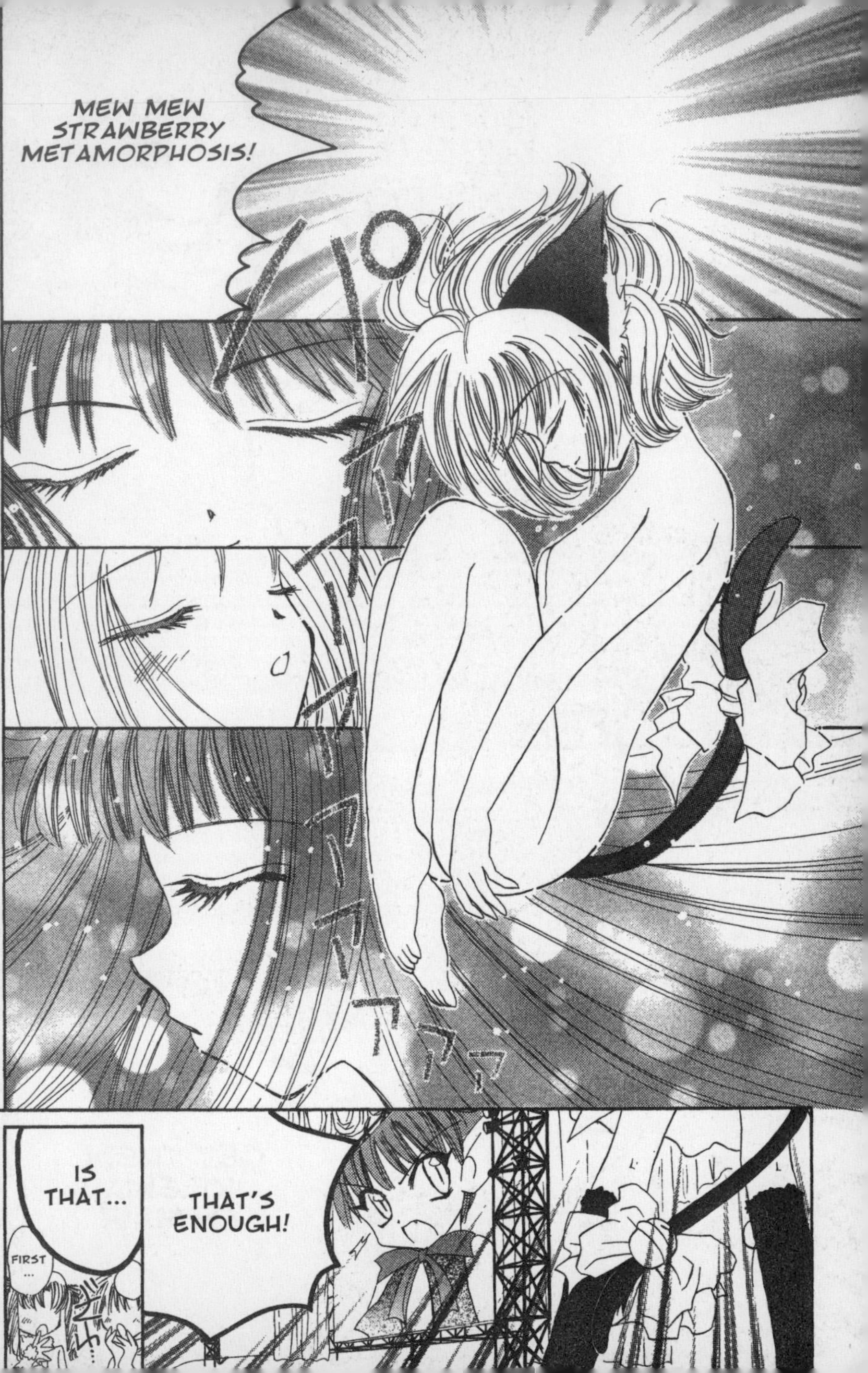
MEW MEW STRAWBERRY METAMORPHOSIS!
THAT'S ENOUGH!
IS THAT...
FIRST ...

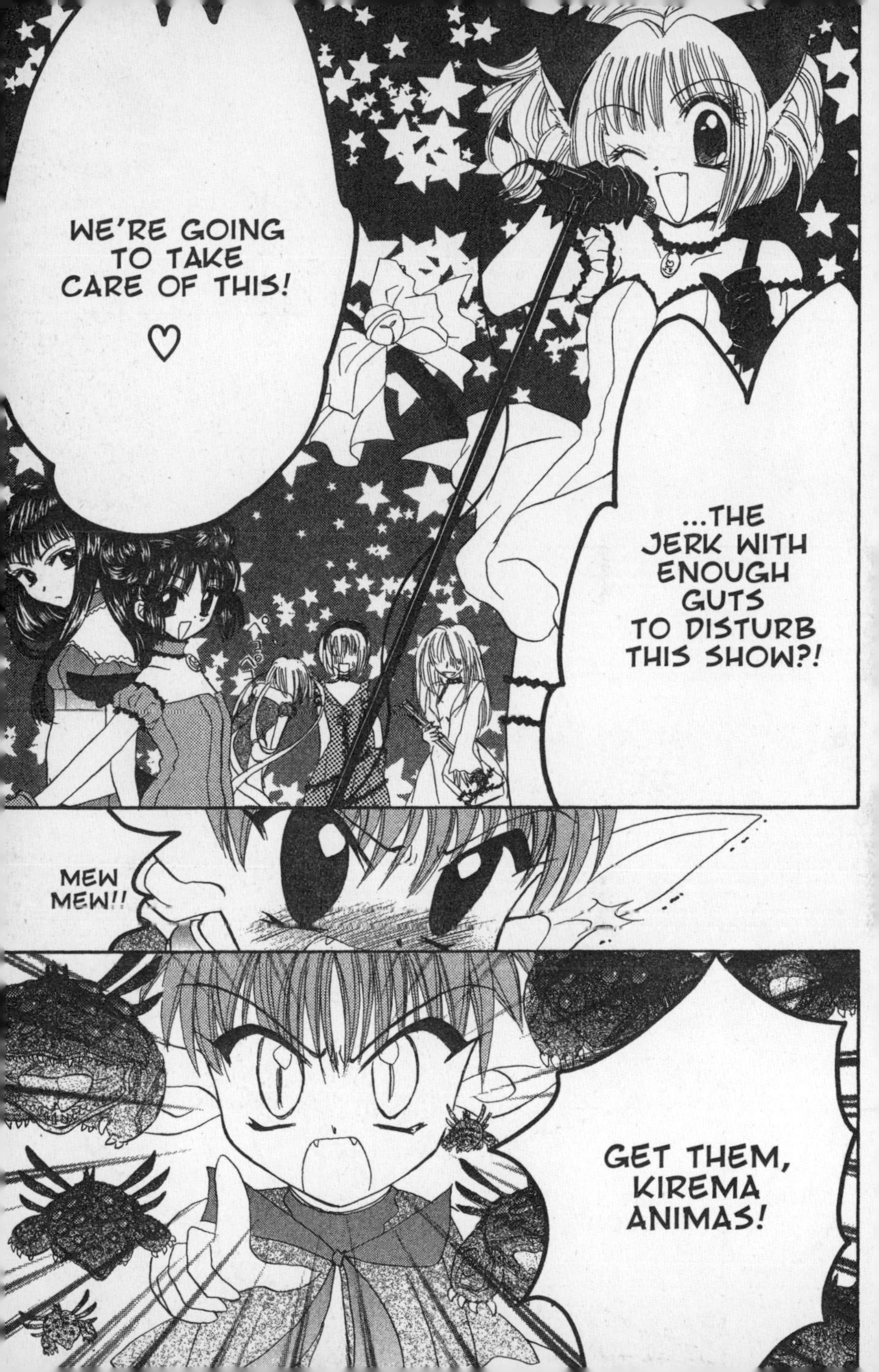
...THE JERK WITH ENOUGH GUTS TO DISTURB THIS SHOW?!
WE'RE GOING TO TAKE CARE OF THIS! ♡
MEW MEW!!
GET THEM, KIREMA ANIMAS!

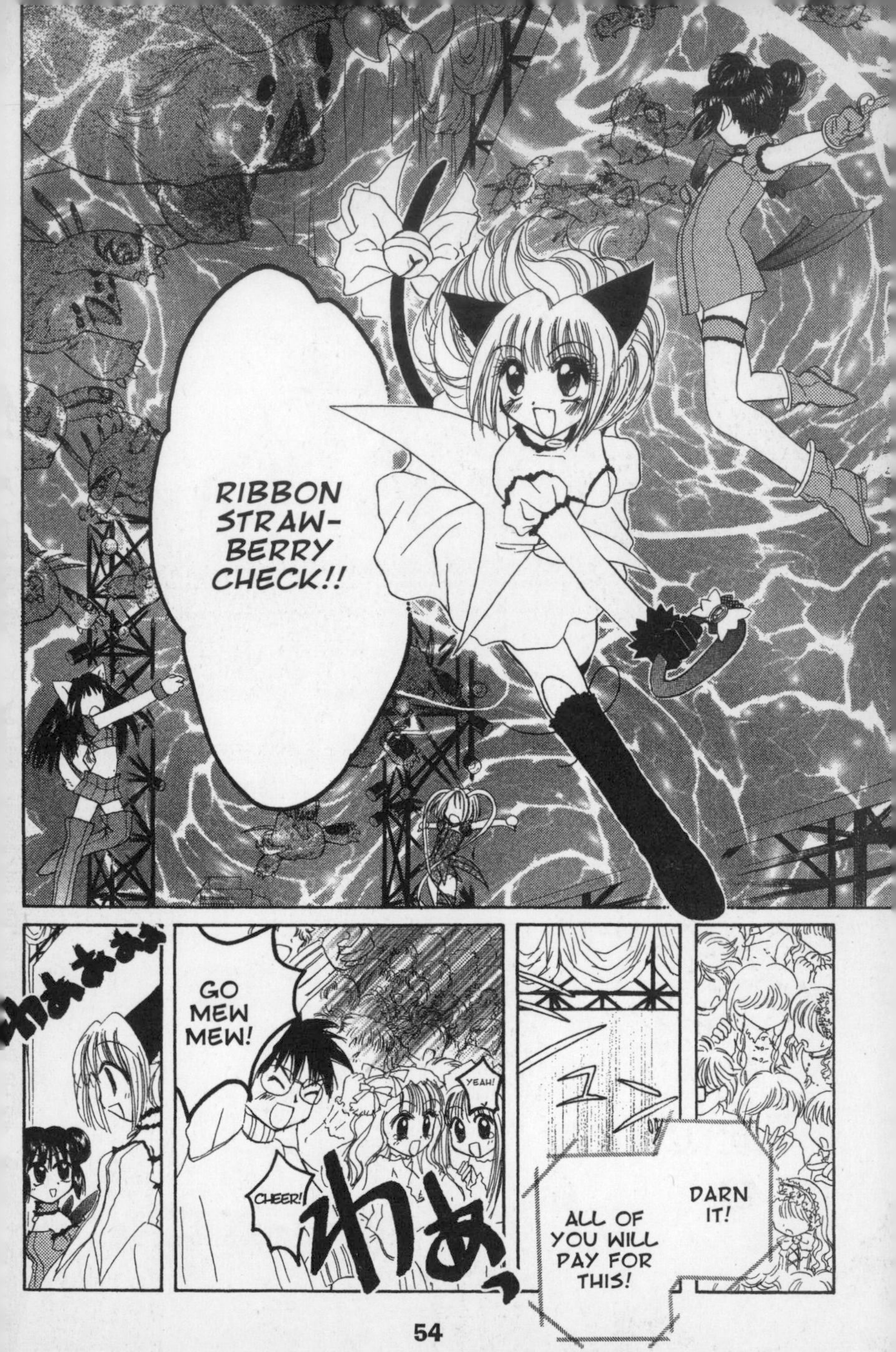
RIBBON STRAWBERRY CHECK!!
DARN IT! ALL OF YOU WILL PAY FOR THIS!
GO MEW MEW!
YEAH!
CHEER!

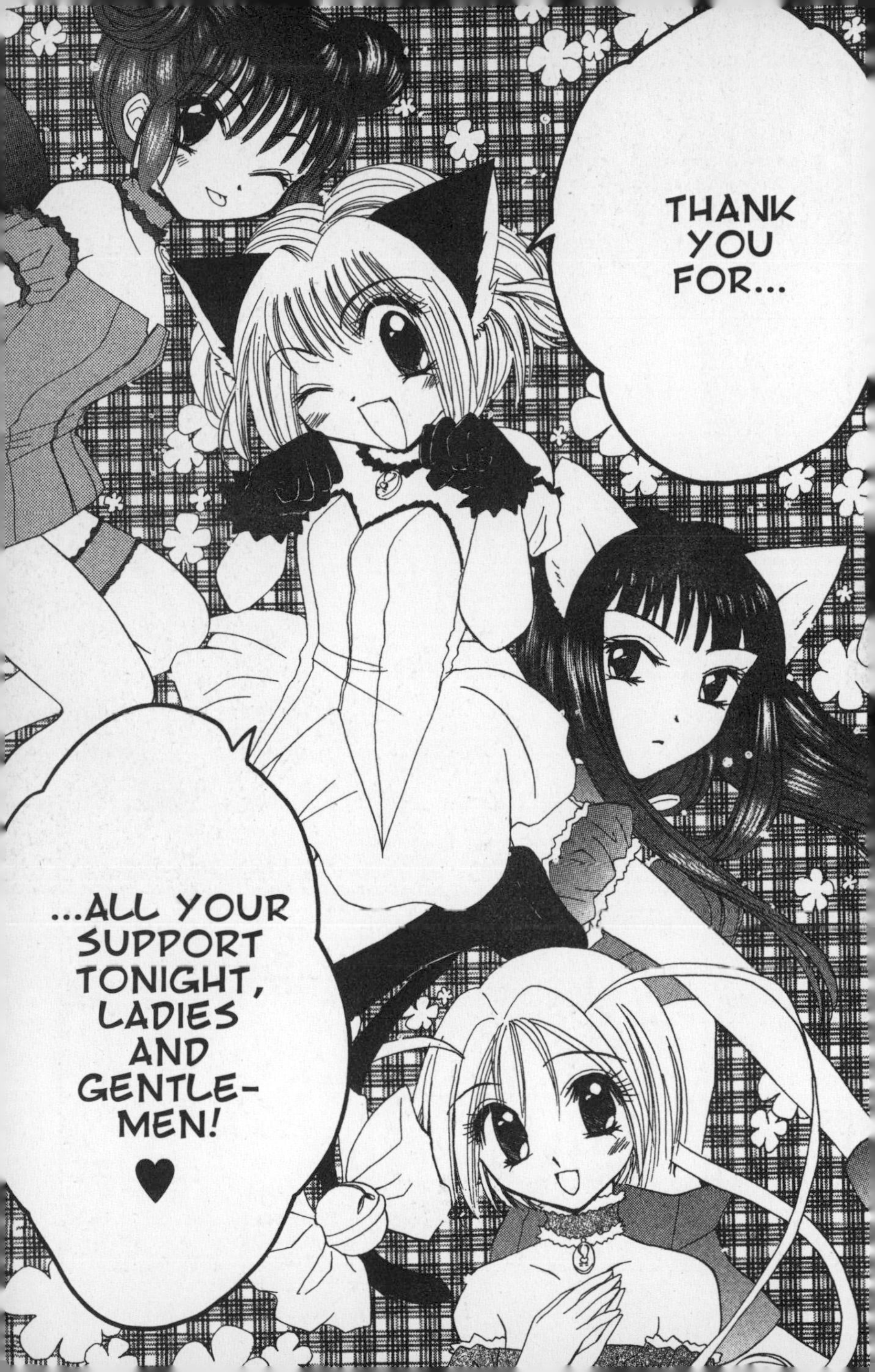
THANK YOU FOR...
...ALL YOUR SUPPORT TONIGHT, LADIES AND GENTLE-MEN! ♥

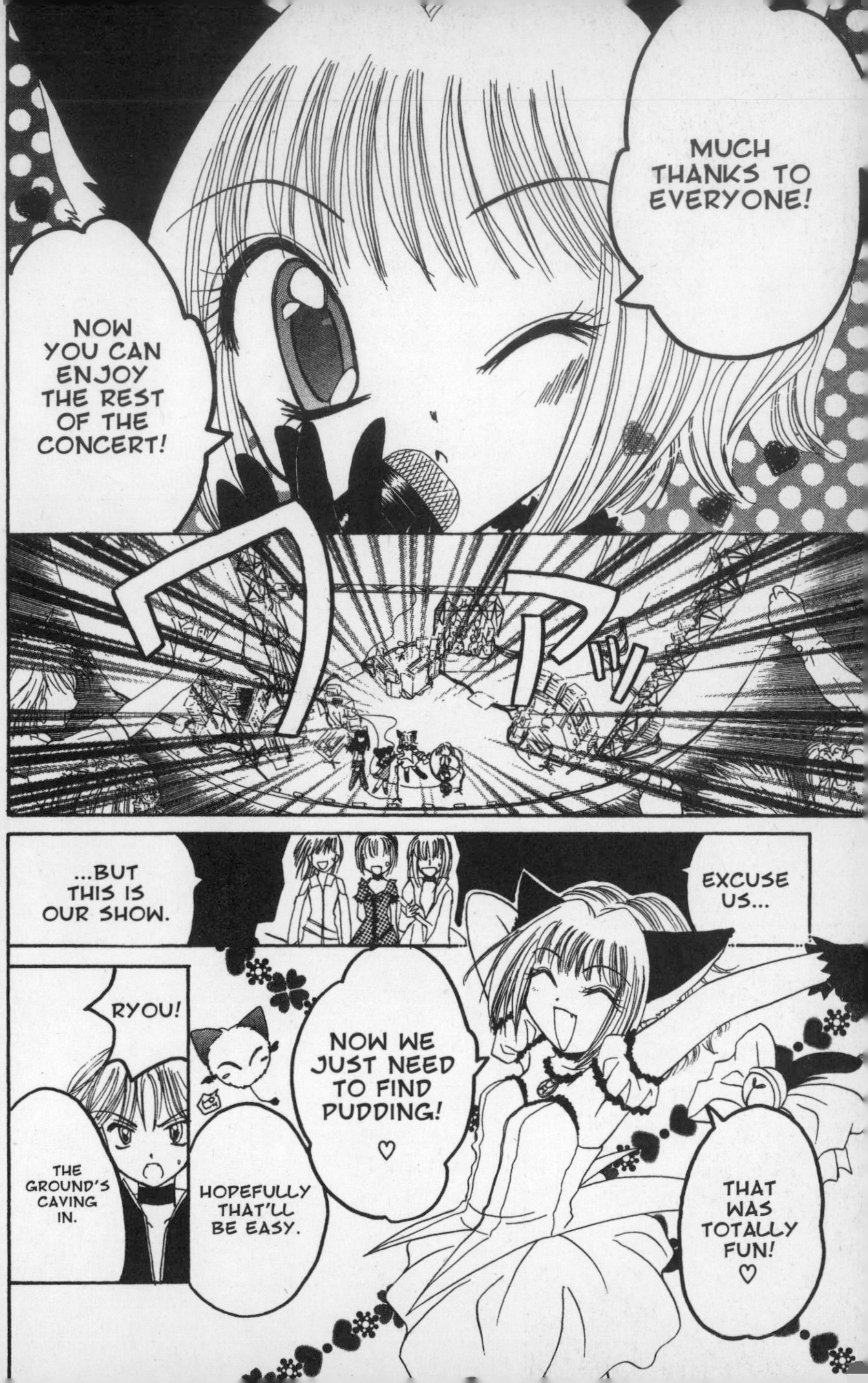
MUCH THANKS TO EVERYONE!
NOW YOU CAN ENJOY THE REST OF THE CONCERT!
ワァッ
EXCUSE US...
...BUT THIS IS OUR SHOW.
THAT WAS TOTALLY FUN! ♡
NOW WE JUST NEED TO FIND PUDDING! ♡
HOPEFULLY THAT'LL BE EASY.
RYOU!
THE GROUND'S CAVING IN.

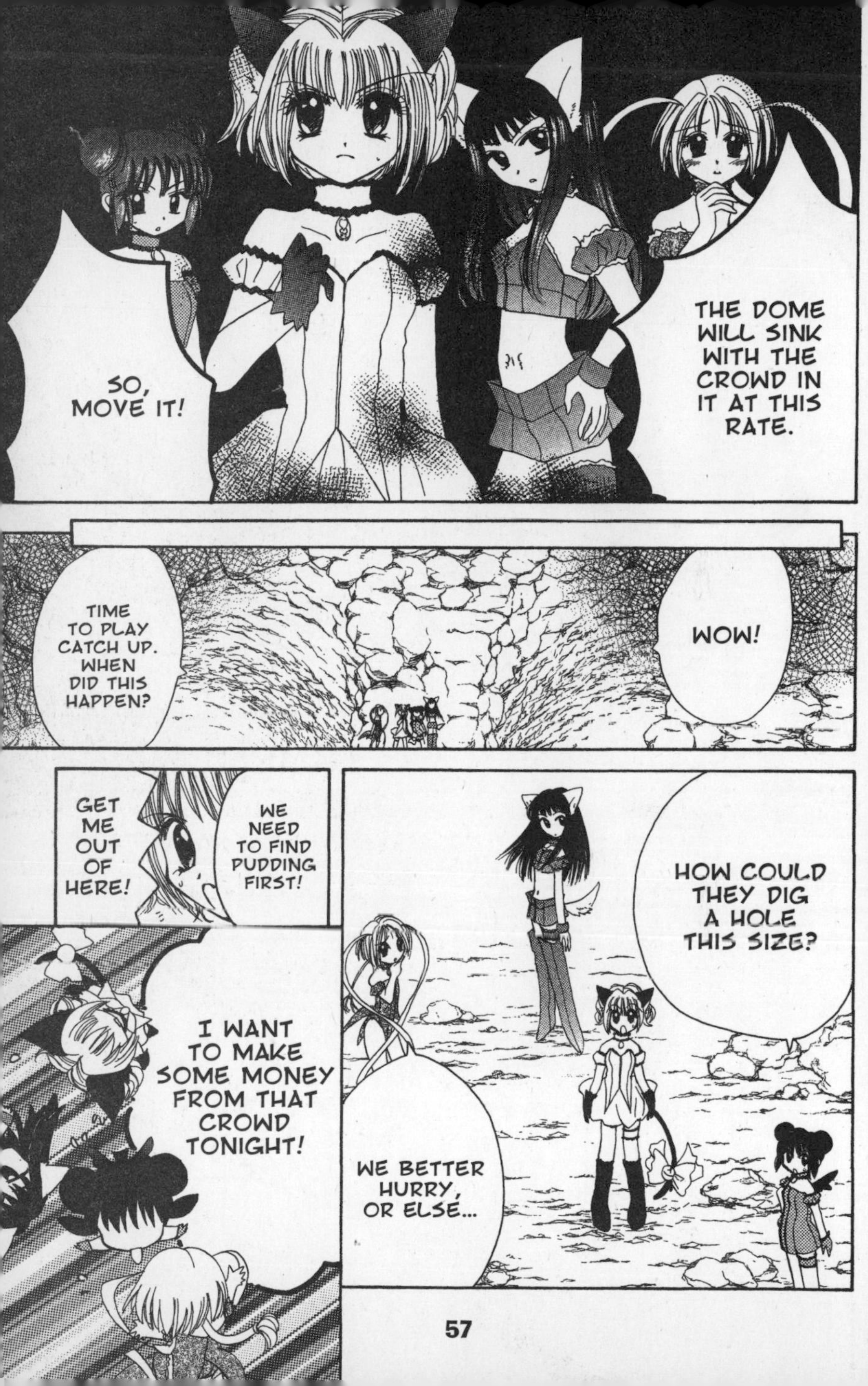
THE DOME WILL SINK WITH THE CROWD IN IT AT THIS RATE.
SO, MOVE IT!
WOW!
TIME TO PLAY CATCH UP. WHEN DID THIS HAPPEN?
HOW COULD THEY DIG A HOLE THIS SIZE?
WE BETTER HURRY, OR ELSE...
WE NEED TO FIND PUDDING FIRST!
GET ME OUT OF HERE!
I WANT TO MAKE SOME MONEY FROM THAT CROWD TONIGHT!

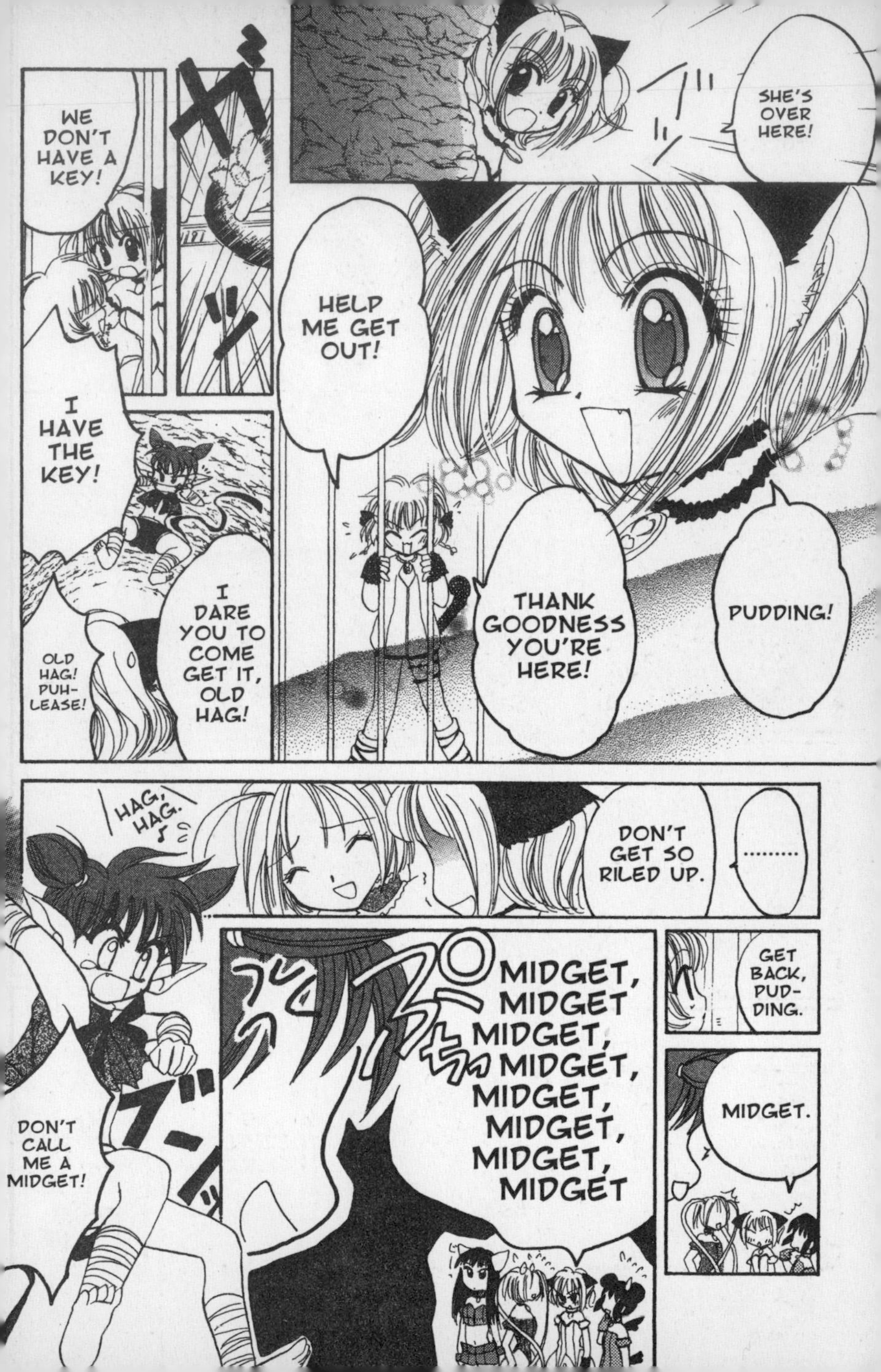
SHE'S OVER HERE!
PUDDING!
THANK GOODNESS YOU'RE HERE!
HELP ME GET OUT!
WE DON'T HAVE A KEY!
I HAVE THE KEY!
I DARE YOU TO COME GET IT, OLD HAG!
OLD HAG! PUH-LEASE!
....
DON'T GET SO RILED UP.
HAG, HAG. ♪
GET BACK, PUD-DING.
MIDGET.
MIDGET, MIDGET MIDGET, MIDGET, MIDGET, MIDGET, MIDGET, MIDGET
DON'T CALL ME A MIDGET!

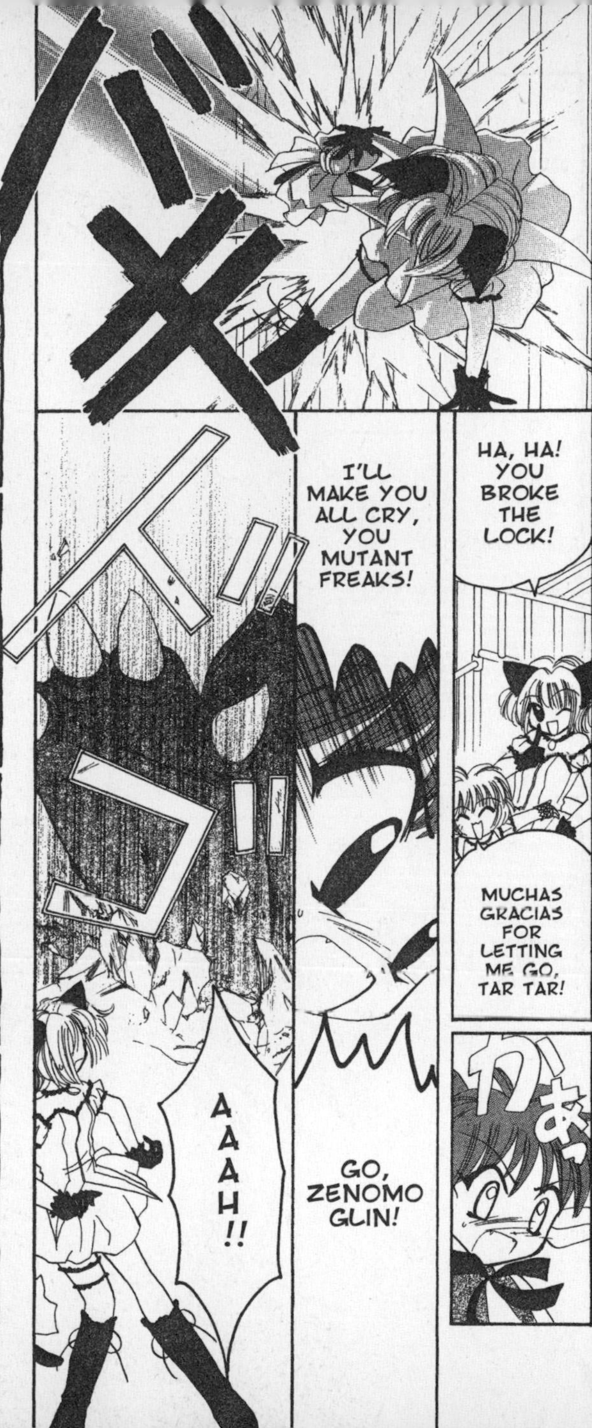
HA, HA! YOU BROKE THE LOCK!
MUCHAS GRACIAS FOR LETTING ME GO, TAR TAR!
かあっ
I'LL MAKE YOU ALL CRY, YOU MUTANT FREAKS!
GO, ZENOMO GLIN!
AAAH!!

Go, go, Masha! ☆

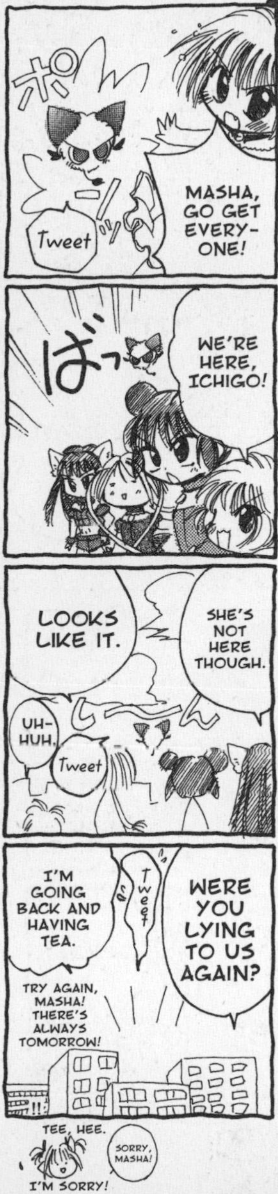
ポ
MASHA, GO GET EVERY-ONE!
Tweet
WE'RE HERE, ICHIGO!
ばっ
SHE'S NOT HERE THOUGH.
LOOKS LIKE IT.
UH-HUH.
Tweet
WERE YOU LYING TO US AGAIN?
Tweet
I'M GOING BACK AND HAVING TEA.
TRY AGAIN, MASHA! THERE'S ALWAYS TOMORROW!
TEE, HEE.
SORRY, MASHA!
I'M SORRY!

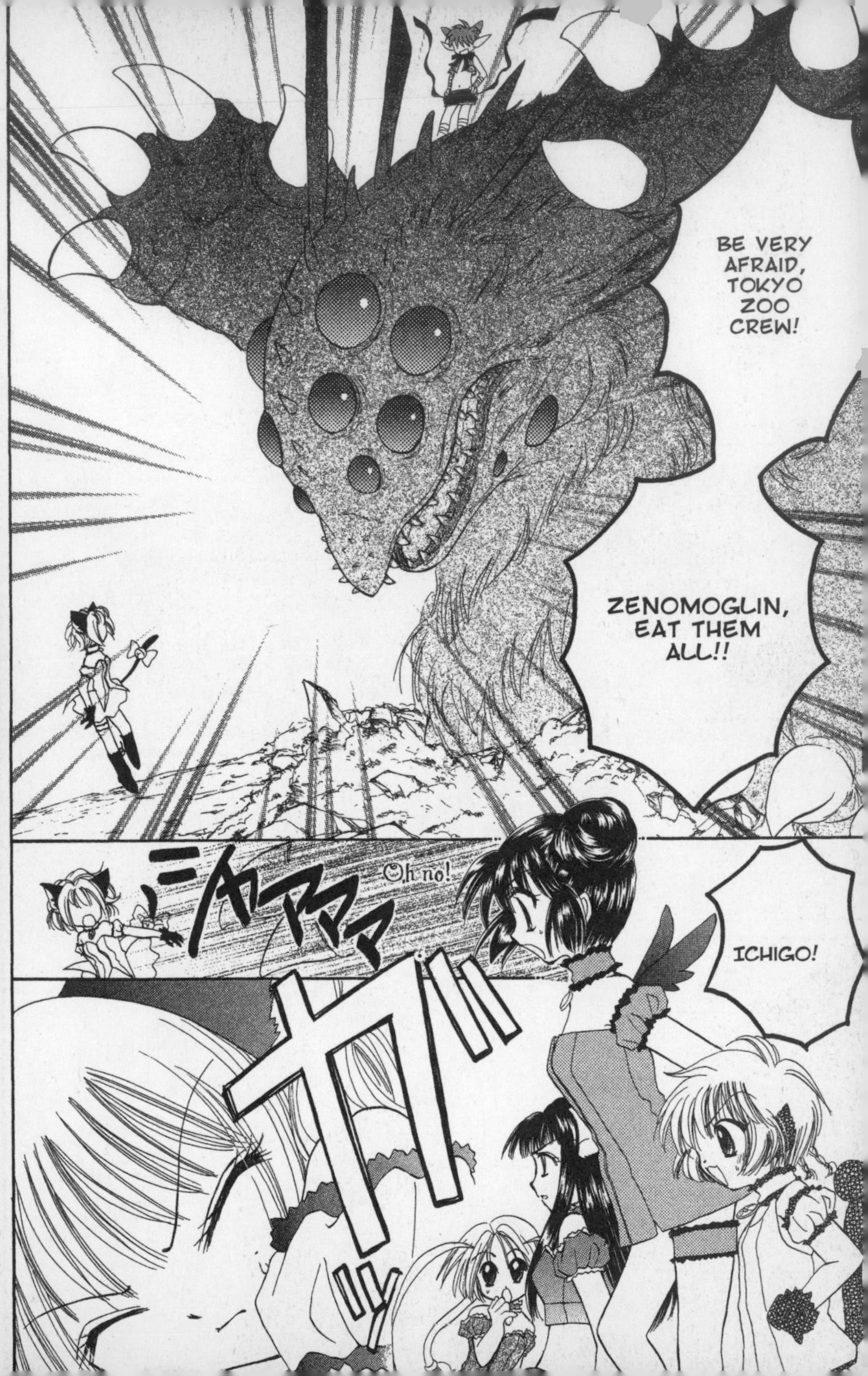
BE VERY AFRAID, TOKYO ZOO CREW!
ZENOMOGLIN, EAT THEM ALL!!
ICHIGO!
Oh no!

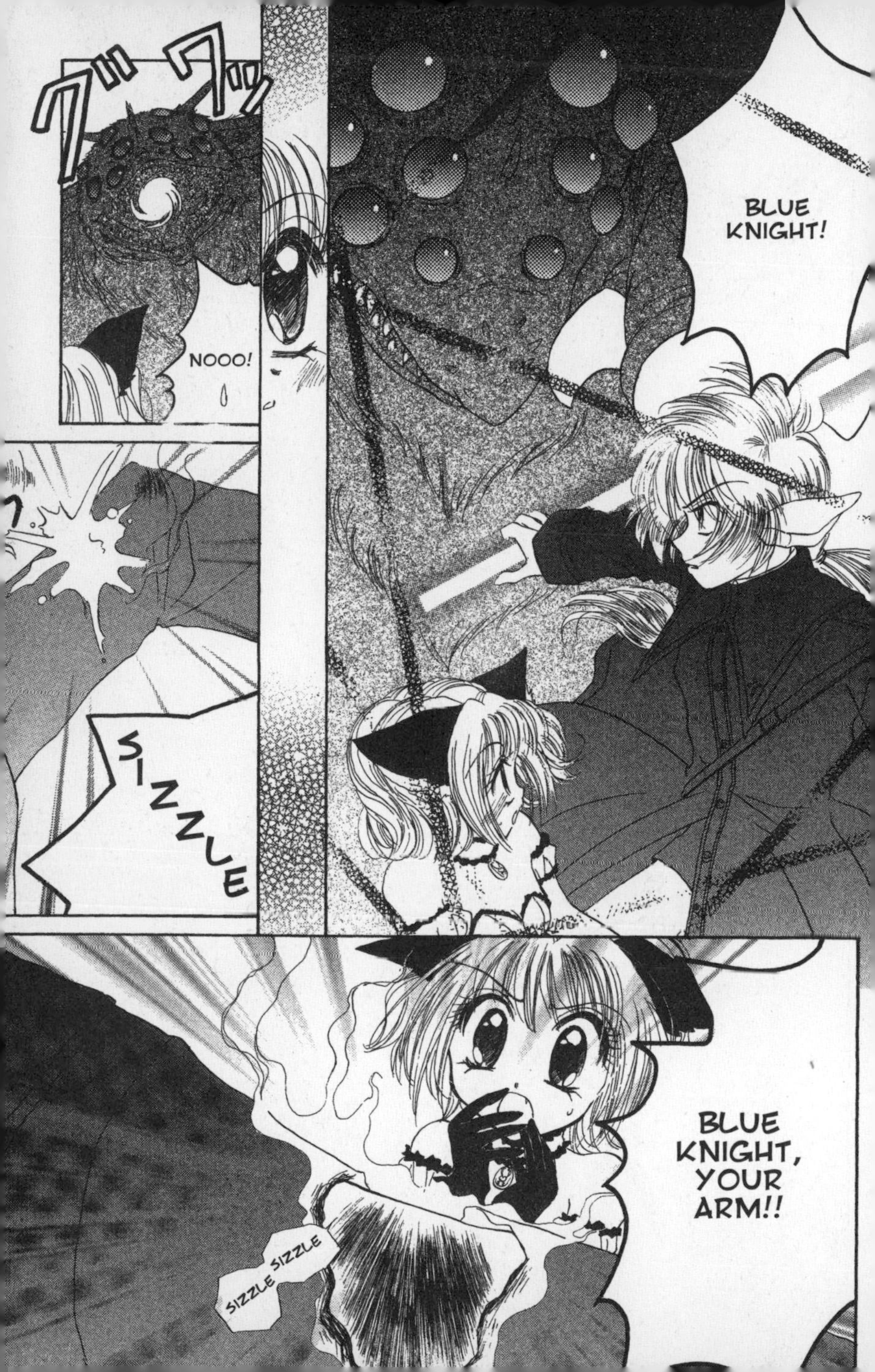
BLUE KNIGHT!
ブワッ
NOOO!
SIZZLE
BLUE KNIGHT, YOUR ARM!!
SIZZLE SIZZLE SIZZLE

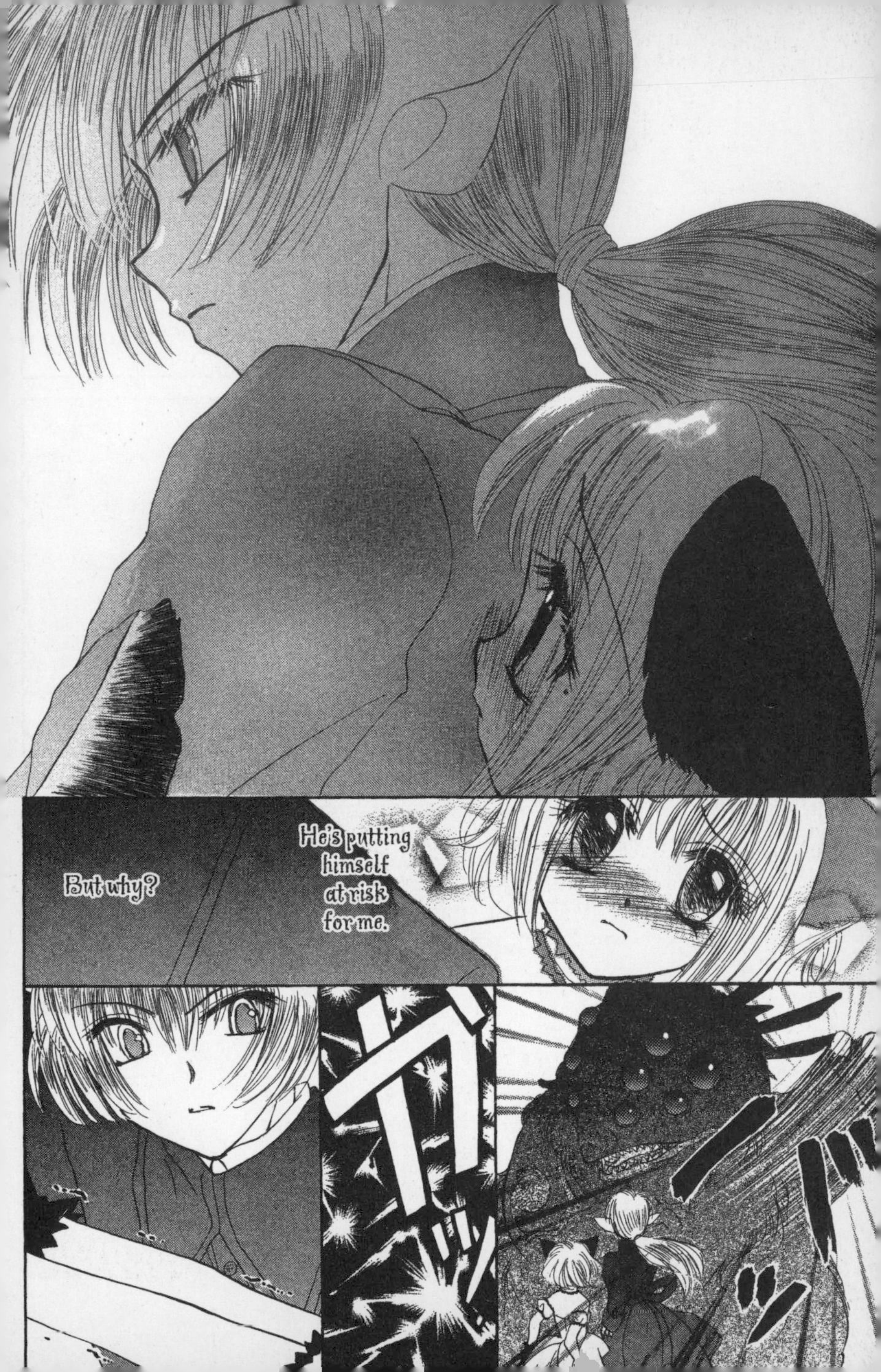
He's putting himself at risk for me.
But why?

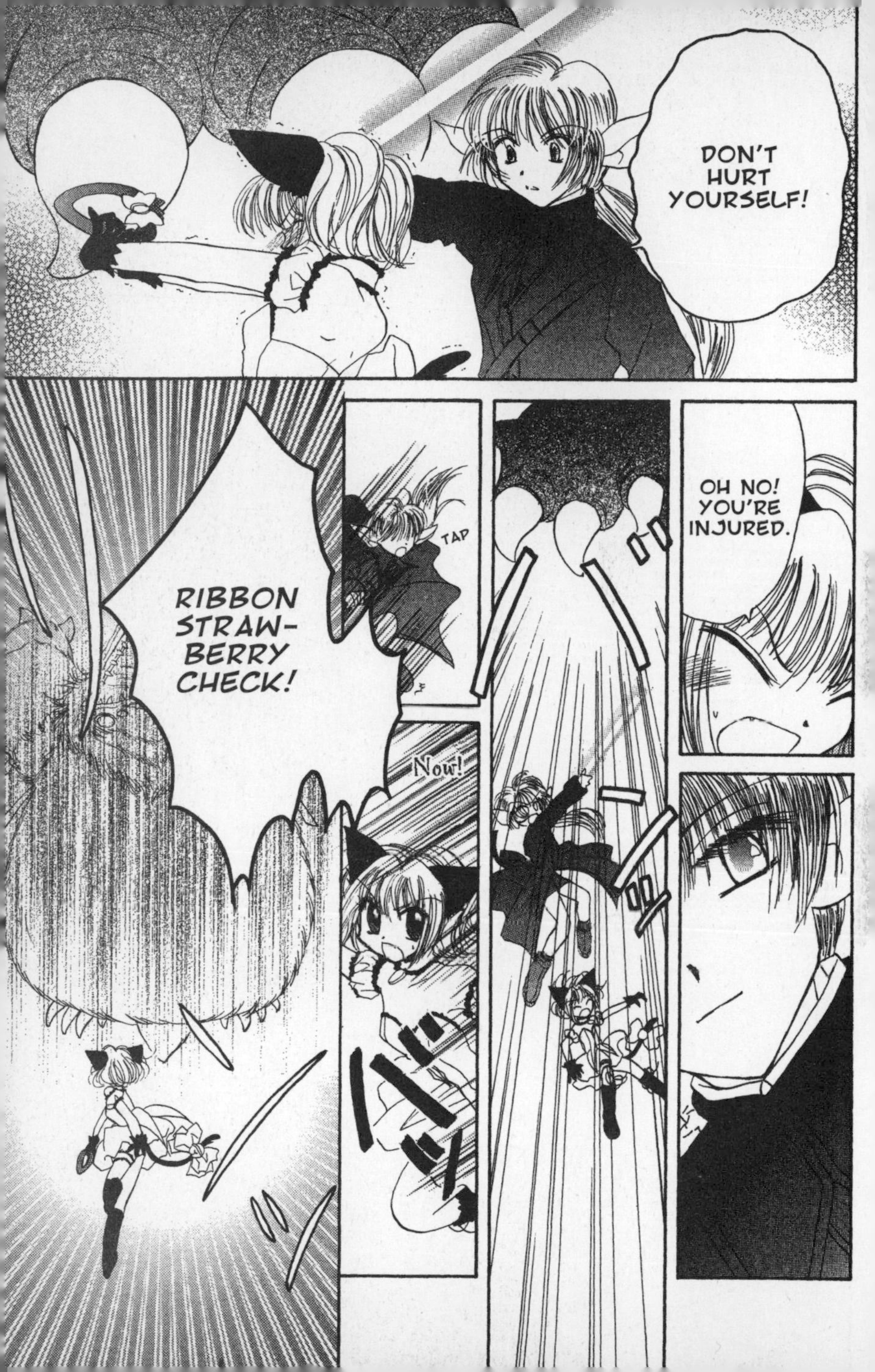
DON'T HURT YOURSELF!
OH NO! YOU'RE INJURED.
TAP
Now!
RIBBON STRAW-BERRY CHECK!

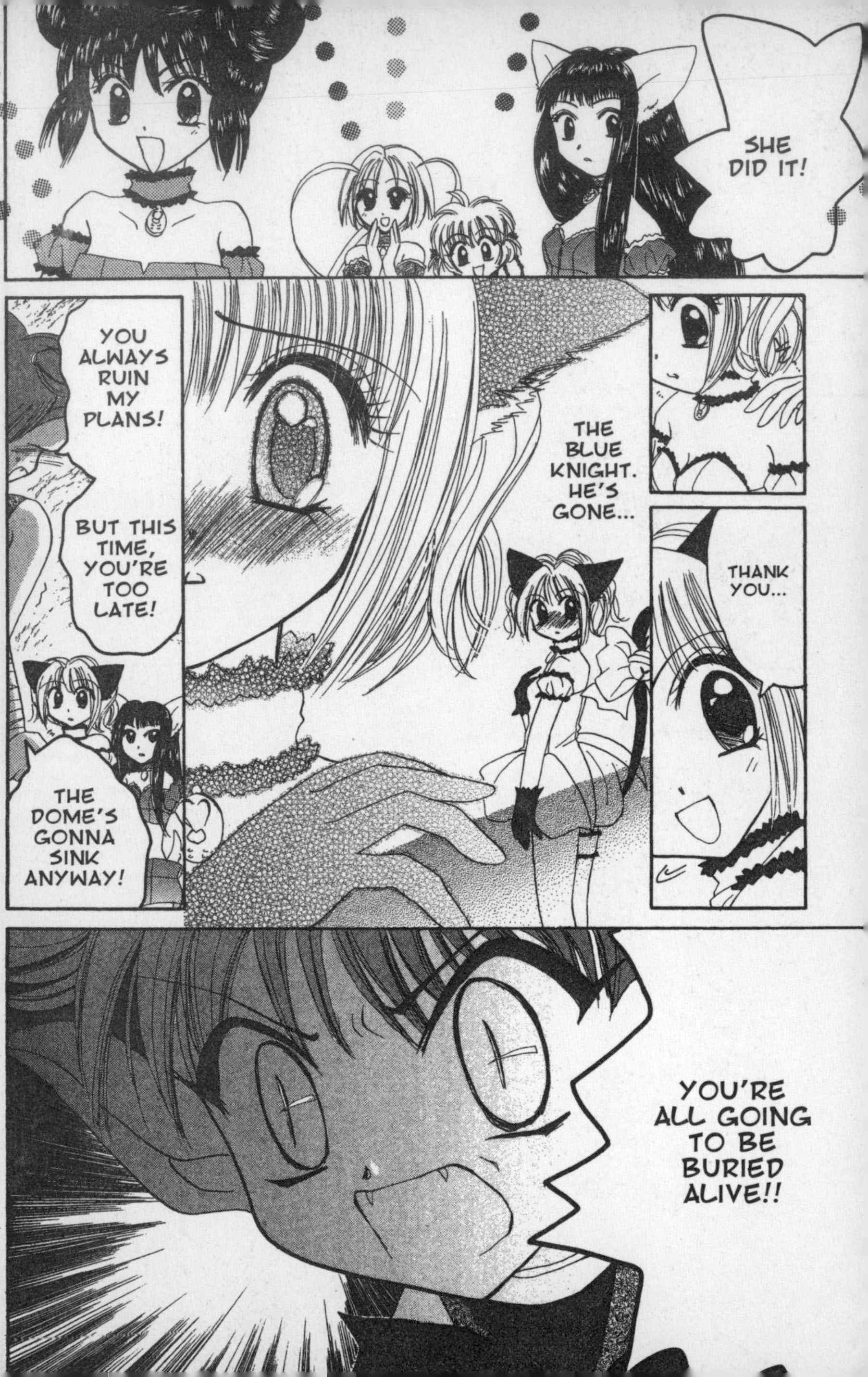
SHE DID IT!
THANK YOU...
THE BLUE KNIGHT. HE'S GONE...
YOU ALWAYS RUIN MY PLANS!
BUT THIS TIME, YOU'RE TOO LATE!
THE DOME'S GONNA SINK ANYWAY!
YOU'RE ALL GOING TO BE BURIED ALIVE!!

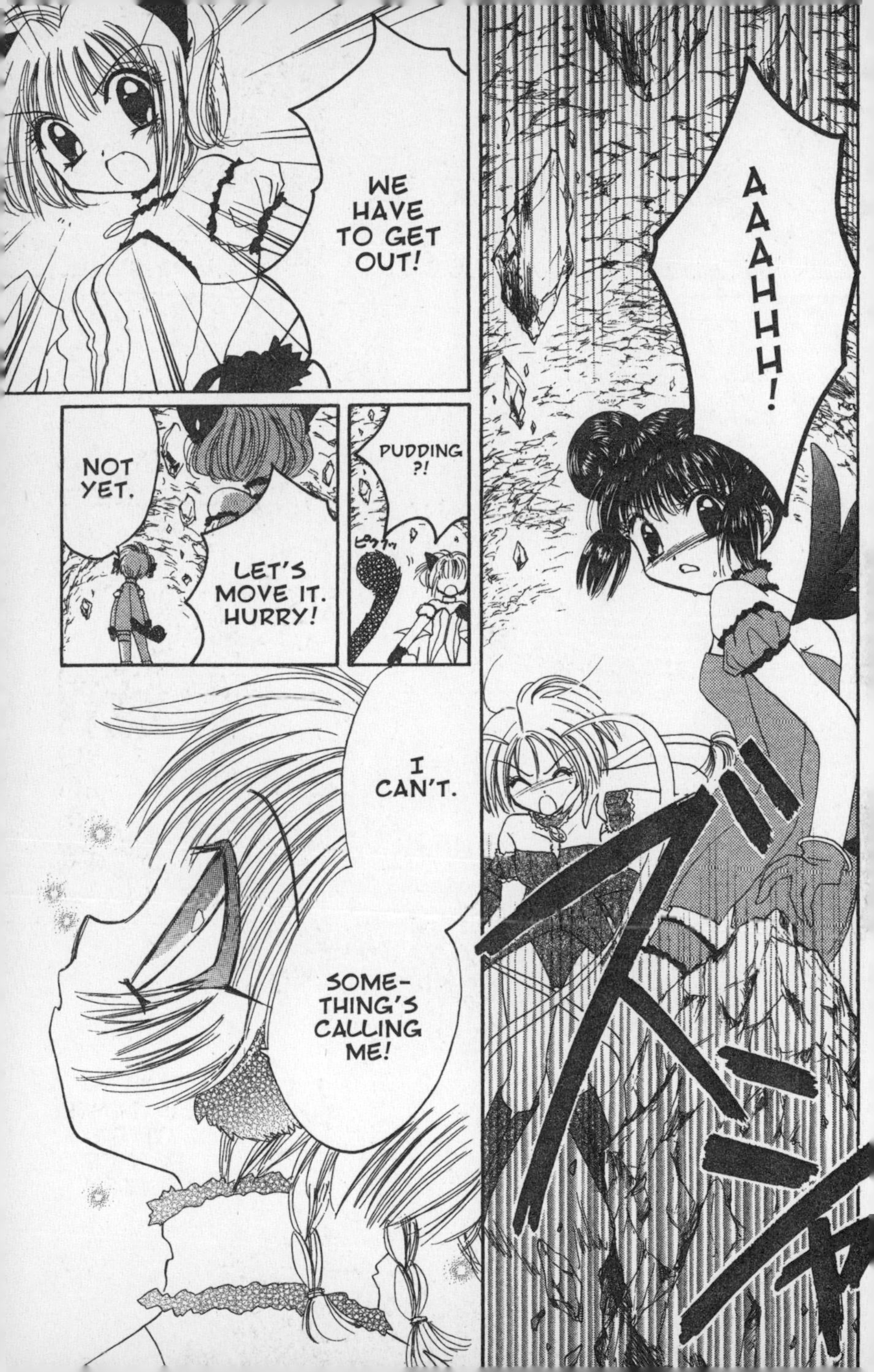
AAAHHH!
WE HAVE TO GET OUT!
PUDDING ?!
NOT YET.
LET'S MOVE IT. HURRY!
I CAN'T.
SOME-THING'S CALLING ME!

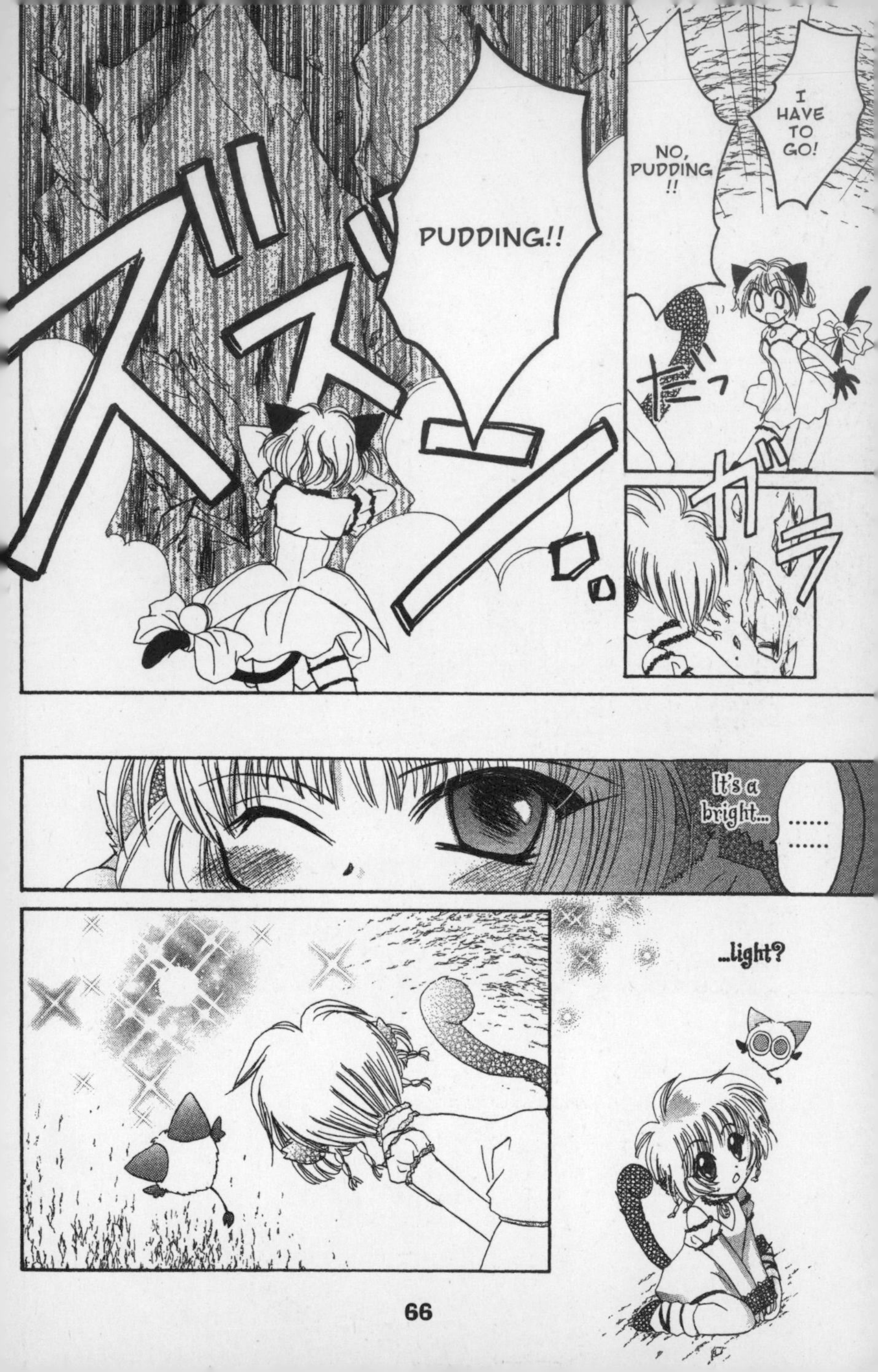
I HAVE TO GO!
NO, PUDDING!!
PUDDING!!
......
......
It's a bright...
...light?

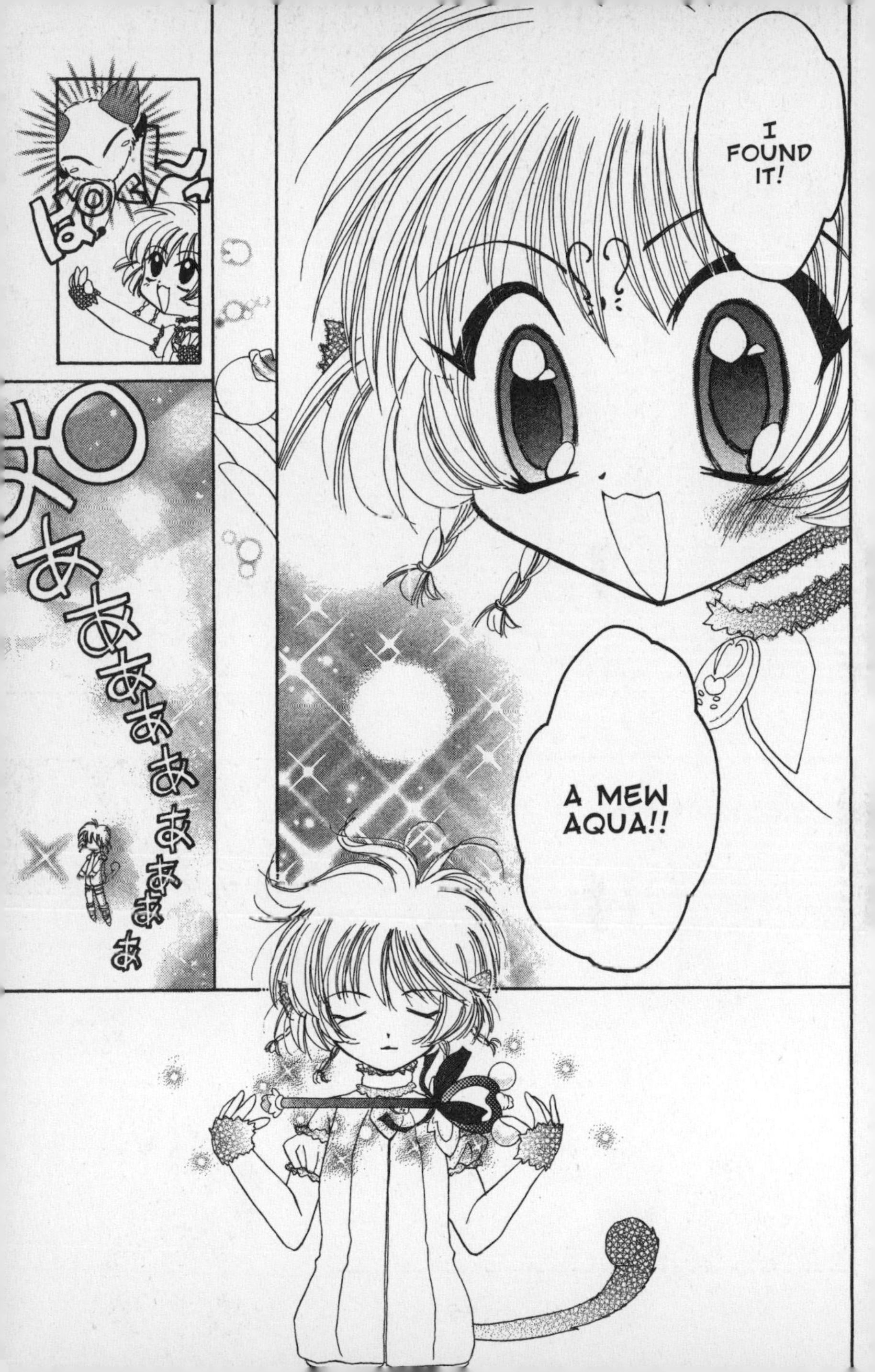
I FOUND IT!
A MEW AQUA!!

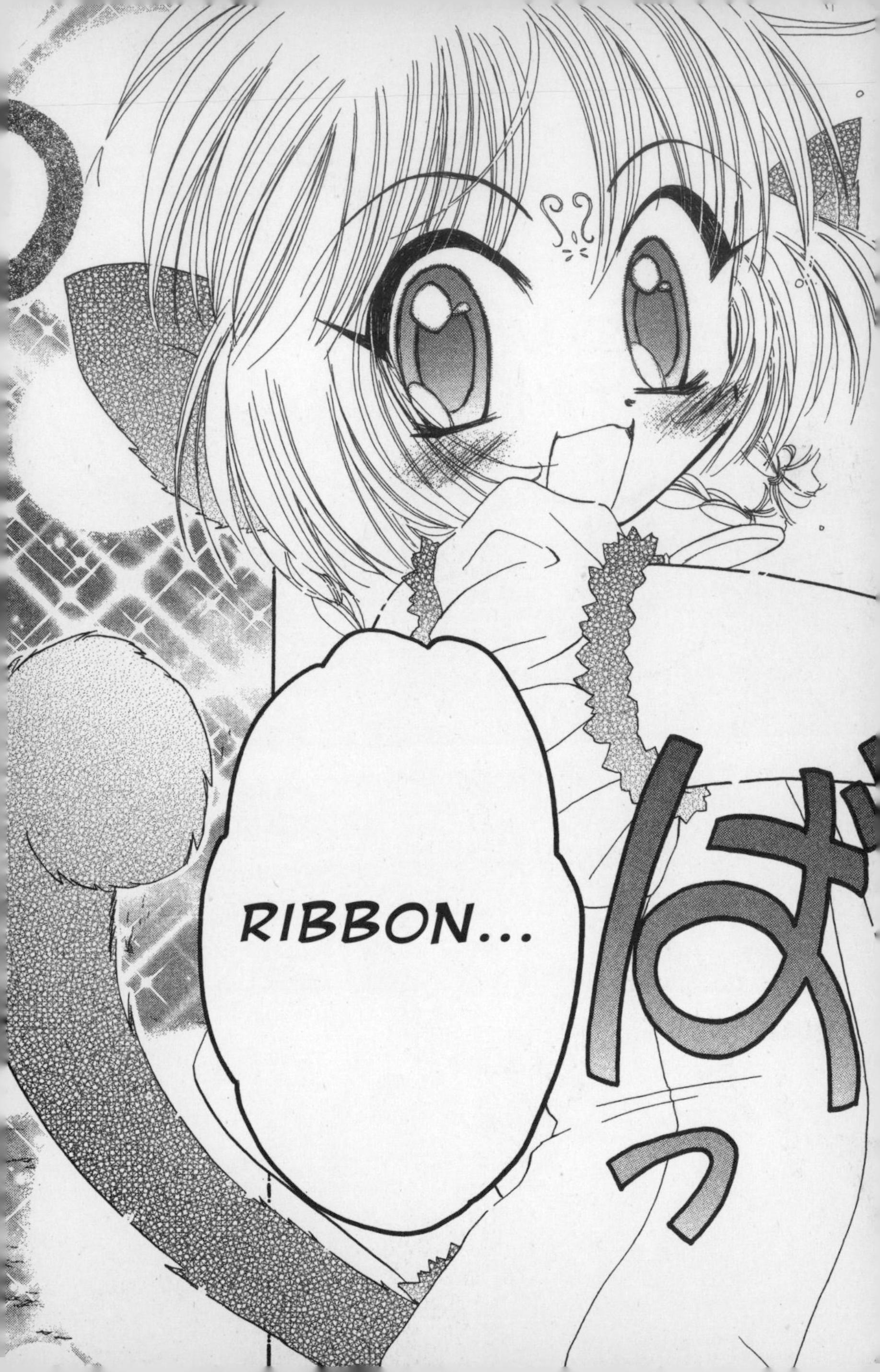
RIBBON...
ぱっ

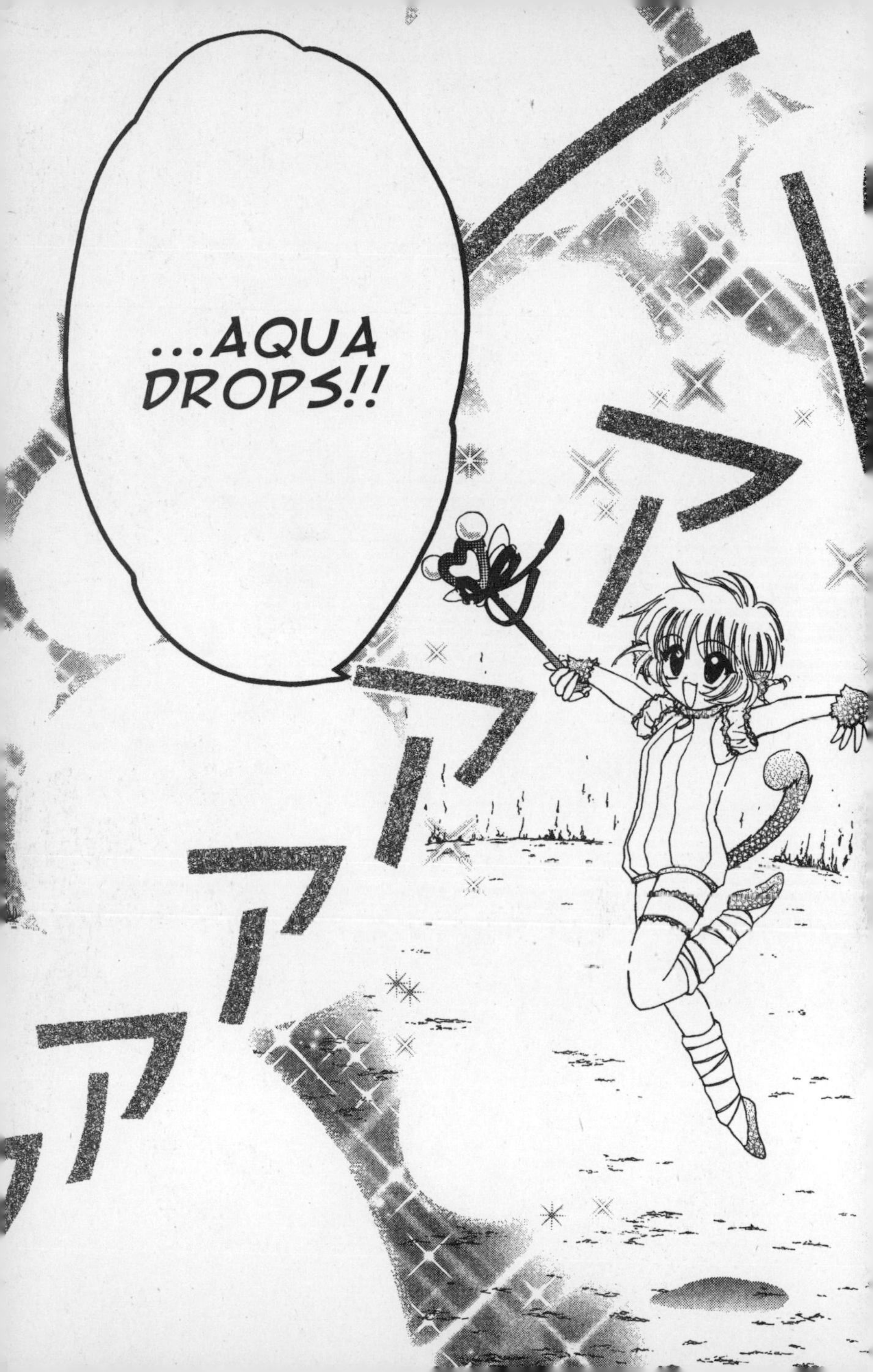
...AQUA DROPS!!

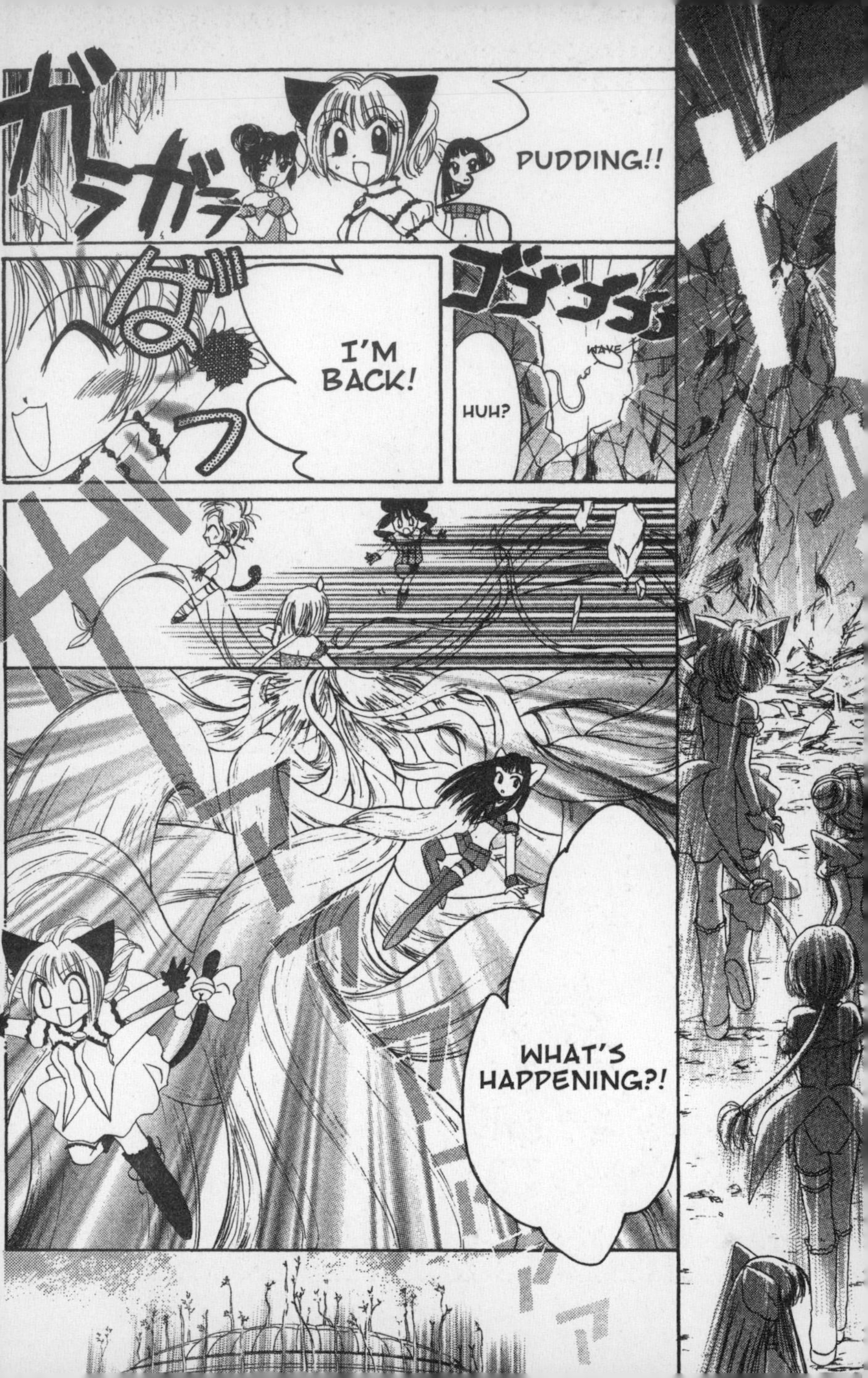
PUDDING!!
HUH?
WAVE
I'M BACK!
WHAT'S HAPPENING?!

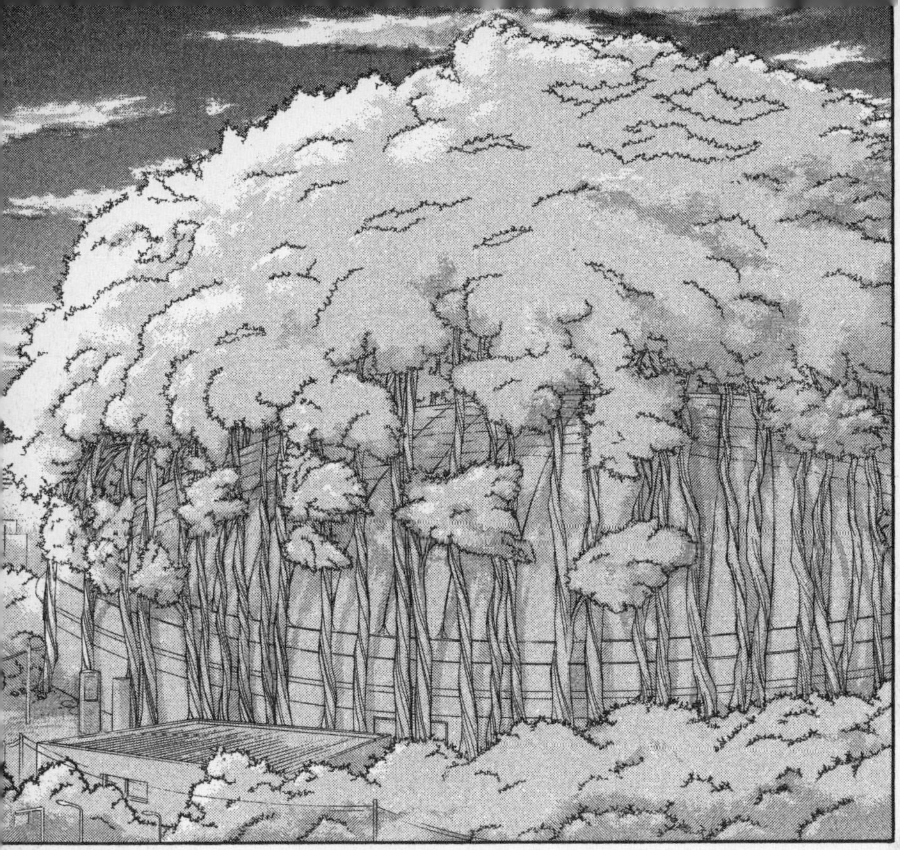

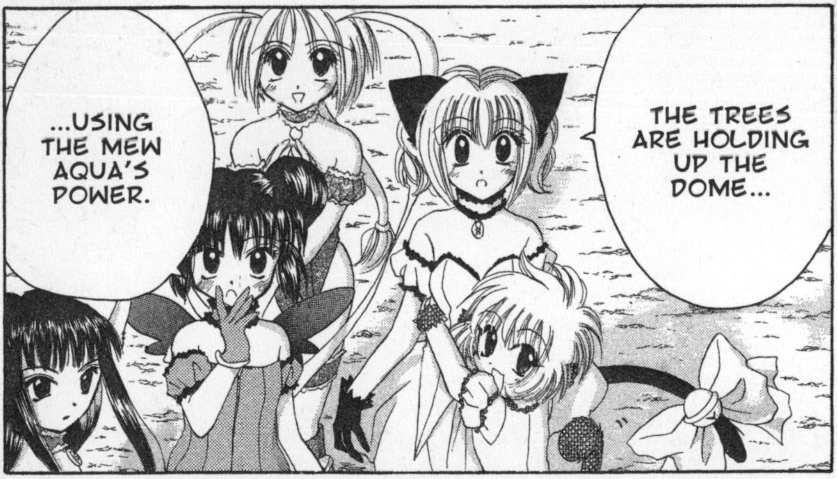
THE TREES ARE HOLDING UP THE DOME...
...USING THE MEW AQUA'S POWER.

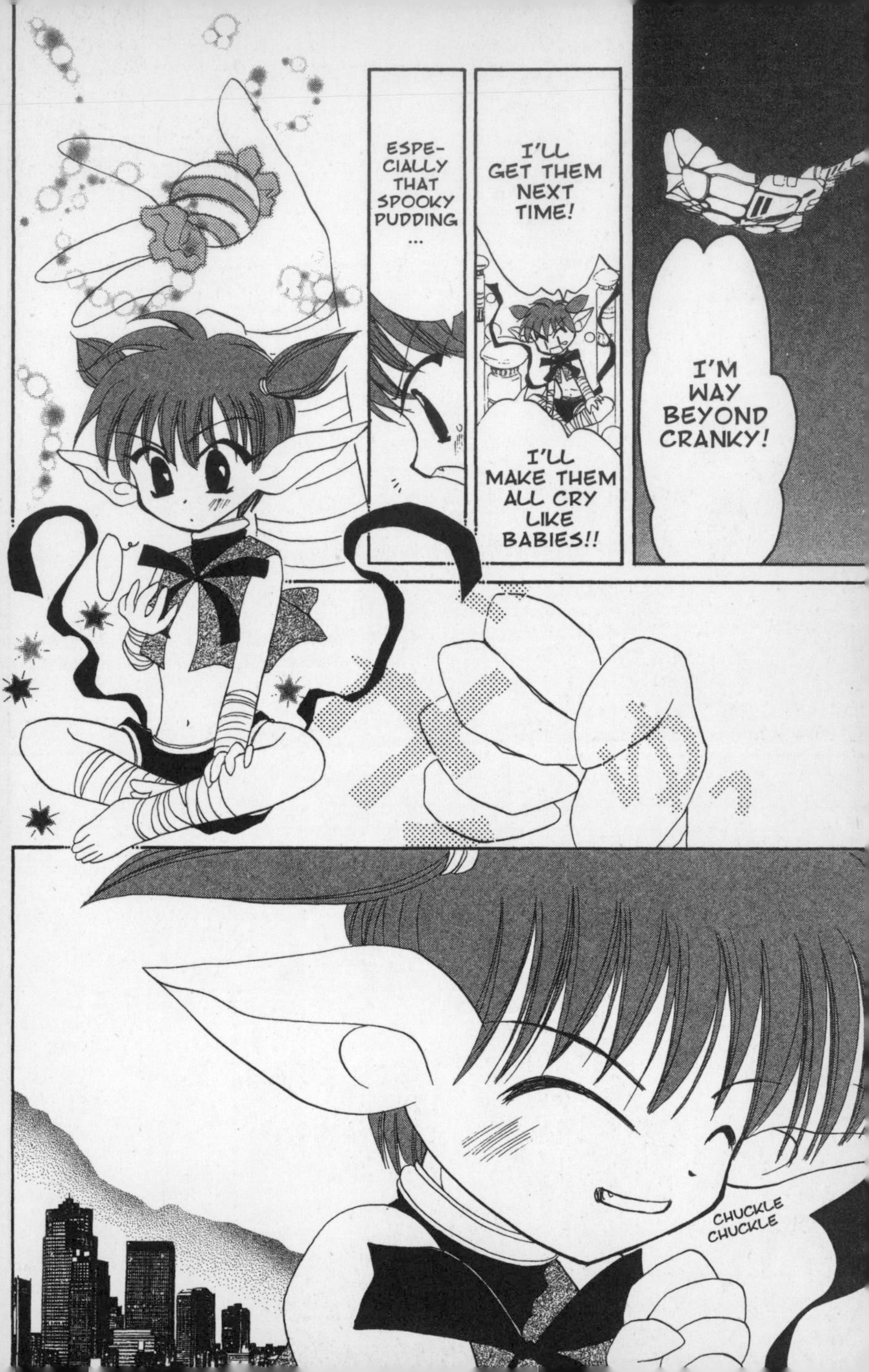
I'M WAY BEYOND CRANKY!
I'LL GET THEM NEXT TIME!
I'LL MAKE THEM ALL CRY LIKE BABIES!!
ESPE-CIALLY THAT SPOOKY PUDDING ...
CHUCKLE CHUCKLE

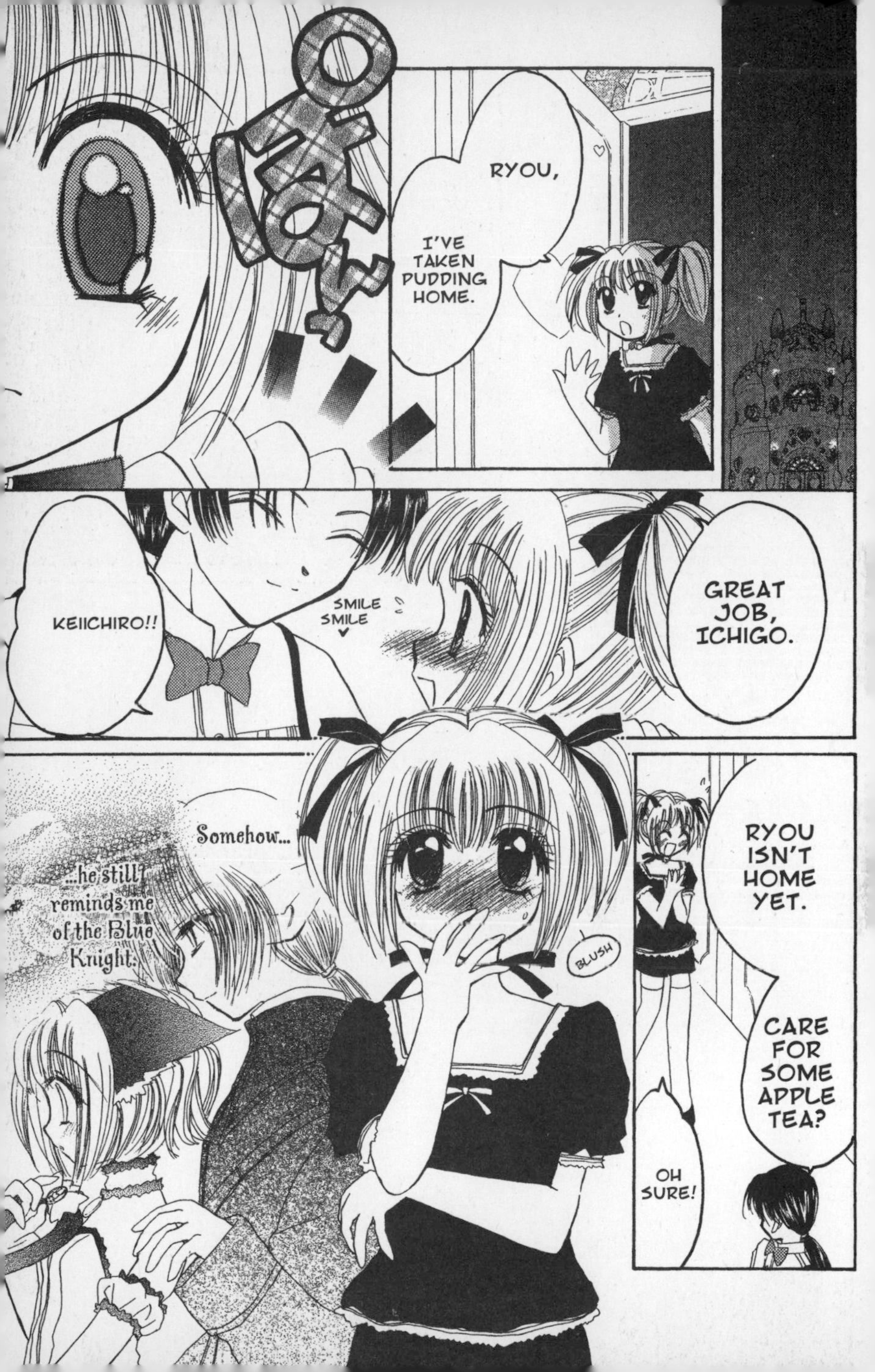
RYOU,
I'VE TAKEN PUDDING HOME.
GREAT JOB, ICHIGO.
SMILE SMILE
KEIICHIRO!!
RYOU ISN'T HOME YET.
CARE FOR SOME APPLE TEA?
OH SURE!
BLUSH
Somehow...
...he still reminds me of the Blue Knight.

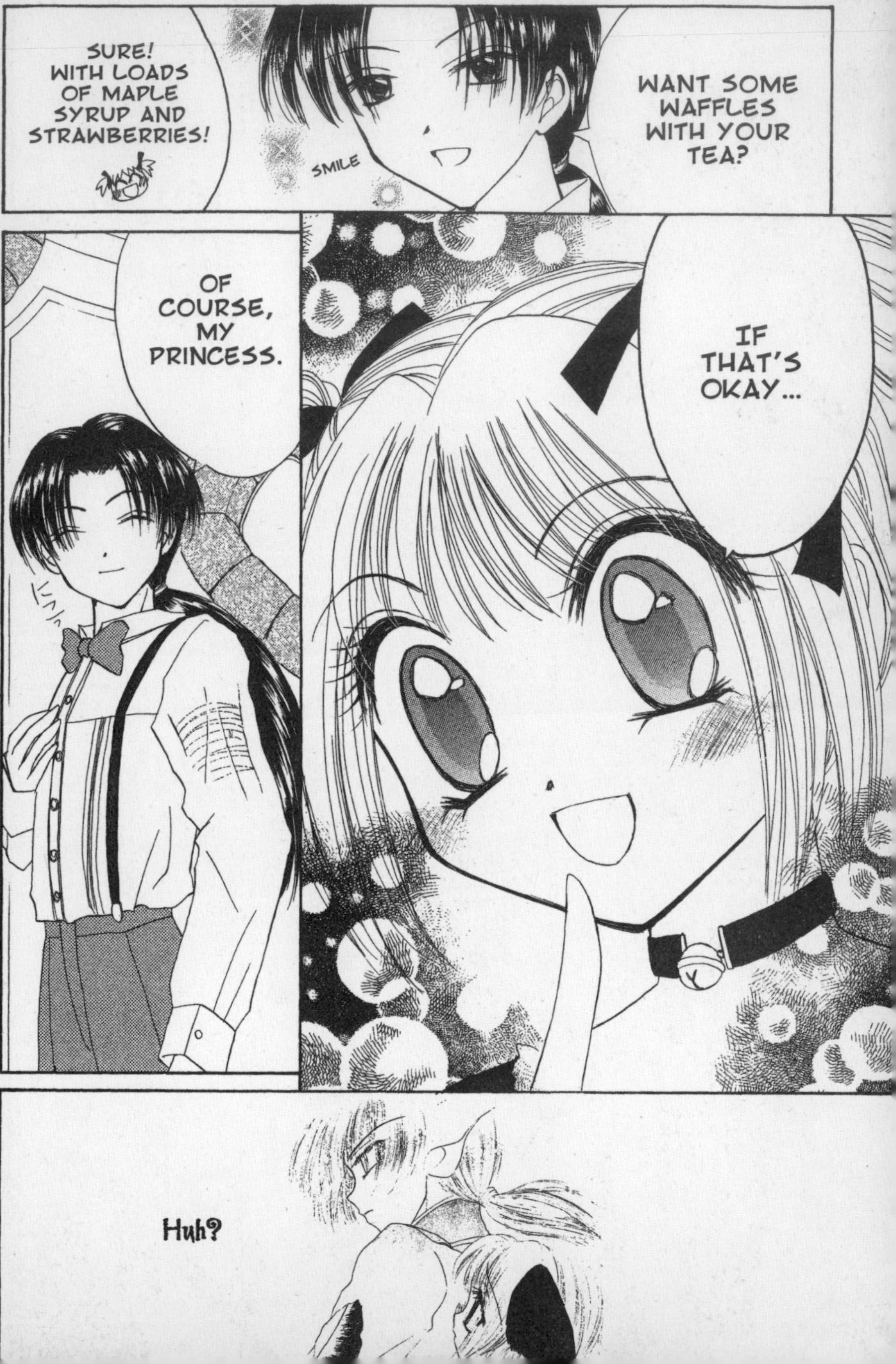
WANT SOME WAFFLES WITH YOUR TEA?
SMILE
SURE! WITH LOADS OF MAPLE SYRUP AND STRAWBERRIES!
IF THAT'S OKAY...
OF COURSE, MY PRINCESS.
Huh?

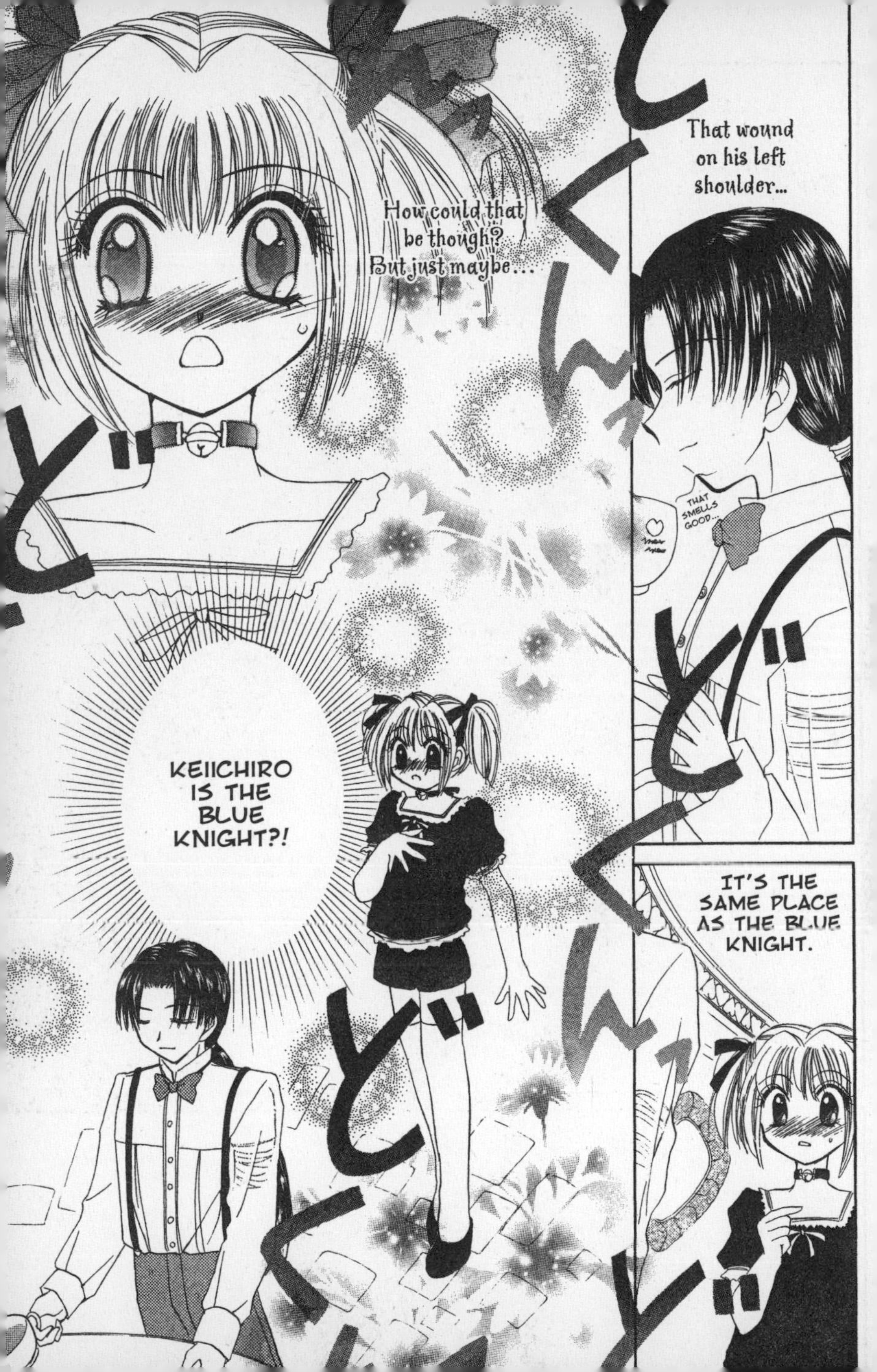
That wound on his left shoulder...
THAT SMELLS GOOD...
IT'S THE SAME PLACE AS THE BLUE KNIGHT.
How could that be though? But just maybe...
KEIICHIRO IS THE BLUE KNIGHT?!

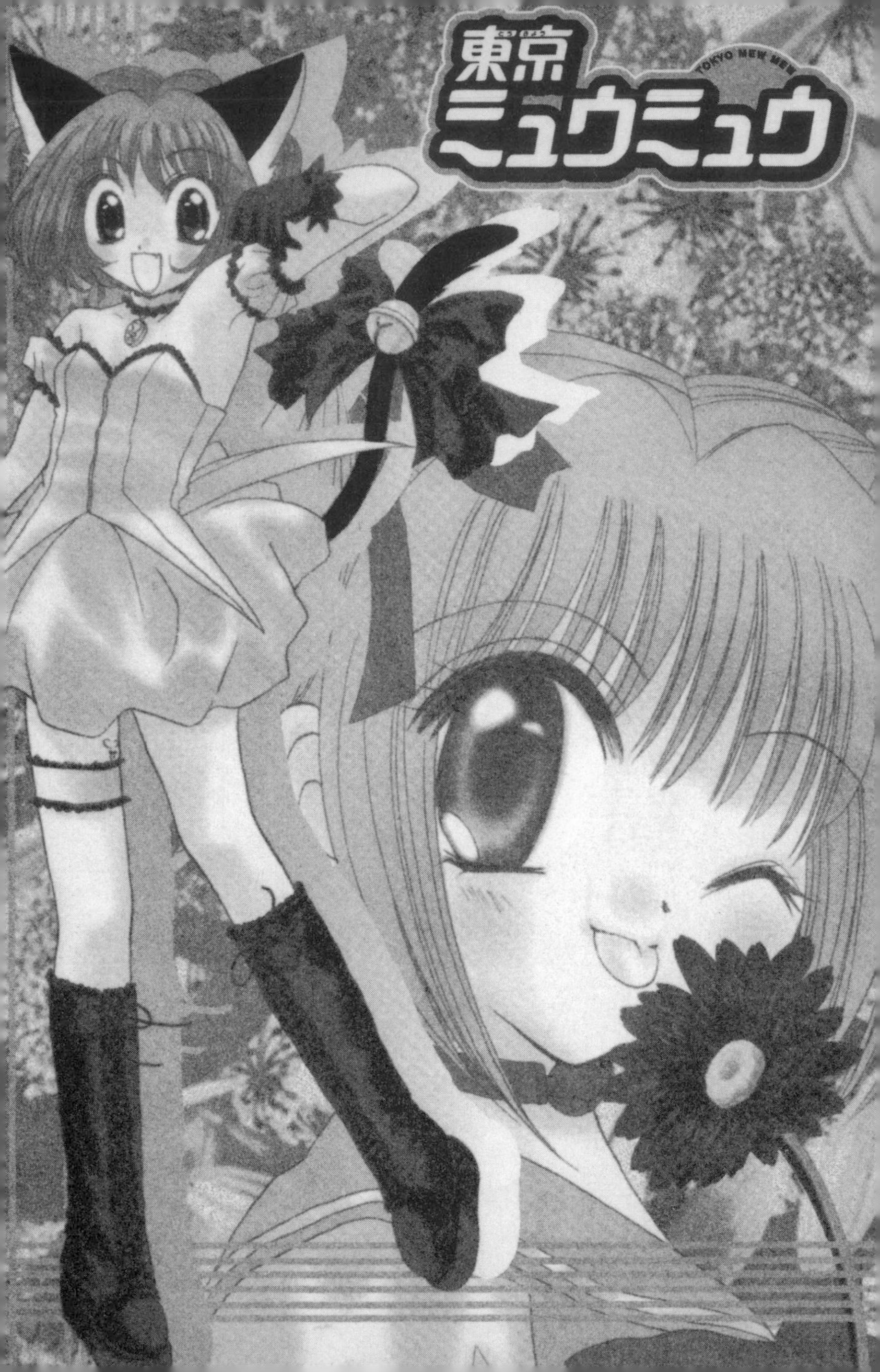
東京ミュウミュウ
TOKYO MEW MEW

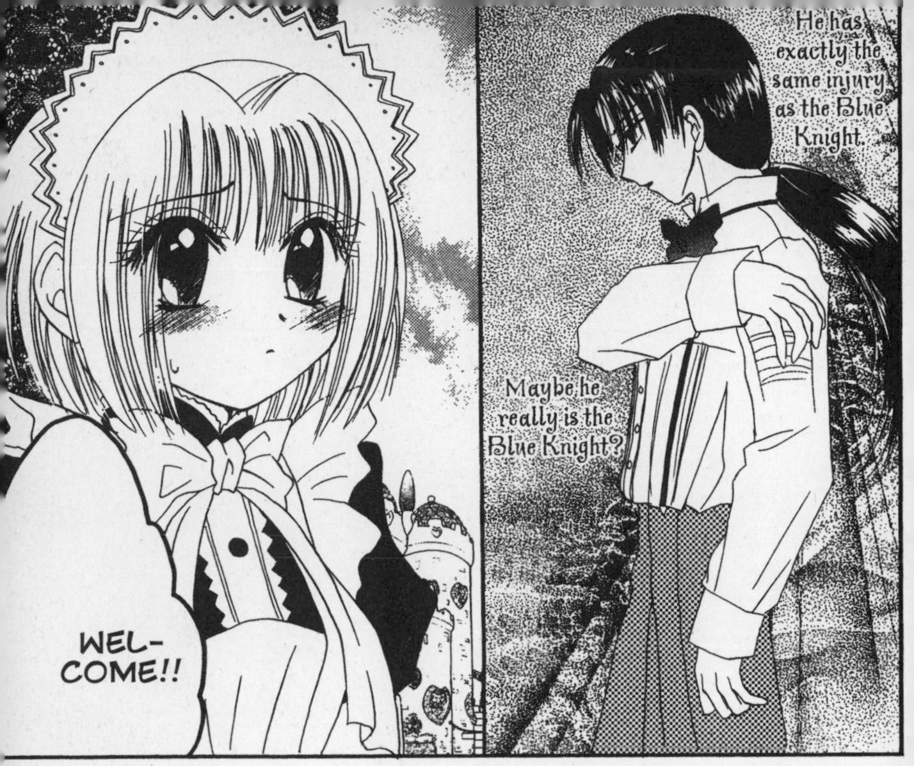
He has exactly the same injury as the Blue Knight.
Maybe he really is the Blue Knight?
WEL-COME!!

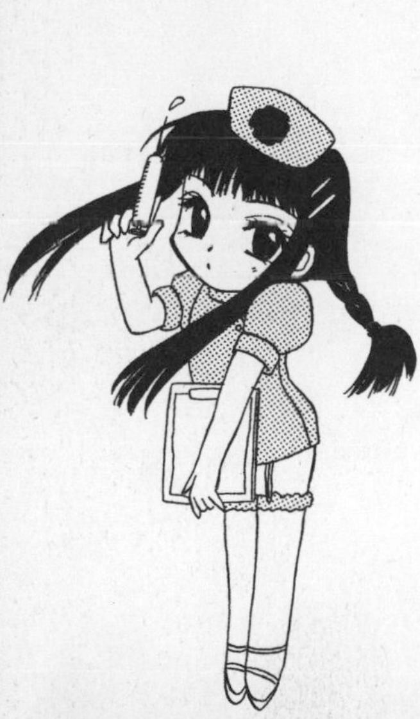

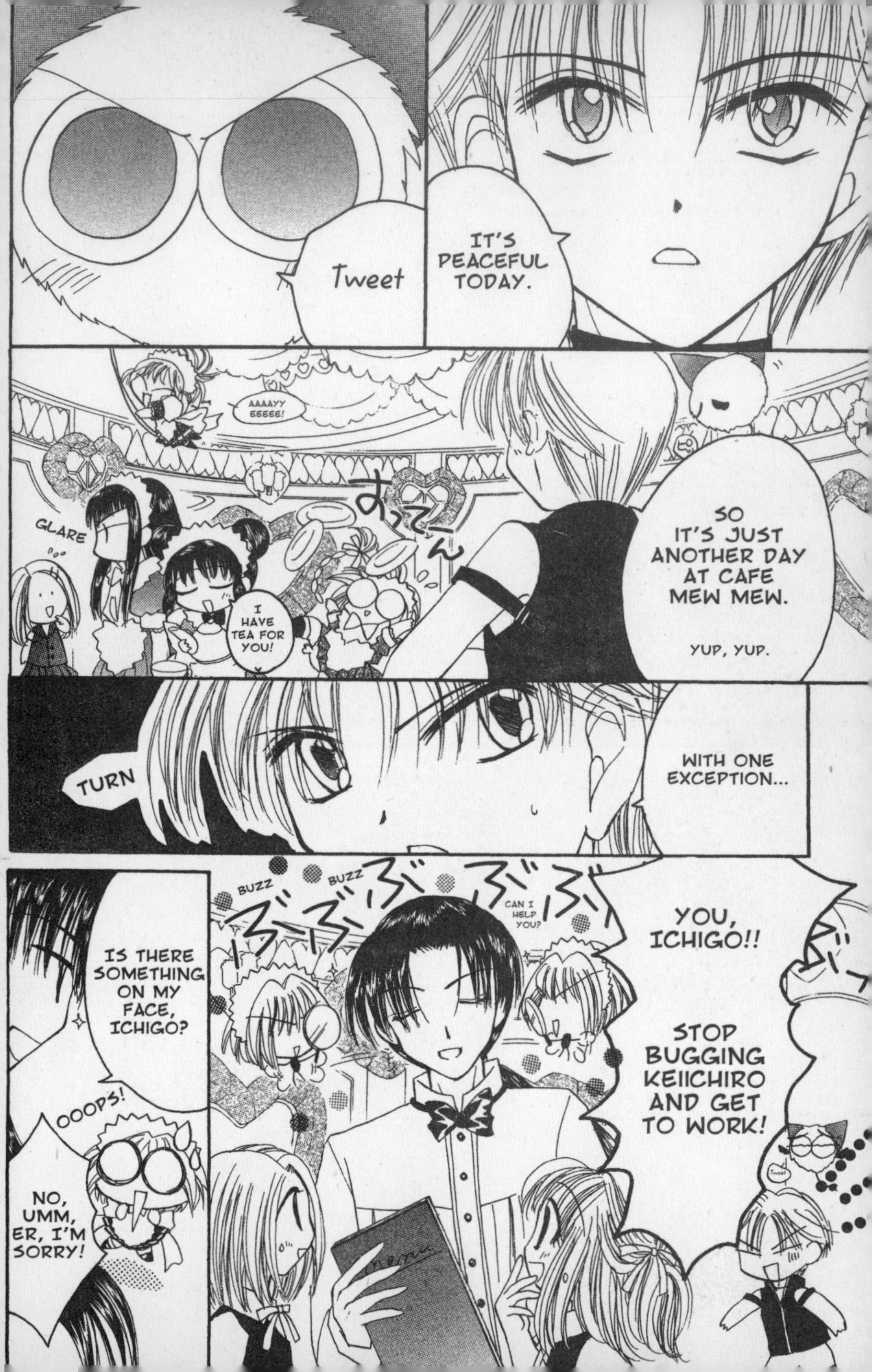
IT'S PEACEFUL TODAY.
Tweet
SO IT'S JUST ANOTHER DAY AT CAFE MEW MEW.
YUP, YUP.
すってーん
AAAAYY EEEEE!
I HAVE TEA FOR YOU!
GLARE
WITH ONE EXCEPTION...
TURN
YOU, ICHIGO!!
STOP BUGGING KEIICHIRO AND GET TO WORK!
Tweet
CAN I HELP YOU?
BUZZ
BUZZ
IS THERE SOMETHING ON MY FACE, ICHIGO?
OOOPS!
NO, UMM, ER, I'M SORRY!

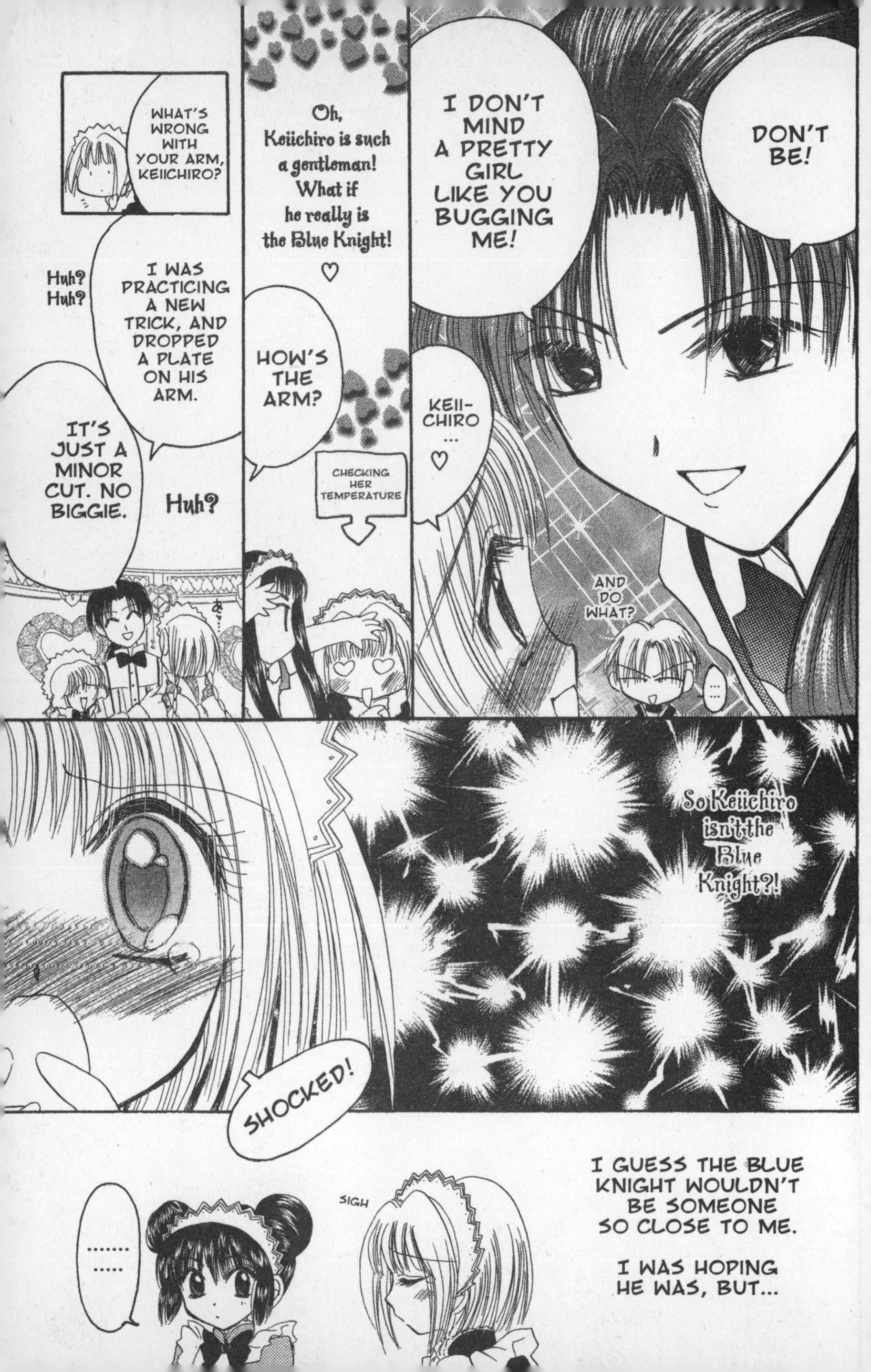
DON'T BE!
I DON'T MIND A PRETTY GIRL LIKE YOU BUGGING ME!
KEII-CHIRO ... ♡
AND DO WHAT?
...
Oh, Keiichiro is such a gentleman! What if he really is the Blue Knight! ♡
HOW'S THE ARM?
CHECKING HER TEMPERATURE
WHAT'S WRONG WITH YOUR ARM, KEIICHIRO?
I WAS PRACTICING A NEW TRICK, AND DROPPED A PLATE ON HIS ARM.
Huh? Huh?
IT'S JUST A MINOR CUT. NO BIGGIE.
Huh?
So Keiichiro isn't the Blue Knight?!
SHOCKED!
I GUESS THE BLUE KNIGHT WOULDN'T BE SOMEONE SO CLOSE TO ME.
I WAS HOPING HE WAS, BUT...
SIGH
....

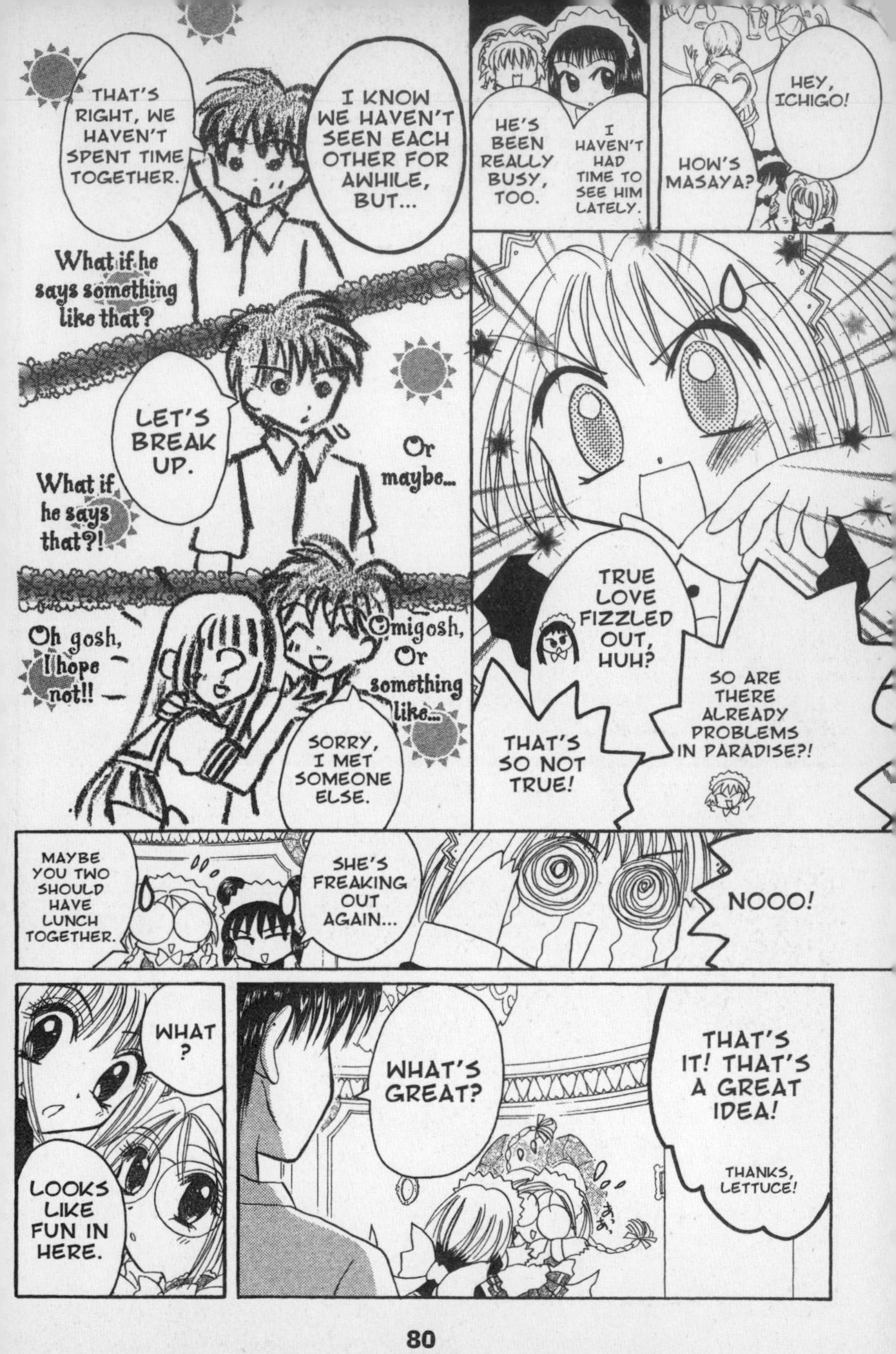
HEY, ICHIGO!
HOW'S MASAYA?
HE'S BEEN REALLY BUSY, TOO.
I HAVEN'T HAD TIME TO SEE HIM LATELY.
SO ARE THERE ALREADY PROBLEMS IN PARADISE?!
TRUE LOVE FIZZLED OUT, HUH?
THAT'S SO NOT TRUE!
I KNOW WE HAVEN'T SEEN EACH OTHER FOR AWHILE, BUT...
THAT'S RIGHT, WE HAVEN'T SPENT TIME TOGETHER.
What if he says something like that?
Or maybe...
LET'S BREAK UP.
What if he says that?!
Omigosh, Or something like...
SORRY, I MET SOMEONE ELSE.
Oh gosh, I hope not!!
NOOO!
SHE'S FREAKING OUT AGAIN...
MAYBE YOU TWO SHOULD HAVE LUNCH TOGETHER.
THAT'S IT! THAT'S A GREAT IDEA!
THANKS, LETTUCE!
WHAT'S GREAT?
WHAT?
LOOKS LIKE FUN IN HERE.

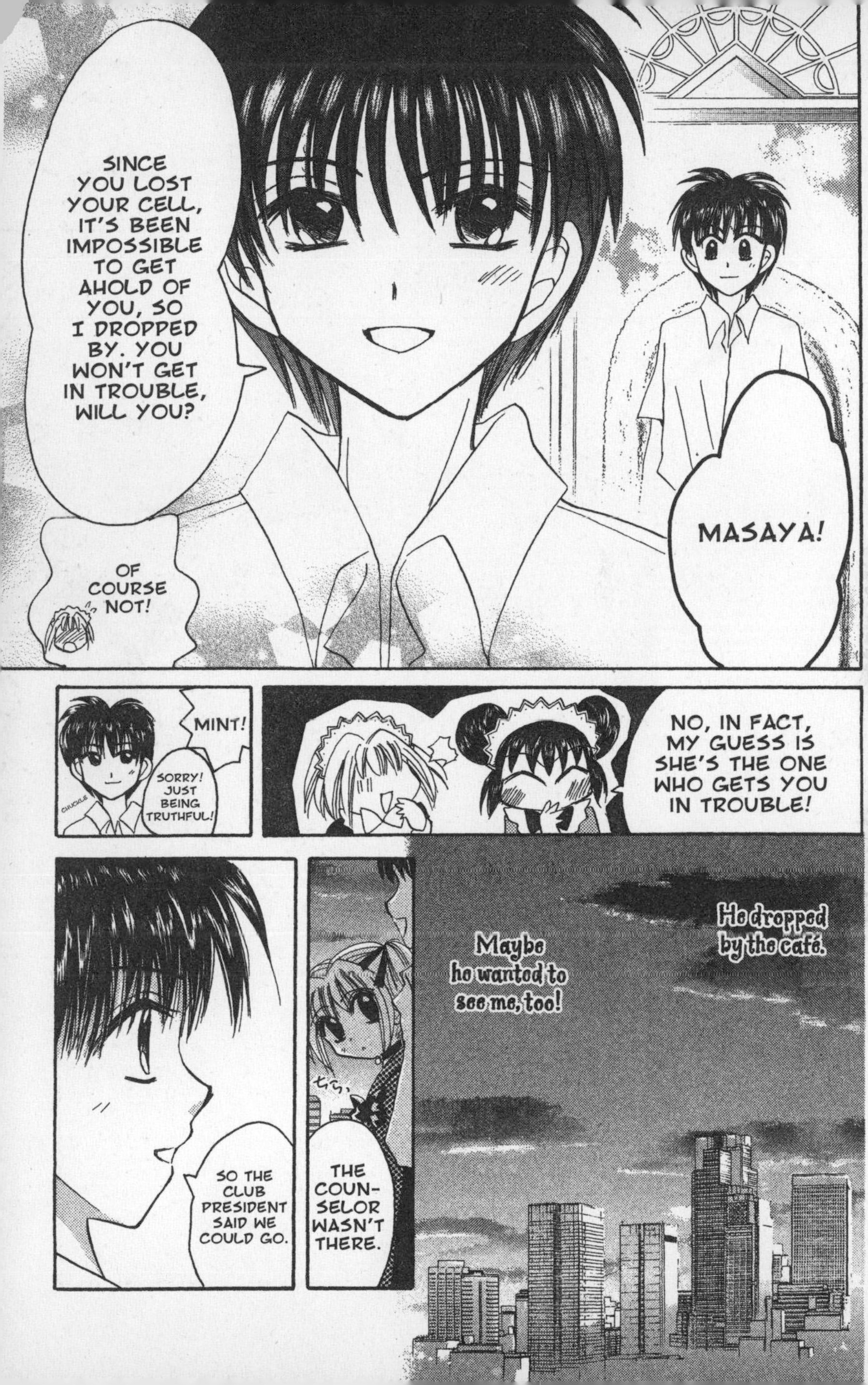
MASAYA!
SINCE YOU LOST YOUR CELL, IT'S BEEN IMPOSSIBLE TO GET AHOLD OF YOU, SO I DROPPED BY. YOU WON'T GET IN TROUBLE, WILL YOU?
OF COURSE NOT!
NO, IN FACT, MY GUESS IS SHE'S THE ONE WHO GETS YOU IN TROUBLE!
MINT!
SORRY! JUST BEING TRUTHFUL!
CHUCKLE
He dropped by the café.
Maybe he wanted to see me, too!
THE COUN-SELOR WASN'T THERE.
SO THE CLUB PRESIDENT SAID WE COULD GO.

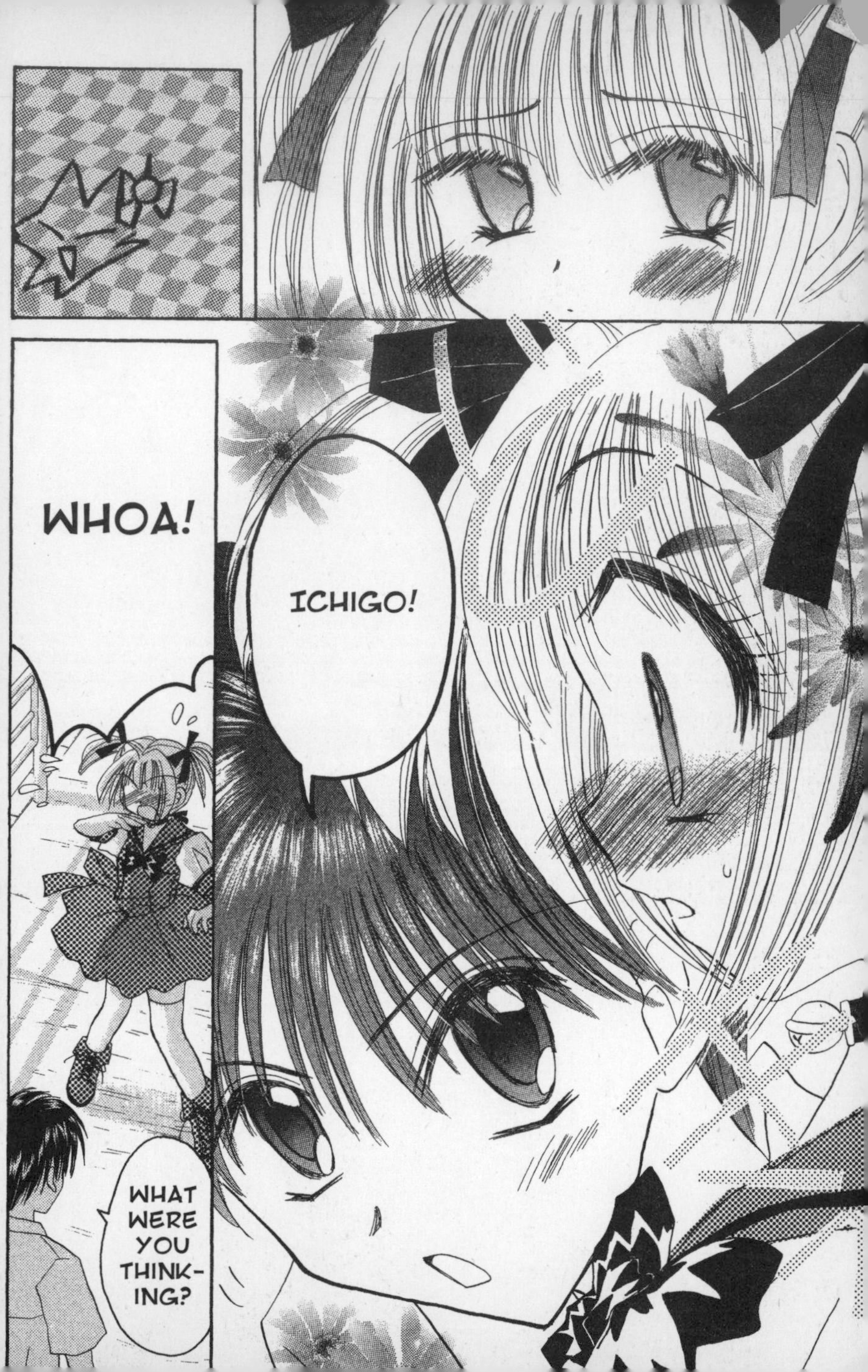
ICHIGO!
WHOA!
WHAT WERE YOU THINKING?

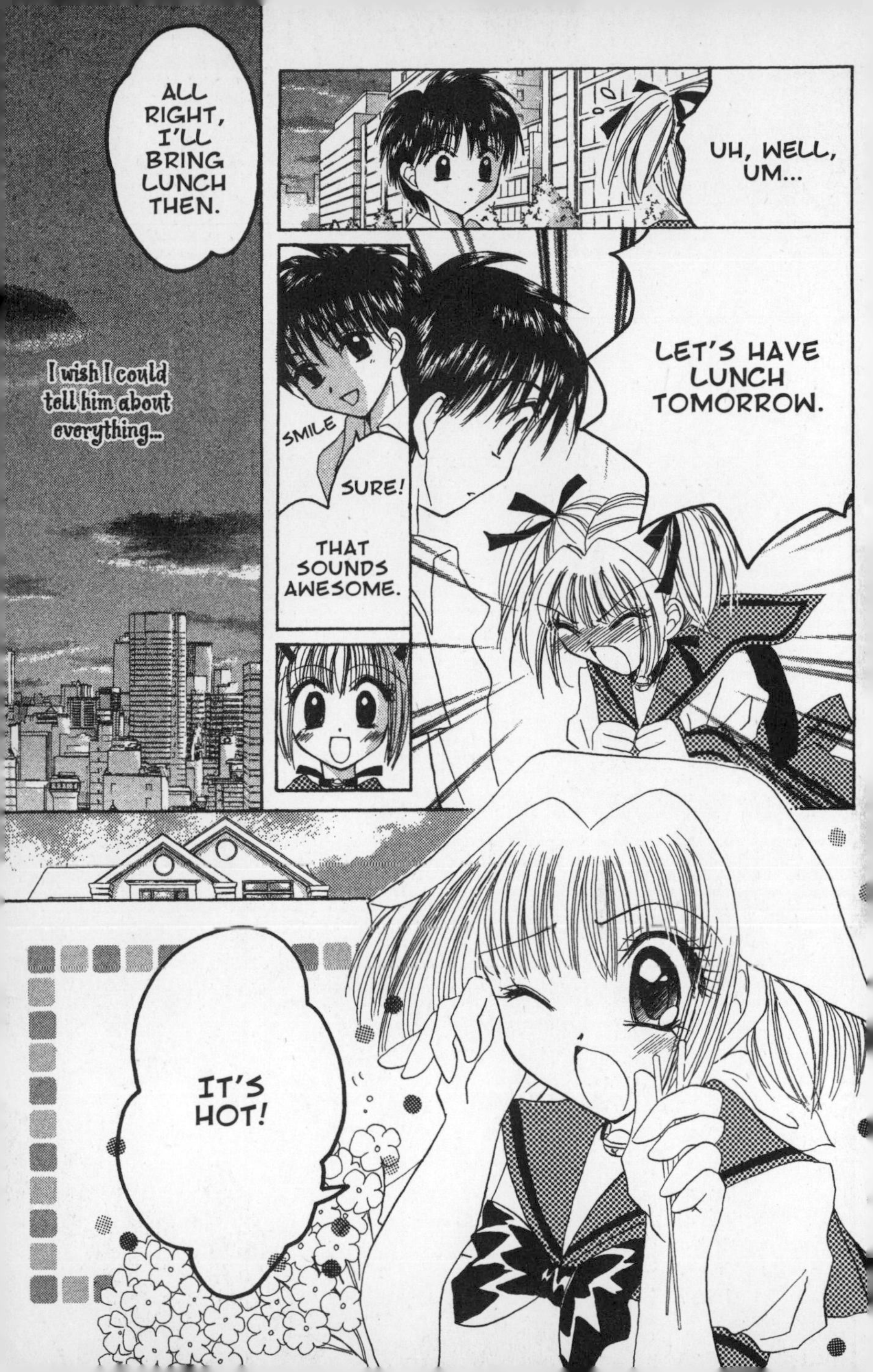
UH, WELL, UM...
LET'S HAVE LUNCH TOMORROW.
SMILE
SURE!
THAT SOUNDS AWESOME.
ALL RIGHT, I'LL BRING LUNCH THEN.
I wish I could tell him about everything...
IT'S HOT!

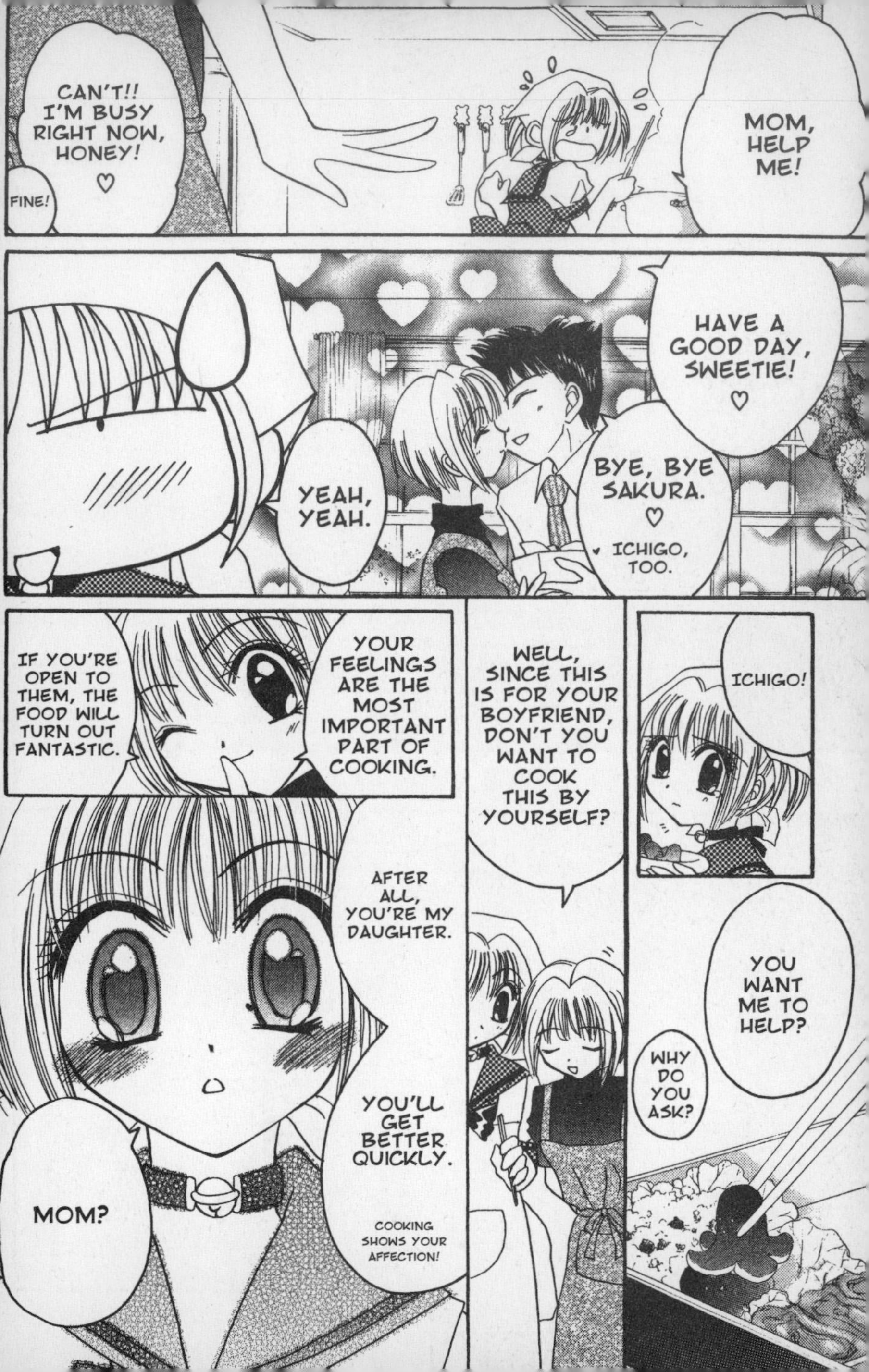
MOM, HELP ME!
CAN'T!! I'M BUSY RIGHT NOW, HONEY! ♡
FINE!
HAVE A GOOD DAY, SWEETIE! ♡
BYE, BYE SAKURA. ♡
ICHIGO, TOO.
YEAH, YEAH.
ICHIGO!
YOU WANT ME TO HELP?
WHY DO YOU ASK?
WELL, SINCE THIS IS FOR YOUR BOYFRIEND, DON'T YOU WANT TO COOK THIS BY YOURSELF?
YOUR FEELINGS ARE THE MOST IMPORTANT PART OF COOKING.
IF YOU'RE OPEN TO THEM, THE FOOD WILL TURN OUT FANTASTIC.
AFTER ALL, YOU'RE MY DAUGHTER.
YOU'LL GET BETTER QUICKLY.
COOKING SHOWS YOUR AFFECTION!
MOM?

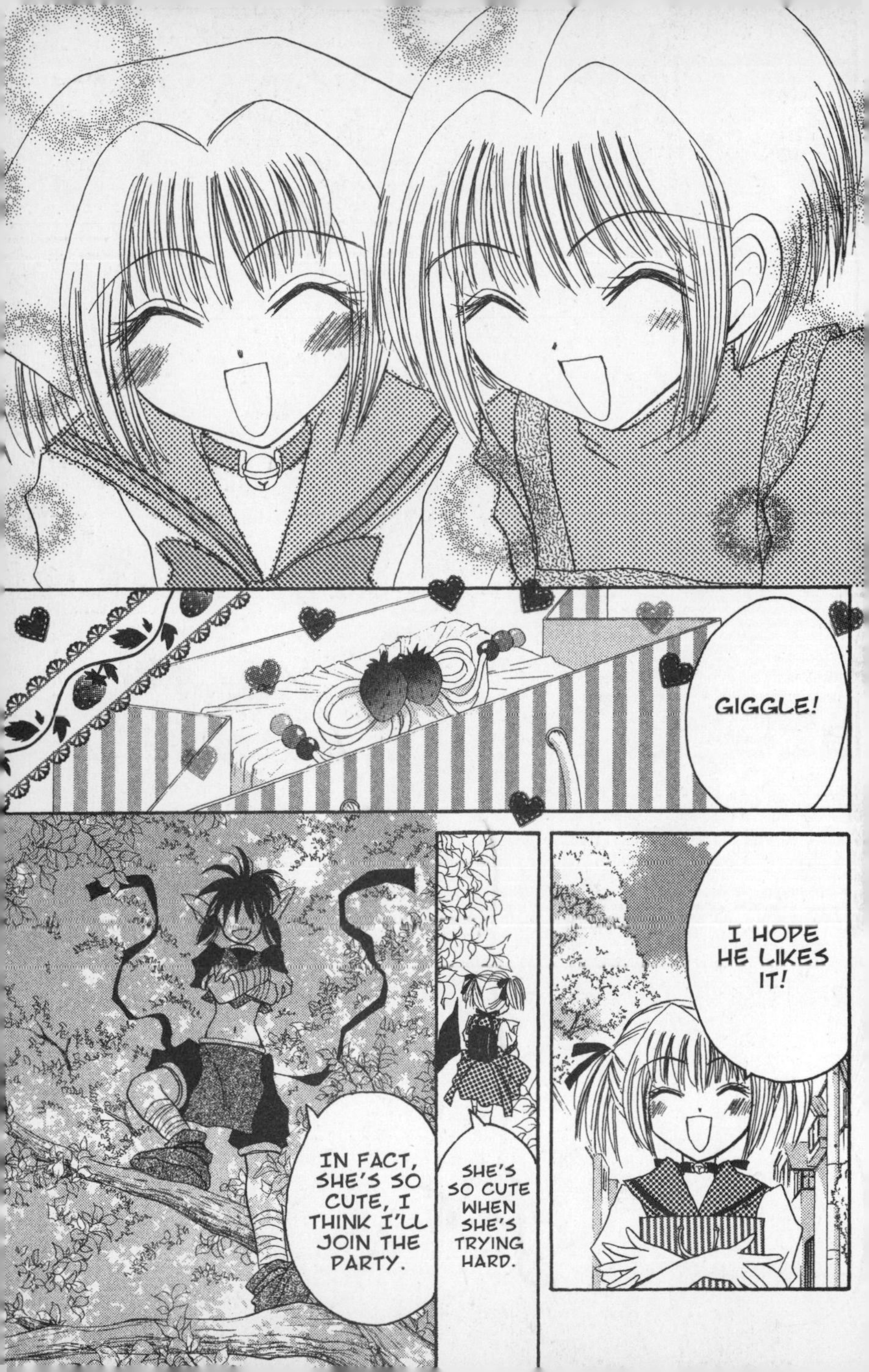
GIGGLE!
I HOPE HE LIKES IT!
SHE'S SO CUTE WHEN SHE'S TRYING HARD.
IN FACT, SHE'S SO CUTE, I THINK I'LL JOIN THE PARTY.

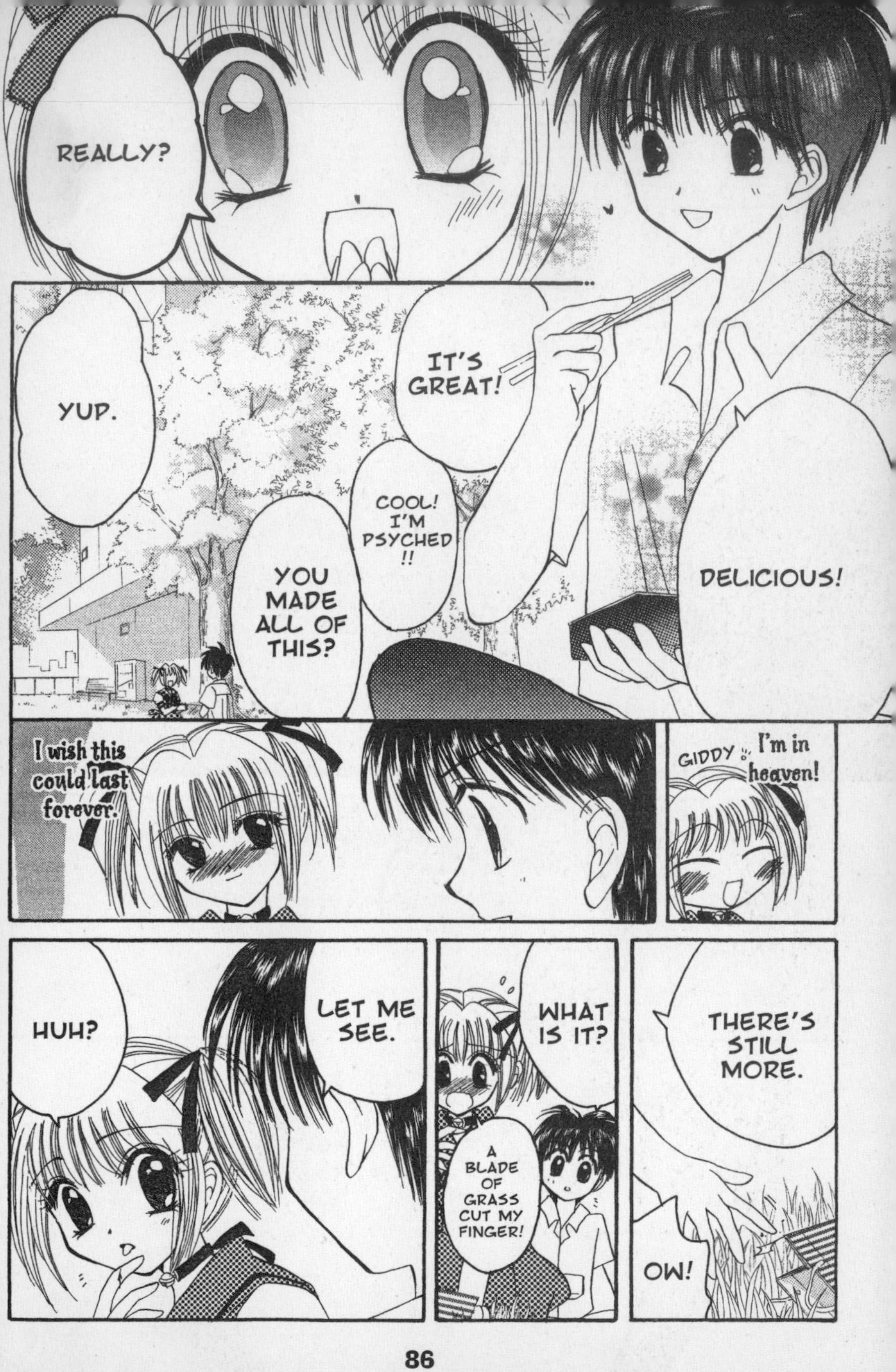
REALLY?
DELICIOUS!
IT'S GREAT!
COOL! I'M PSYCHED!!
YOU MADE ALL OF THIS?
YUP.
GIDDY
I'm in heaven!
I wish this could last forever.
THERE'S STILL MORE.
OW!
WHAT IS IT?
A BLADE OF GRASS CUT MY FINGER!
LET ME SEE.
HUH?

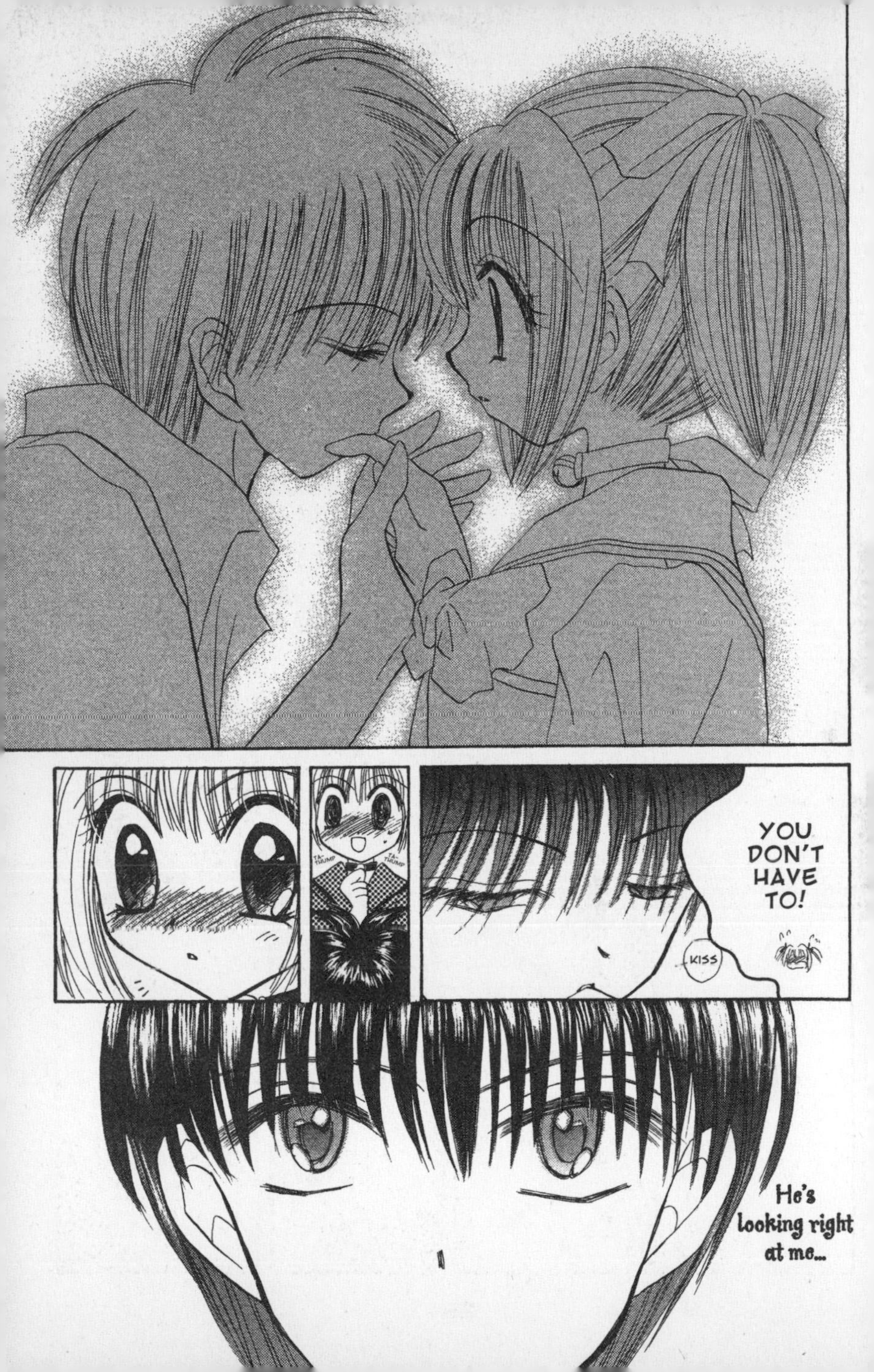
YOU DON'T HAVE TO!
KISS
TA-THUMP
TA-THUMP
He's looking right at me...

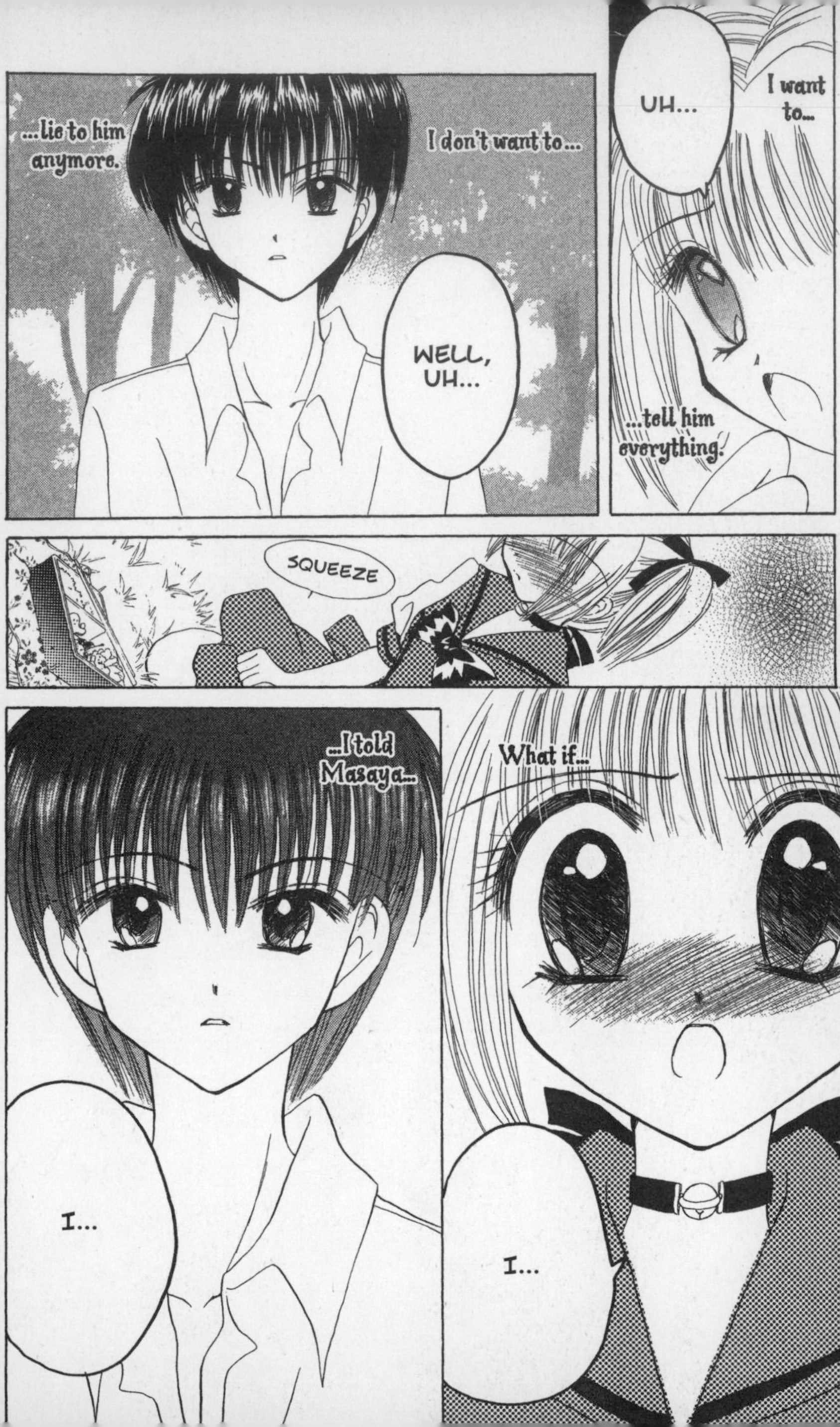
UH...
I want to...
...tell him everything.
I don't want to...
...lie to him anymore.
WELL, UH...
SQUEEZE
What if...
I...
...I told Masaya...
I...

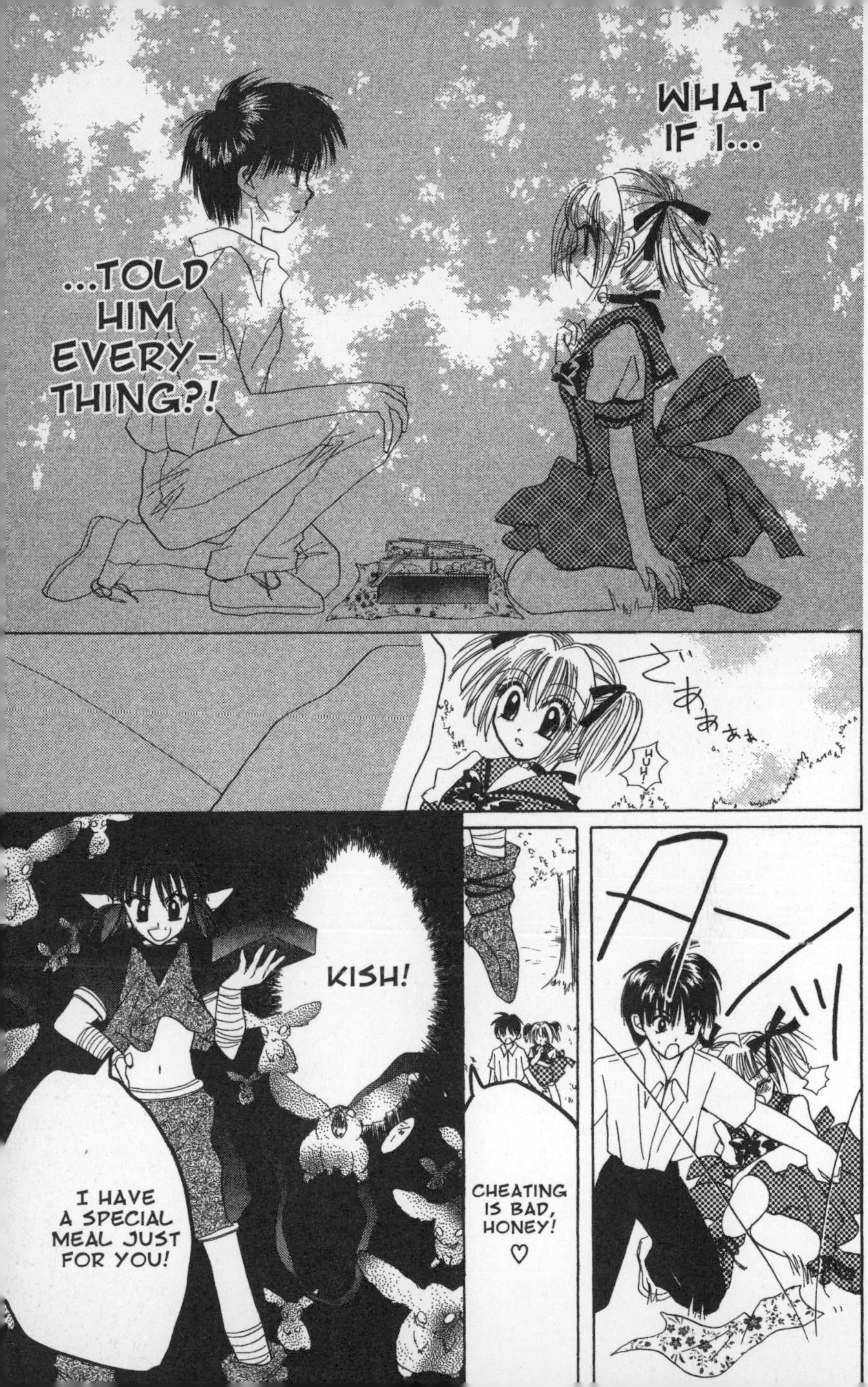
WHAT IF I...
...TOLD HIM EVERY-THING?!
ざあああ
HUH!
CHEATING IS BAD, HONEY! ♡
KISH!
I HAVE A SPECIAL MEAL JUST FOR YOU!

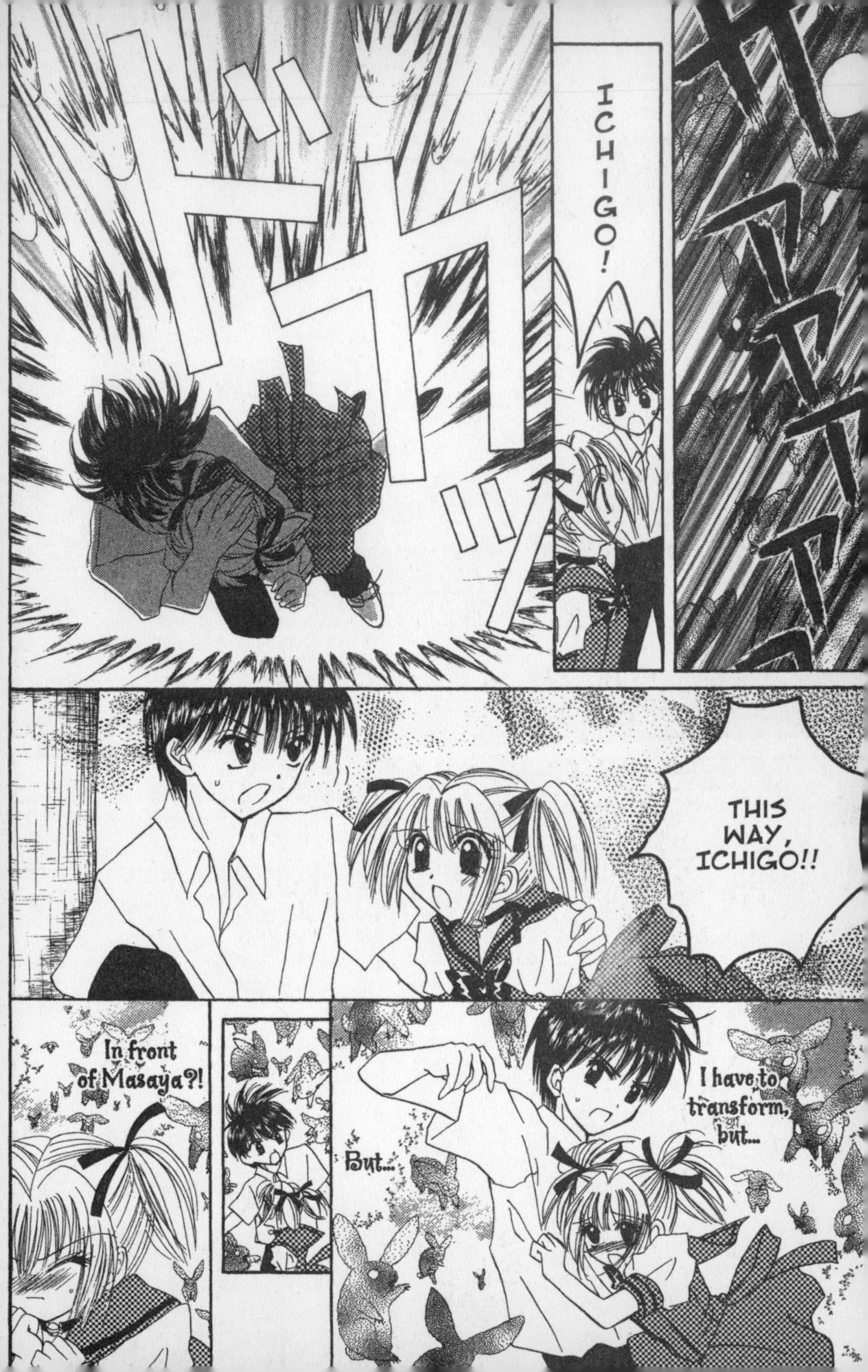
ICHIGO!
THIS WAY, ICHIGO!!
I have to transform, but...
But...
In front of Masaya?!

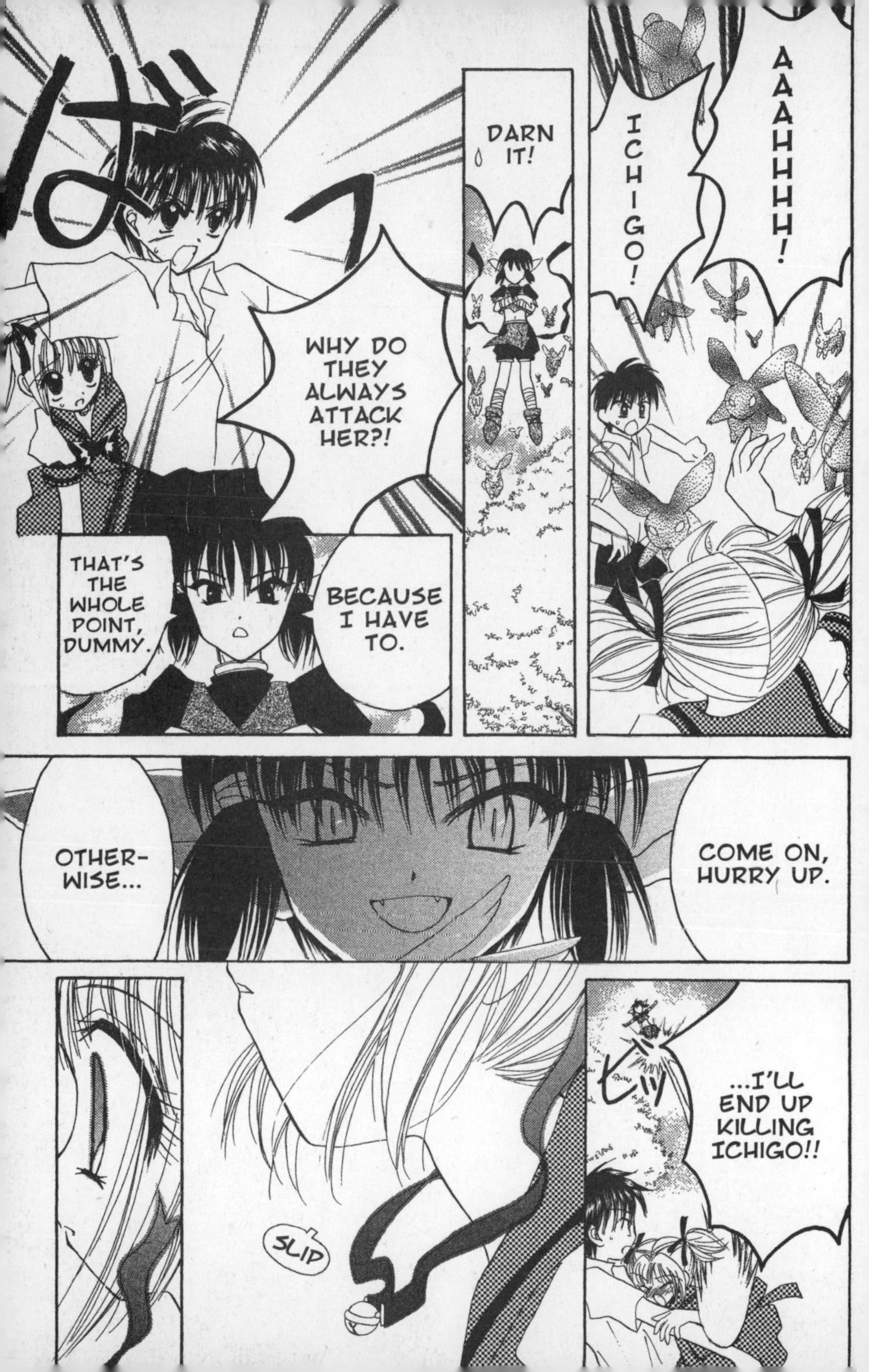

AAAHHHH!
ICHIGO!
DARN IT!
ばっ
WHY DO THEY ALWAYS ATTACK HER?!
BECAUSE I HAVE TO.
THAT'S THE WHOLE POINT, DUMMY.
COME ON, HURRY UP.
OTHER-WISE...
...I'LL END UP KILLING ICHIGO!!
SLIP

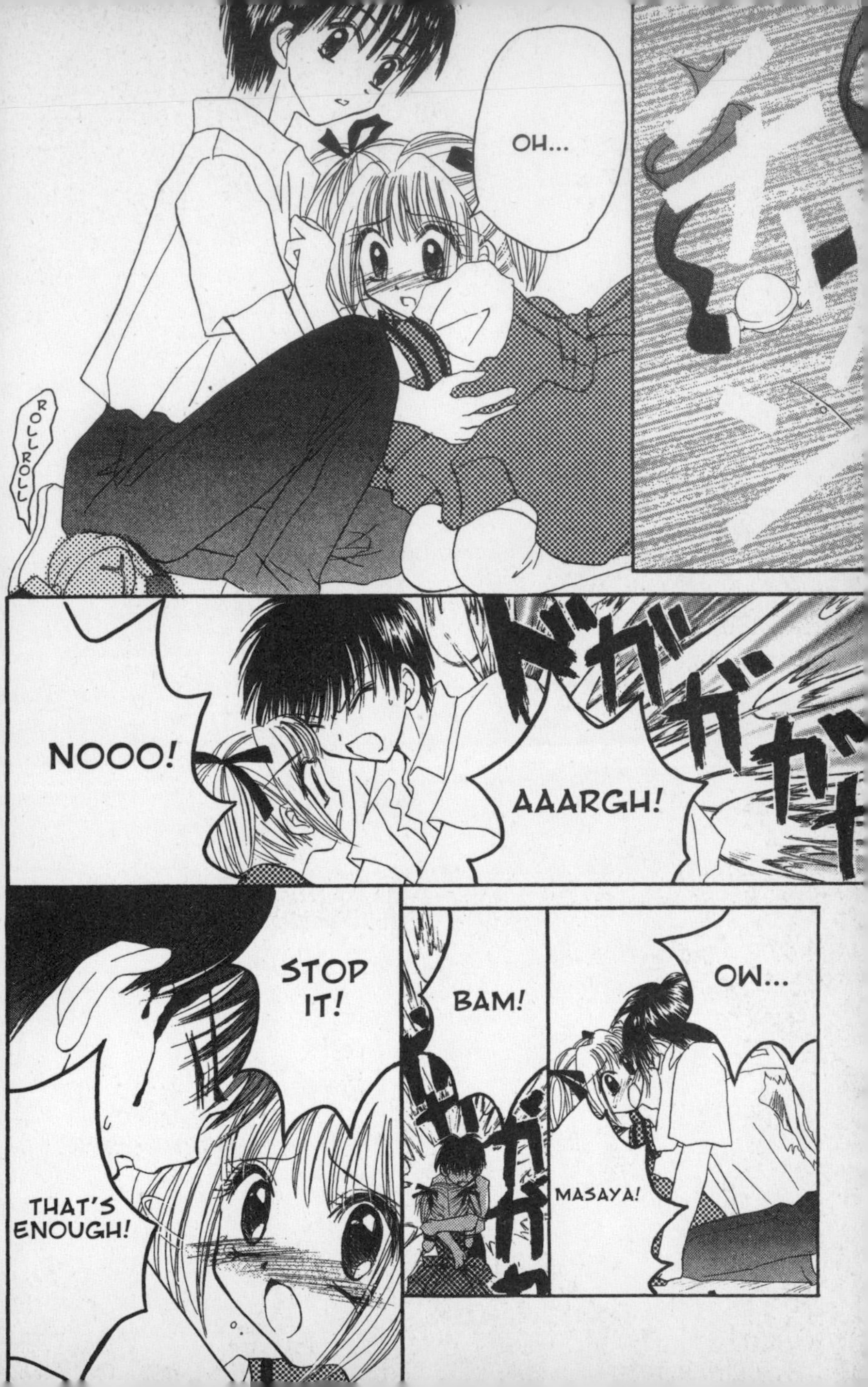
OH...
ROLL ROLL
AAARGH!
NOOO!
OW...
MASAYA!
BAM!
STOP IT!
THAT'S ENOUGH!

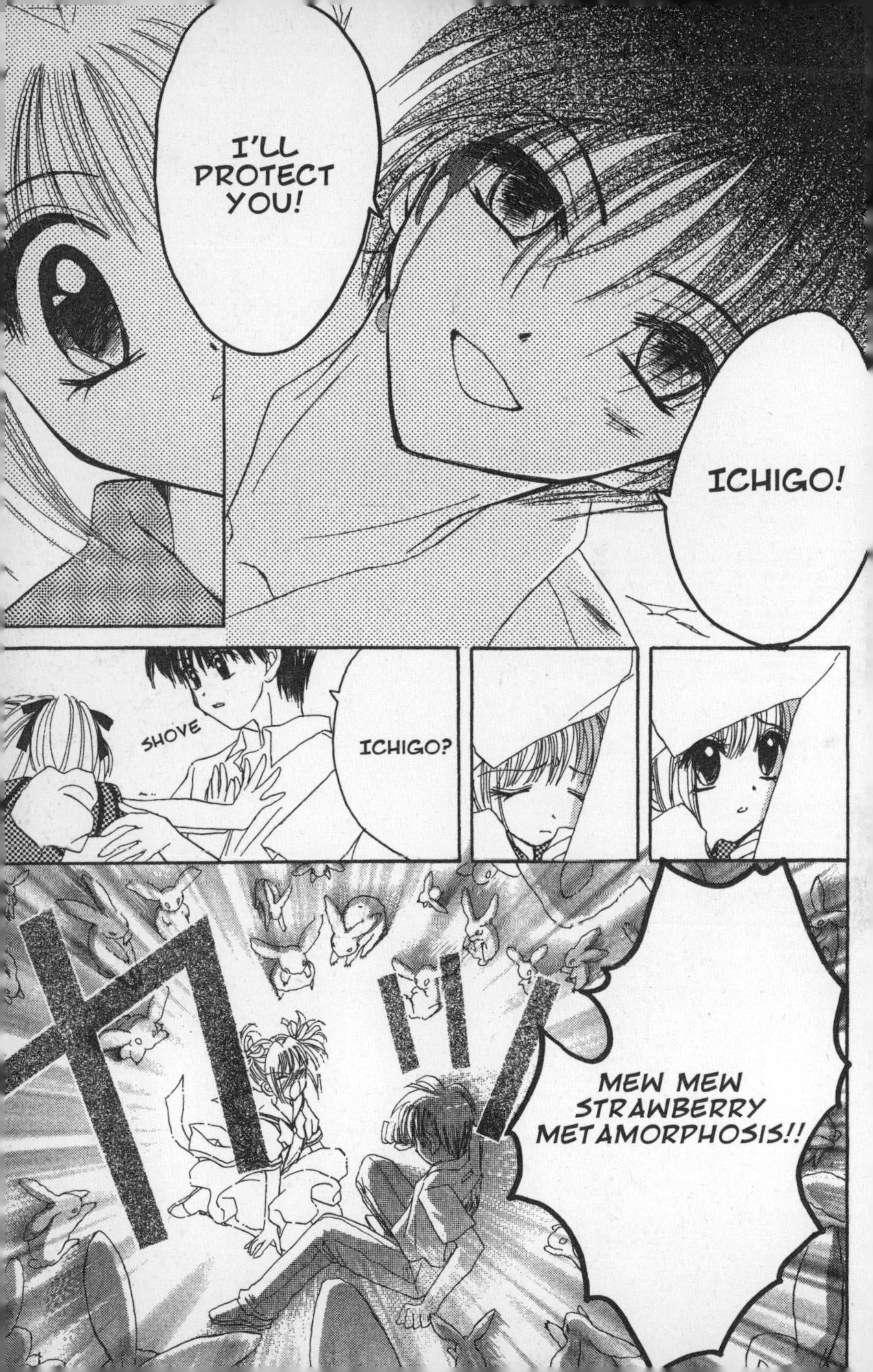
ICHIGO!
I'LL PROTECT YOU!
ICHIGO?
SHOVE
MEW MEW STRAWBERRY METAMORPHOSIS!!

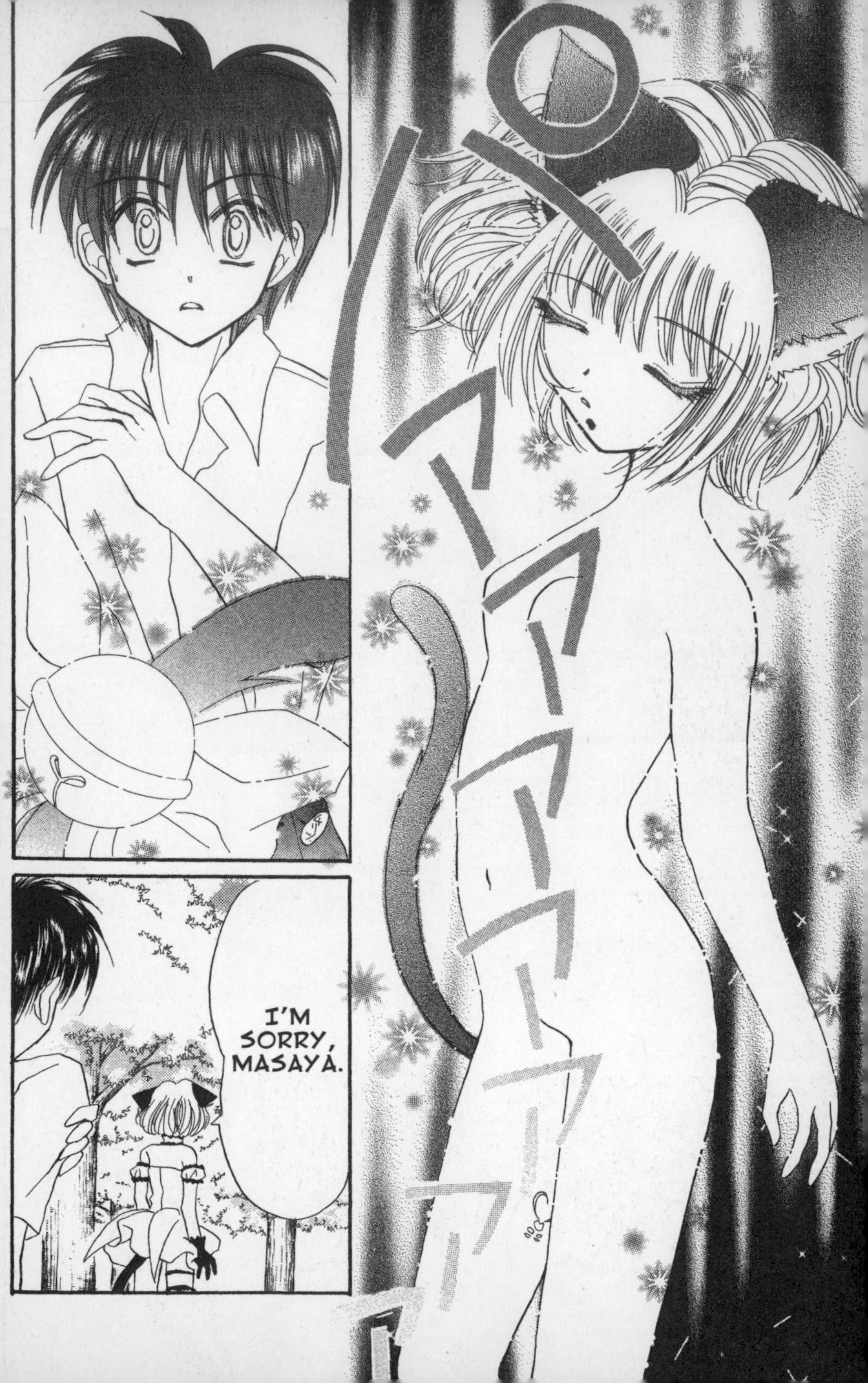
I'M SORRY, MASAYA.

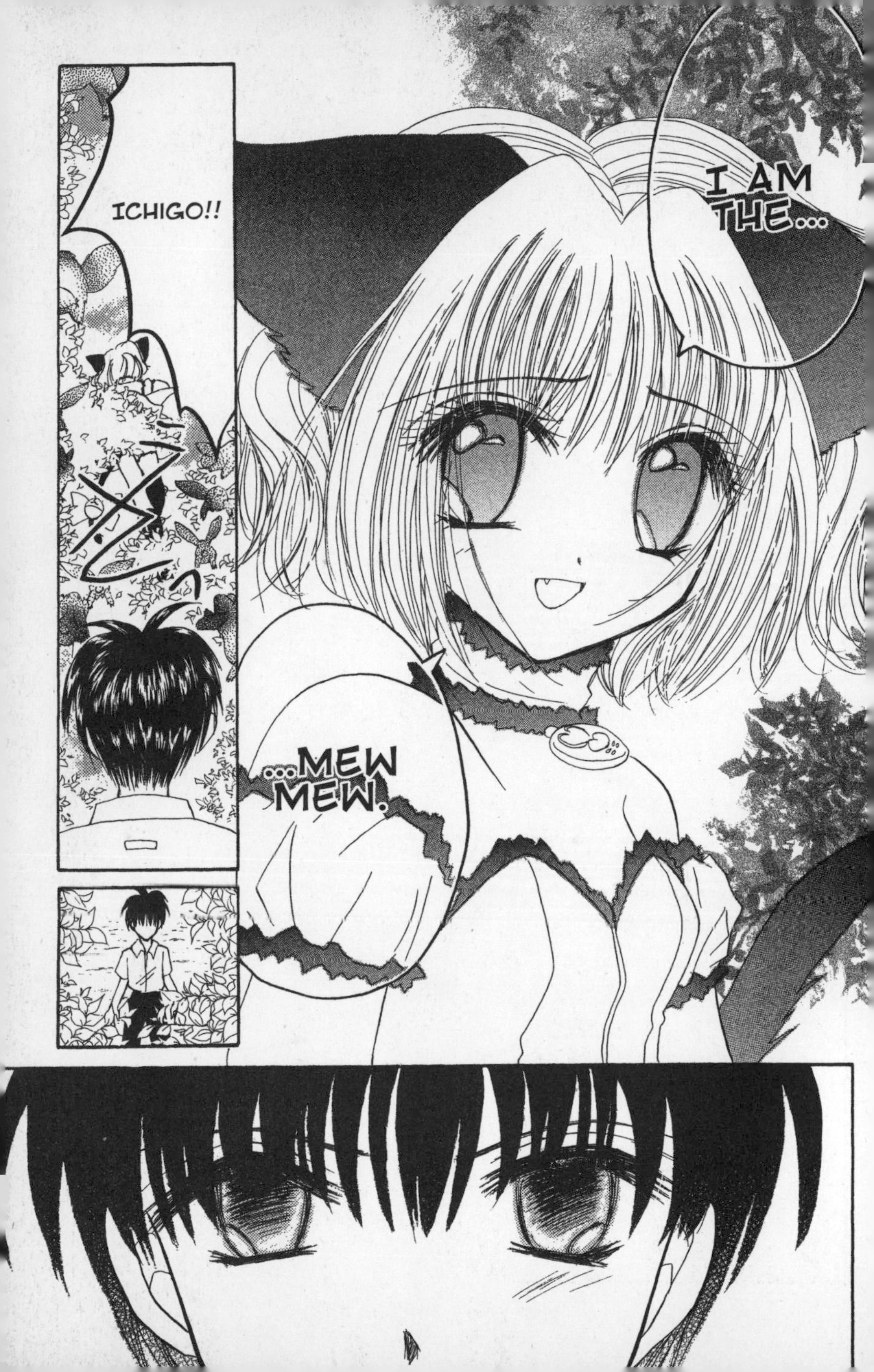
I AM THE...
...MEW MEW.
ICHIGO!!

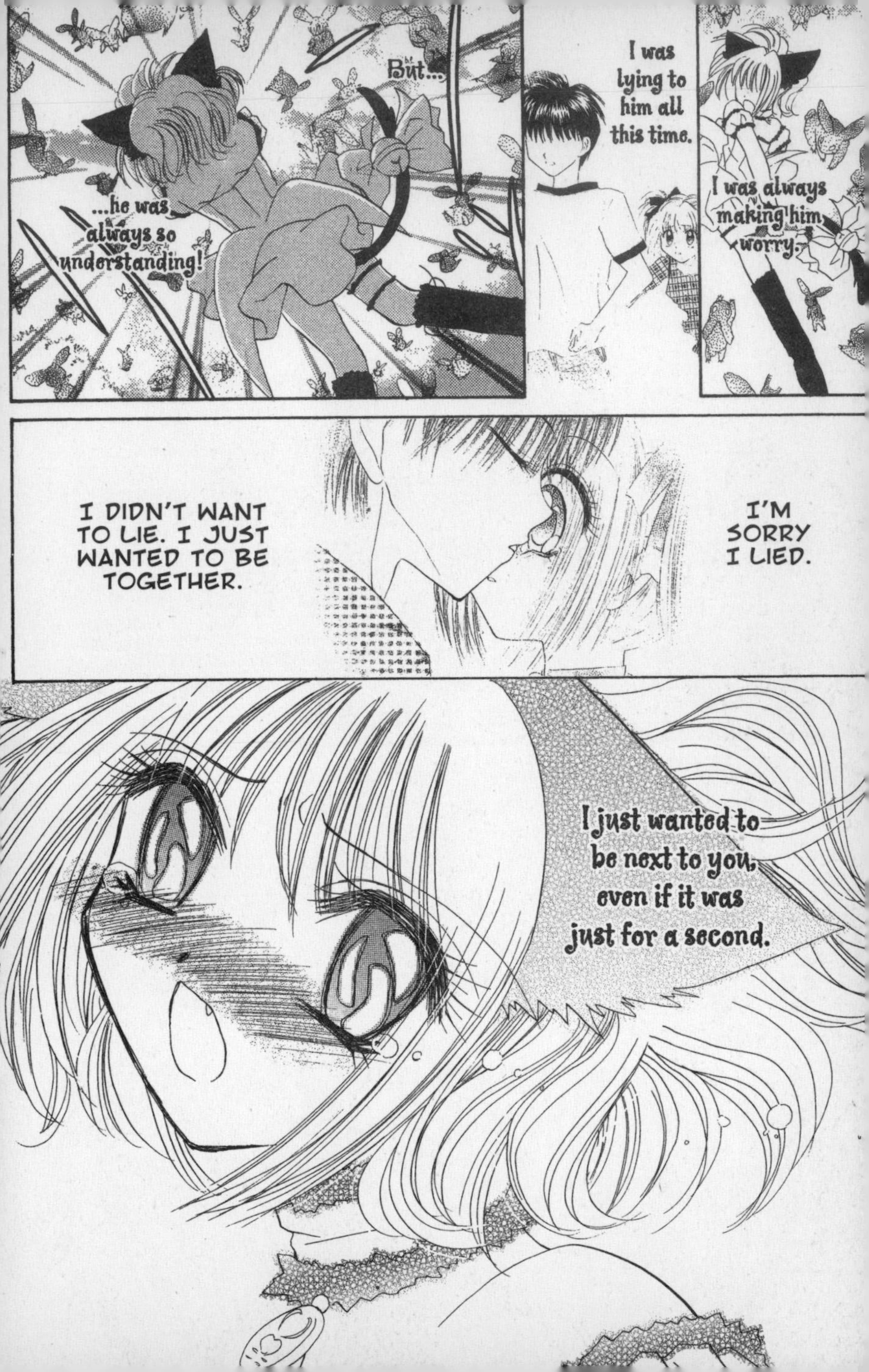
I was always making him worry.
I was lying to him all this time.
But...
...he was always so understanding!
I'M SORRY I LIED.
I DIDN'T WANT TO LIE. I JUST WANTED TO BE TOGETHER.
I just wanted to be next to you, even if it was just for a second.

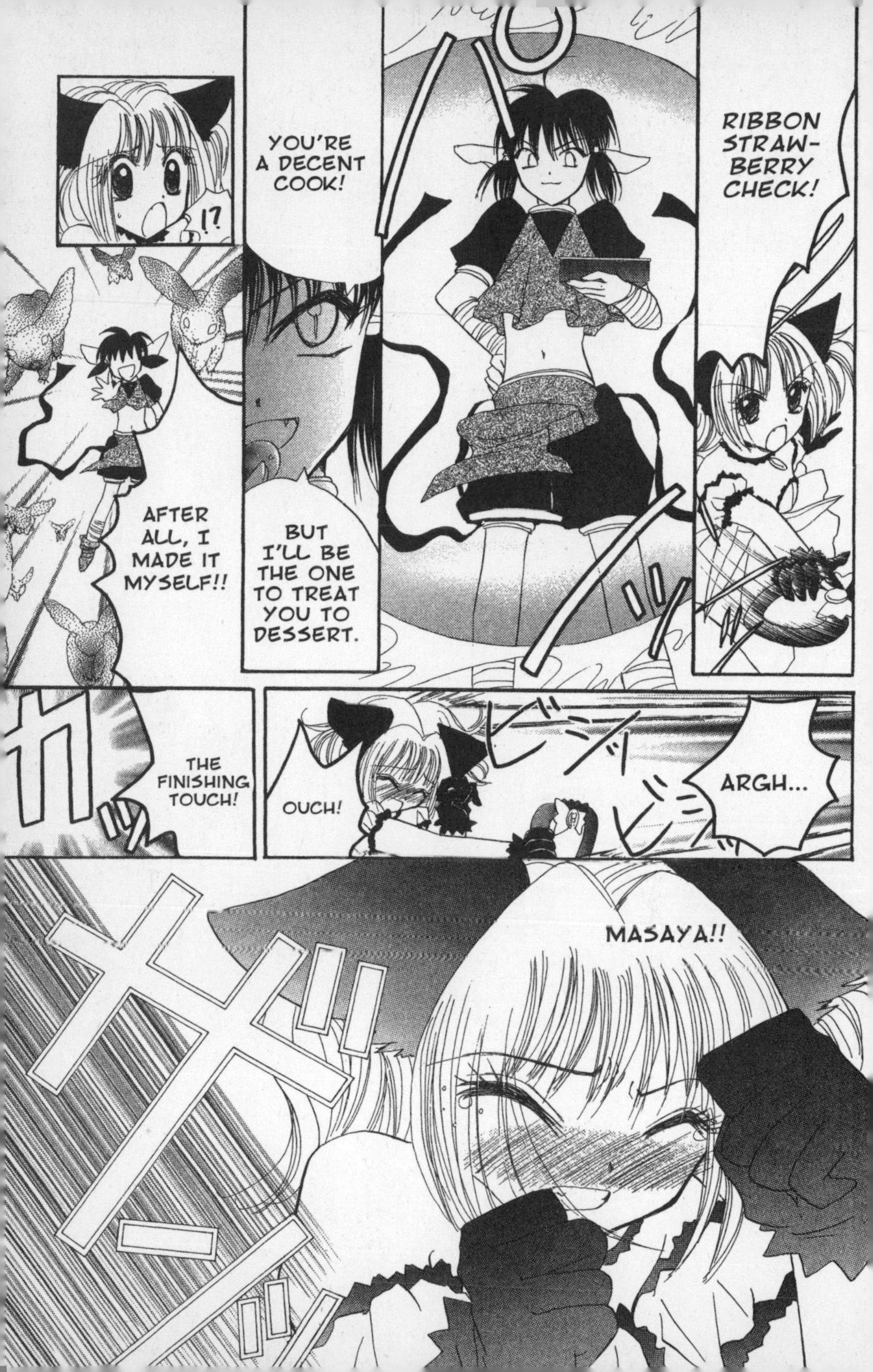
RIBBON STRAW-BERRY CHECK!
YOU'RE A DECENT COOK!
BUT I'LL BE THE ONE TO TREAT YOU TO DESSERT.
!?
AFTER ALL, I MADE IT MYSELF!!
ARGH...
OUCH!
THE FINISHING TOUCH!
MASAYA!!

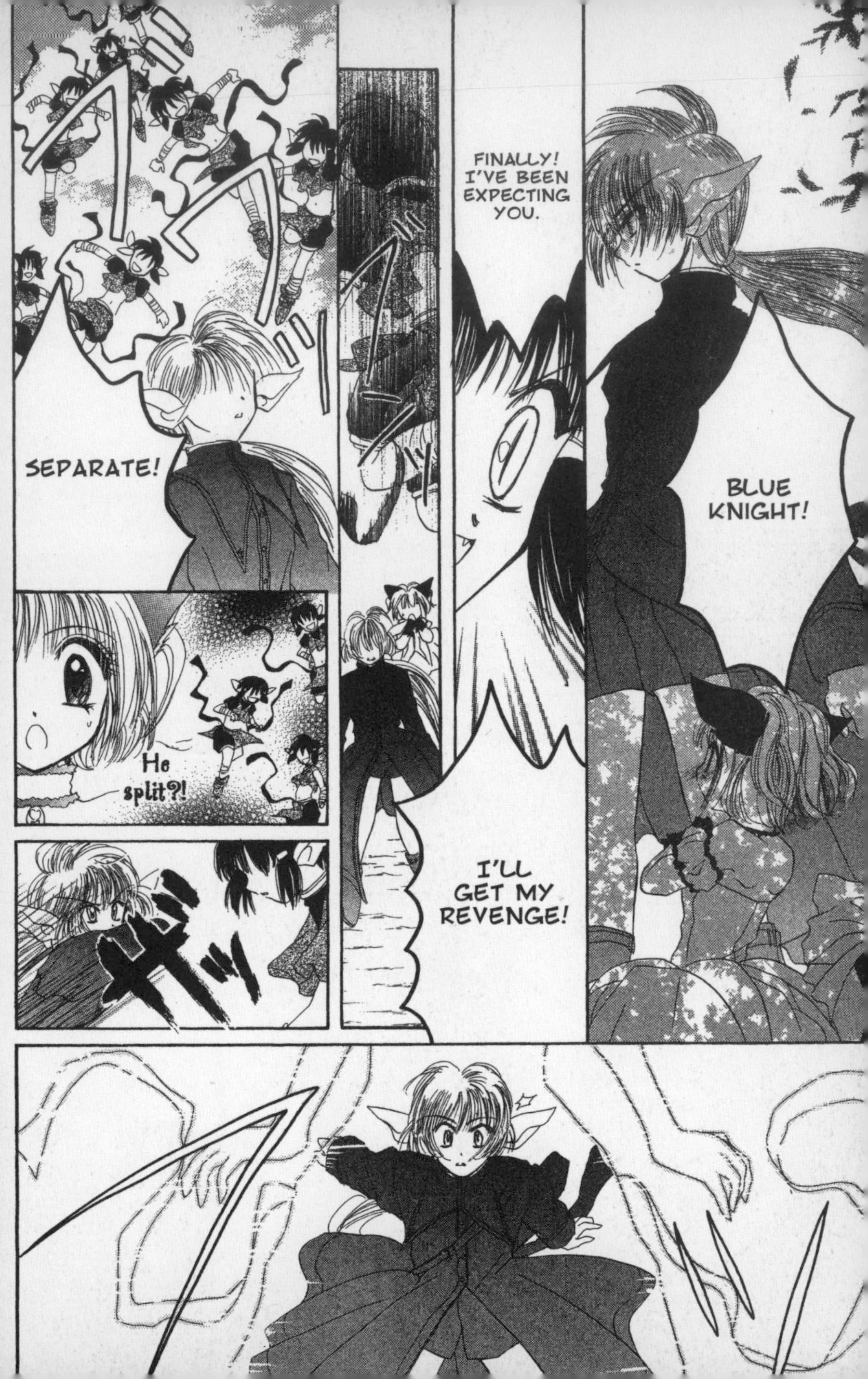
BLUE KNIGHT!
FINALLY! I'VE BEEN EXPECTING YOU.
I'LL GET MY REVENGE!
SEPARATE!
He split?!

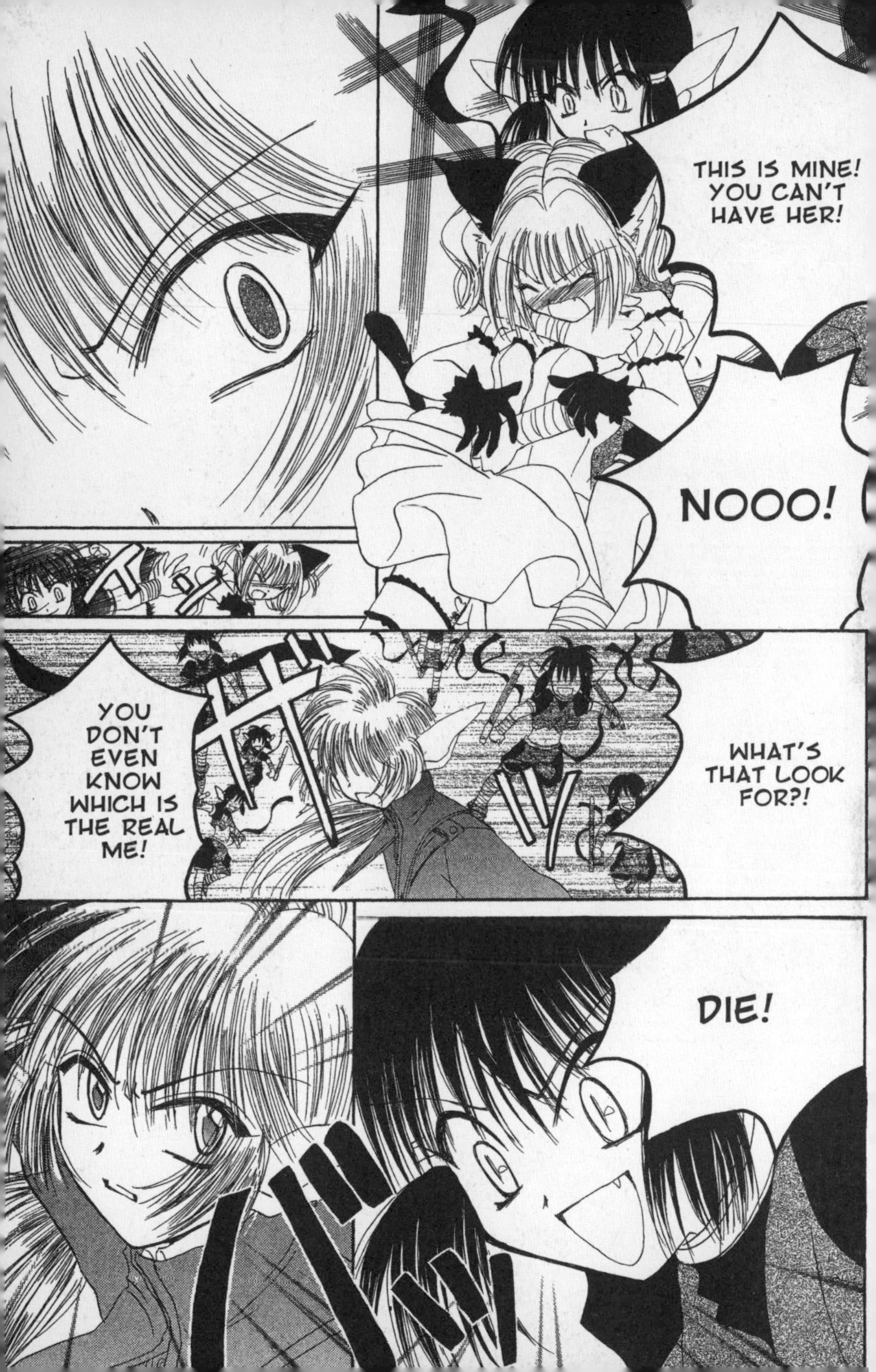
THIS IS MINE! YOU CAN'T HAVE HER!
NOOO!
WHAT'S THAT LOOK FOR?!
YOU DON'T EVEN KNOW WHICH IS THE REAL ME!
DIE!

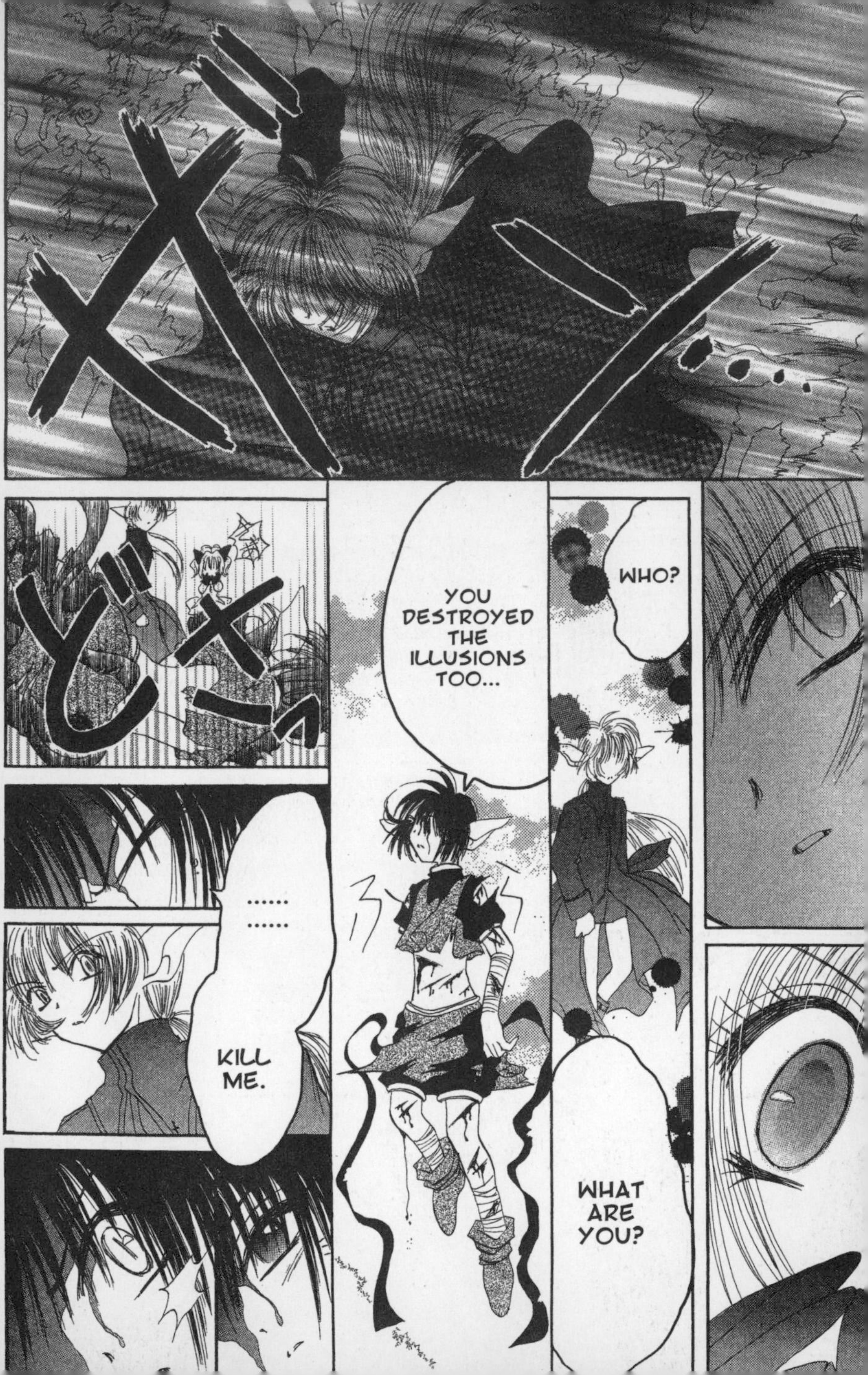
WHO?
WHAT ARE YOU?
YOU DESTROYED THE ILLUSIONS TOO...
....
KILL ME.

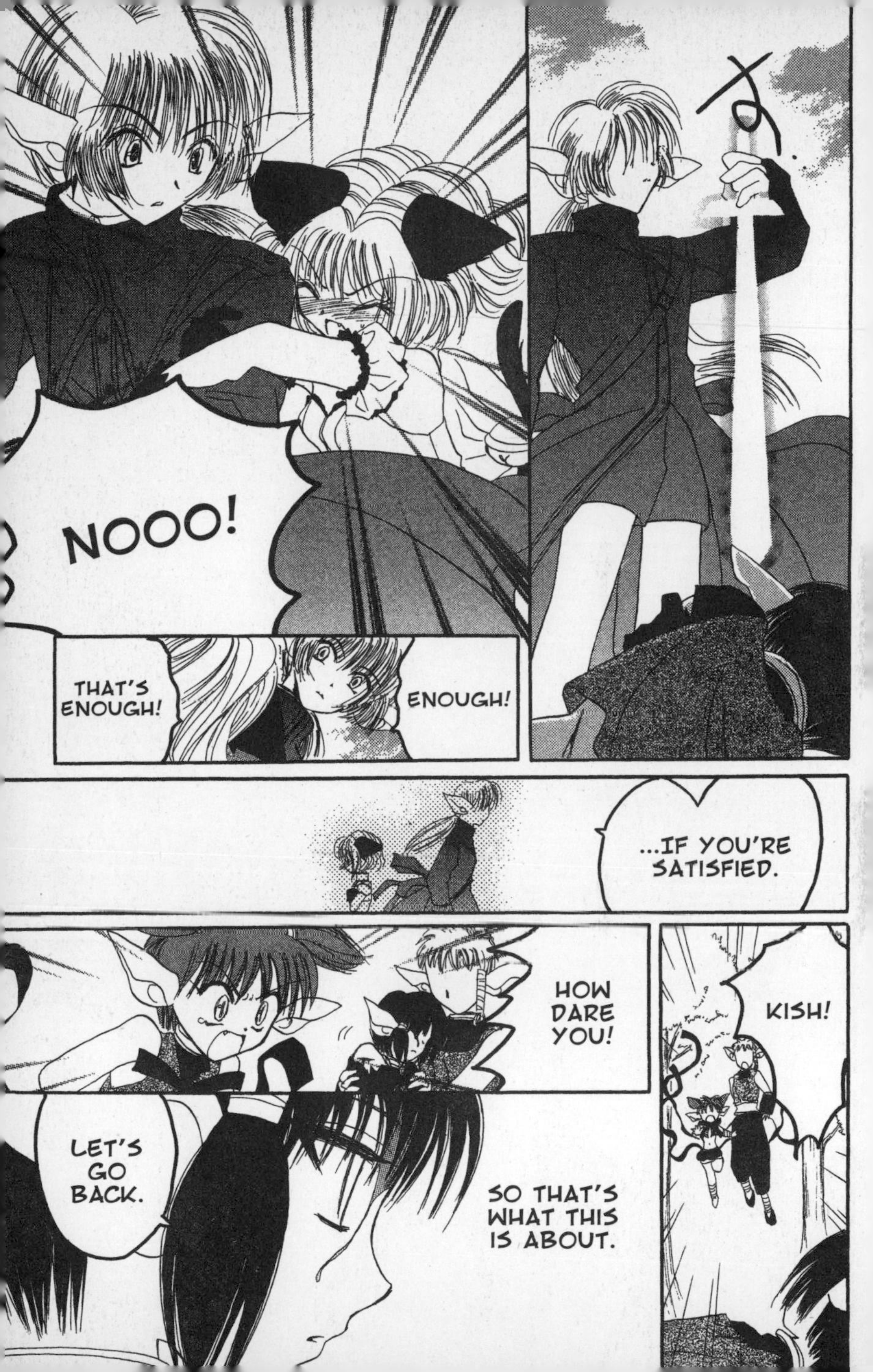
NOOO!
ENOUGH!
THAT'S ENOUGH!
...IF YOU'RE SATISFIED.
KISH!
HOW DARE YOU!
SO THAT'S WHAT THIS IS ABOUT.
LET'S GO BACK.

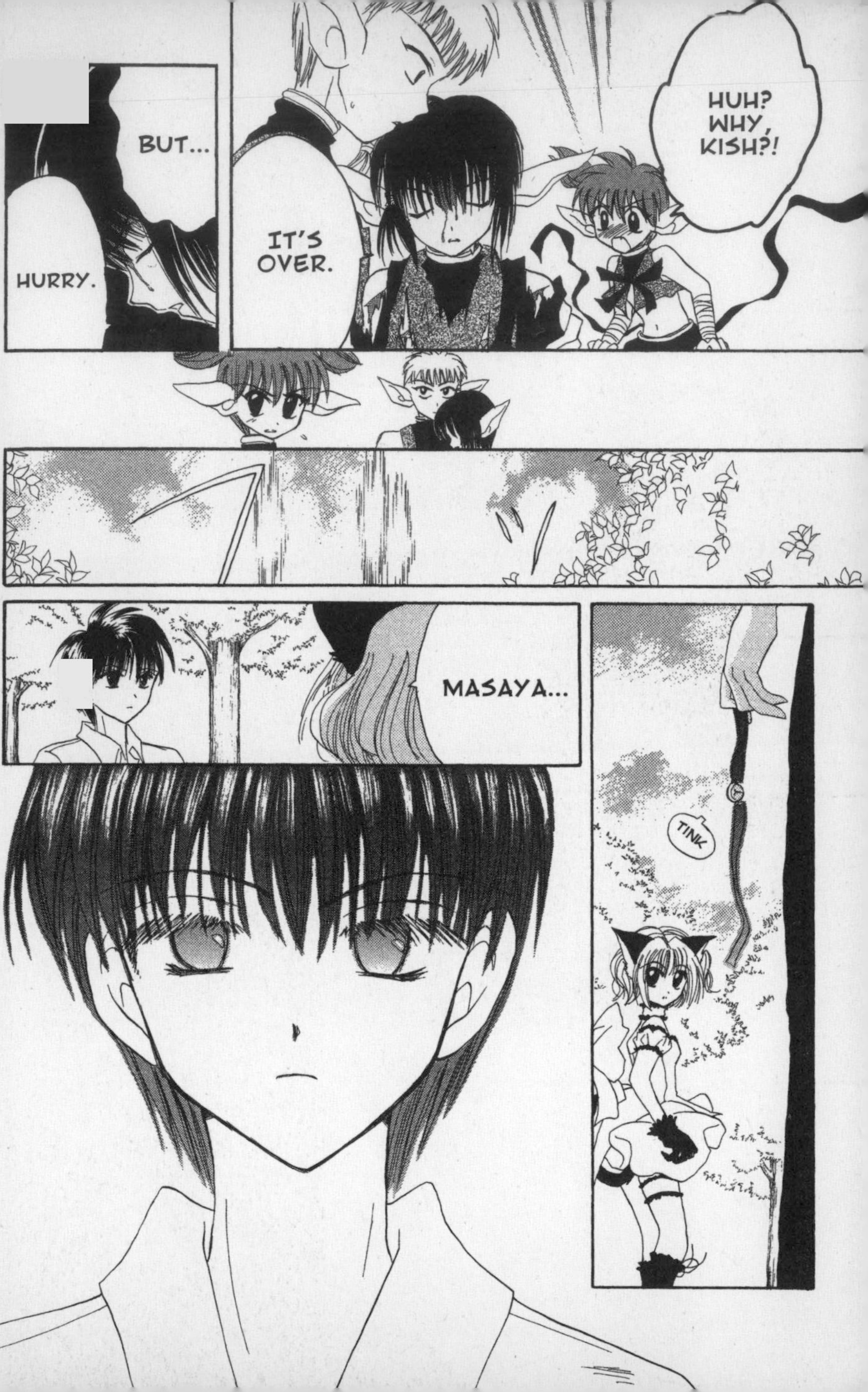
HUH? WHY, KISH?!
IT'S OVER.
BUT...
HURRY.
TINK
MASAYA...

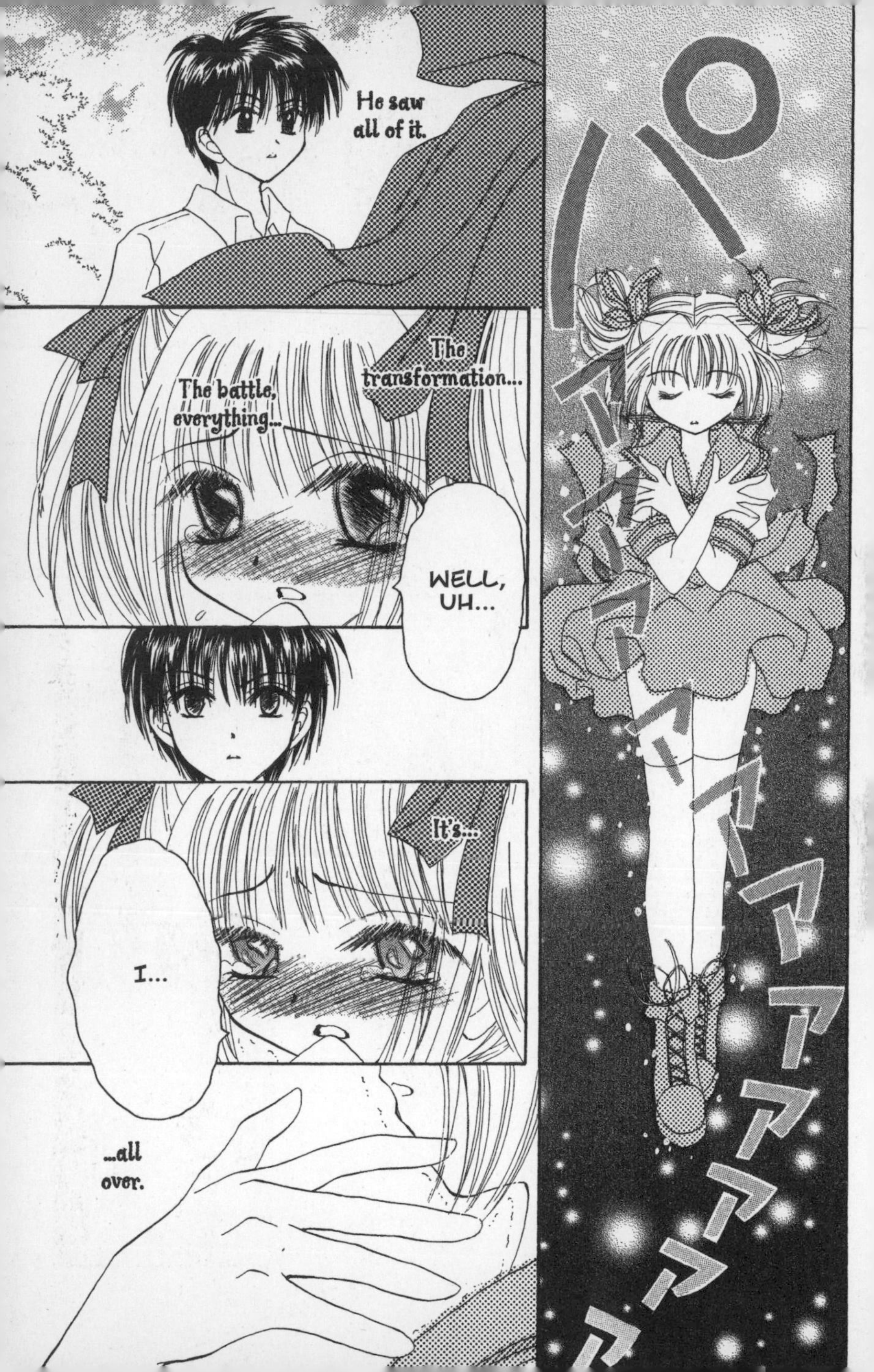
パアアアアアアアアアアアア
He saw all of it.
The transformation...
The battle, everything...
WELL, UH...
It's...
I...
...all over.

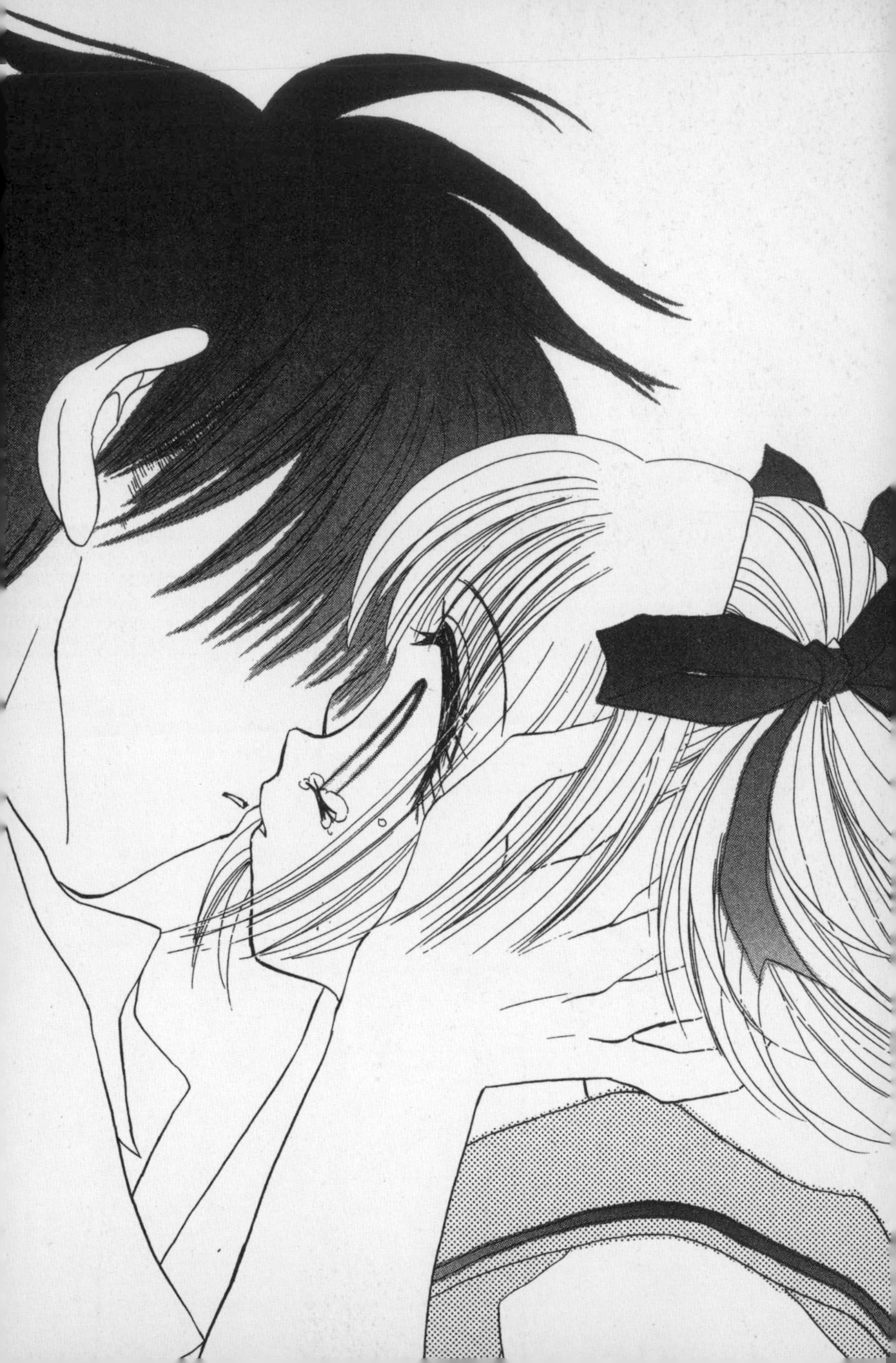

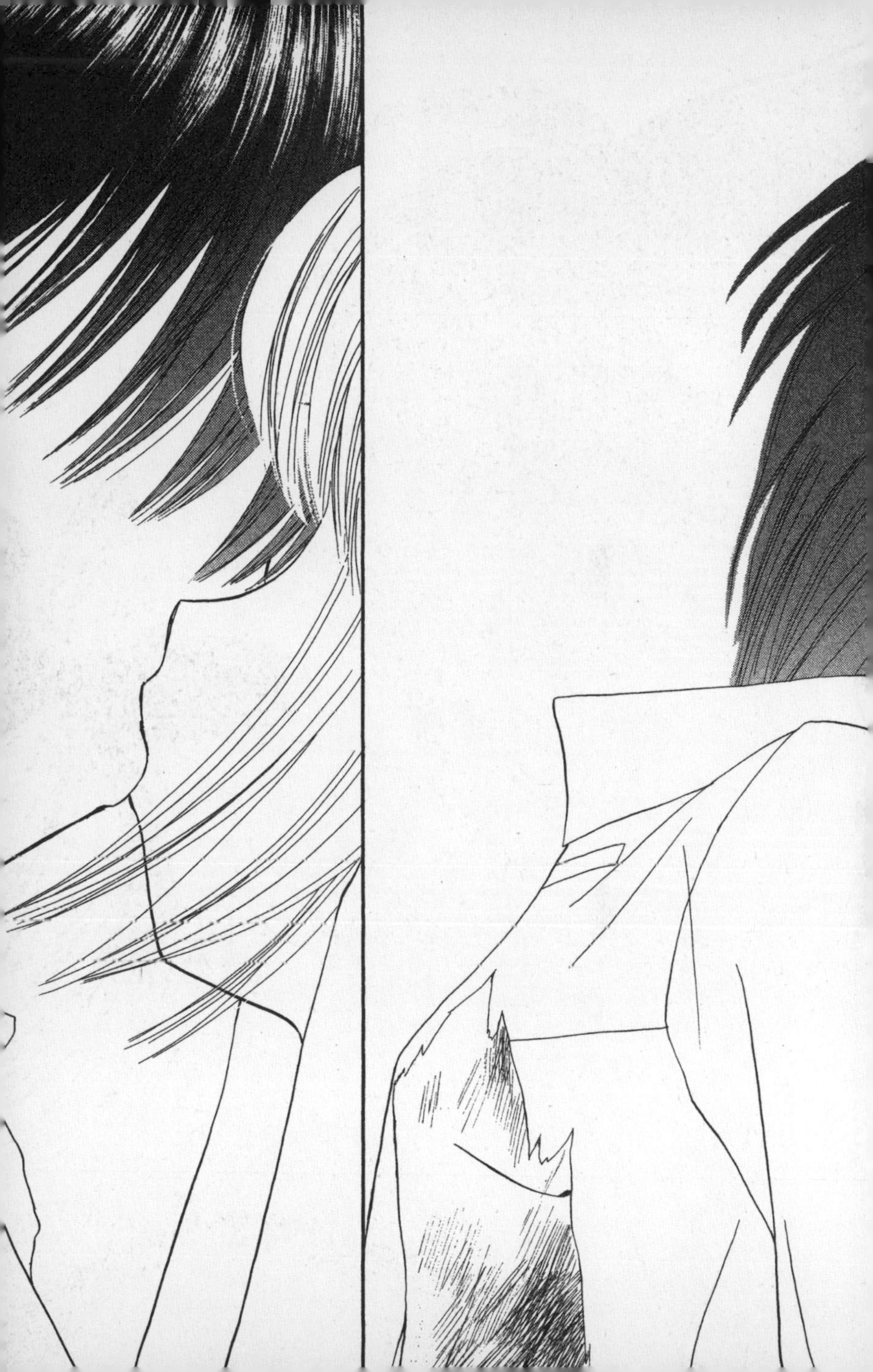

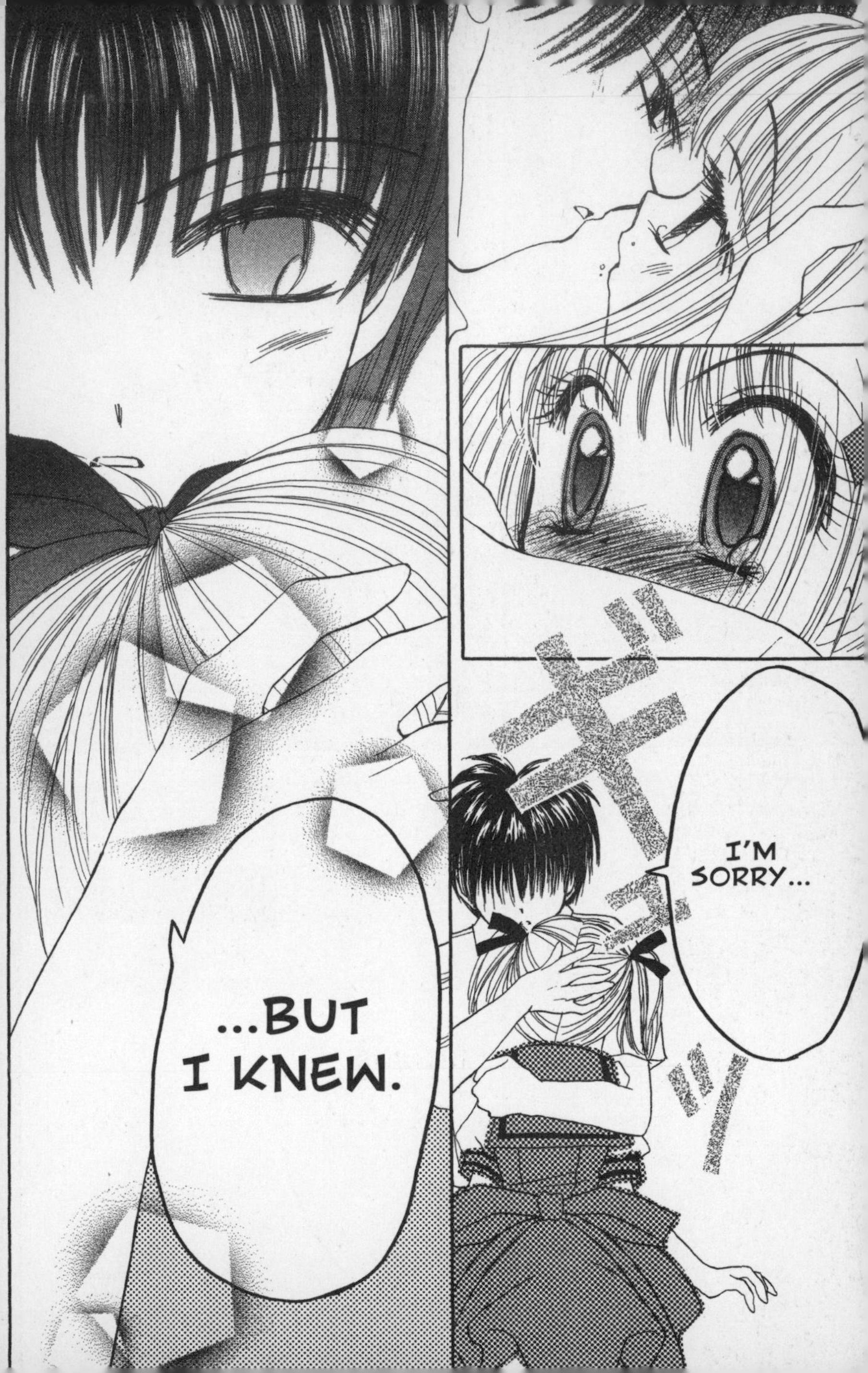
I'M SORRY...
...BUT I KNEW.

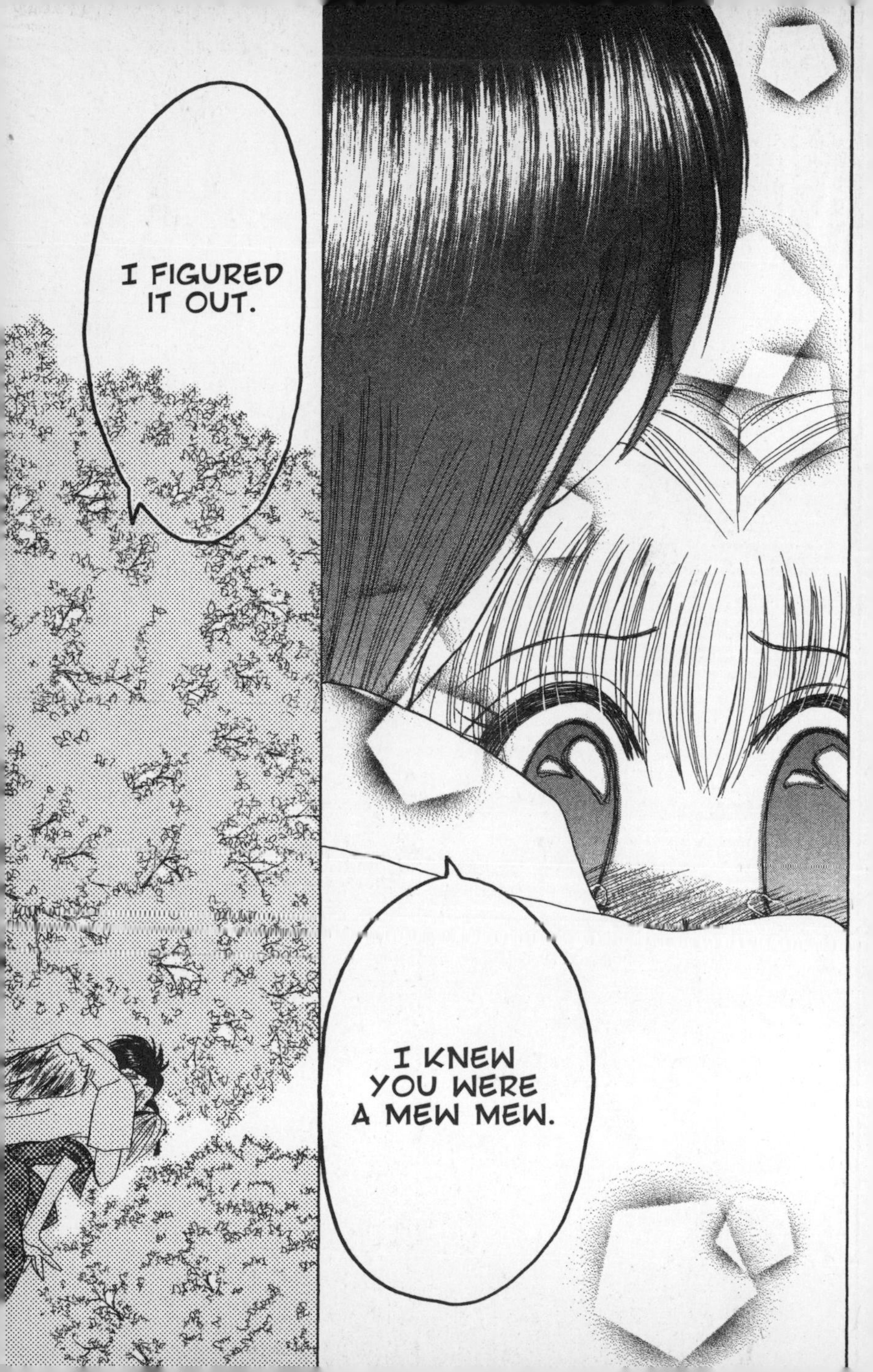
I KNEW YOU WERE A MEW MEW.
I FIGURED IT OUT.

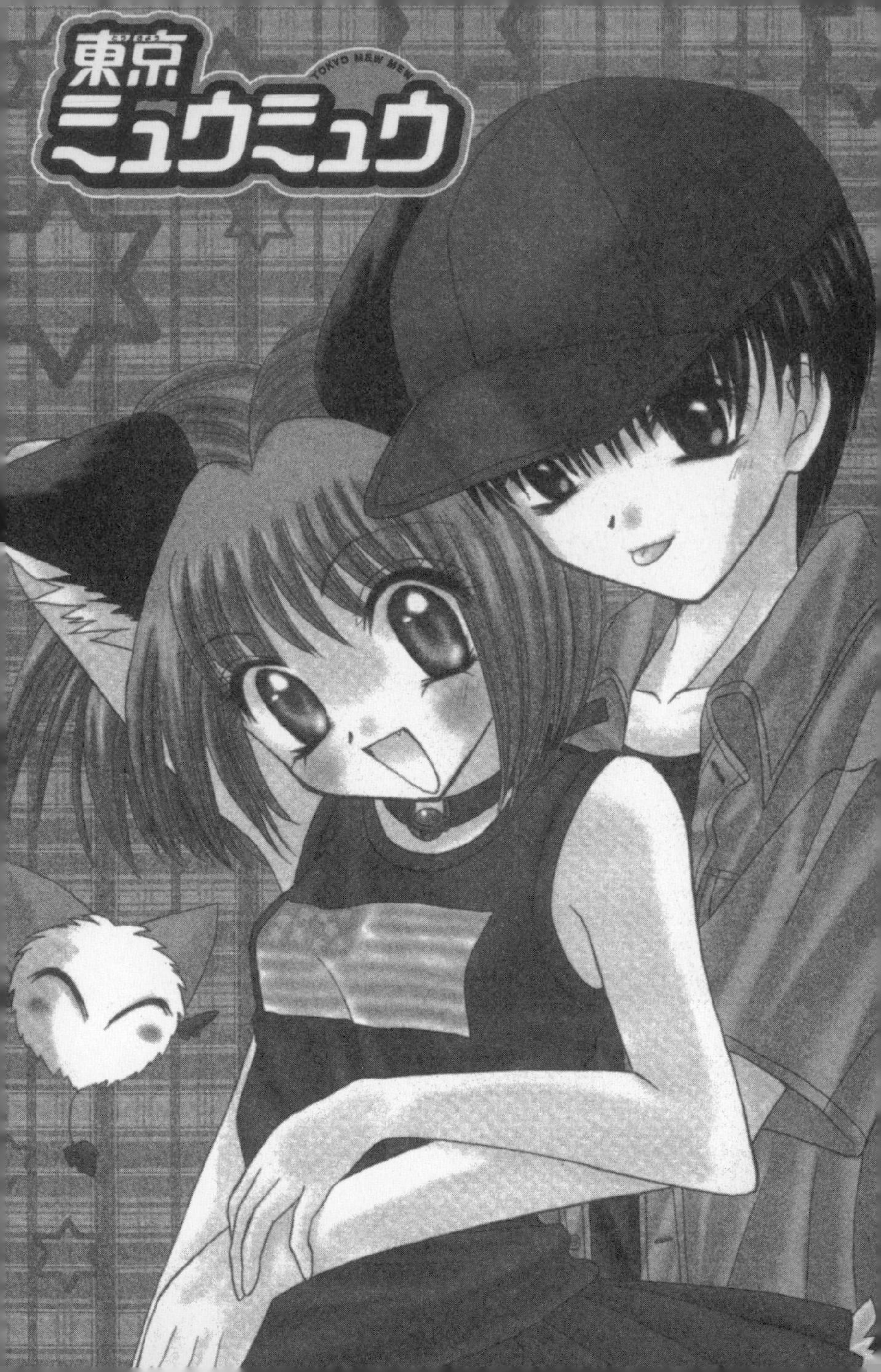
東京ミュウミュウ
TOKYO MEW MEW

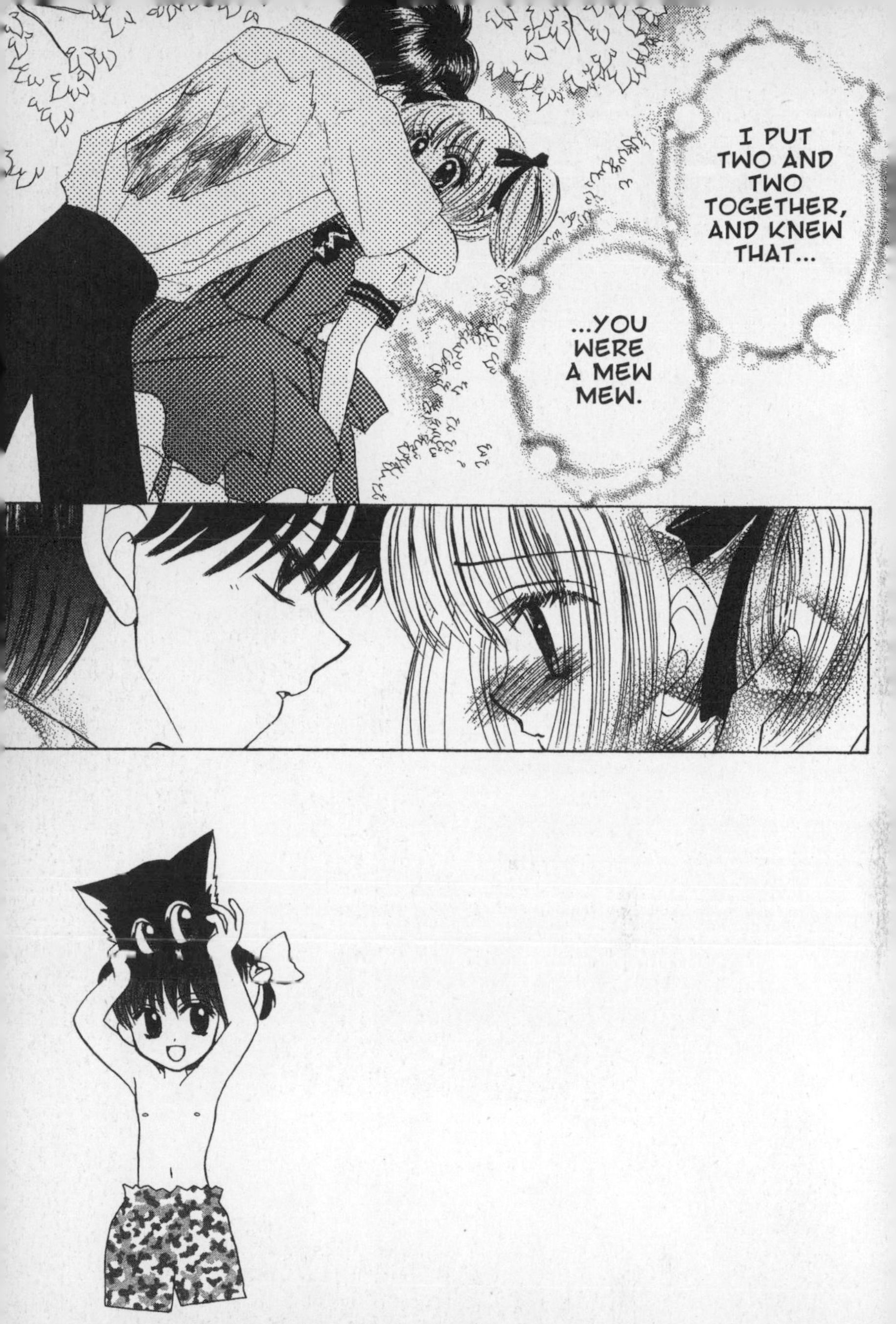
I PUT TWO AND TWO TOGETHER, AND KNEW THAT...
...YOU WERE A MEW MEW.

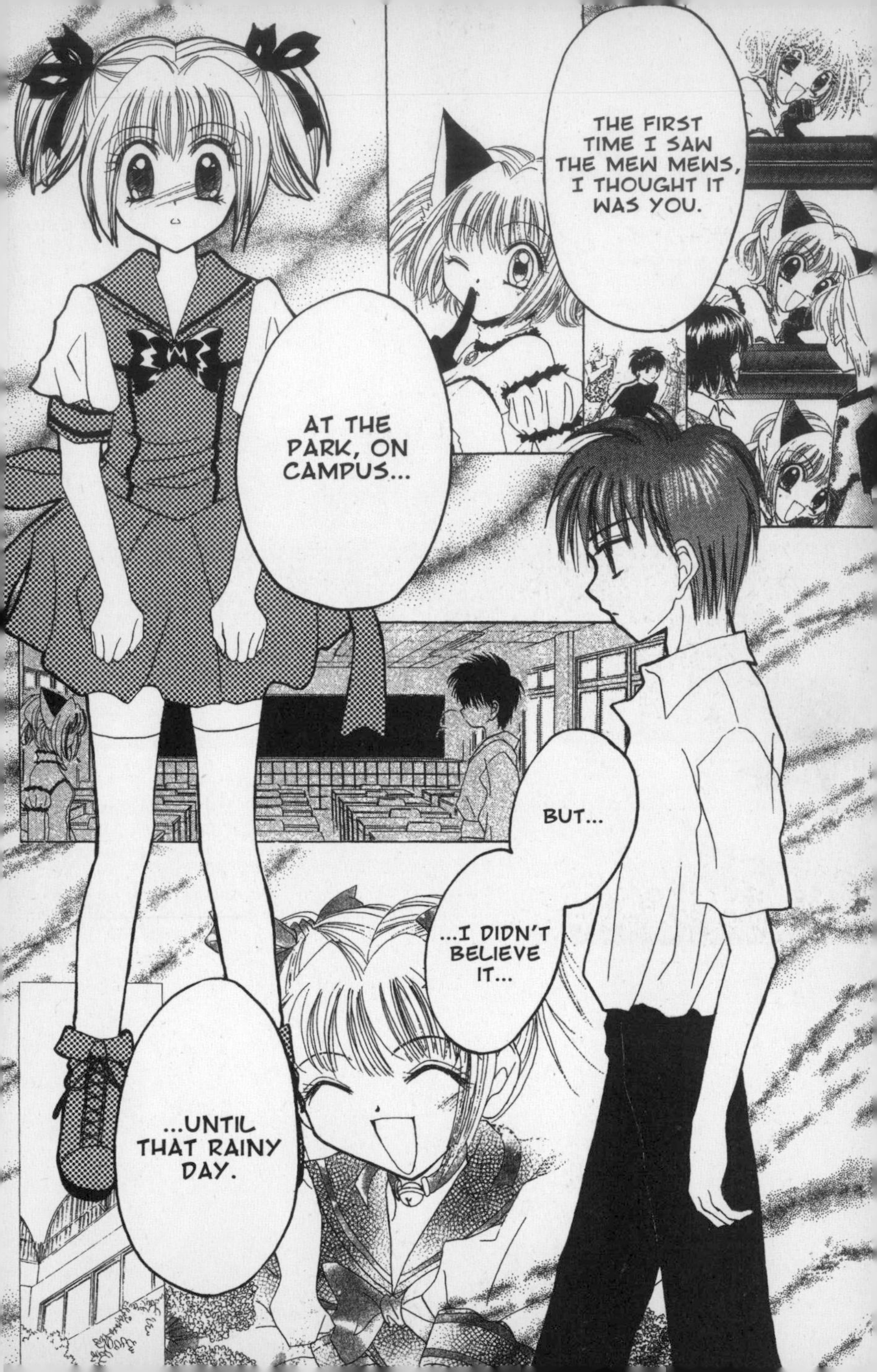
THE FIRST TIME I SAW THE MEW MEWS, I THOUGHT IT WAS YOU.
AT THE PARK, ON CAMPUS...
BUT...
...I DIDN'T BELIEVE IT...
...UNTIL THAT RAINY DAY.

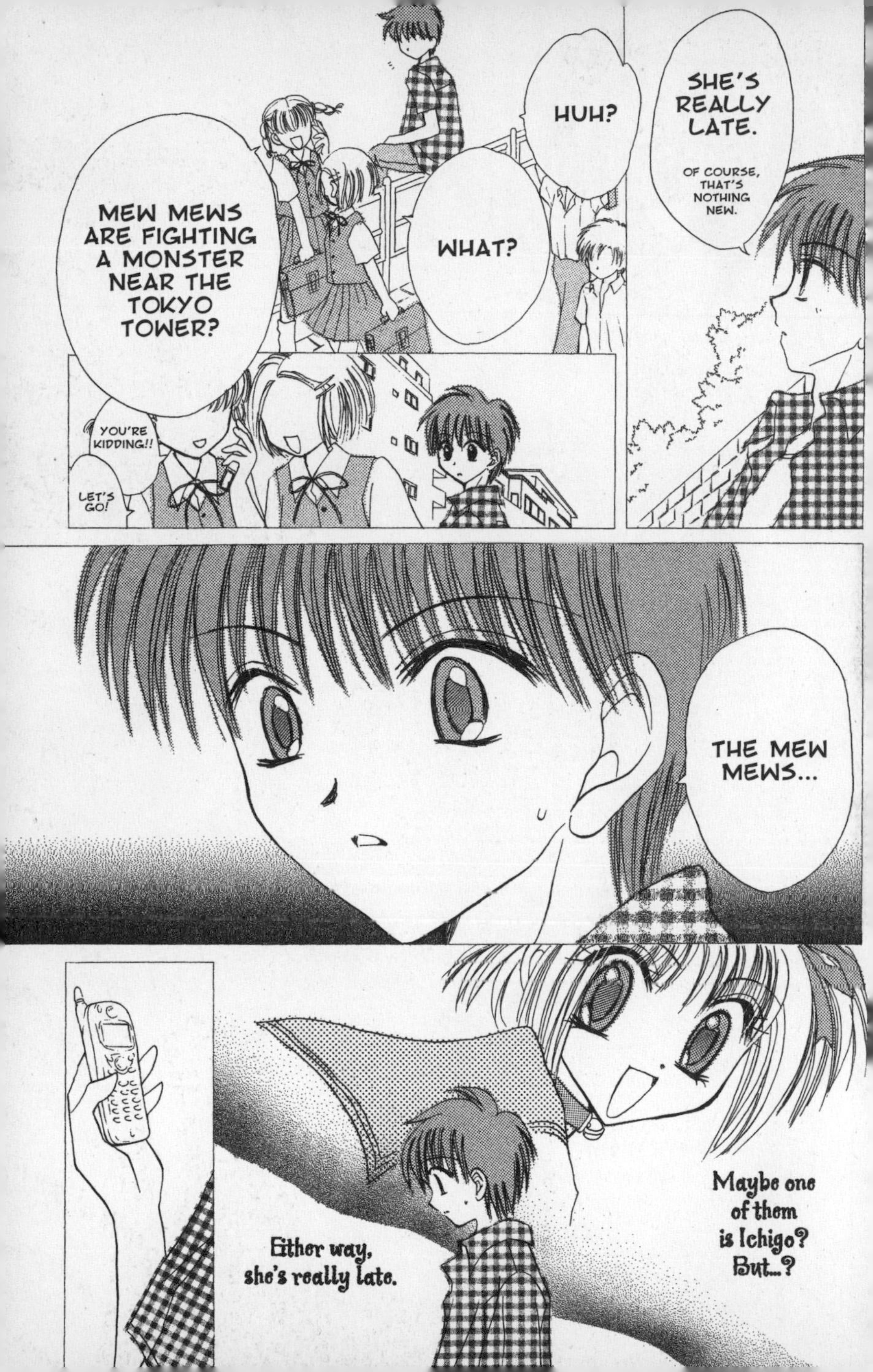
SHE'S REALLY LATE.
OF COURSE, THAT'S NOTHING NEW.
HUH?
WHAT?
MEW MEWS ARE FIGHTING A MONSTER NEAR THE TOKYO TOWER?
YOU'RE KIDDING!!
LET'S GO!
THE MEW MEWS...
Maybe one of them is Ichigo? But...?
Either way, she's really late.

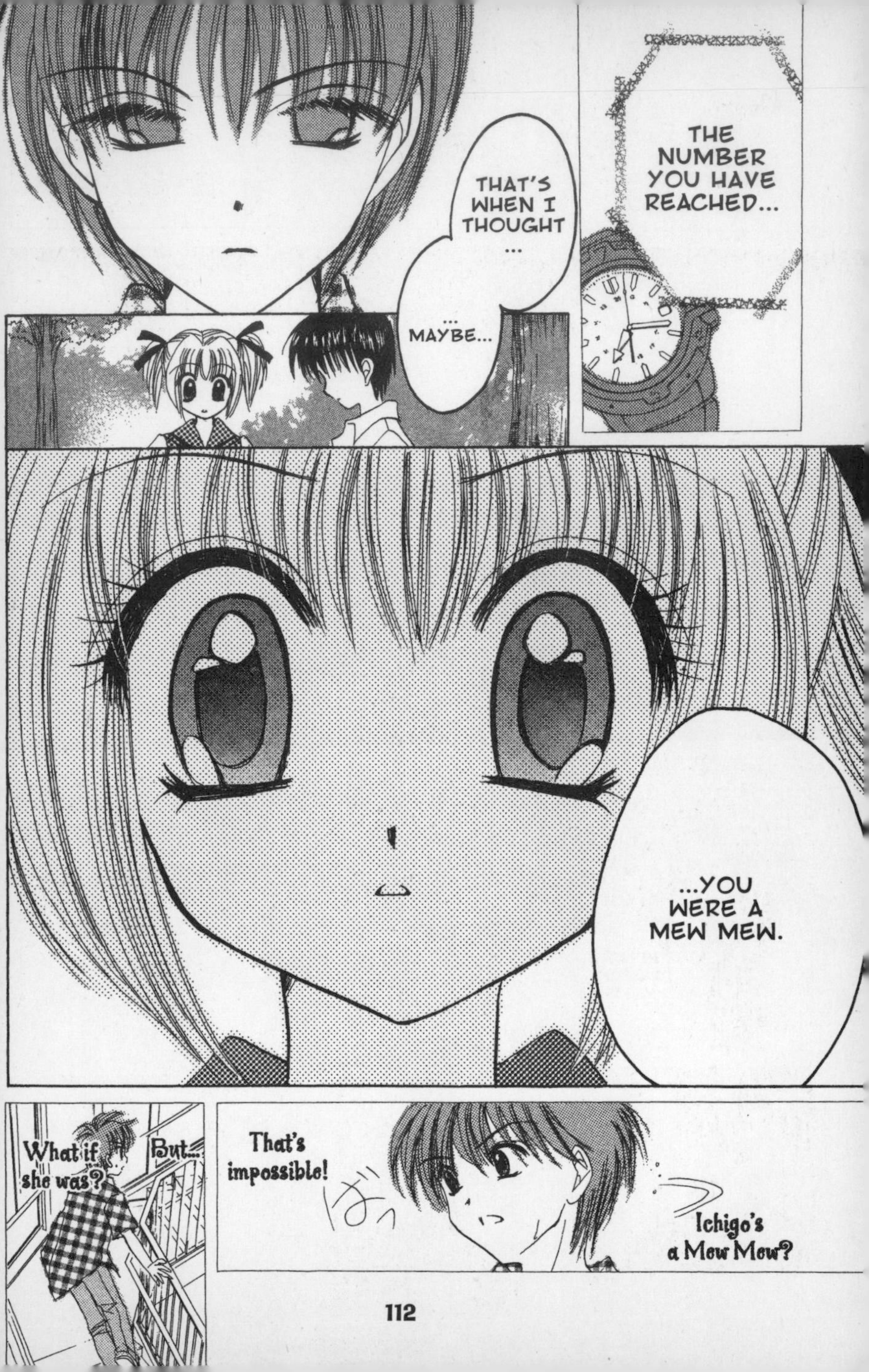
THE NUMBER YOU HAVE REACHED...
THAT'S WHEN I THOUGHT ...
... MAYBE...
...YOU WERE A MEW MEW.
Ichigo's a Mew Mew?
ばっ
That's impossible!
But...
What if she was?

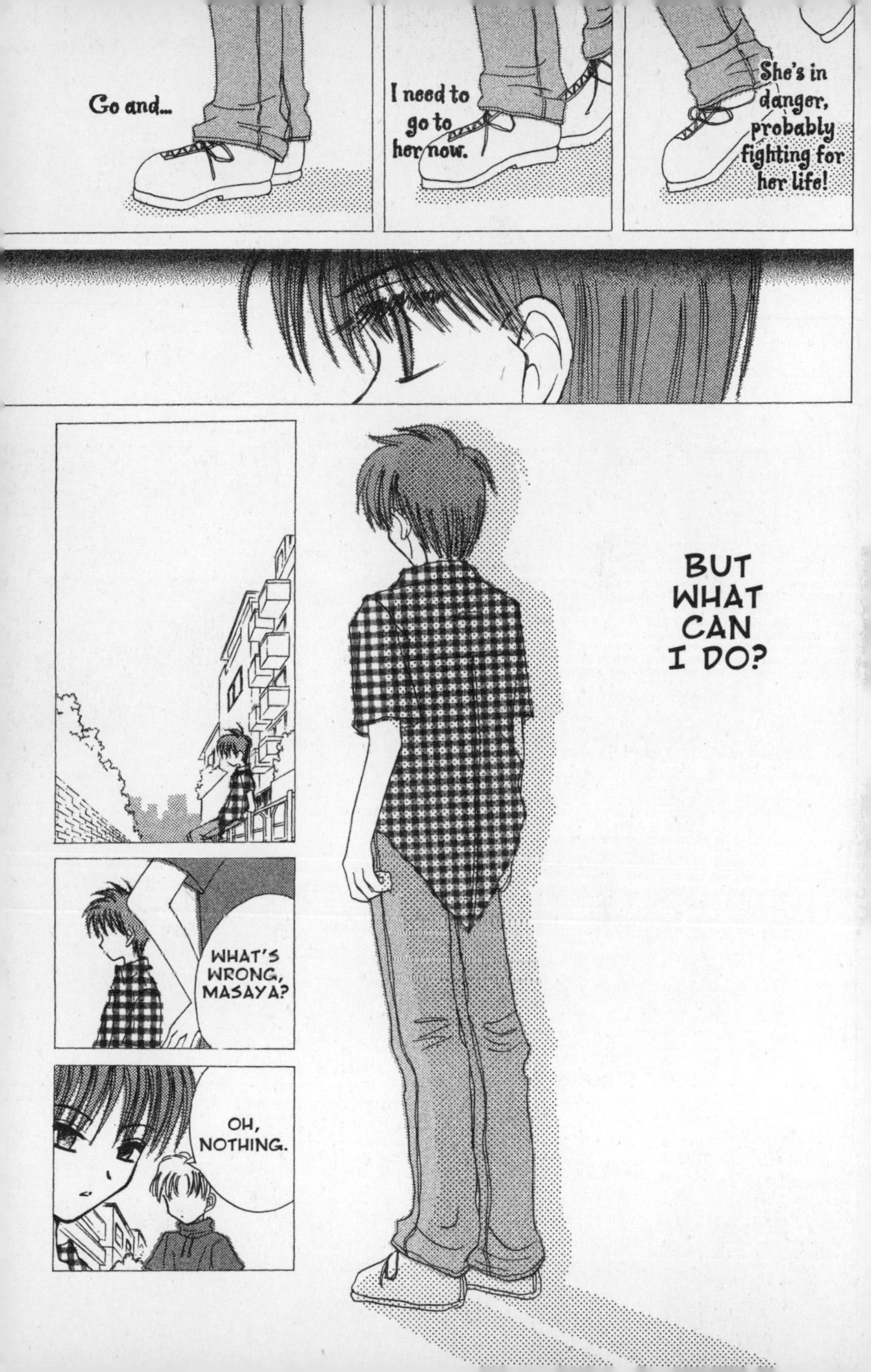
She's in danger, probably fighting for her life!
I need to go to her now.
Go and...
BUT WHAT CAN I DO?
WHAT'S WRONG, MASAYA?
OH, NOTHING.

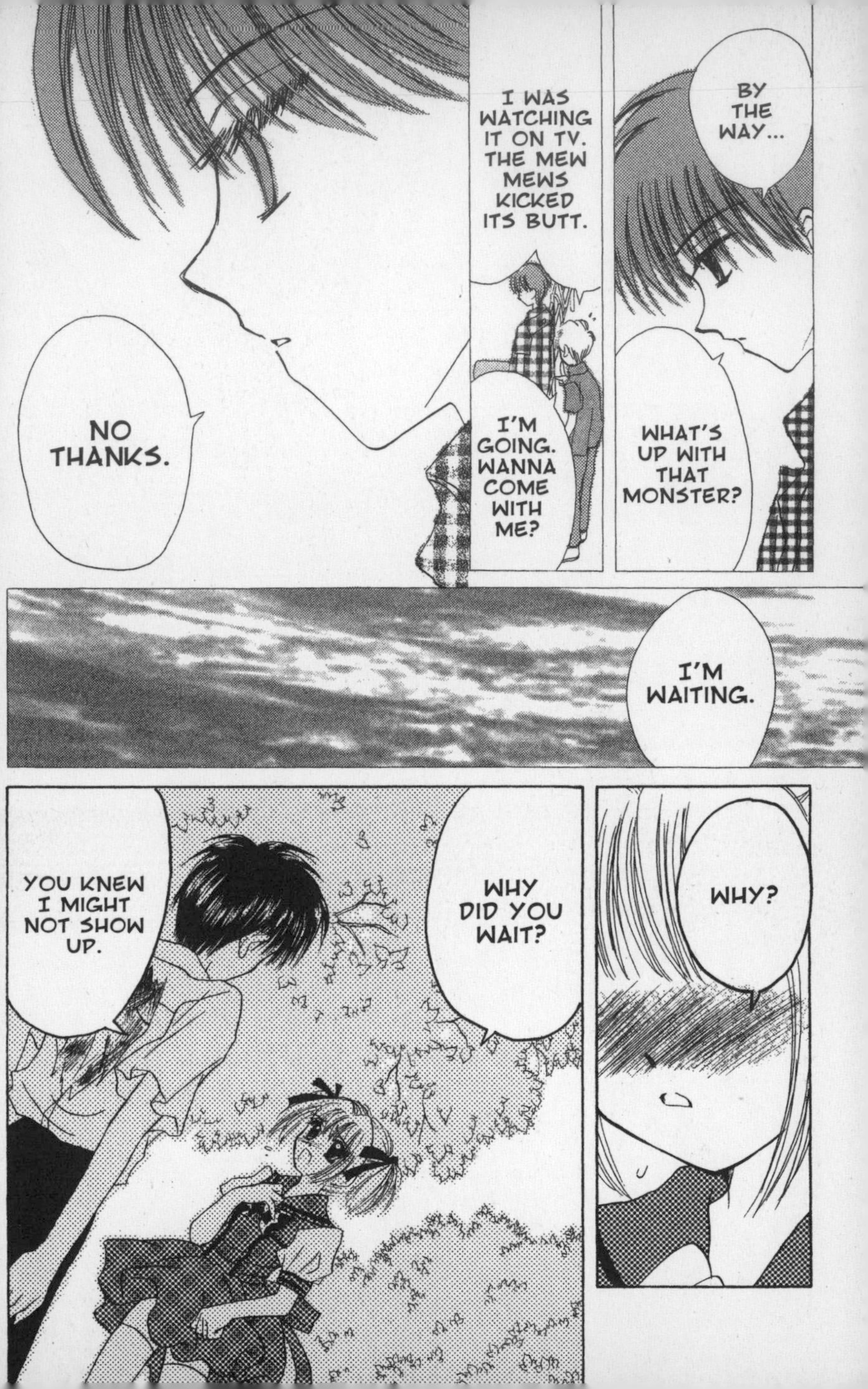
BY THE WAY...
WHAT'S UP WITH THAT MONSTER?
I WAS WATCHING IT ON TV. THE MEW MEWS KICKED ITS BUTT.
I'M GOING. WANNA COME WITH ME?
NO THANKS.
I'M WAITING.
WHY?
WHY DID YOU WAIT?
YOU KNEW I MIGHT NOT SHOW UP.

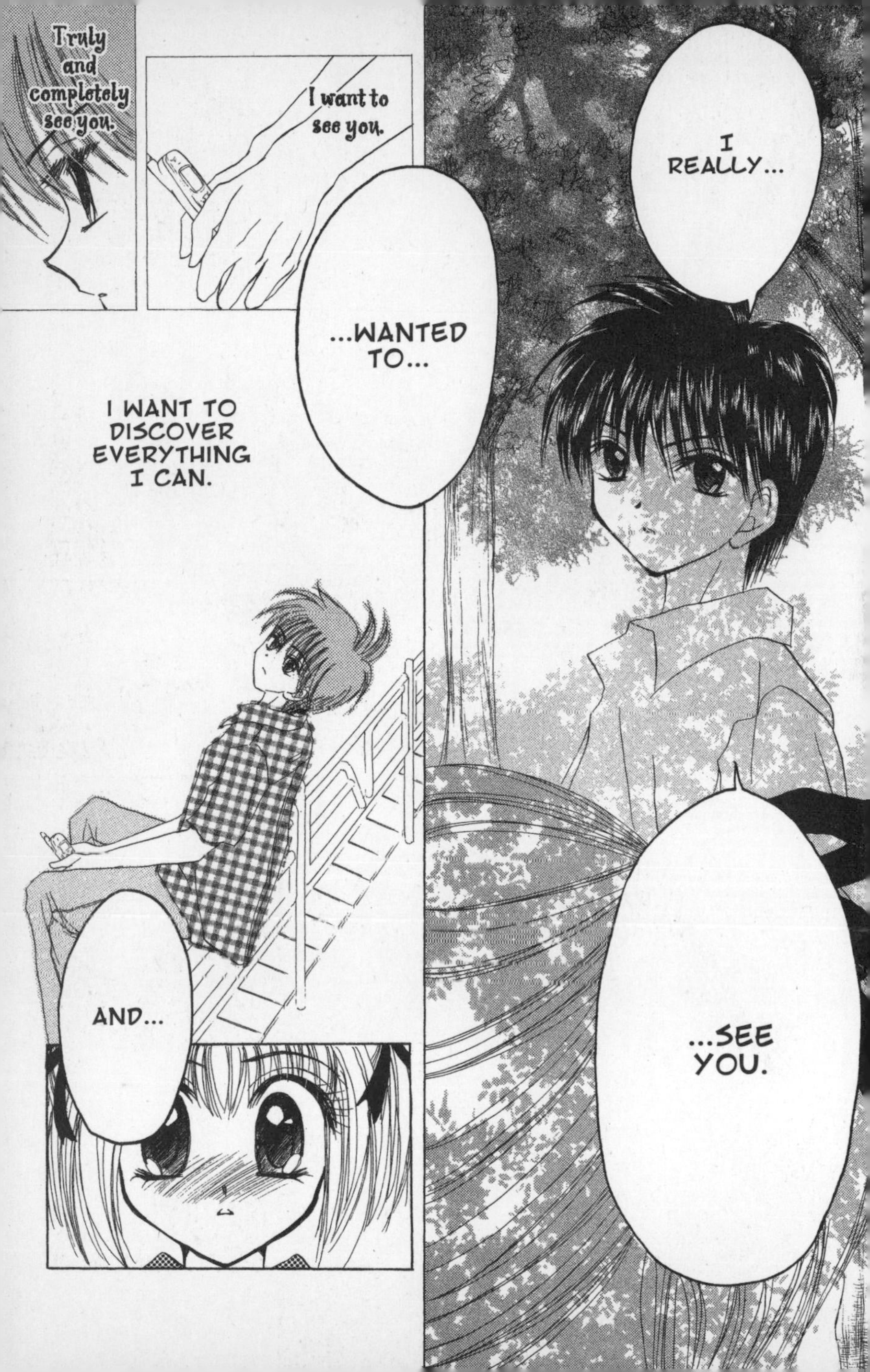
I REALLY...
...WANTED TO...
...SEE YOU.
I want to see you.
Truly and completely see you.
I WANT TO DISCOVER EVERYTHING I CAN.
AND...

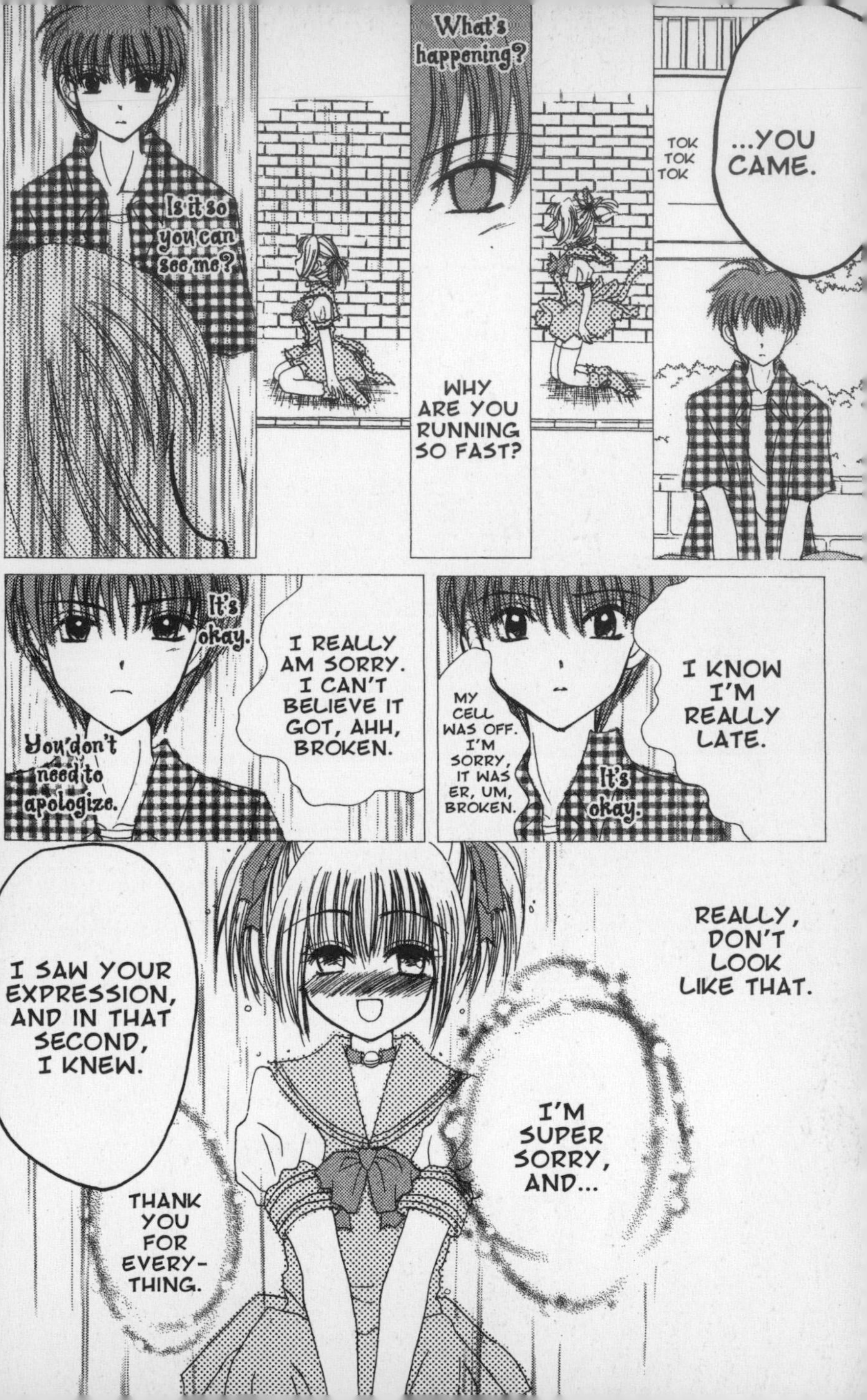

...YOU CAME.
TOK TOK TOK
What's happening?
WHY ARE YOU RUNNING SO FAST?
Is it so you can see me?
I KNOW I'M REALLY LATE.
MY CELL WAS OFF. I'M SORRY, IT WAS ER, UM, BROKEN.
It's okay.
I REALLY AM SORRY. I CAN'T BELIEVE IT GOT, AHH, BROKEN.
It's okay.
You don't need to apologize.
REALLY, DON'T LOOK LIKE THAT.
I'M SUPER SORRY, AND...
I SAW YOUR EXPRESSION, AND IN THAT SECOND, I KNEW.
THANK YOU FOR EVERYTHING.

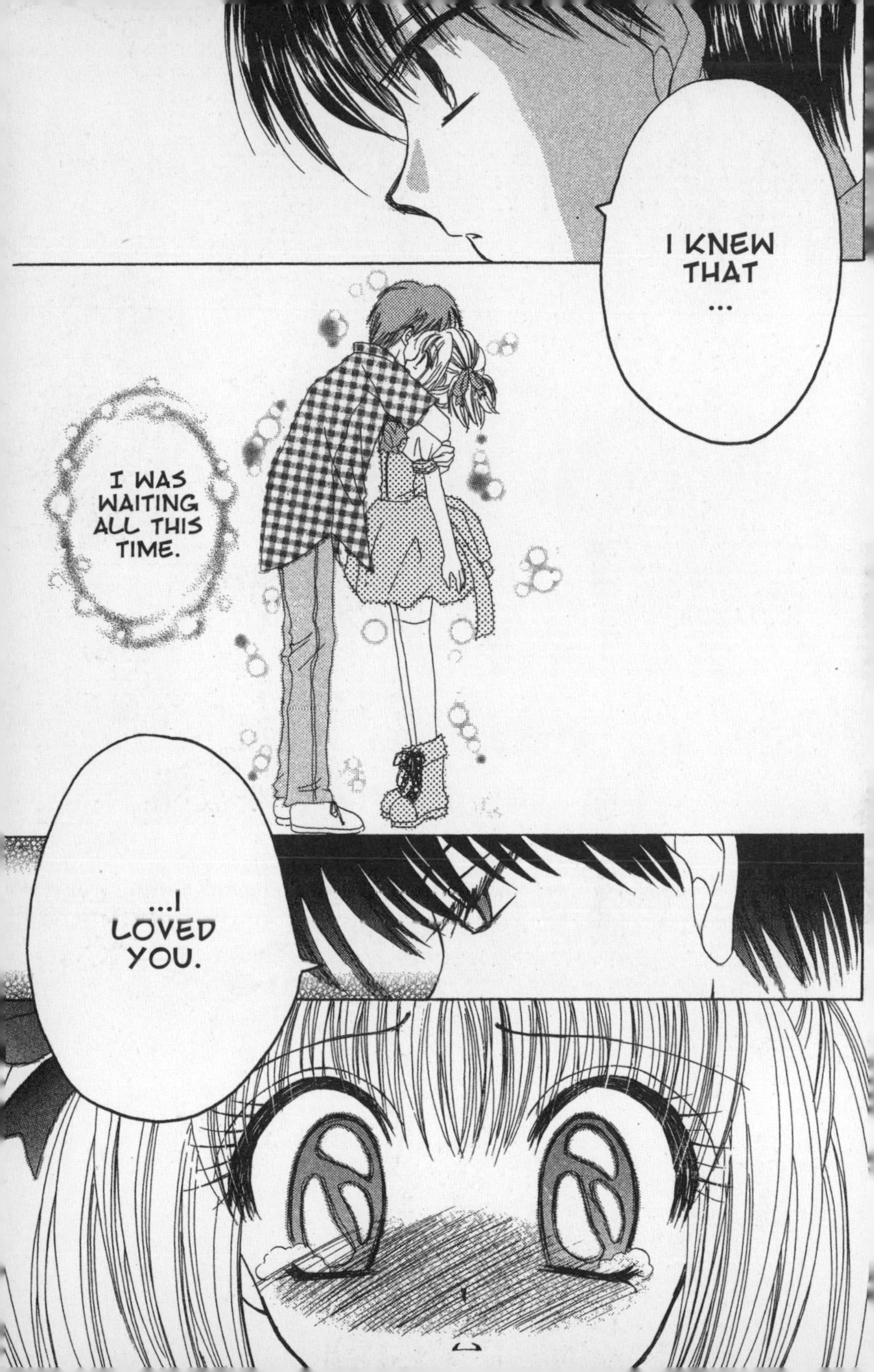
I KNEW THAT ...
I WAS WAITING ALL THIS TIME.
...I LOVED YOU.

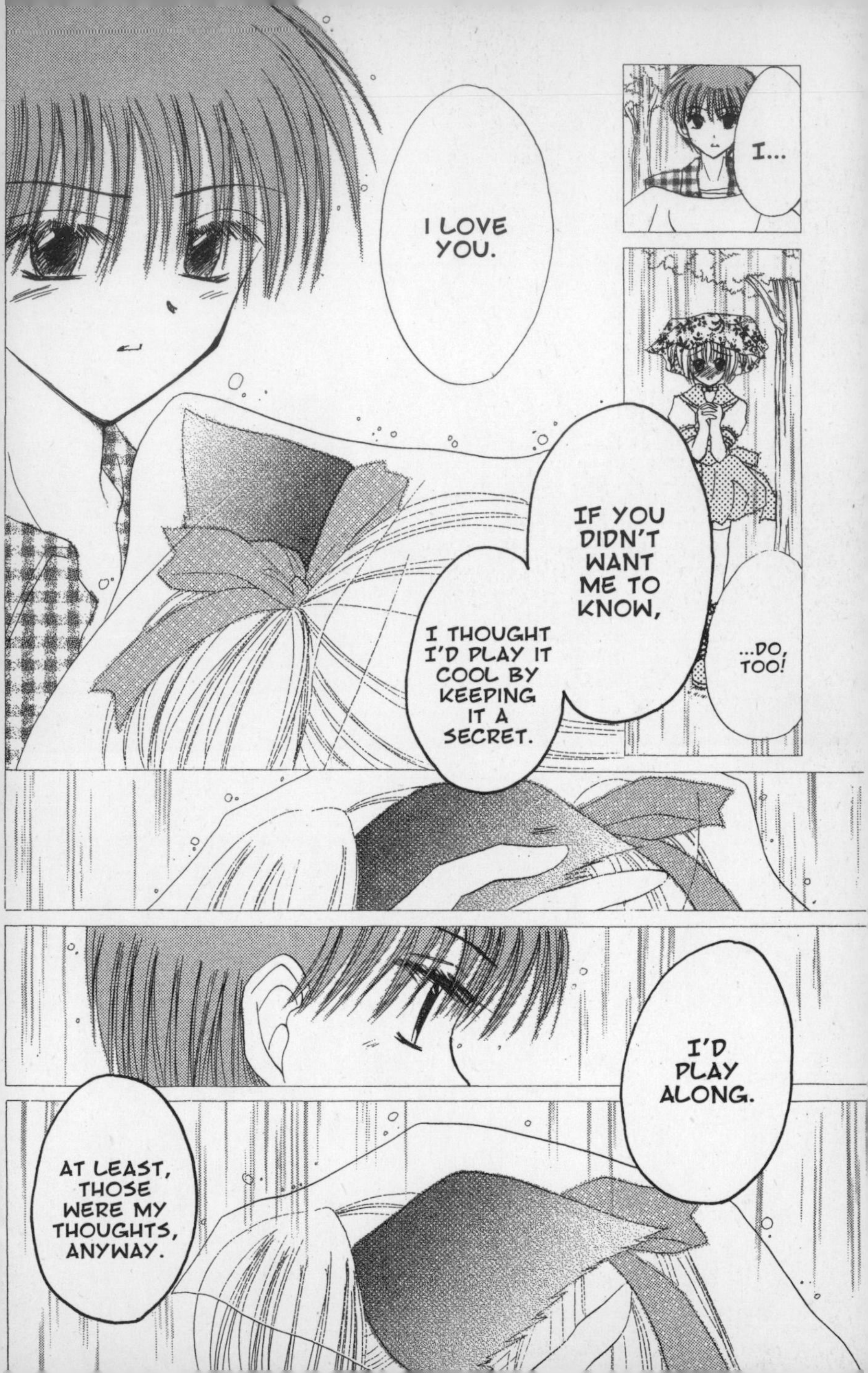
I...
...DO, TOO!
I LOVE YOU.
IF YOU DIDN'T WANT ME TO KNOW, I THOUGHT I'D PLAY IT COOL BY KEEPING IT A SECRET.
I'D PLAY ALONG.
AT LEAST, THOSE WERE MY THOUGHTS, ANYWAY.

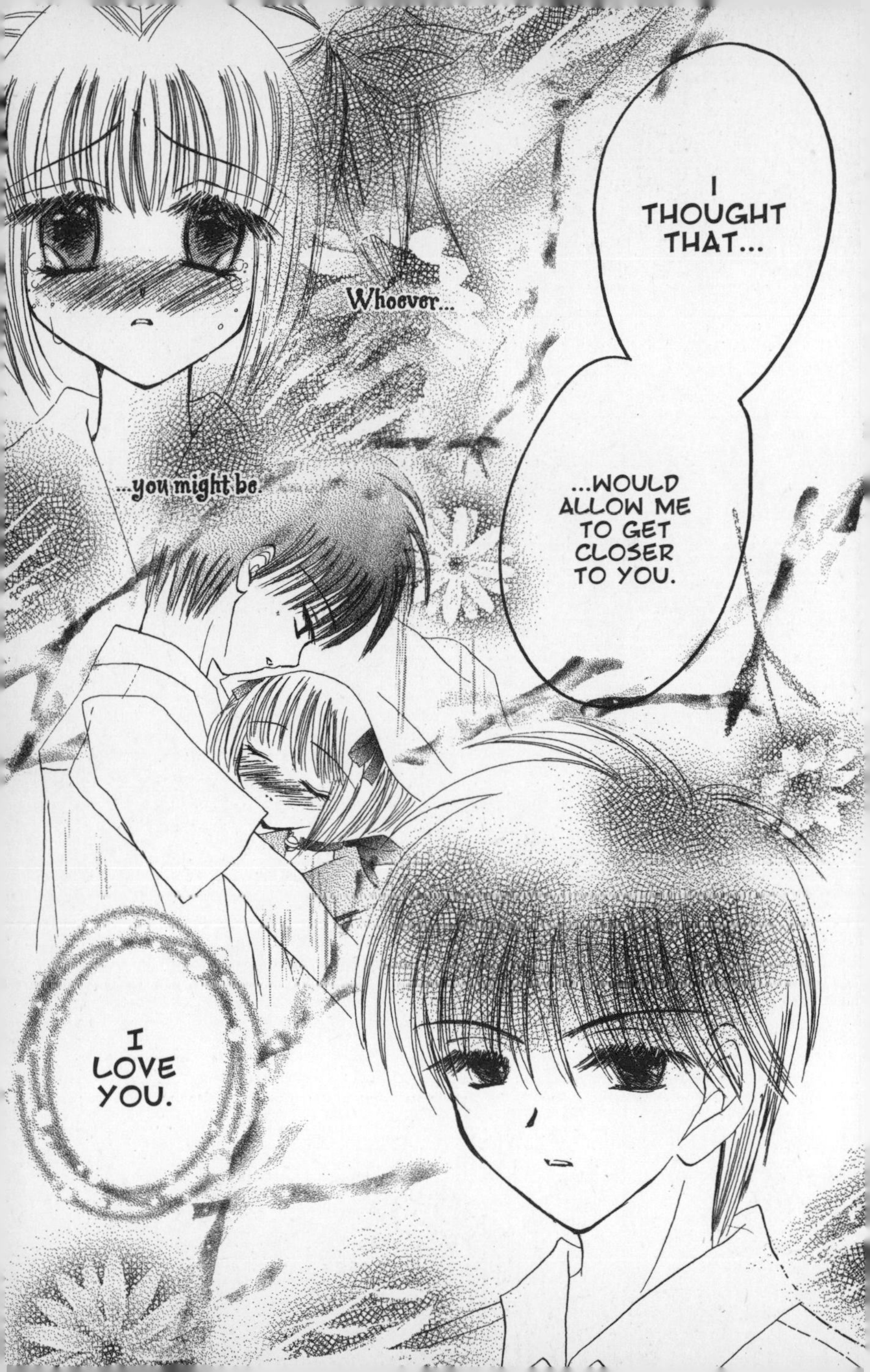
I THOUGHT THAT...
Whoever...
...WOULD ALLOW ME TO GET CLOSER TO YOU.
...you might be.
I LOVE YOU.

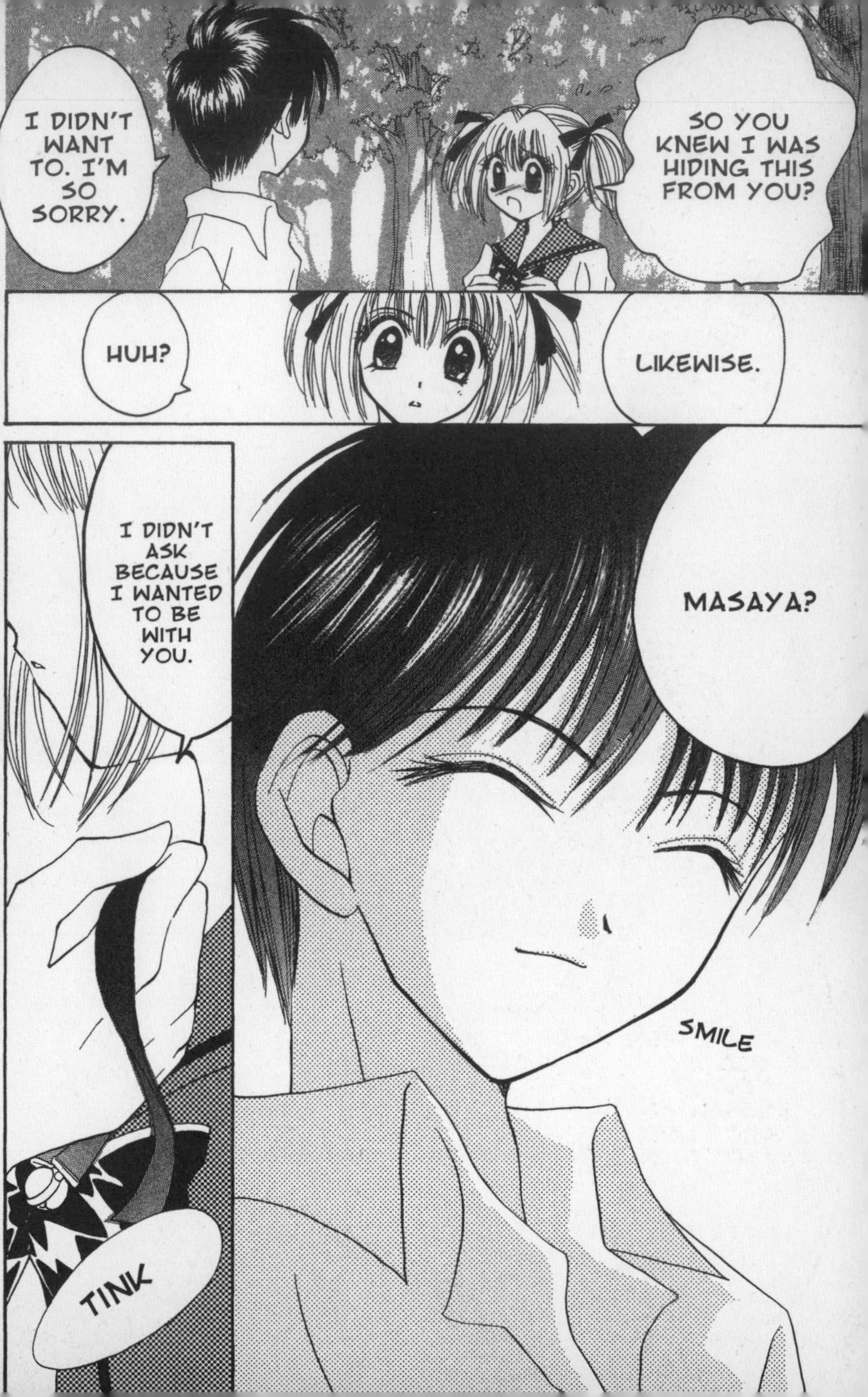
SO YOU KNEW I WAS HIDING THIS FROM YOU?
I DIDN'T WANT TO. I'M SO SORRY.
LIKEWISE.
HUH?
MASAYA?
SMILE
I DIDN'T ASK BECAUSE I WANTED TO BE WITH YOU.
TINK

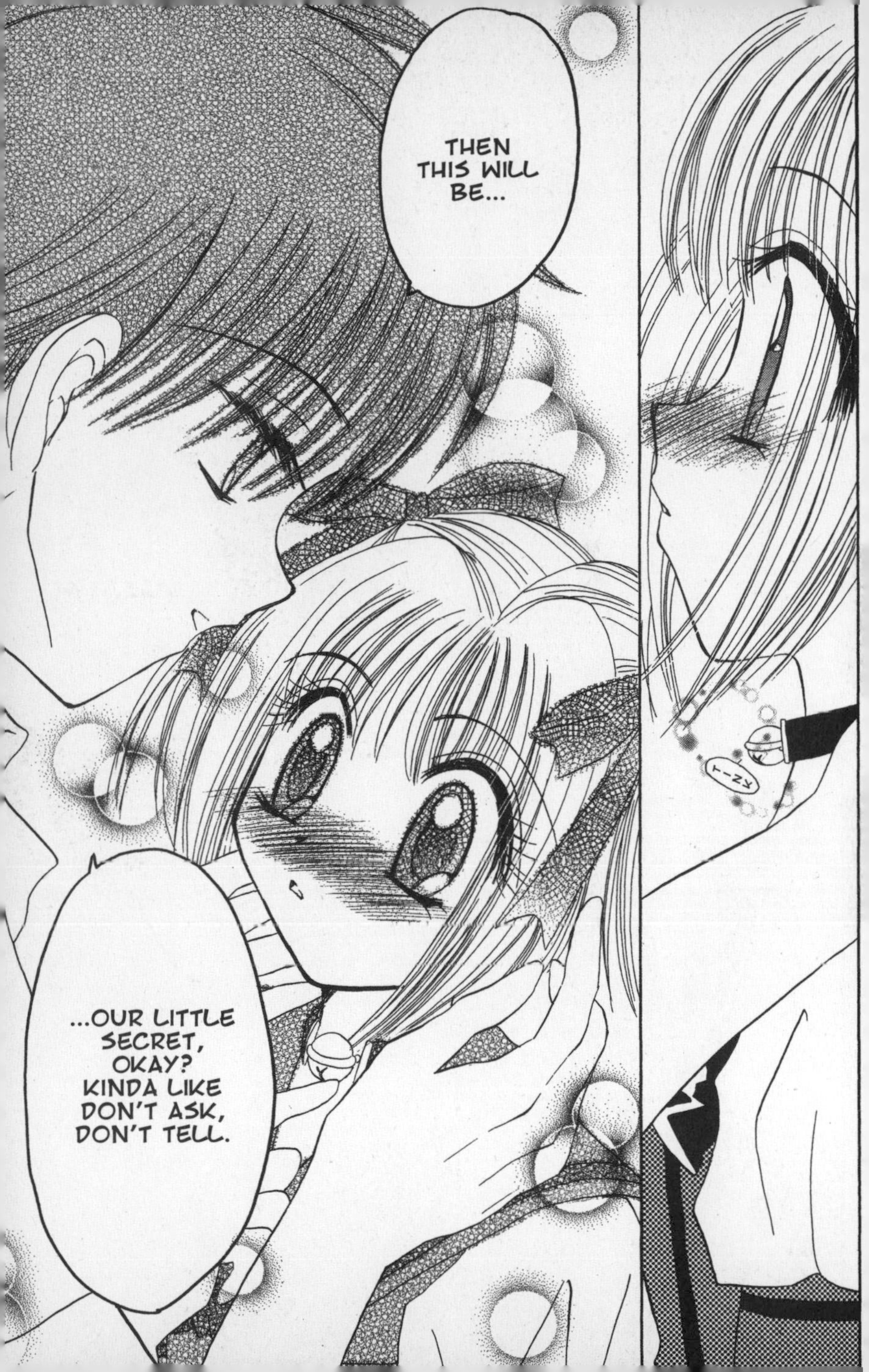
THEN THIS WILL BE...
...OUR LITTLE SECRET, OKAY? KINDA LIKE DON'T ASK, DON'T TELL.

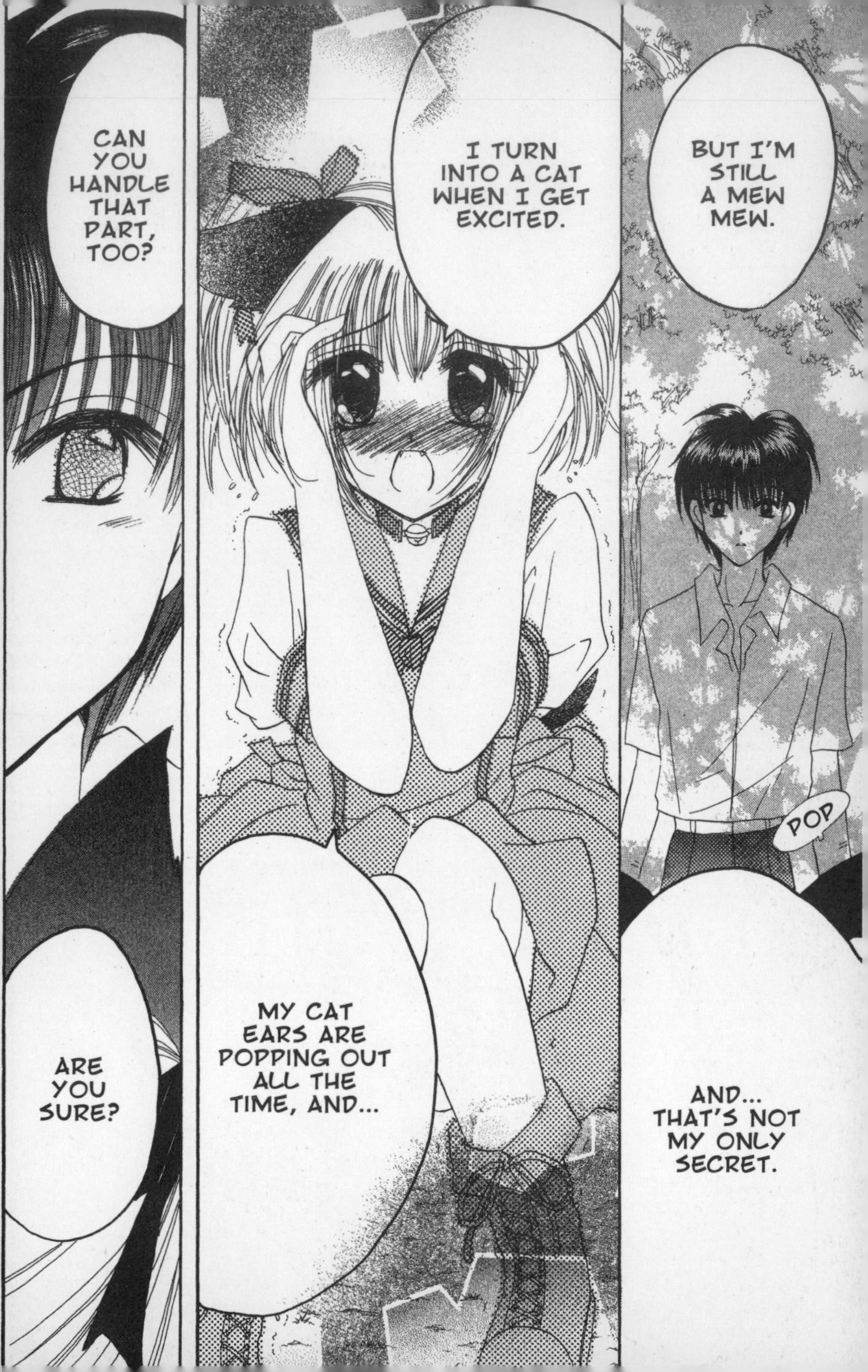
BUT I'M STILL A MEW MEW.
POP
AND... THAT'S NOT MY ONLY SECRET.
I TURN INTO A CAT WHEN I GET EXCITED.
MY CAT EARS ARE POPPING OUT ALL THE TIME, AND...
CAN YOU HANDLE THAT PART, TOO?
ARE YOU SURE?

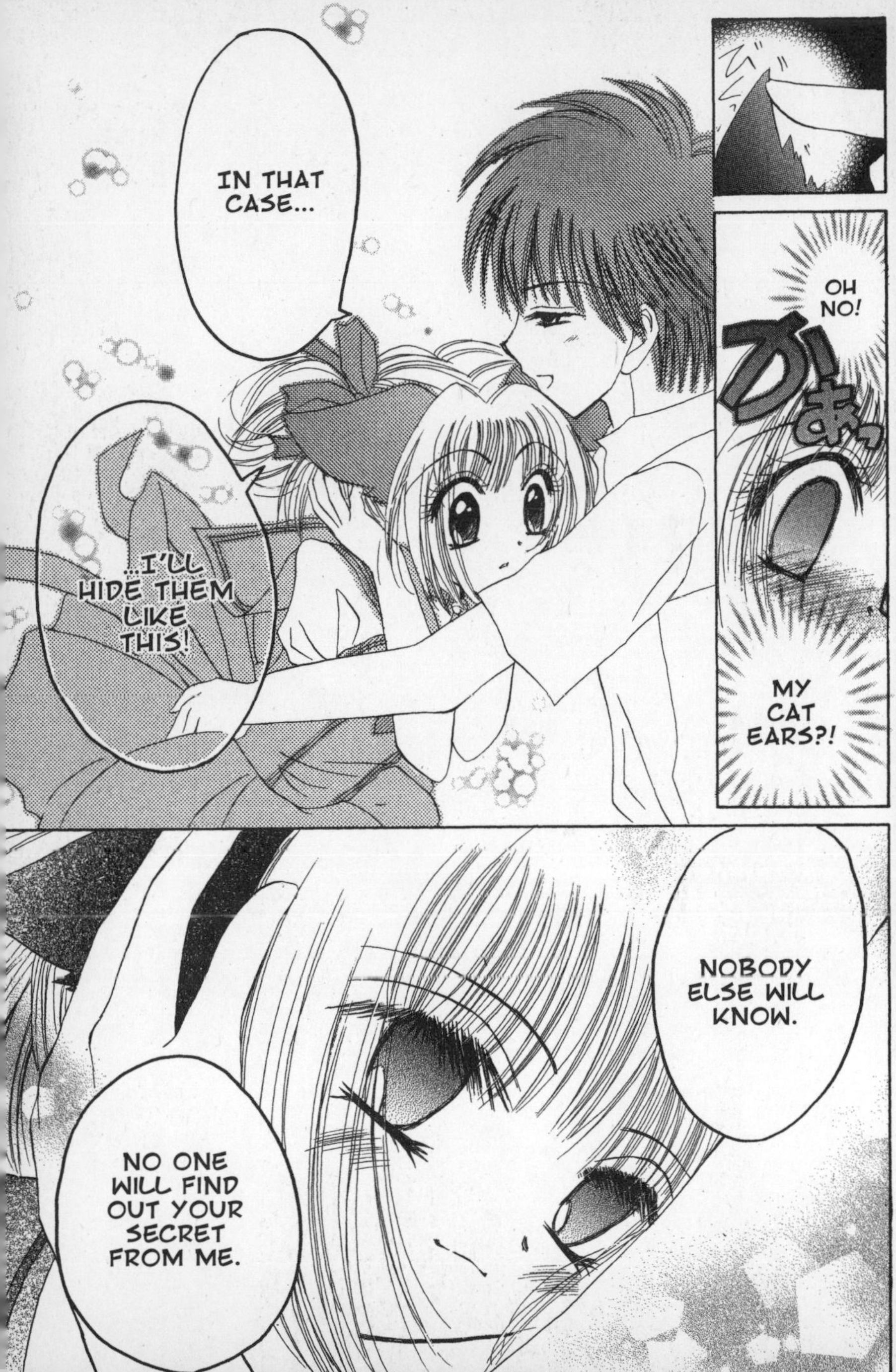
OH NO!
かぁっ
MY CAT EARS?!
IN THAT CASE...
...I'LL HIDE THEM LIKE THIS!
NOBODY ELSE WILL KNOW.
NO ONE WILL FIND OUT YOUR SECRET FROM ME.

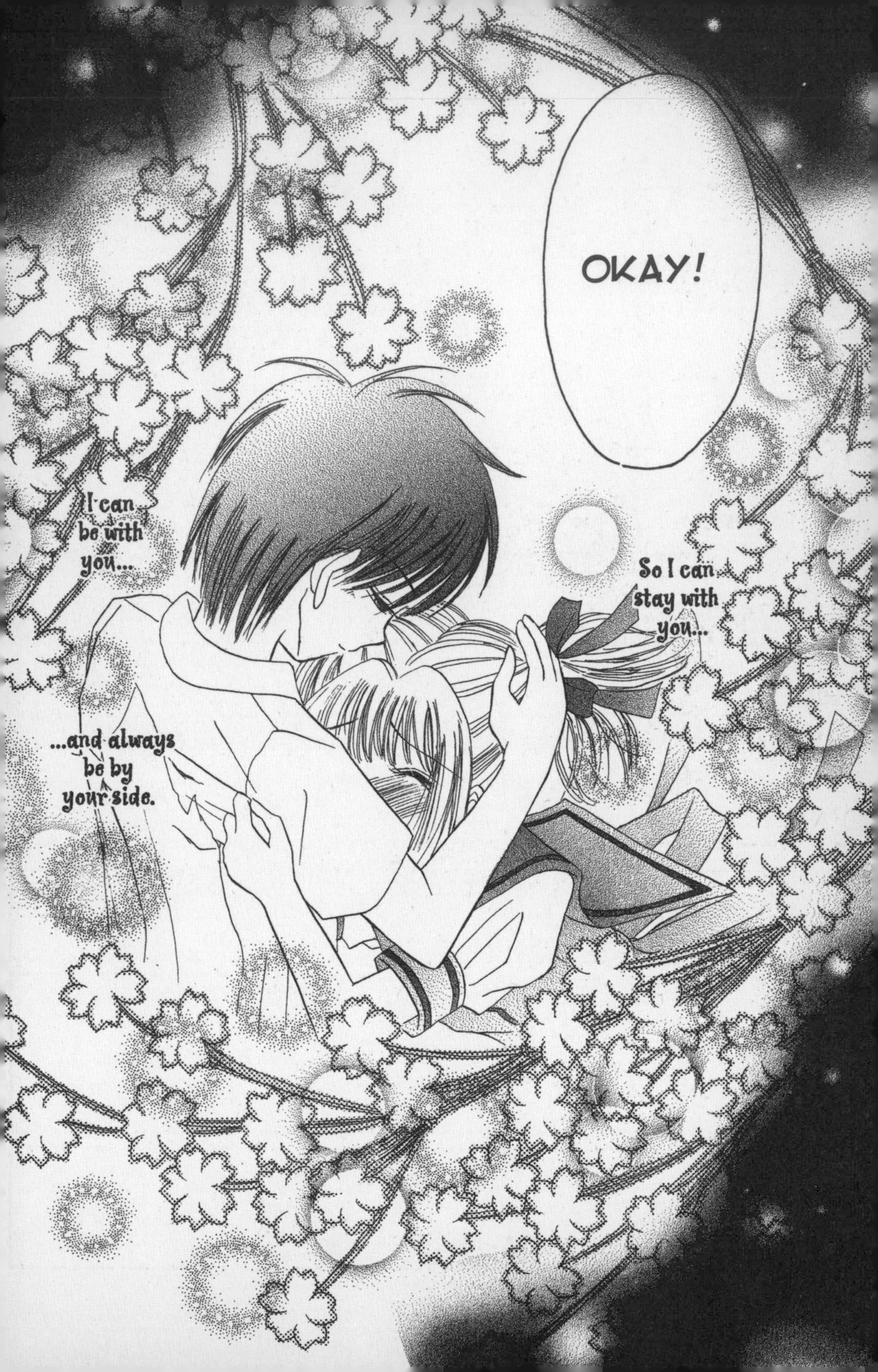
OKAY!
So I can stay with you...
I can be with you...
...and always be by your side.

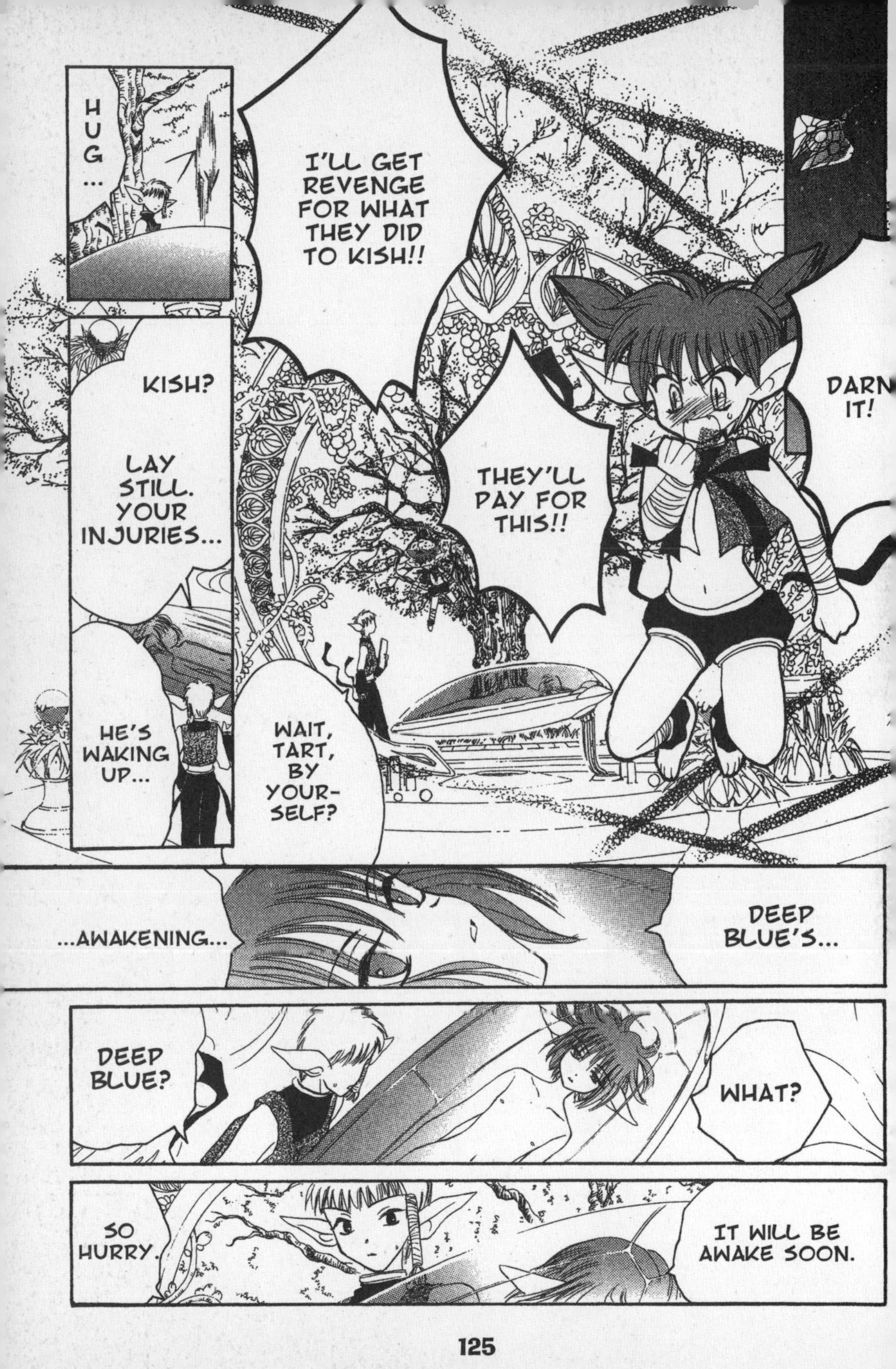
DARN IT!
I'LL GET REVENGE FOR WHAT THEY DID TO KISH!!
THEY'LL PAY FOR THIS!!
WAIT, TART, BY YOURSELF?
HUG...
KISH?
LAY STILL. YOUR INJURIES...
HE'S WAKING UP...
DEEP BLUE'S...
...AWAKENING...
WHAT?
DEEP BLUE?
IT WILL BE AWAKE SOON.
SO HURRY.

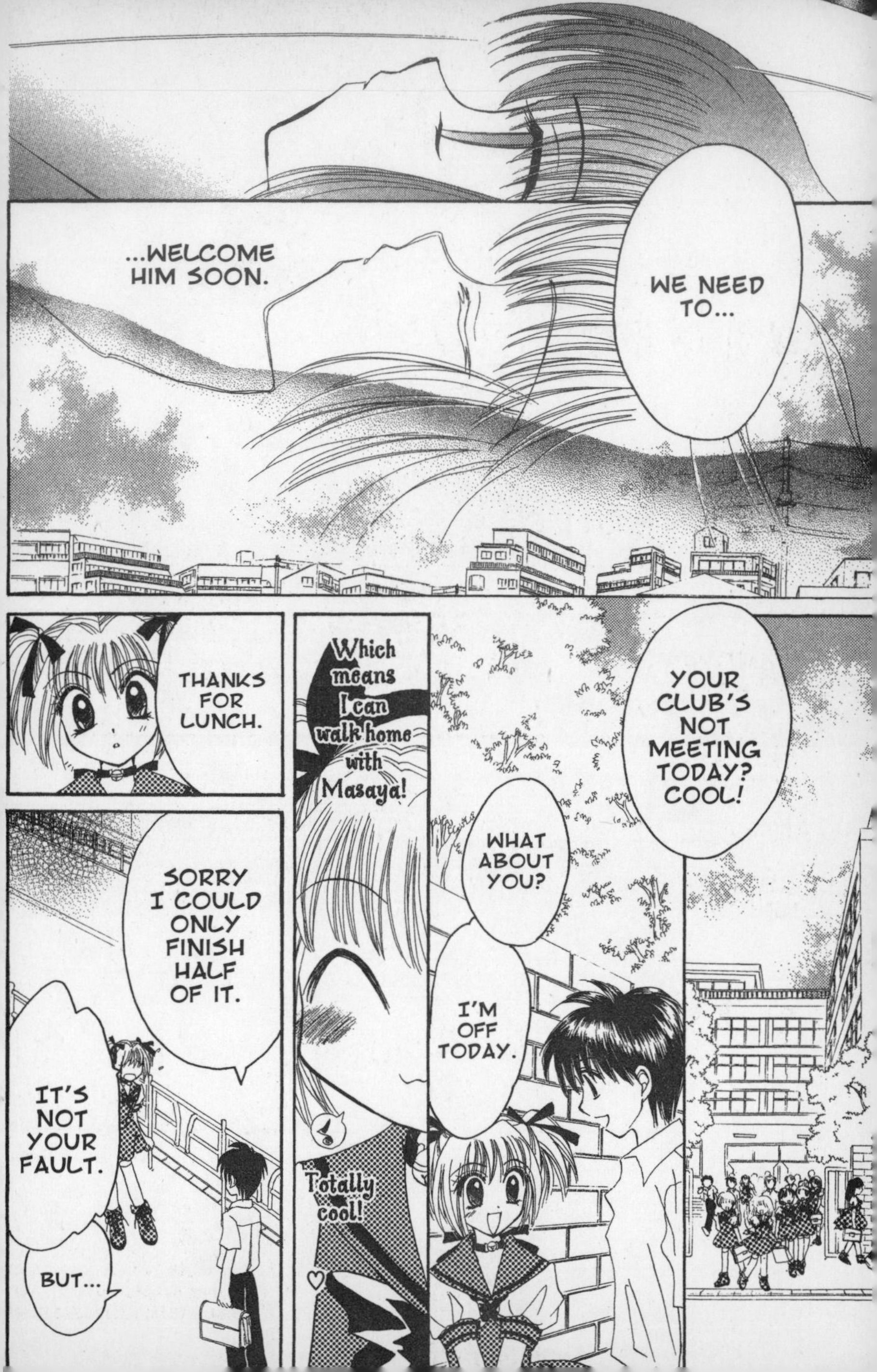
WE NEED TO...
...WELCOME HIM SOON.
YOUR CLUB'S NOT MEETING TODAY? COOL!
WHAT ABOUT YOU?
I'M OFF TODAY.
Which means I can walk home with Masaya!
Totally cool!
THANKS FOR LUNCH.
SORRY I COULD ONLY FINISH HALF OF IT.
IT'S NOT YOUR FAULT.
BUT...

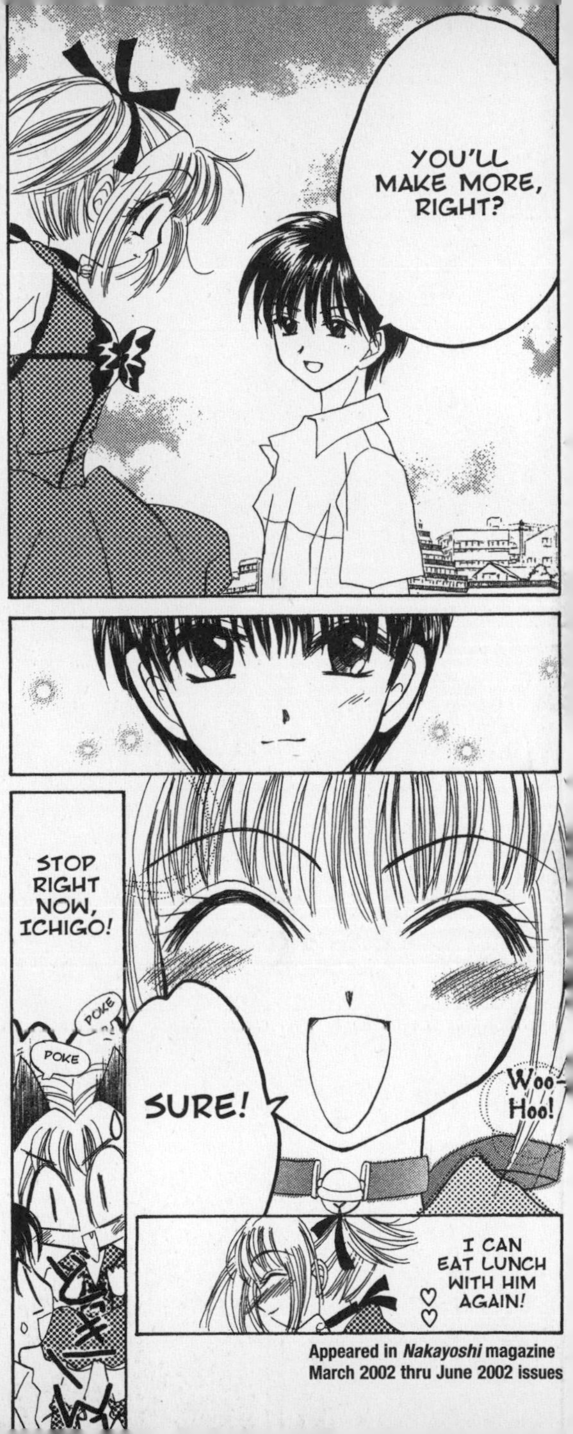
YOU'LL MAKE MORE, RIGHT?
SURE!
Woo-Hoo!
STOP RIGHT NOW, ICHIGO!
POKE
POKE
I CAN EAT LUNCH WITH HIM AGAIN!

Appeared in *Nakayoshi* magazine March 2002 thru June 2002 issues

SPECIAL THANKS!!

R.YOSHIDA

H.MATSUMOTO
M.OMORI

S.NAOHARA
A.SUZUKI
K.HONDA

H.OIKAWA

M.SEKIYA
S.SUDA

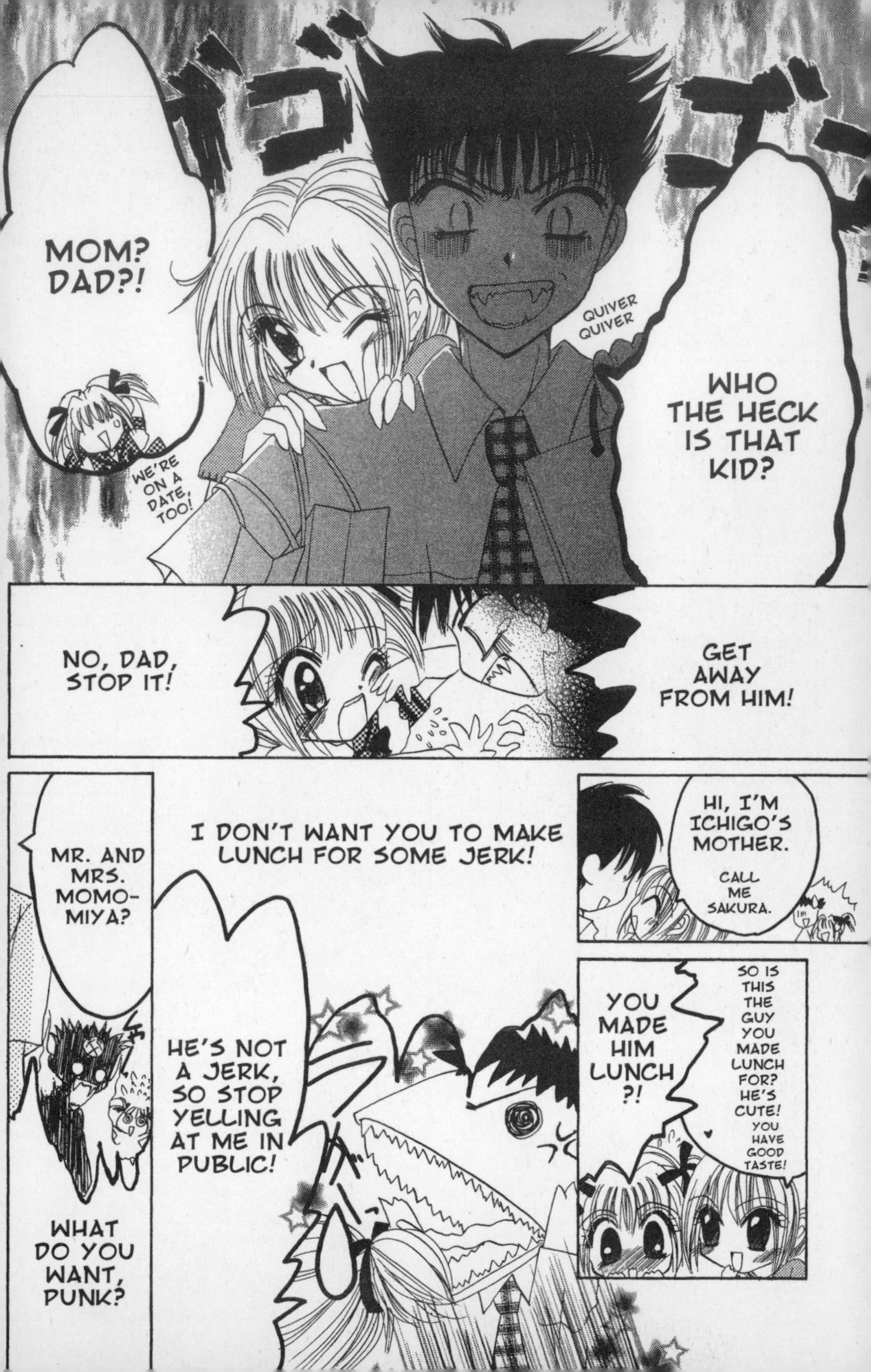
WHO THE HECK IS THAT KID?
QUIVER QUIVER
MOM? DAD?!
WE'RE ON A DATE, TOO!
GET AWAY FROM HIM!
NO, DAD, STOP IT!
HI, I'M ICHIGO'S MOTHER.
CALL ME SAKURA.
SO IS THIS THE GUY YOU MADE LUNCH FOR? HE'S CUTE!
YOU HAVE GOOD TASTE!
YOU MADE HIM LUNCH?!
I DON'T WANT YOU TO MAKE LUNCH FOR SOME JERK!
HE'S NOT A JERK, SO STOP YELLING AT ME IN PUBLIC!
MR. AND MRS. MOMOMIYA?
WHAT DO YOU WANT, PUNK?

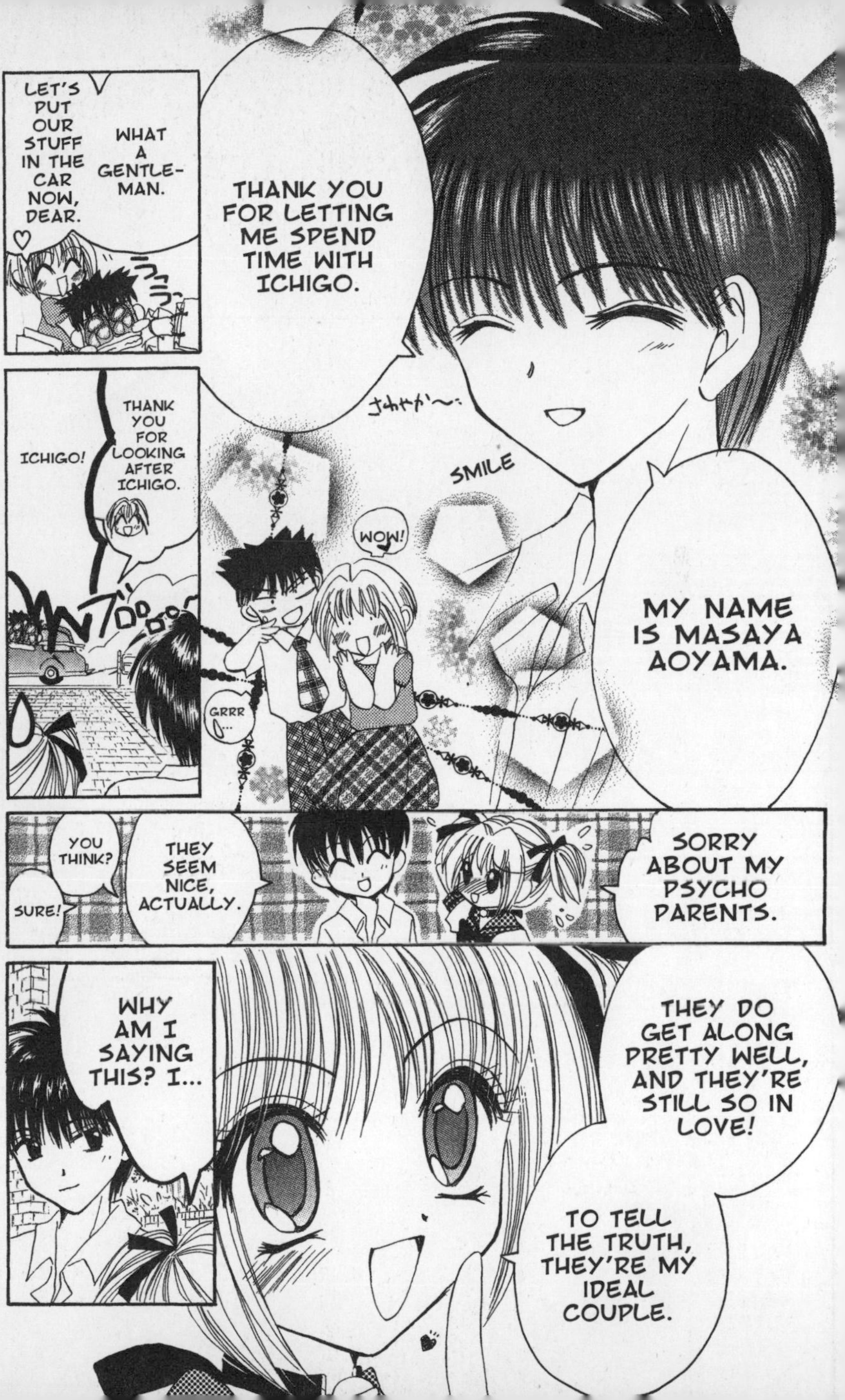
THANK YOU FOR LETTING ME SPEND TIME WITH ICHIGO.
SMILE
MY NAME IS MASAYA AOYAMA.
WOW!
GRRR...
WHAT A GENTLEMAN.
LET'S PUT OUR STUFF IN THE CAR NOW, DEAR.
THANK YOU FOR LOOKING AFTER ICHIGO.
ICHIGO!
SORRY ABOUT MY PSYCHO PARENTS.
THEY SEEM NICE, ACTUALLY.
YOU THINK?
SURE!
THEY DO GET ALONG PRETTY WELL, AND THEY'RE STILL SO IN LOVE!
TO TELL THE TRUTH, THEY'RE MY IDEAL COUPLE.
WHY AM I SAYING THIS? I...

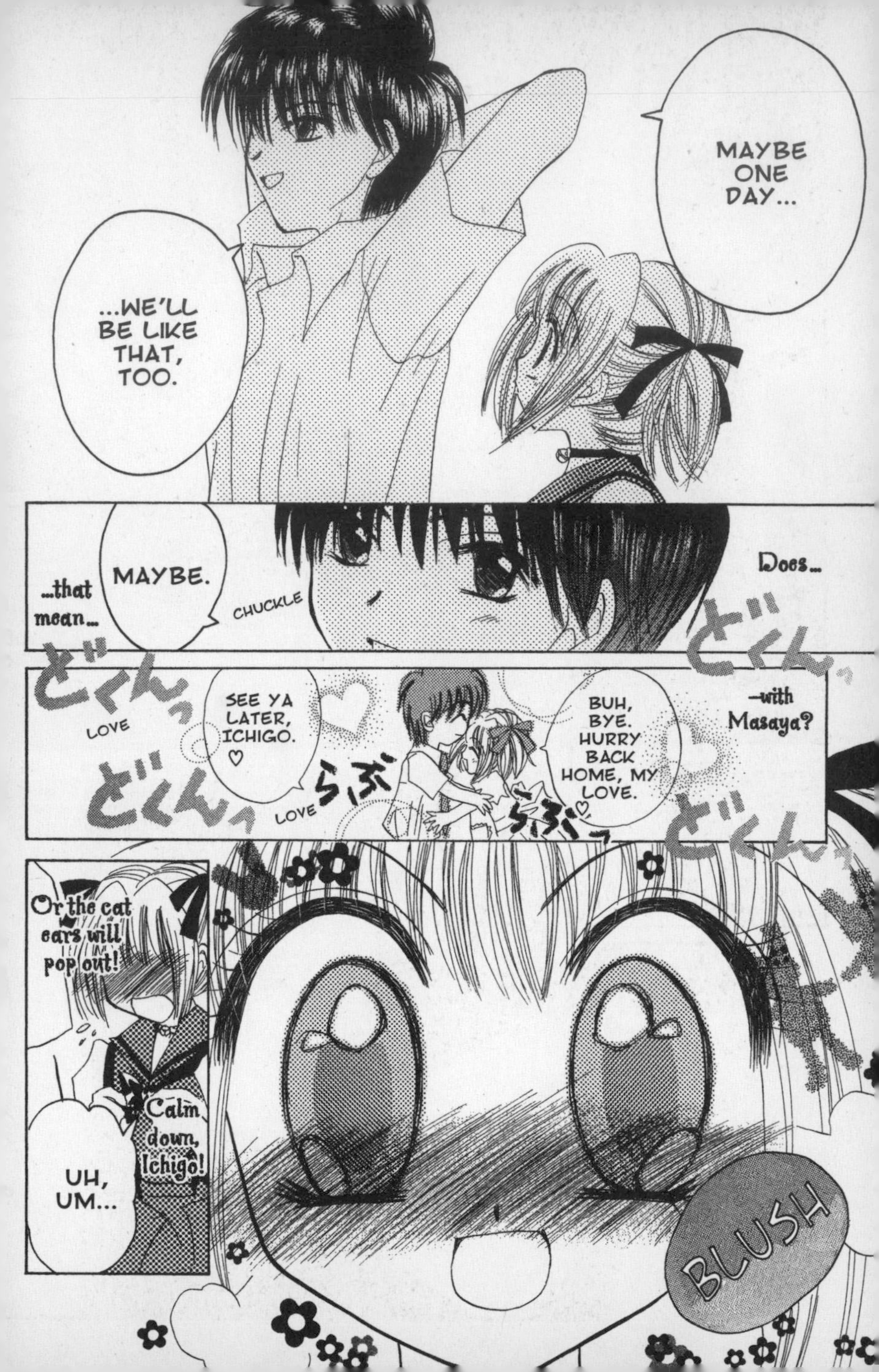
MAYBE ONE DAY...
...WE'LL BE LIKE THAT, TOO.
Does...
どくん
CHUCKLE
MAYBE.
...that mean...
どくん
—with Masaya?
どくん
BUH, BYE. HURRY BACK HOME, MY LOVE.
らぶ
らぶ
LOVE
SEE YA LATER, ICHIGO. ♡
LOVE
どくん
BLUSH
Or the cat ears will pop out!
Calm down, Ichigo!
UH, UM...

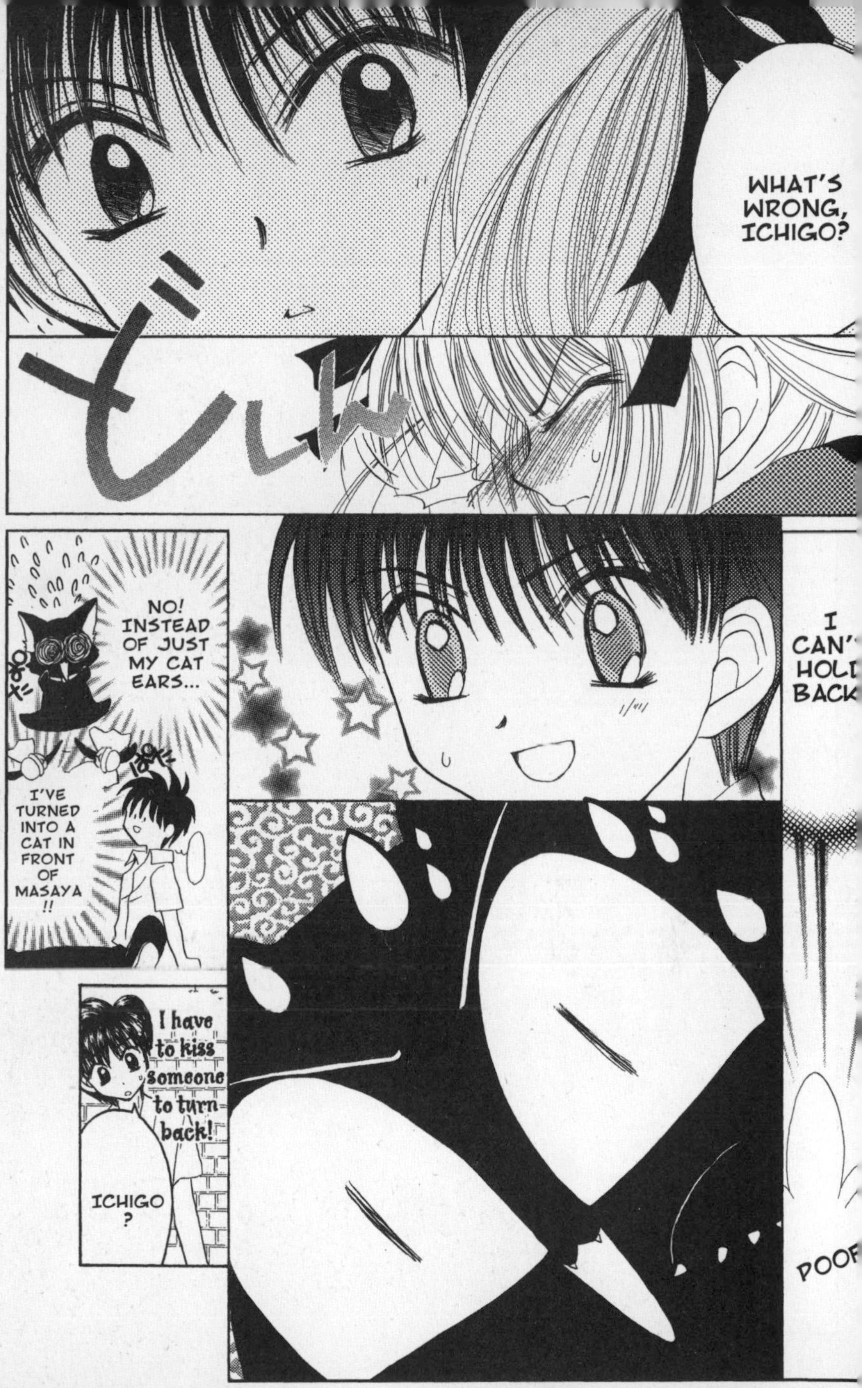
WHAT'S WRONG, ICHIGO?
I CAN' HOLD BACK
POOF
NO! INSTEAD OF JUST MY CAT EARS...
I'VE TURNED INTO A CAT IN FRONT OF MASAYA !!
I have to kiss someone to turn back!
ICHIGO ?

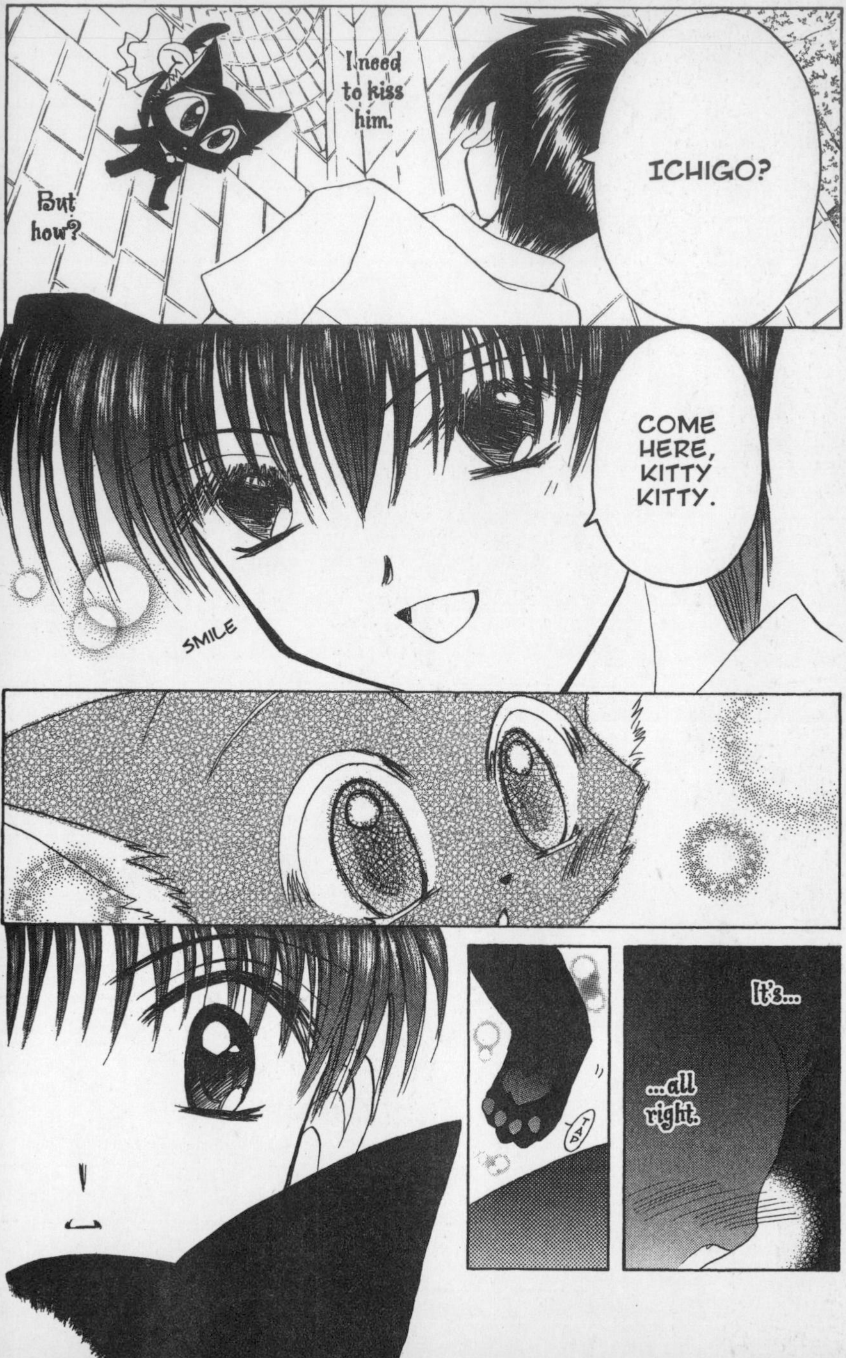
ICHIGO?
I need to kiss him.
But how?
COME HERE, KITTY KITTY.
SMILE
It's...
...all right.
TAP

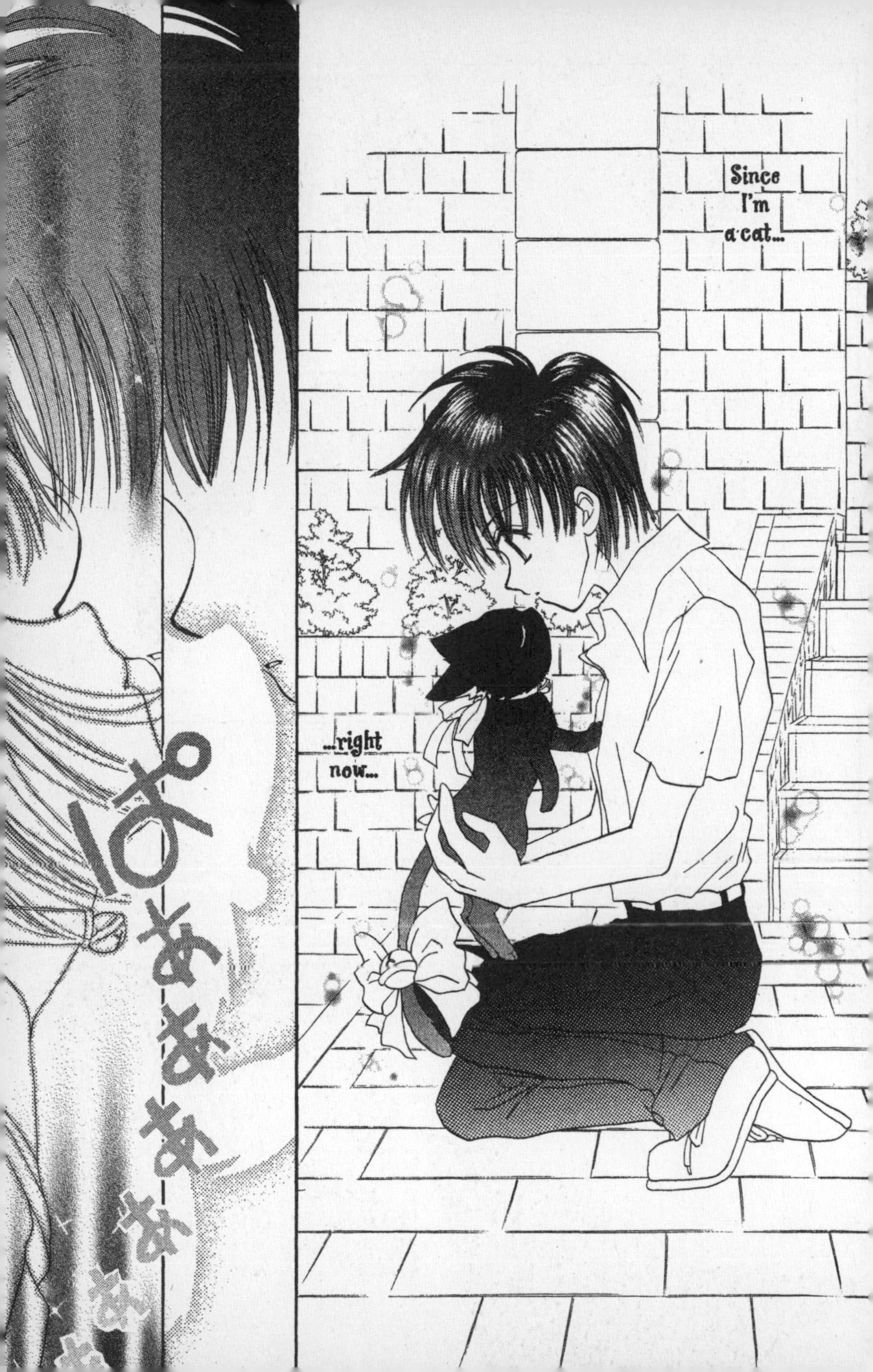
Since I'm a cat...
...right now...

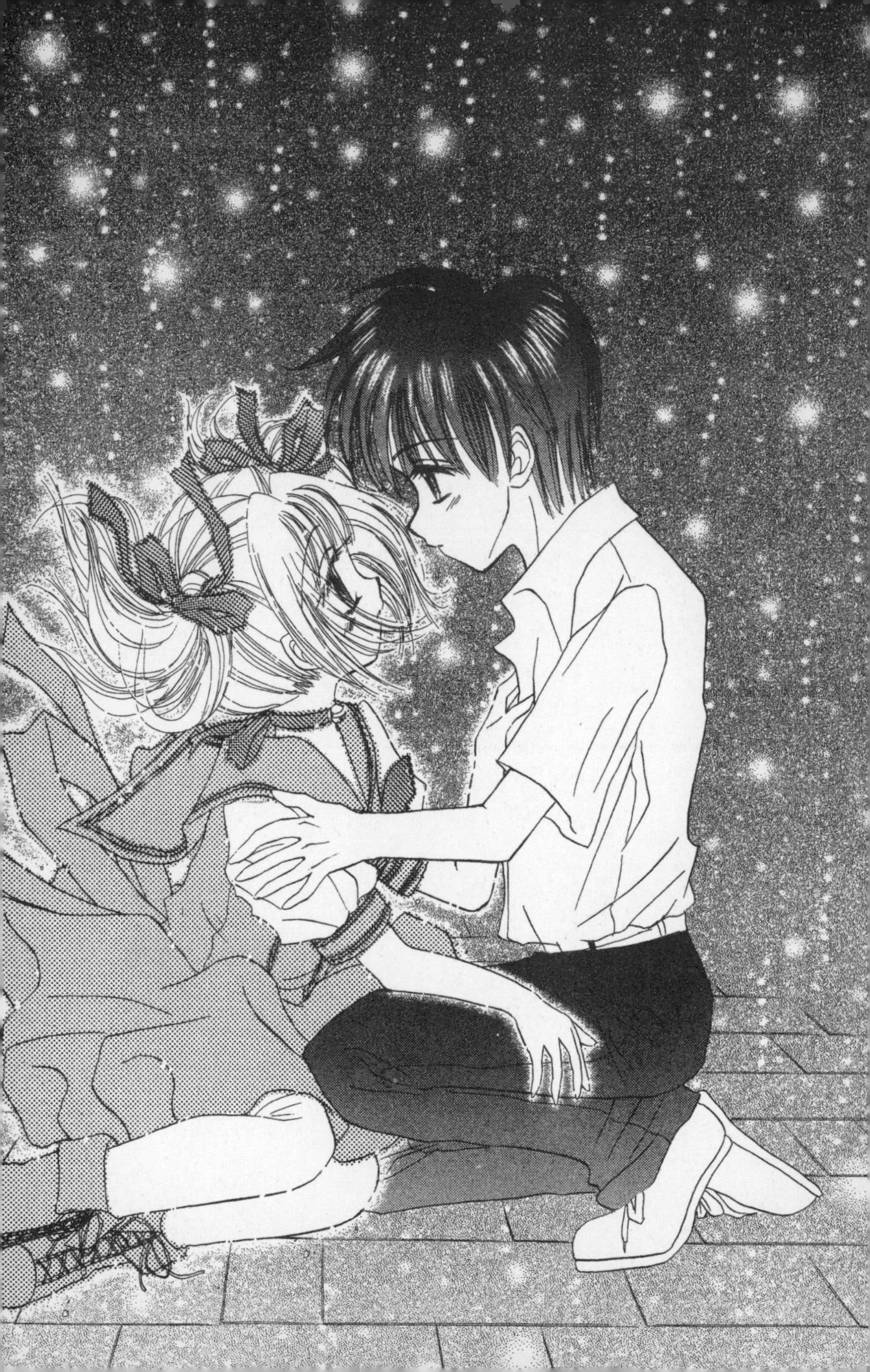

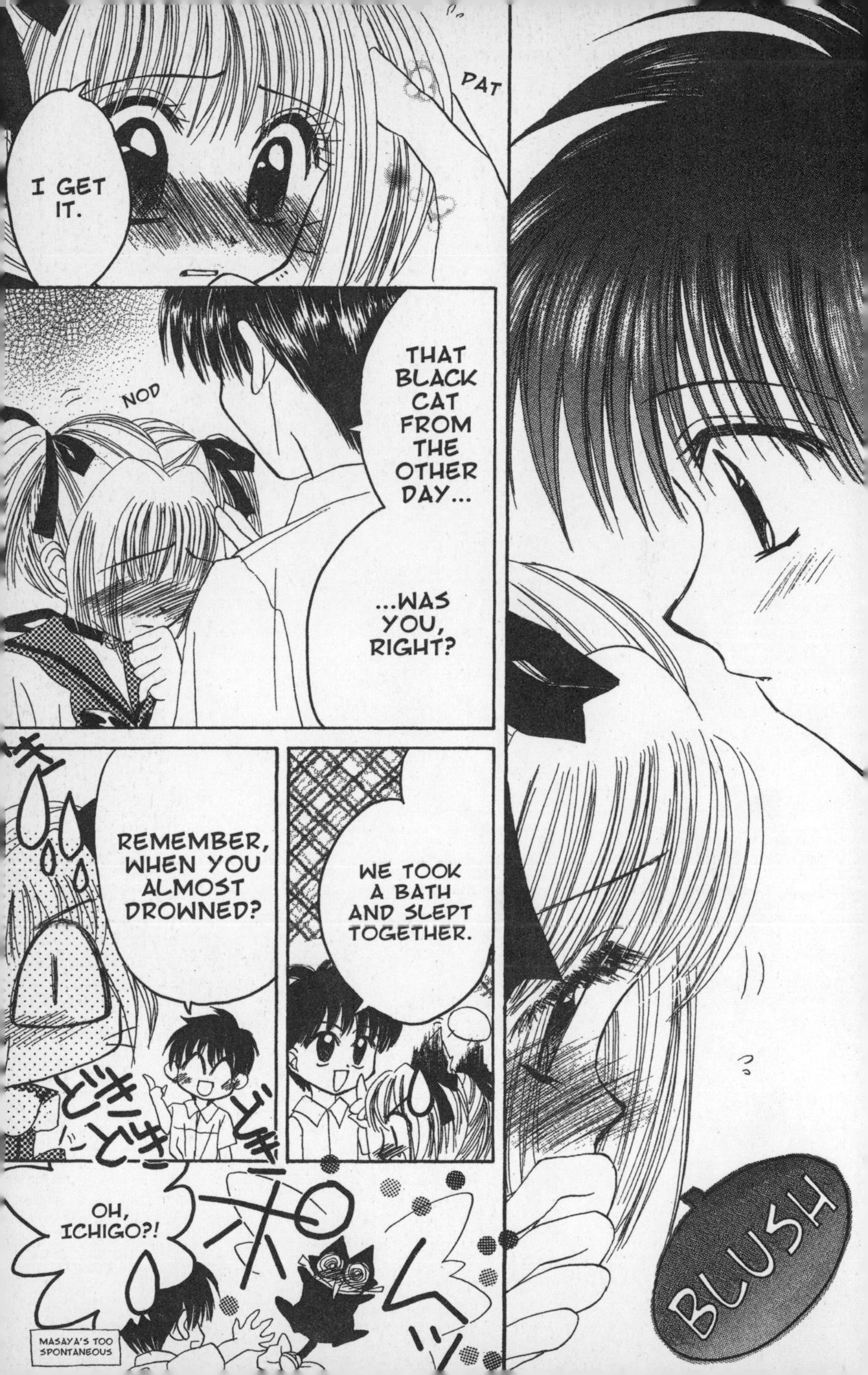
BLUSH
PAT
I GET IT.
NOD
THAT BLACK CAT FROM THE OTHER DAY...
...WAS YOU, RIGHT?
WE TOOK A BATH AND SLEPT TOGETHER.
REMEMBER, WHEN YOU ALMOST DROWNED?
OH, ICHIGO?!
MASAYA'S TOO SPONTANEOUS

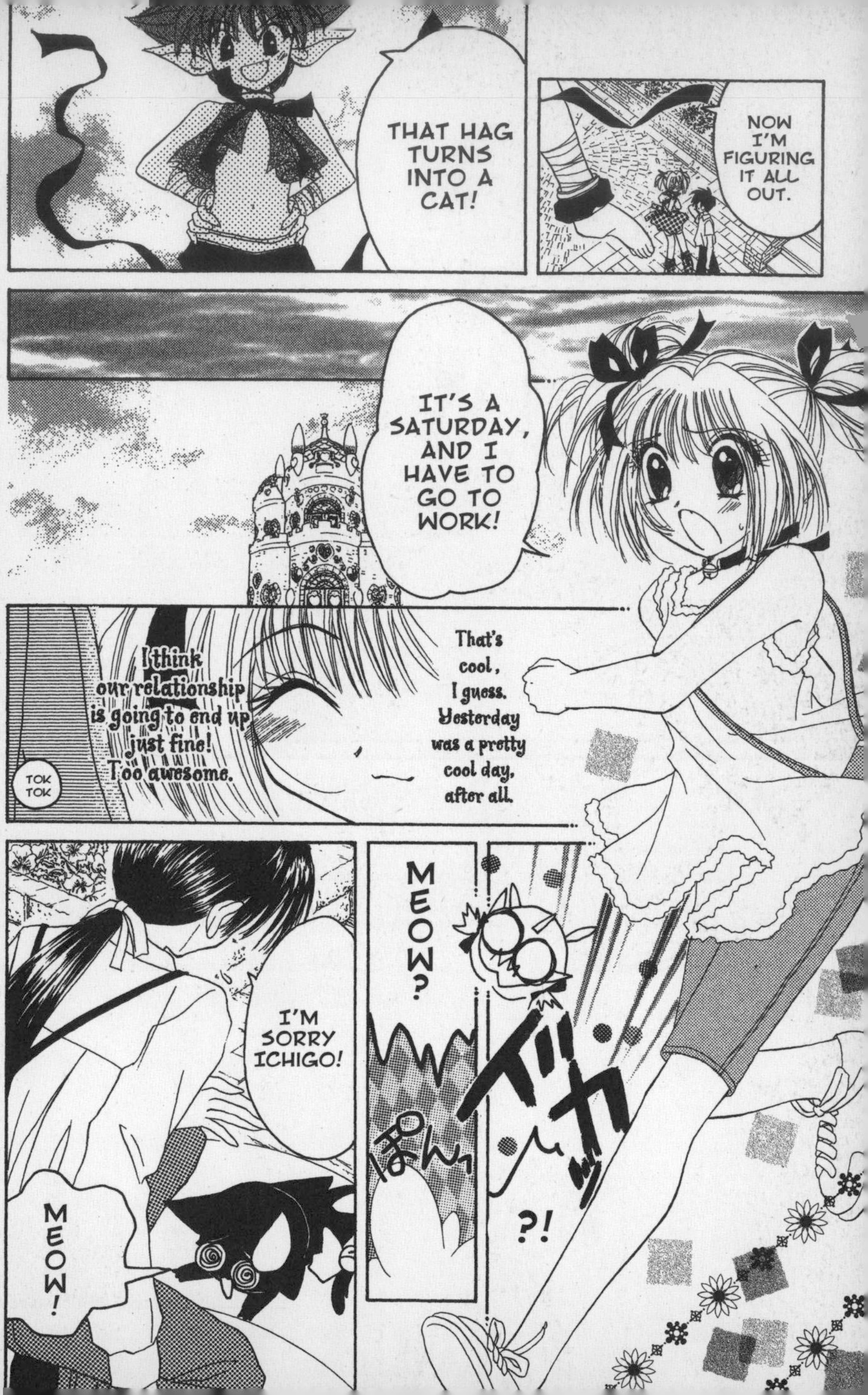
NOW I'M FIGURING IT ALL OUT.
THAT HAG TURNS INTO A CAT!
IT'S A SATURDAY, AND I HAVE TO GO TO WORK!
That's cool, I guess. Yesterday was a pretty cool day, after all.
I think our relationship is going to end up just fine! Too awesome.
TOK TOK
MEOW?
?!
I'M SORRY ICHIGO!
MEOW!

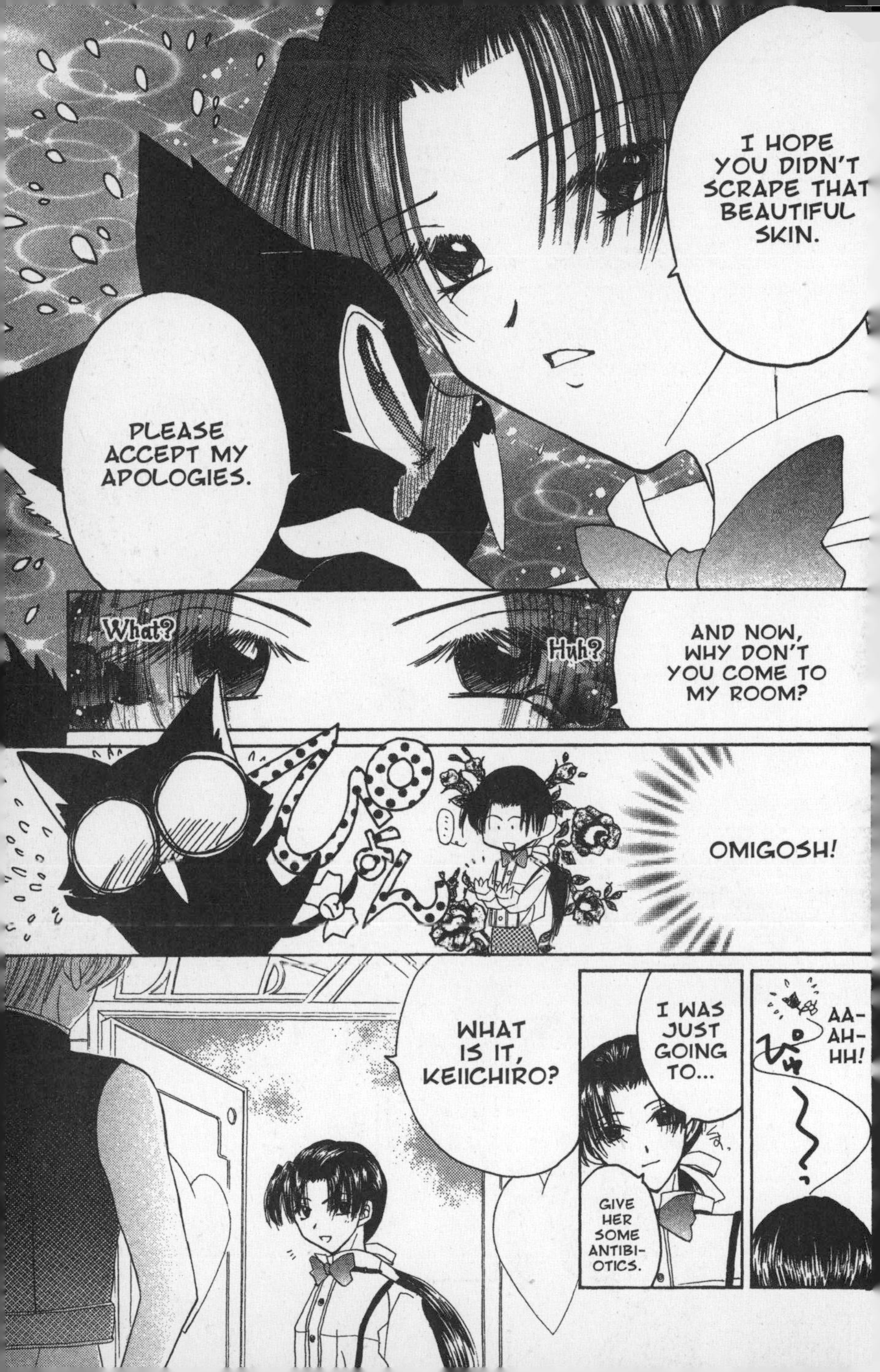
I HOPE YOU DIDN'T SCRAPE THAT BEAUTIFUL SKIN.
PLEASE ACCEPT MY APOLOGIES.
AND NOW, WHY DON'T YOU COME TO MY ROOM?
Huh?
What?
OMIGOSH!
AA-AH-HH!
I WAS JUST GOING TO...
GIVE HER SOME ANTIBI-OTICS.
WHAT IS IT, KEIICHIRO?

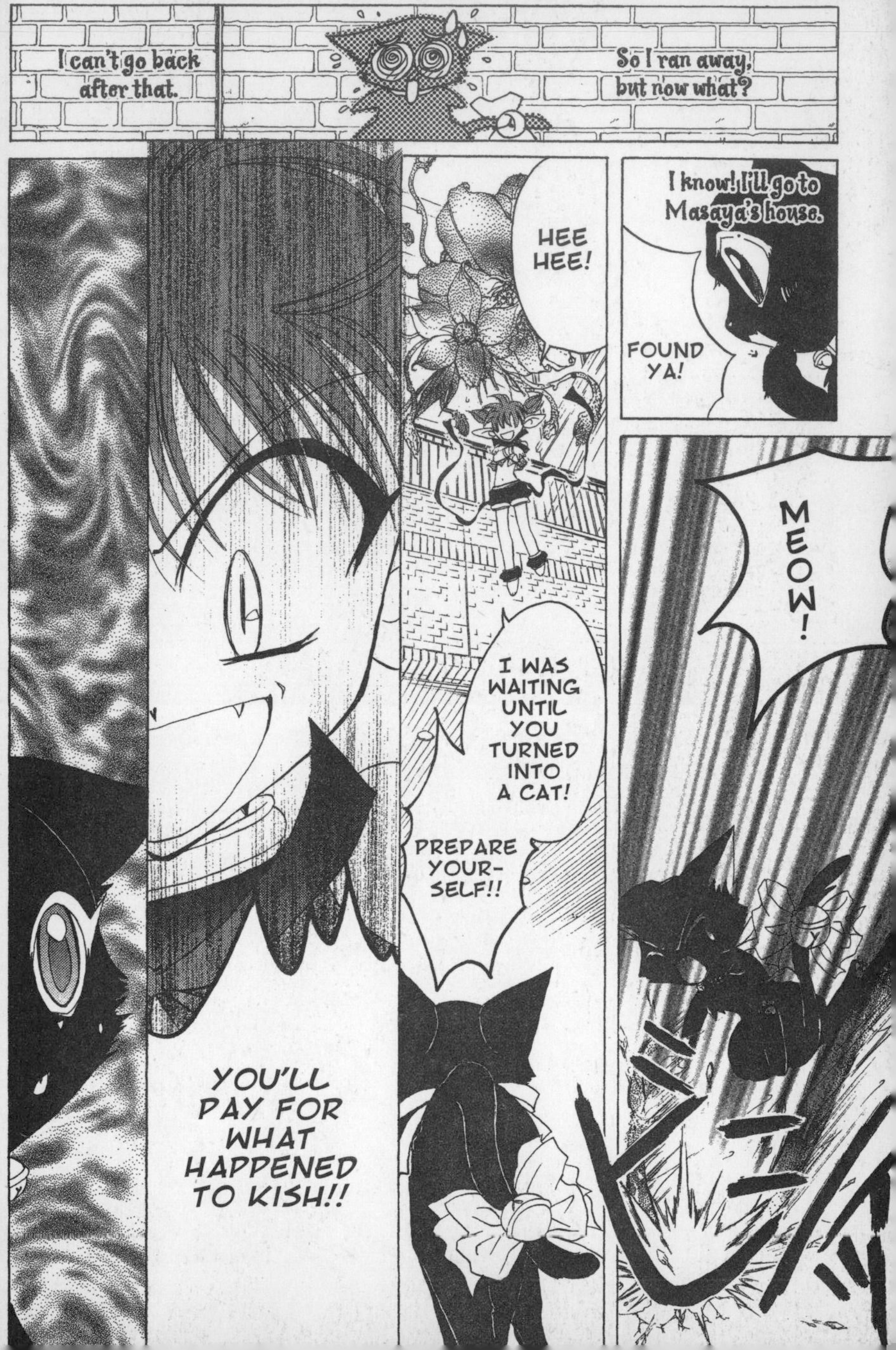
So I ran away, but now what?
I can't go back after that.
I know! I'll go to Masaya's house.
FOUND YA!
MEOW!
HEE HEE!
I WAS WAITING UNTIL YOU TURNED INTO A CAT!
PREPARE YOUR-SELF!!
YOU'LL PAY FOR WHAT HAPPENED TO KISH!!

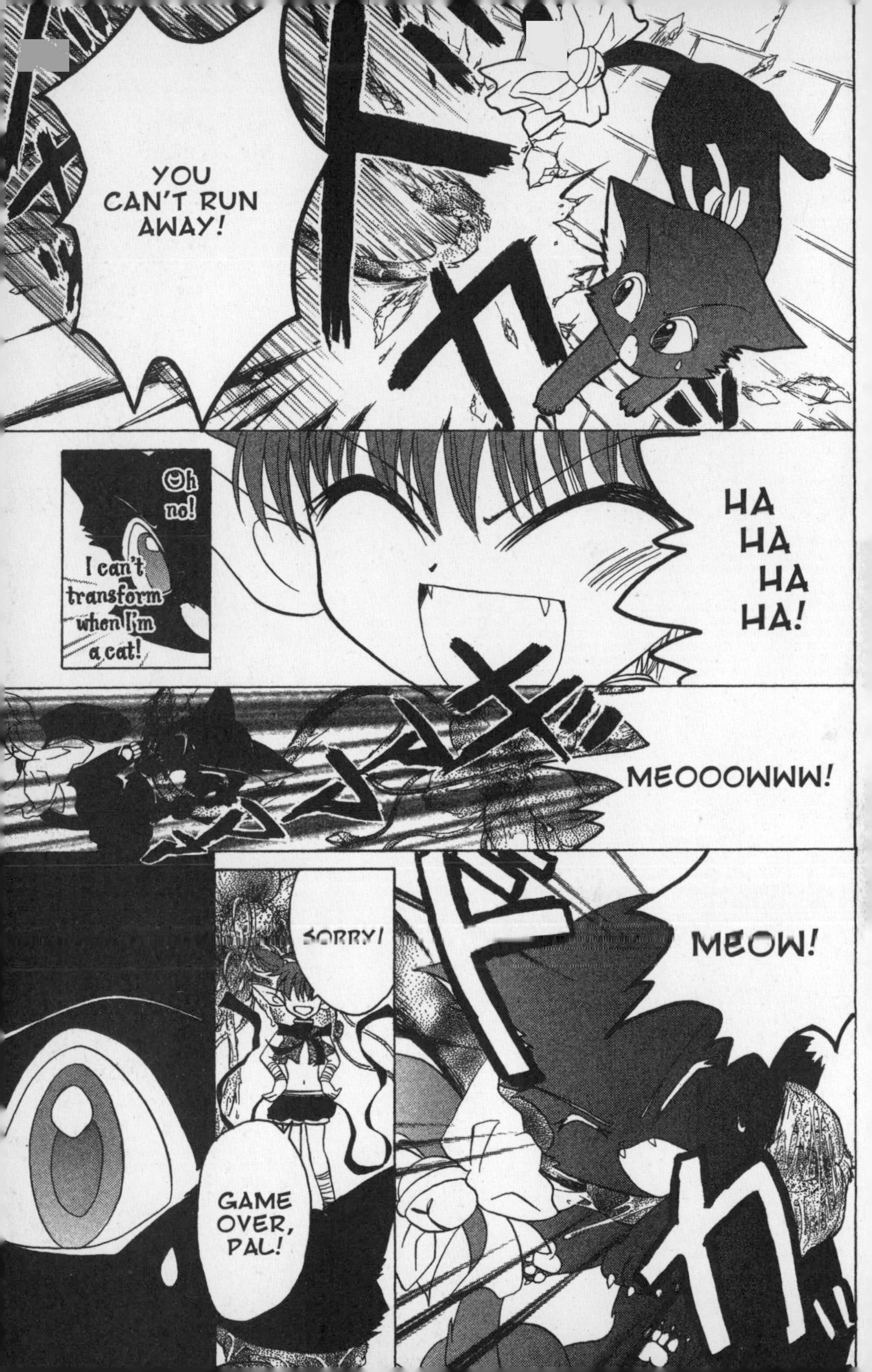
YOU CAN'T RUN AWAY!
HA HA HA HA!
Oh no!
I can't transform when I'm a cat!
MEOOOWWW!
MEOW!
SORRY!
GAME OVER, PAL!

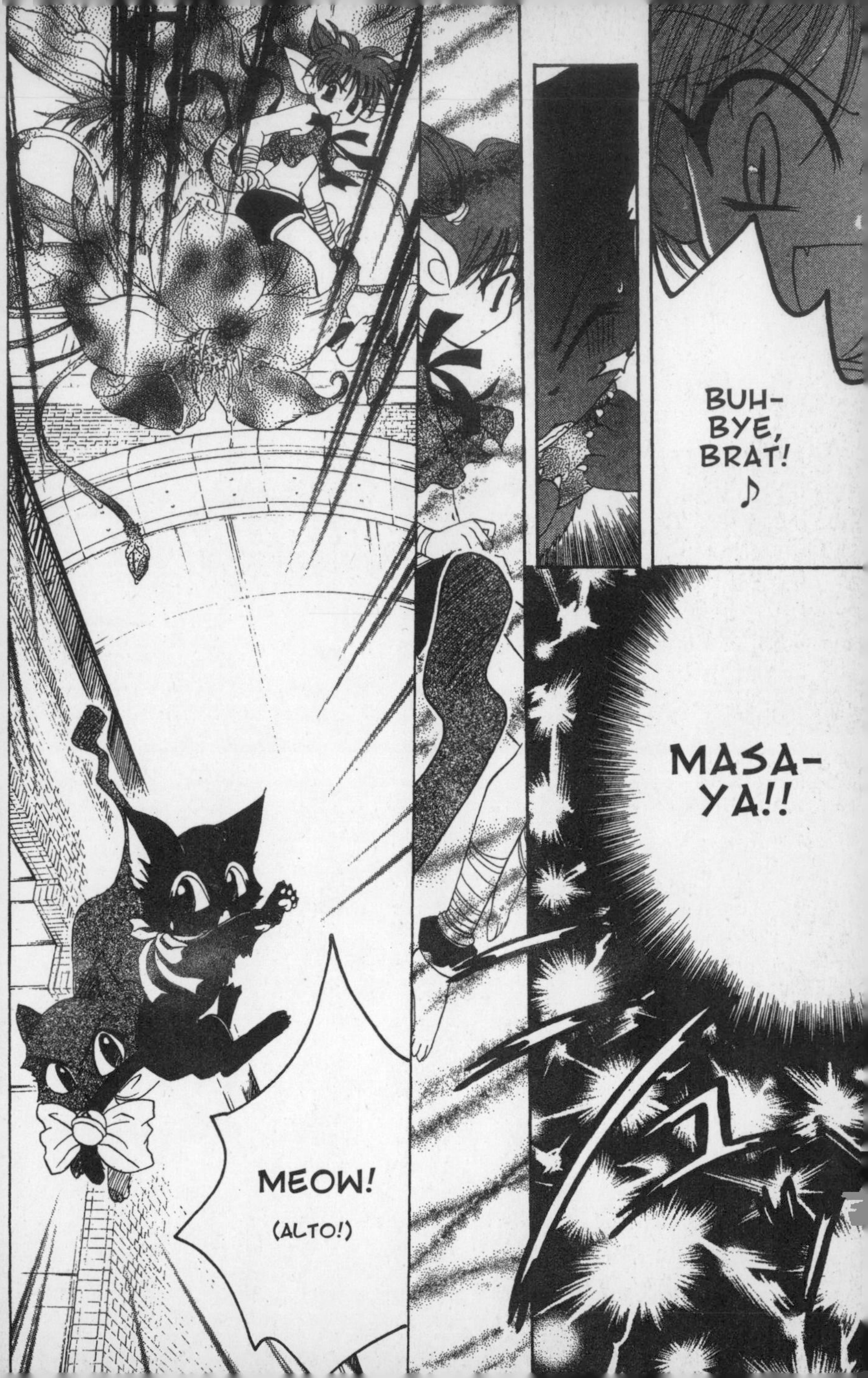
BUH-BYE, BRAT! ♪
MASA-YA!!
MEOW!
(ALTO!)

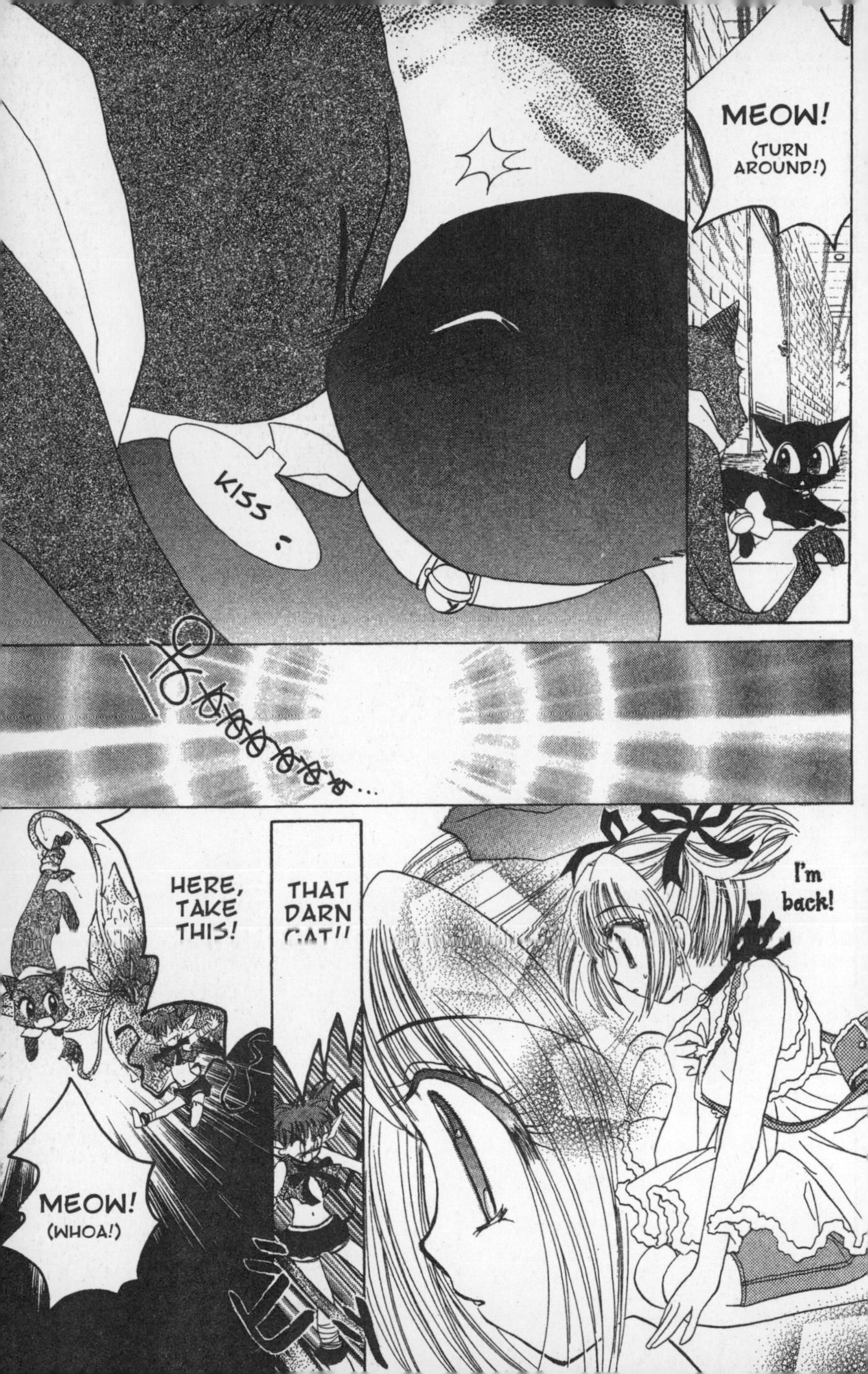

MEOW!
(TURN AROUND!)
KISS!
I'm back!
THAT DARN CAT!!
HERE, TAKE THIS!
MEOW!
(WHOA!)

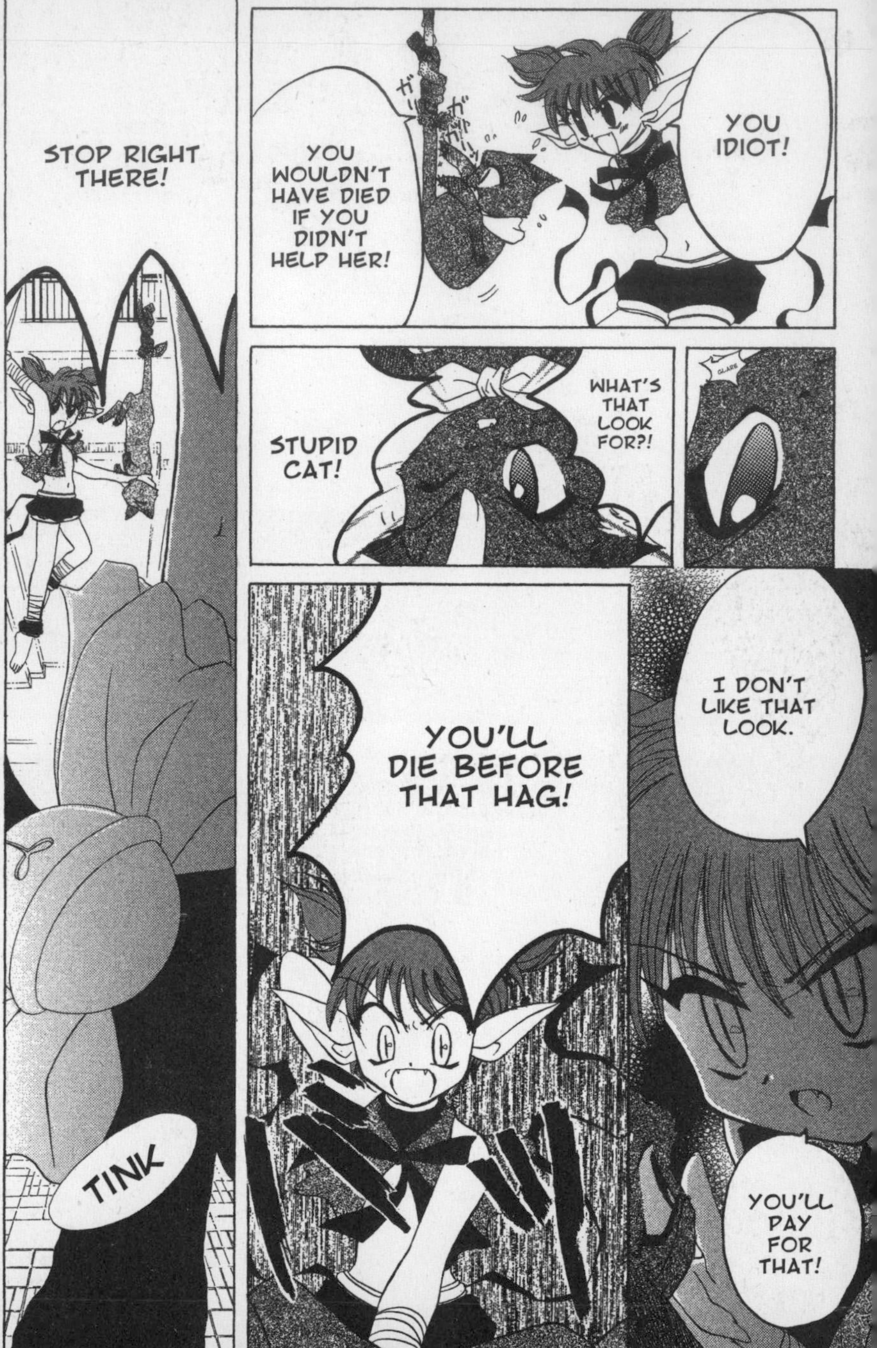
YOU IDIOT!
YOU WOULDN'T HAVE DIED IF YOU DIDN'T HELP HER!
WHAT'S THAT LOOK FOR?!
STUPID CAT!
I DON'T LIKE THAT LOOK.
YOU'LL PAY FOR THAT!
YOU'LL DIE BEFORE THAT HAG!
STOP RIGHT THERE!
TINK

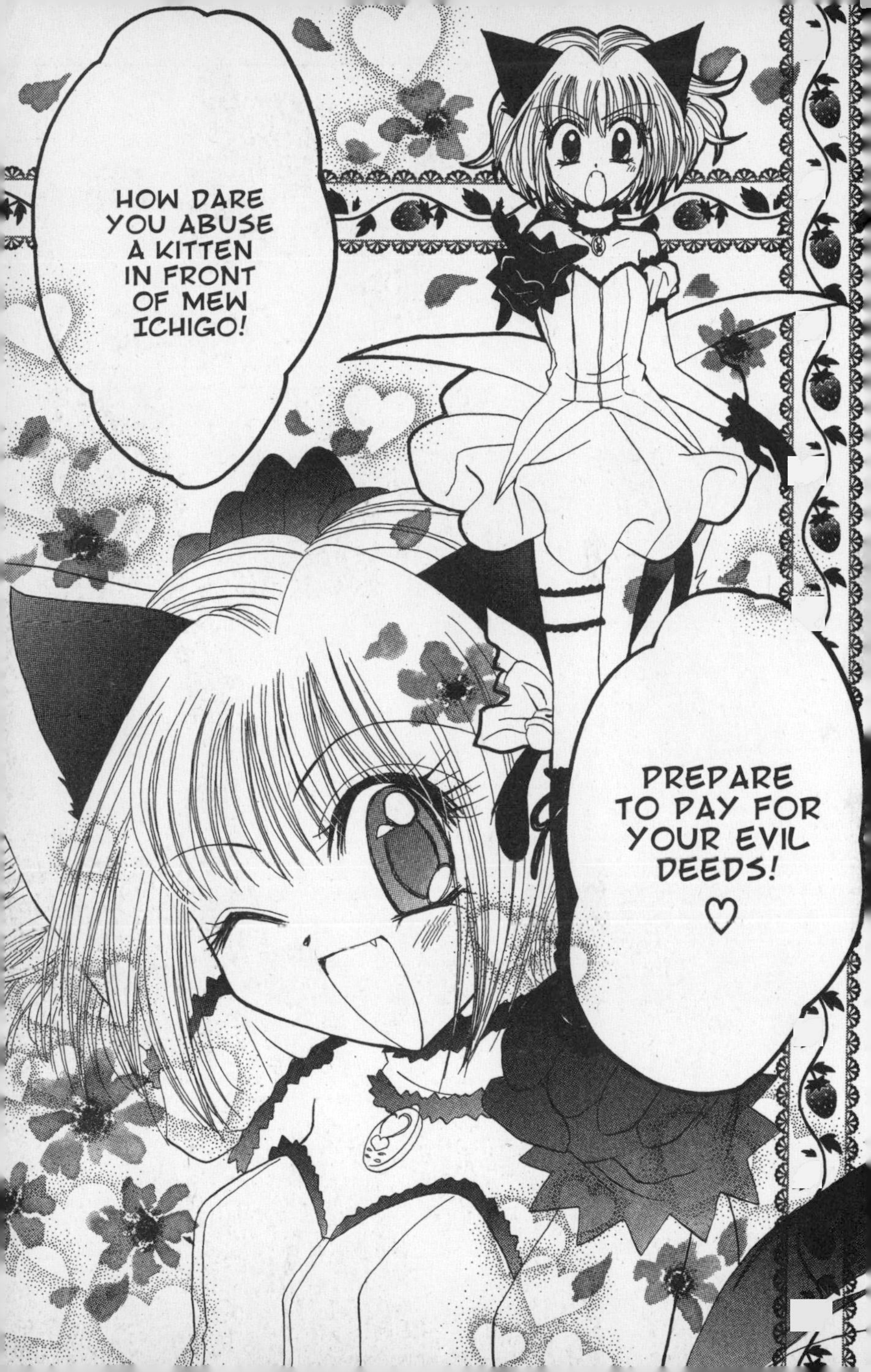
HOW DARE YOU ABUSE A KITTEN IN FRONT OF MEW ICHIGO!
PREPARE TO PAY FOR YOUR EVIL DEEDS! ♡

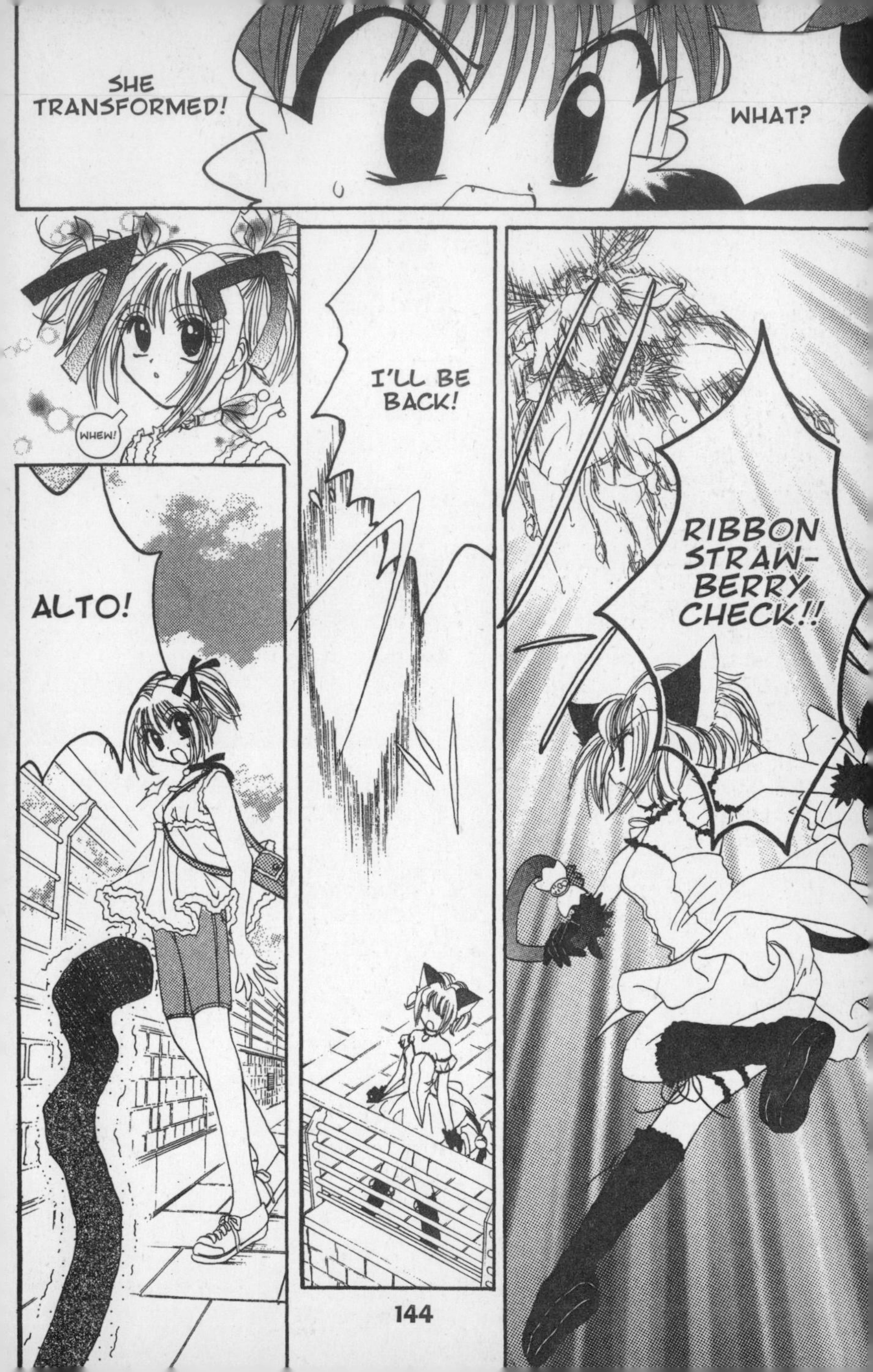
WHAT?
SHE TRANSFORMED!
RIBBON STRAW-BERRY CHECK!!
I'LL BE BACK!
WHEW!
ALTO!

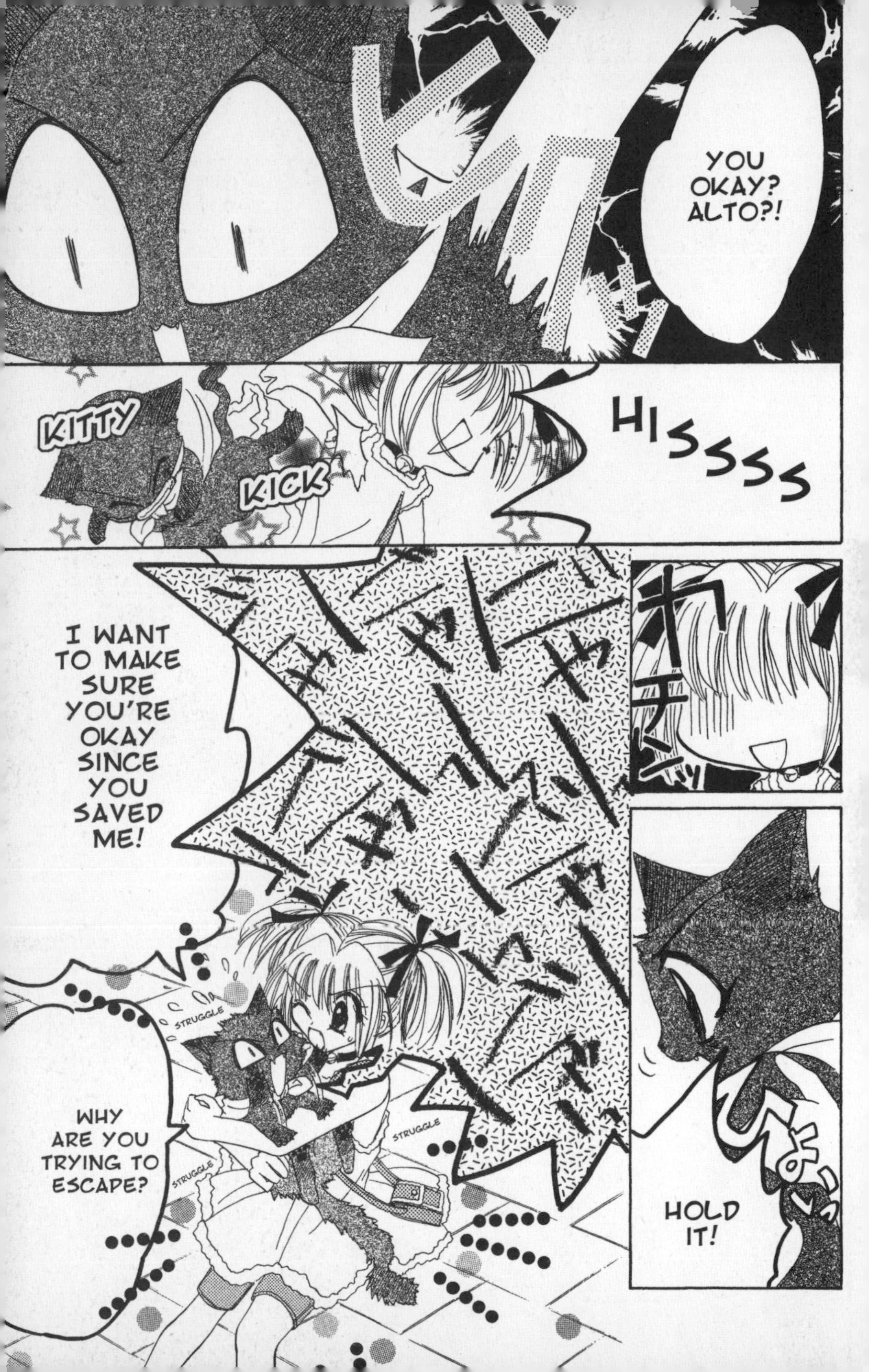
YOU OKAY? ALTO?!
HISSSSS
KITTY
KICK
HOLD IT!
I WANT TO MAKE SURE YOU'RE OKAY SINCE YOU SAVED ME!
STRUGGLE
STRUGGLE
STRUGGLE
WHY ARE YOU TRYING TO ESCAPE?

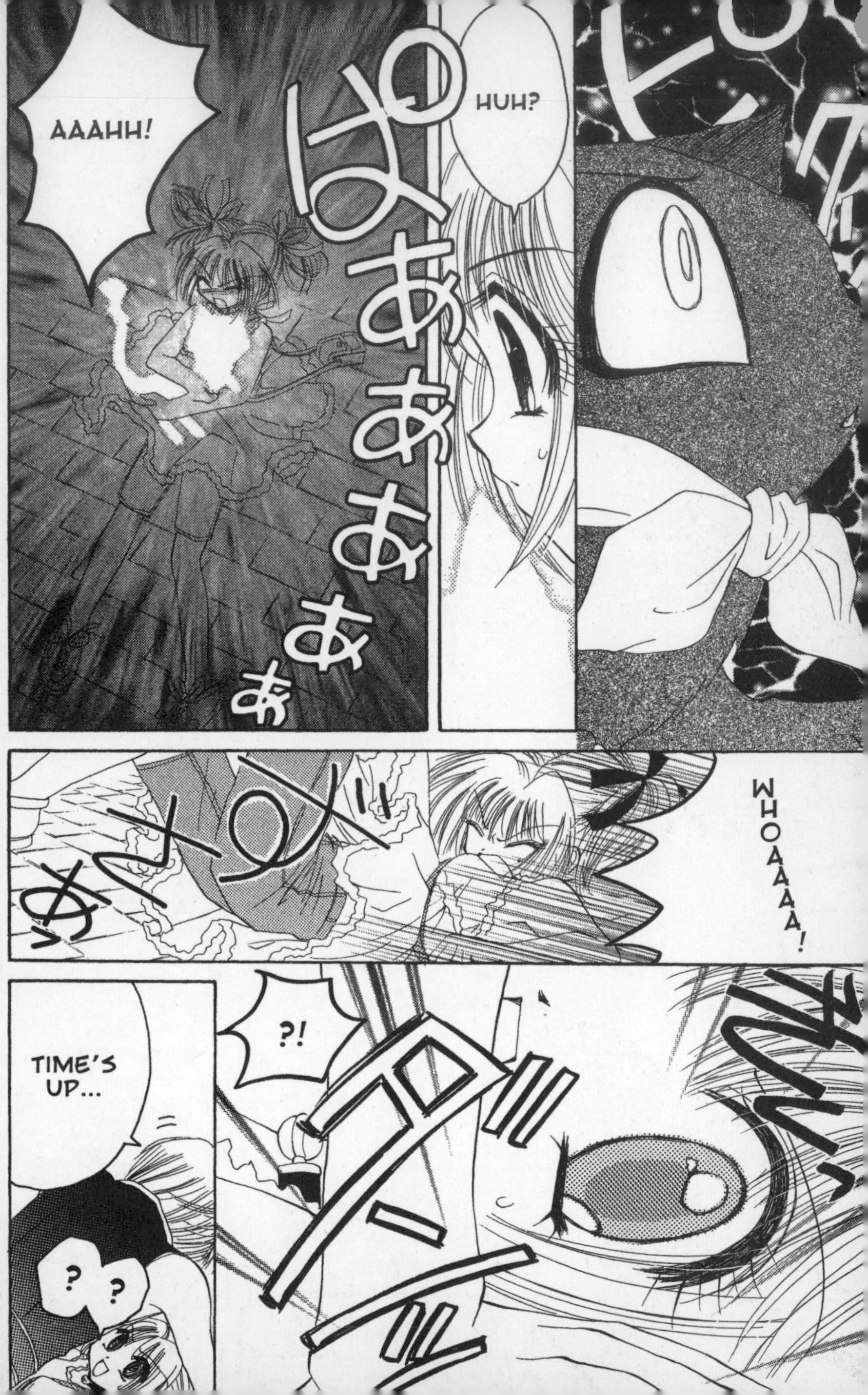
HUH?
AAAHH!
WHOAAAA!
?!
TIME'S UP...
? ?

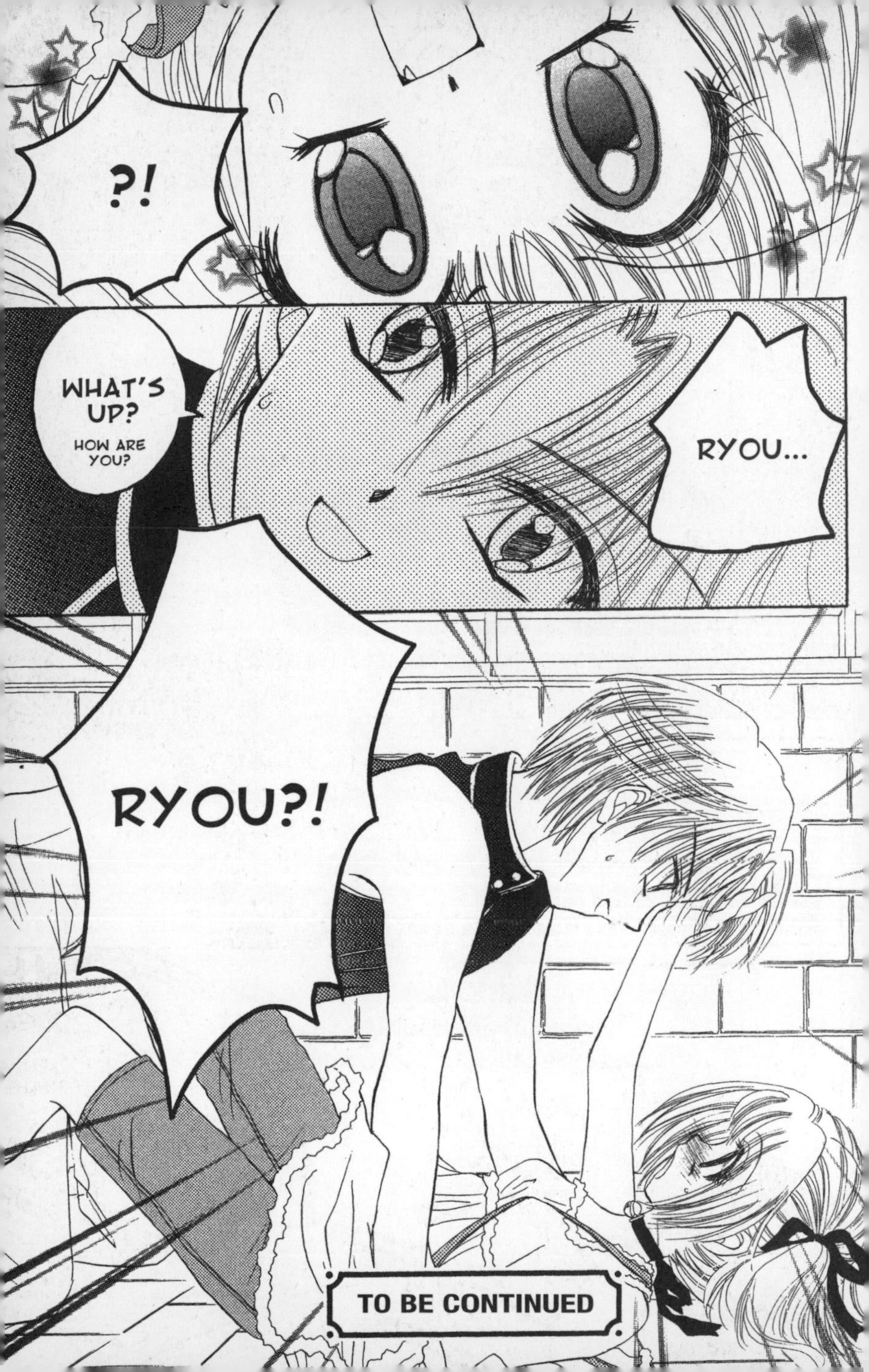
?!
RYOU...
WHAT'S UP? HOW ARE YOU?
RYOU?!
TO BE CONTINUED

About the Fifth Volume
by Reiko Yoshida

Tokyo Mew Mew has a lot of male characters.
Masaya, Ryou, Keiichiro, Pie, Kish, Tart.
Who is your ideal type?
If you want a guy who values work and hobbies
in addition to the relationship, you want someone like
Masaya. However, don't get freaked out if you can't
always figure out what he's feeling. Meanwhile, if you're
headstrong but honest, Ryou might be the right guy for
you. Just be straightforward, and be willing to apologize
whenever you get into an argument. If you're a bit
demanding and want someone who will take care of you,
Keiichiro is definitely your type. If you're passionate, Kish
is the right match. If you're quiet and gentle, Pie might be
your perfect guy. You'll be able to get past his cool
exterior. Tart would be a great partner if you're perky
and active. He'll value your feelings, although he can
be more than a bit childish. There's one more
Francois, the Fat Cat, is a guy, too!
But I don't think he's anybody's type!!!

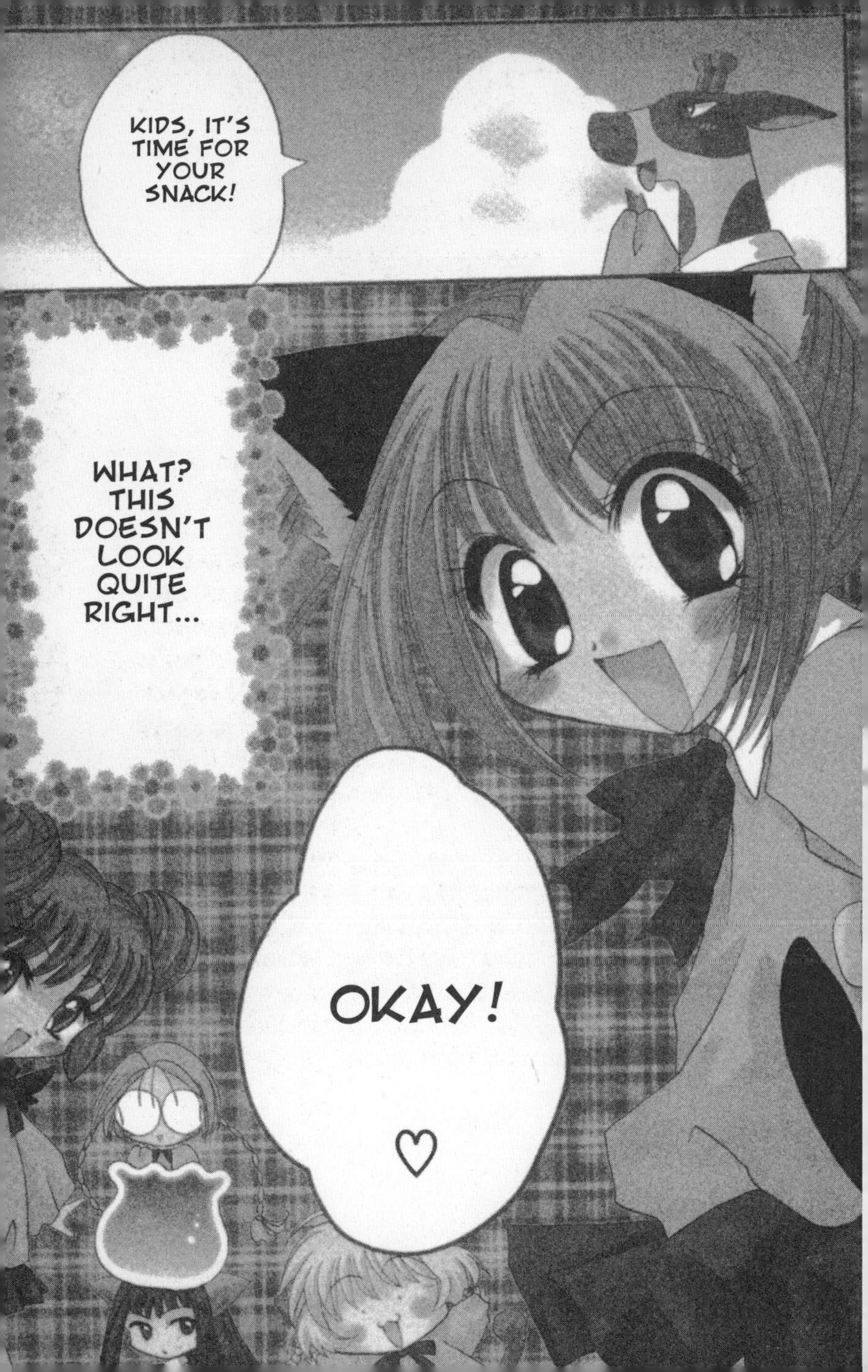
KIDS, IT'S TIME FOR YOUR SNACK!
OKAY! ♡
WHAT? THIS DOESN'T LOOK QUITE RIGHT...

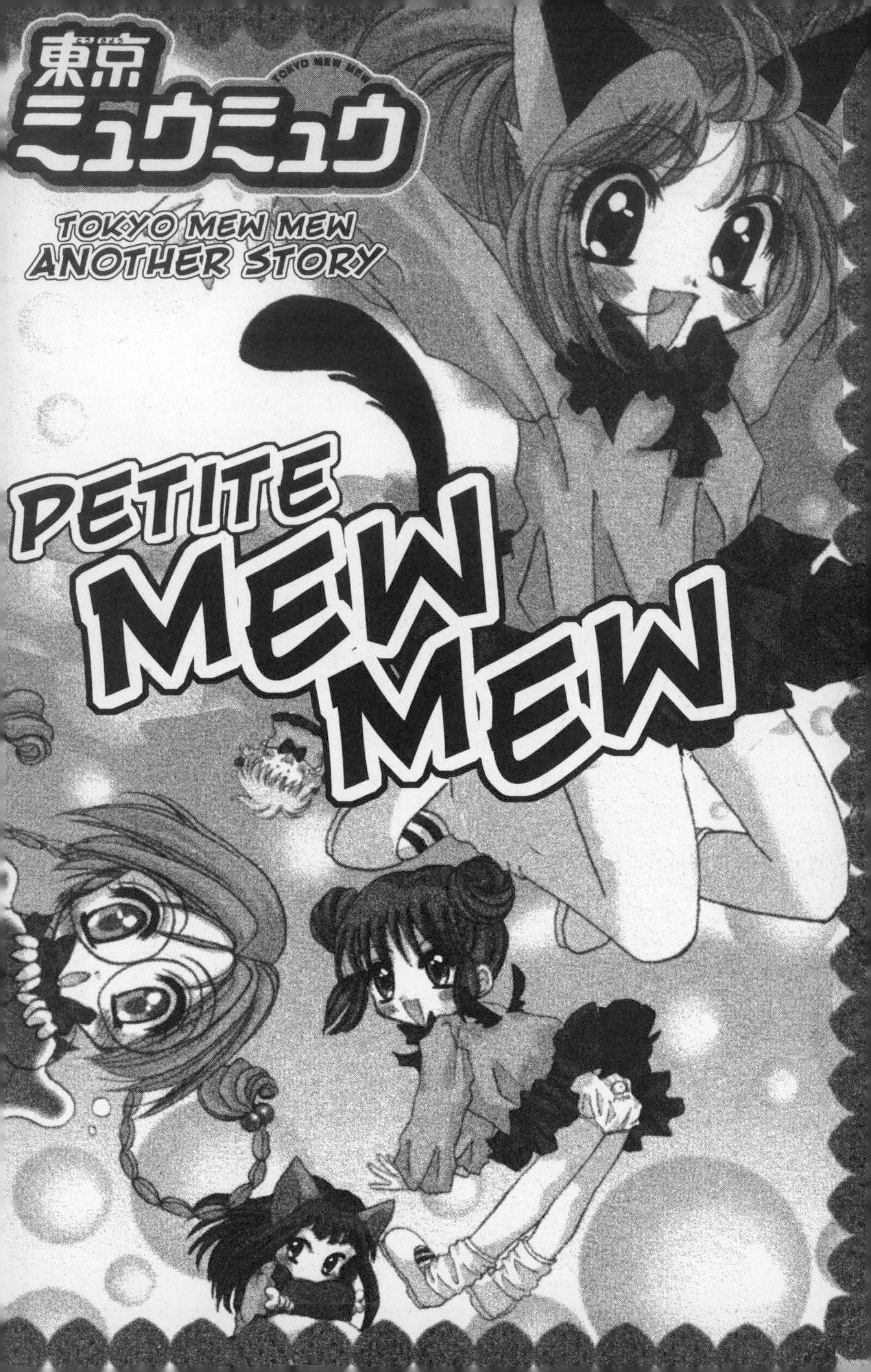
東京ミュウミュウ
TOKYO MEW MEW
TOKYO MEW MEW
ANOTHER STORY
PETITE
MEW
MEW

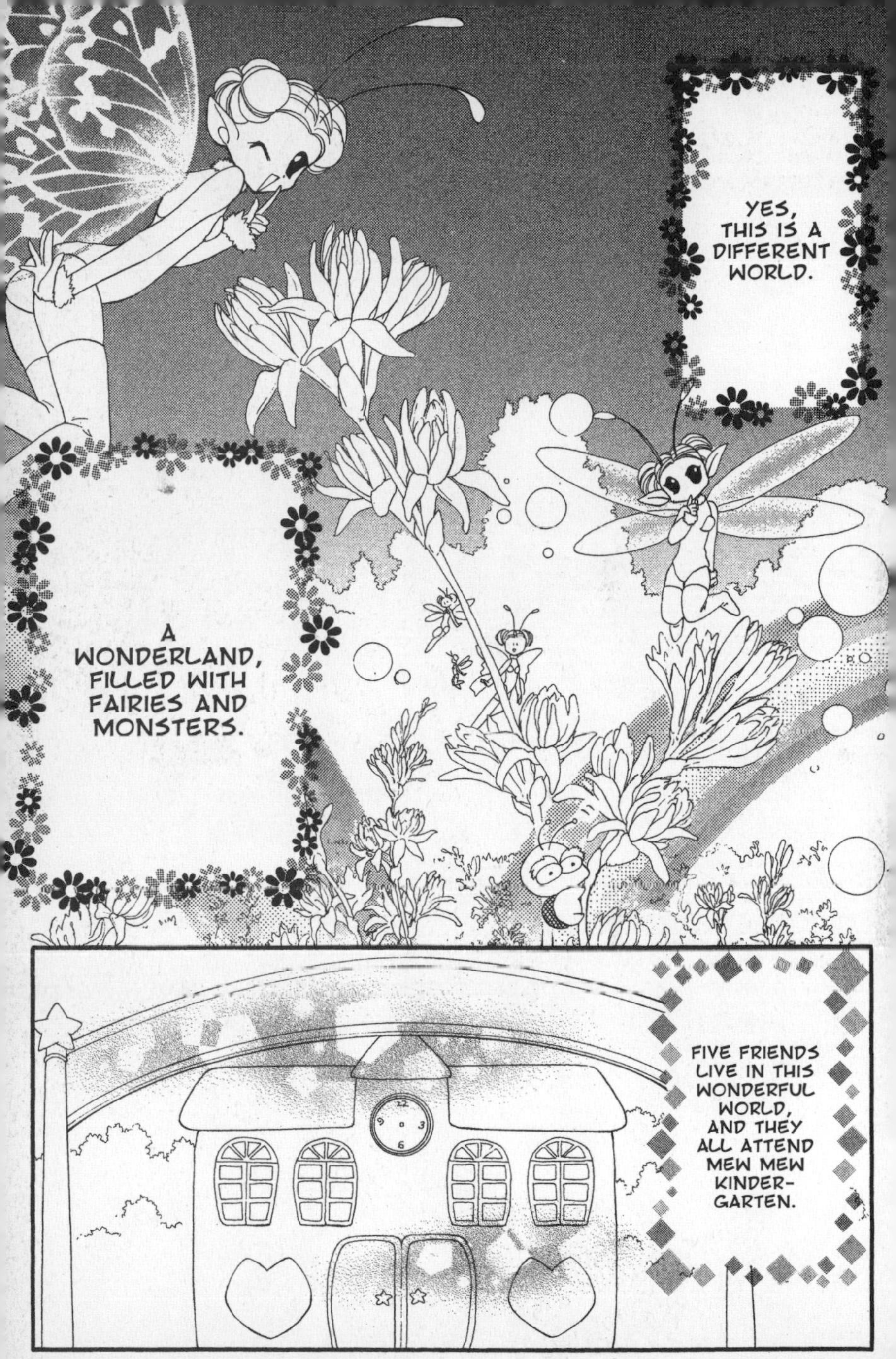
YES, THIS IS A DIFFERENT WORLD.
A WONDERLAND, FILLED WITH FAIRIES AND MONSTERS.
FIVE FRIENDS LIVE IN THIS WONDERFUL WORLD, AND THEY ALL ATTEND MEW MEW KINDER-GARTEN.

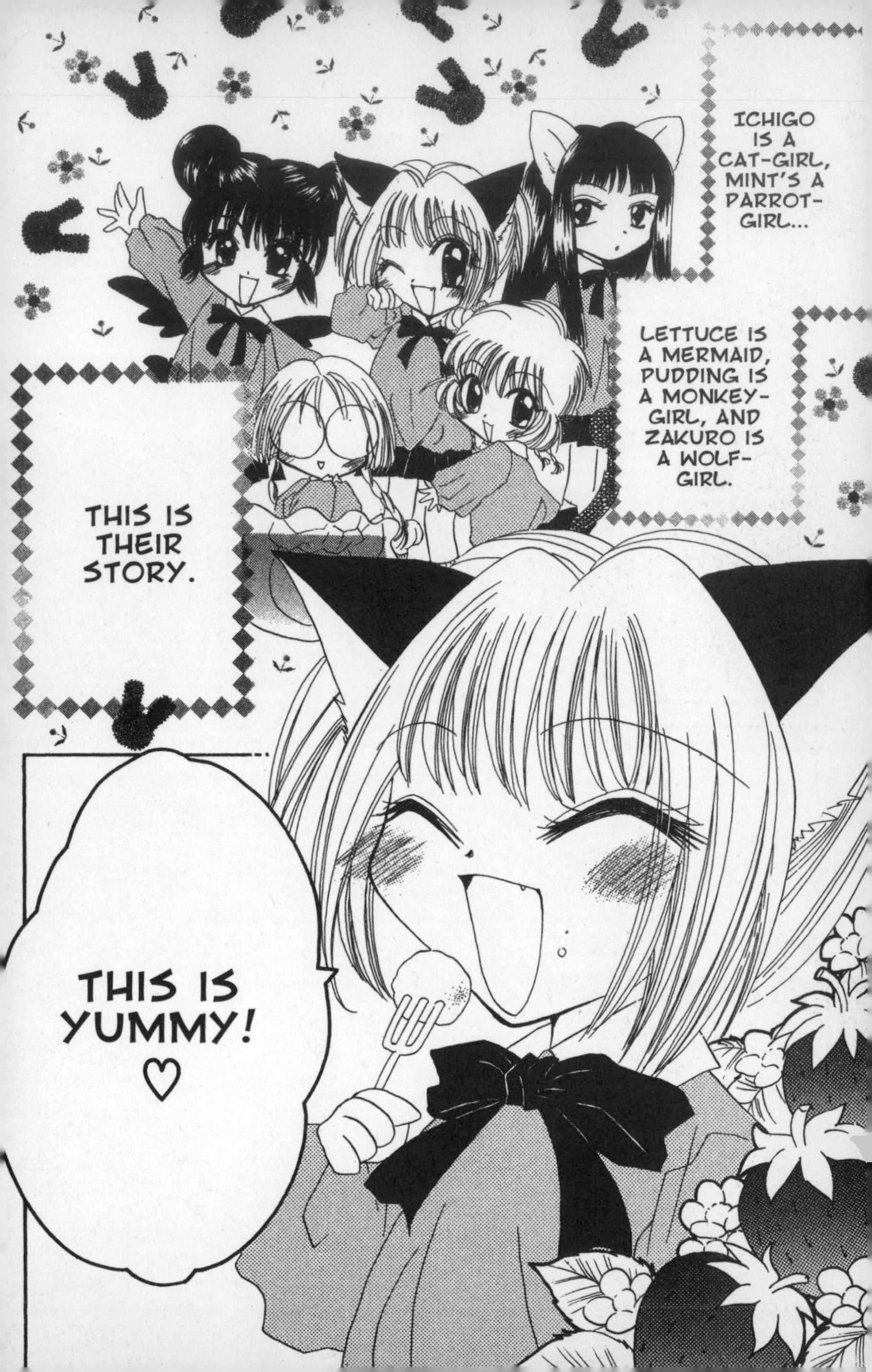
ICHIGO IS A CAT-GIRL, MINT'S A PARROT-GIRL...
LETTUCE IS A MERMAID, PUDDING IS A MONKEY-GIRL, AND ZAKURO IS A WOLF-GIRL.
THIS IS THEIR STORY.
THIS IS YUMMY! ♡

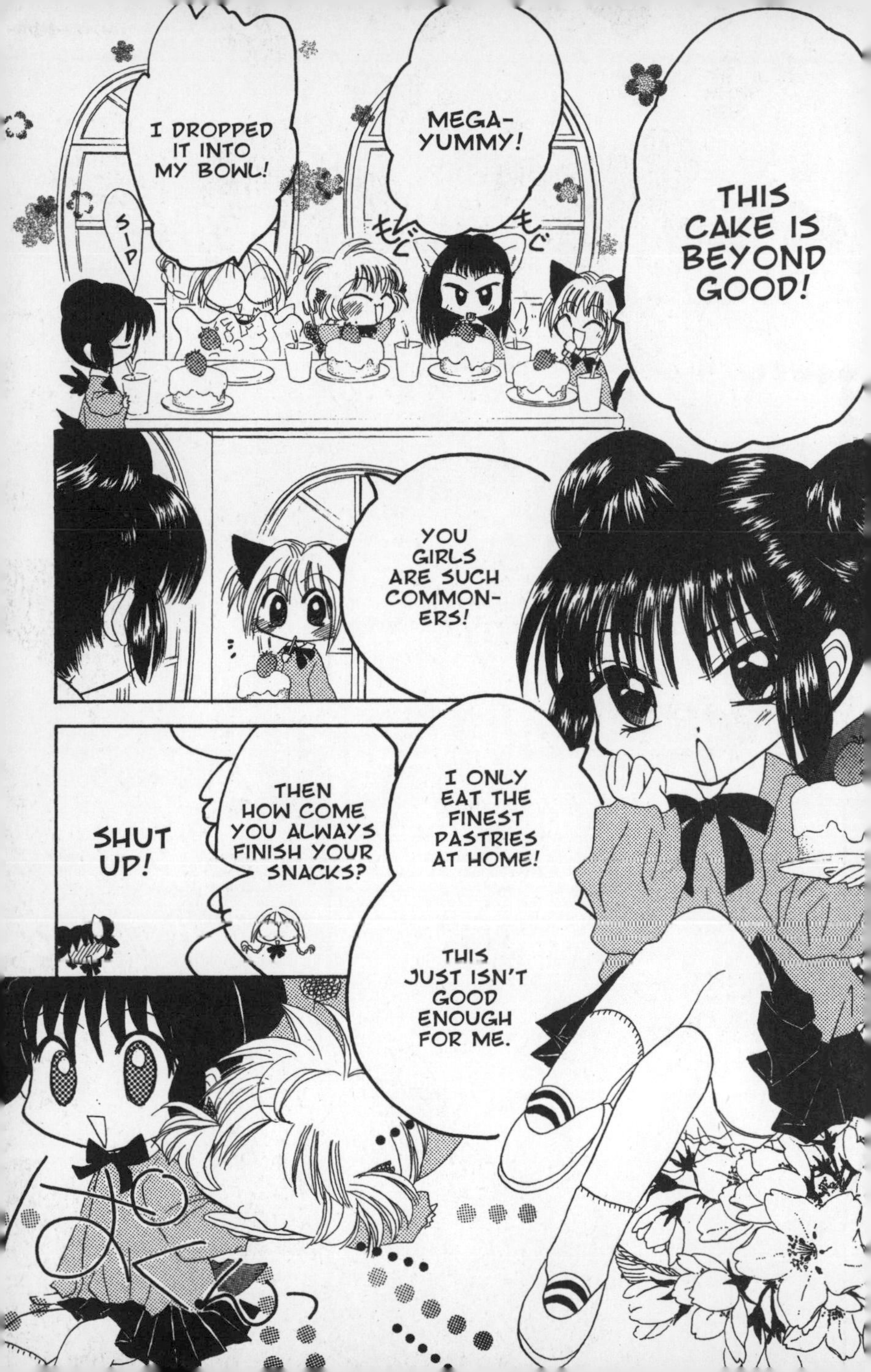

THIS CAKE IS BEYOND GOOD!
MEGA-YUMMY!
もぐ もぐ
I DROPPED IT INTO MY BOWL!
SIP
YOU GIRLS ARE SUCH COMMONERS!
I ONLY EAT THE FINEST PASTRIES AT HOME!
THIS JUST ISN'T GOOD ENOUGH FOR ME.
THEN HOW COME YOU ALWAYS FINISH YOUR SNACKS?
SHUT UP!

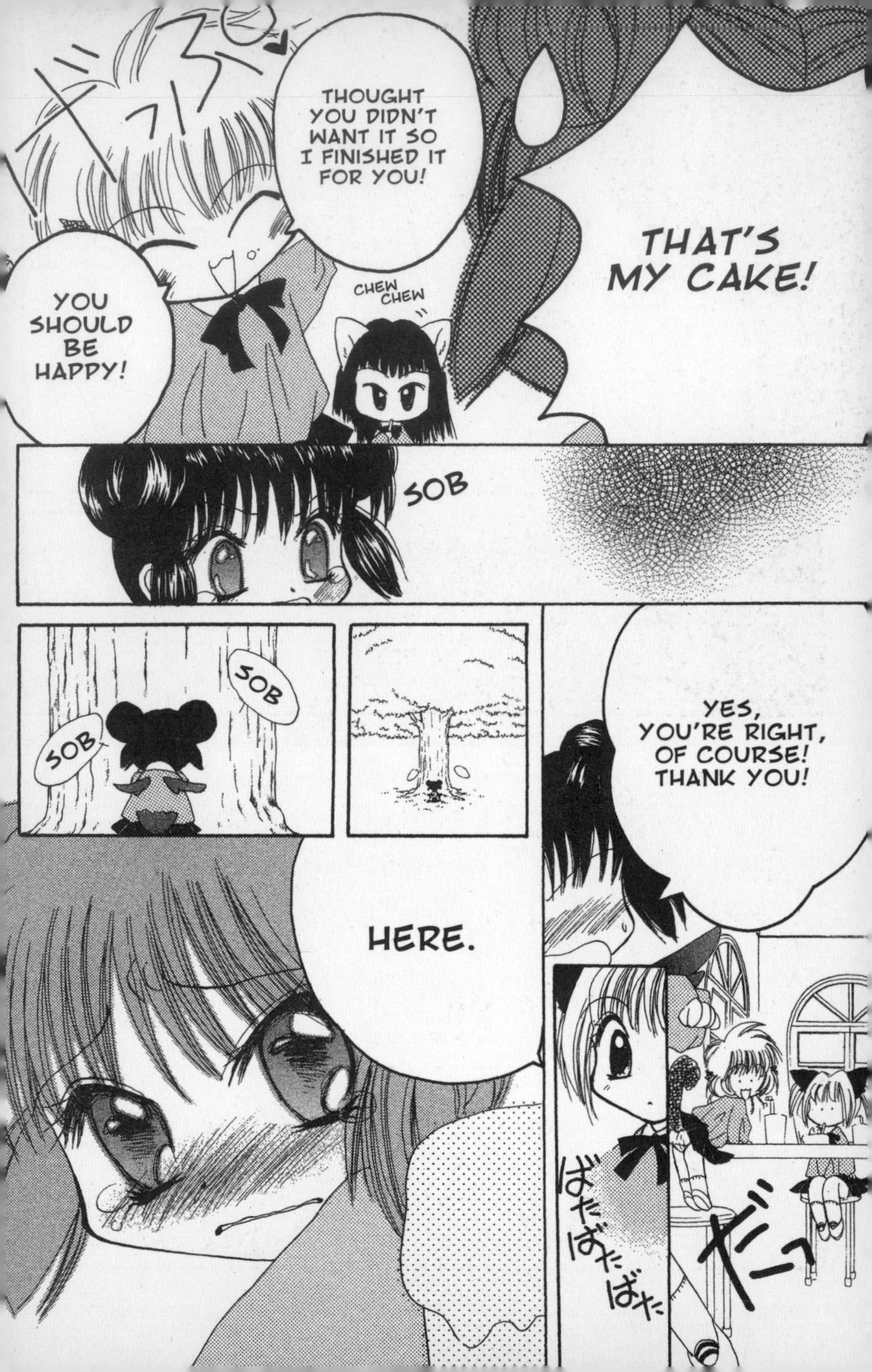
THAT'S MY CAKE!
THOUGHT YOU DIDN'T WANT IT SO I FINISHED IT FOR YOU!
CHEW CHEW
YOU SHOULD BE HAPPY!
SOB
YES, YOU'RE RIGHT, OF COURSE! THANK YOU!
ダーッ
ばだばたばた
SOB
SOB
HERE.

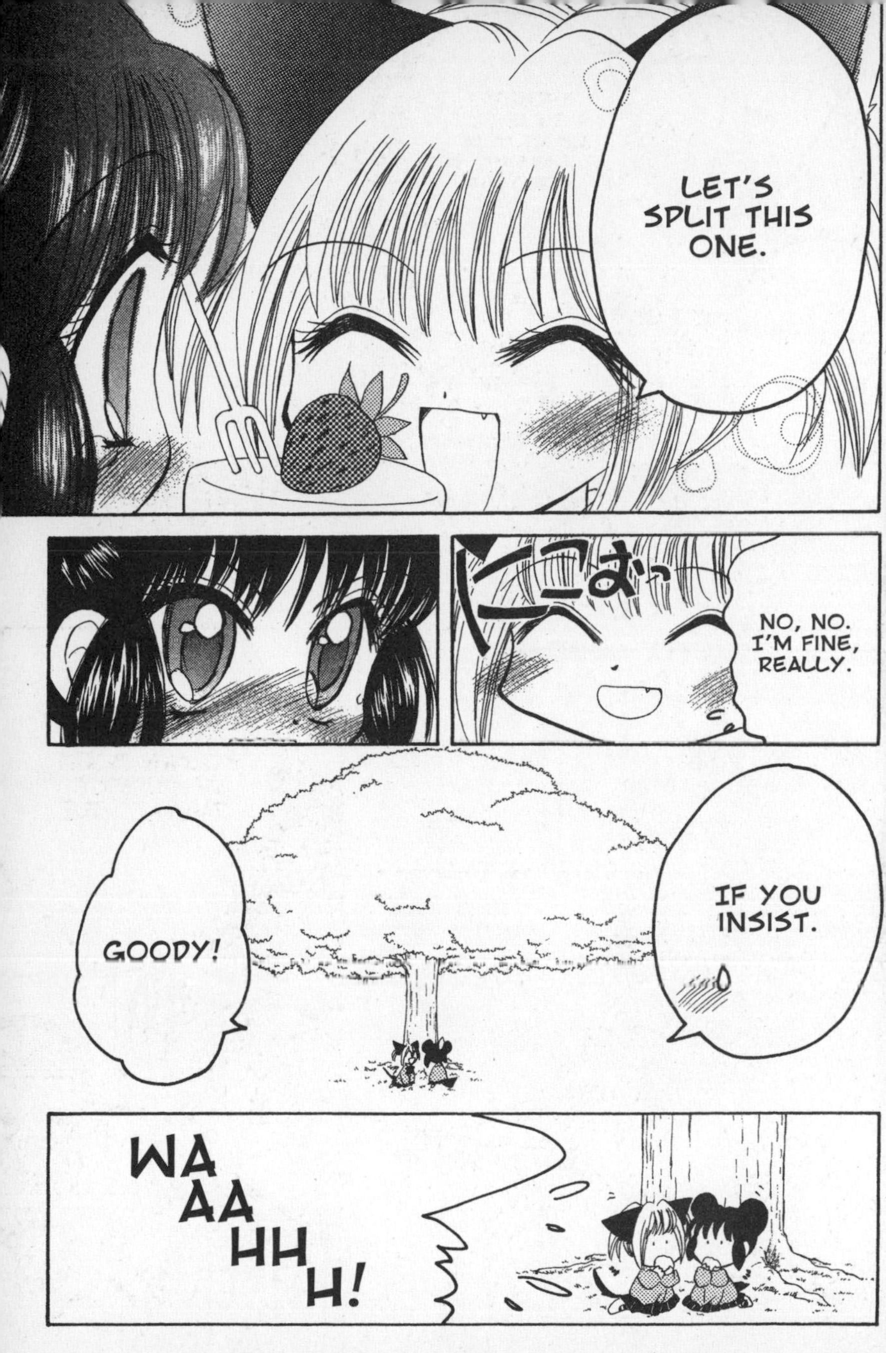
LET'S SPLIT THIS ONE.
NO, NO. I'M FINE, REALLY.
IF YOU INSIST.
GOODY!
WAAAHHHH!

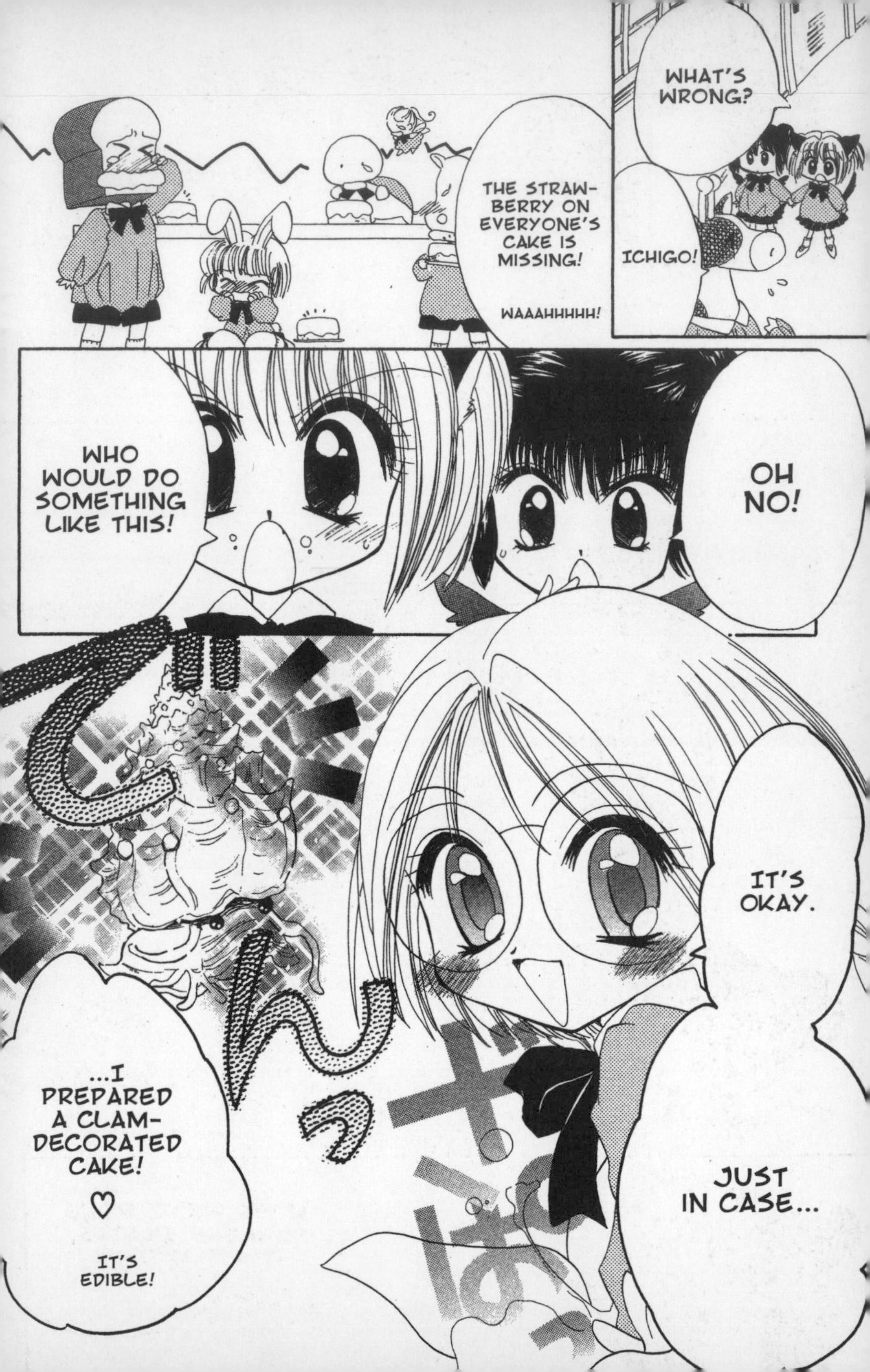
WHAT'S WRONG?
ICHIGO!
THE STRAW-BERRY ON EVERYONE'S CAKE IS MISSING!
WAAAHHHHH!
OH NO!
WHO WOULD DO SOMETHING LIKE THIS!
IT'S OKAY.
JUST IN CASE...
...I PREPARED A CLAM-DECORATED CAKE! ♡
IT'S EDIBLE!

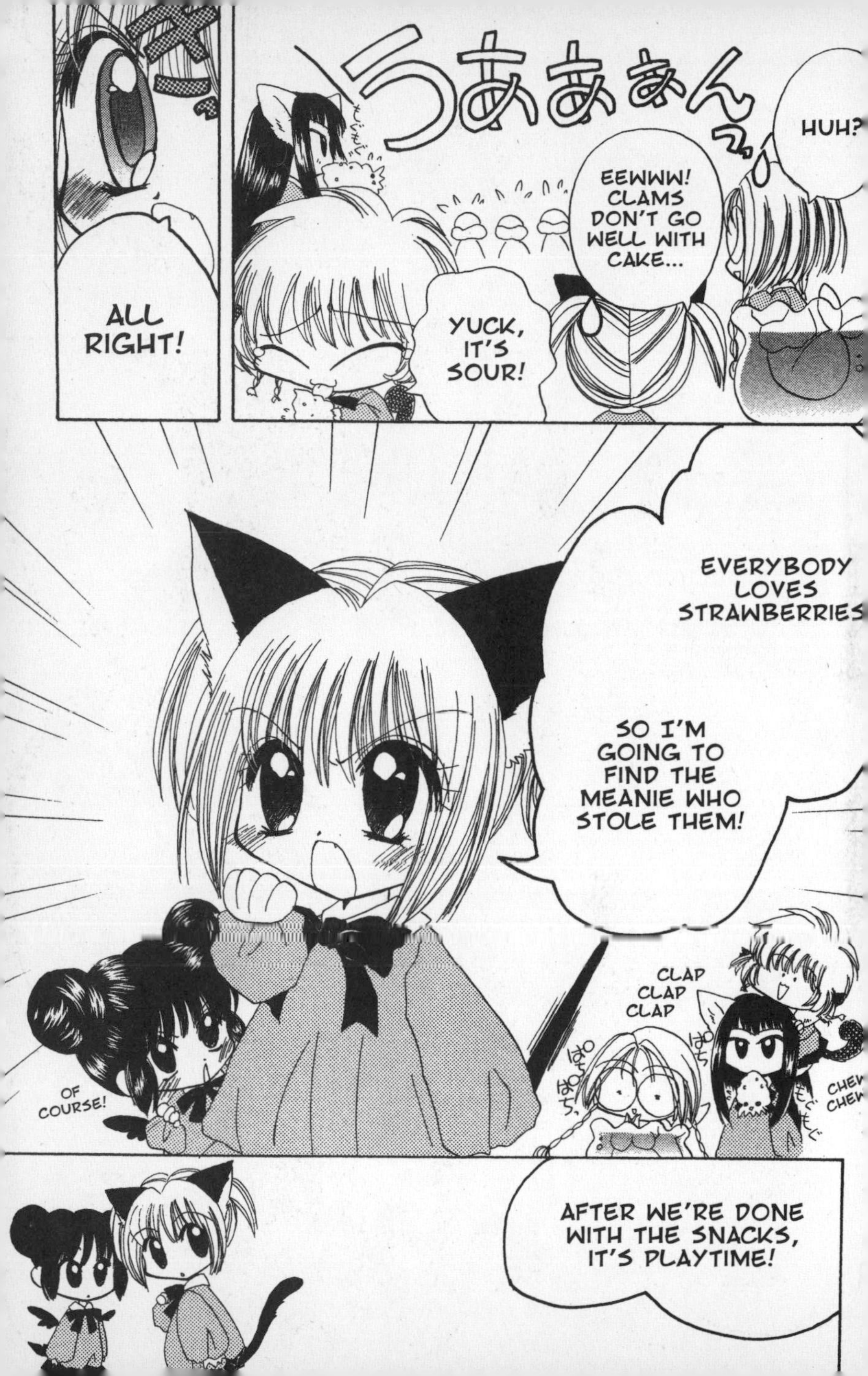
HUH?
うあああん
EEWWW! CLAMS DON'T GO WELL WITH CAKE...
YUCK, IT'S SOUR!
ALL RIGHT!
EVERYBODY LOVES STRAWBERRIES
SO I'M GOING TO FIND THE MEANIE WHO STOLE THEM!
CLAP CLAP CLAP
OF COURSE!
AFTER WE'RE DONE WITH THE SNACKS, IT'S PLAYTIME!

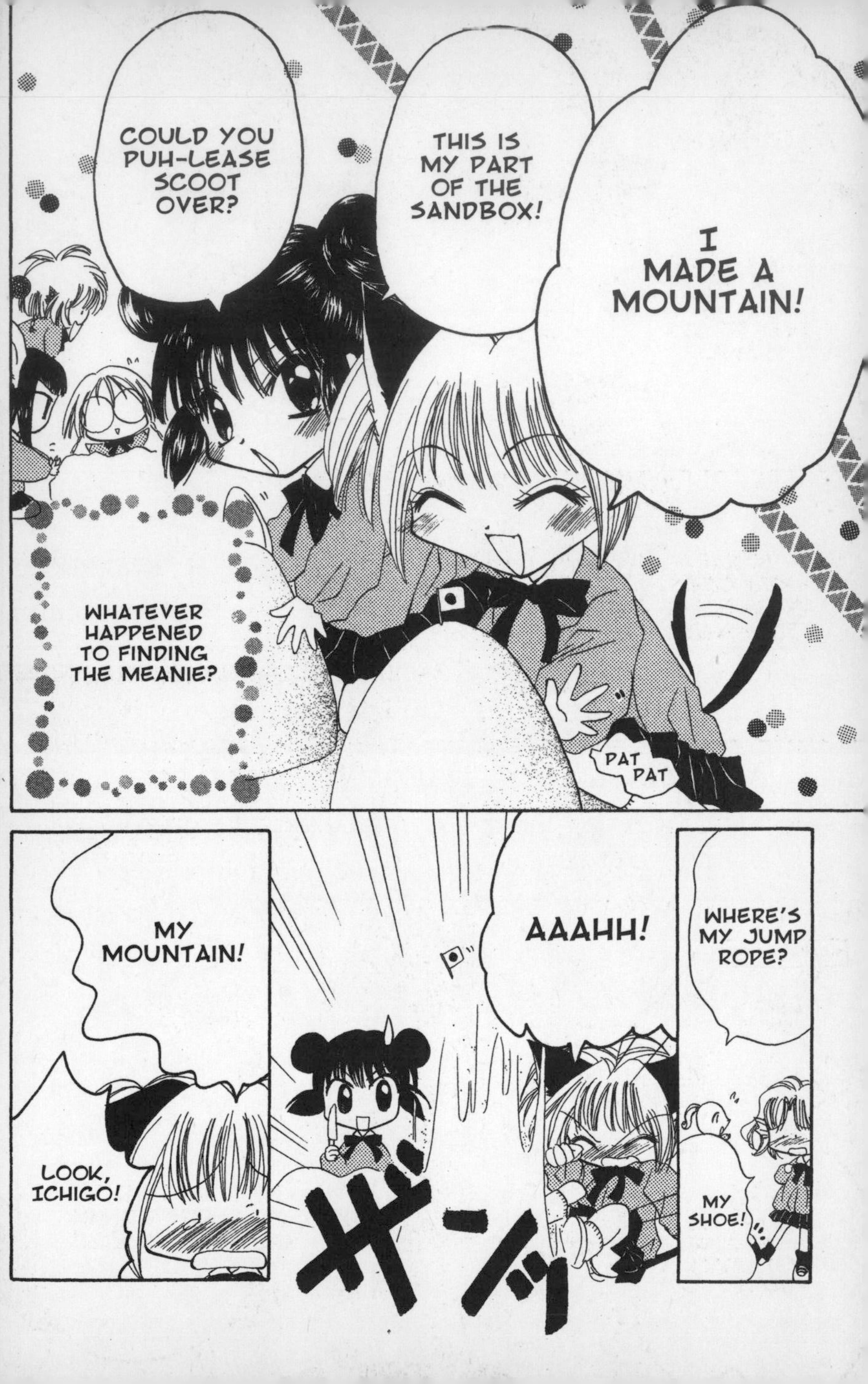
I MADE A MOUNTAIN!
THIS IS MY PART OF THE SANDBOX!
COULD YOU PUH-LEASE SCOOT OVER?
PAT PAT
WHATEVER HAPPENED TO FINDING THE MEANIE?
WHERE'S MY JUMP ROPE?
MY SHOE!
AAAHH!
ザーッ
MY MOUNTAIN!
LOOK, ICHIGO!

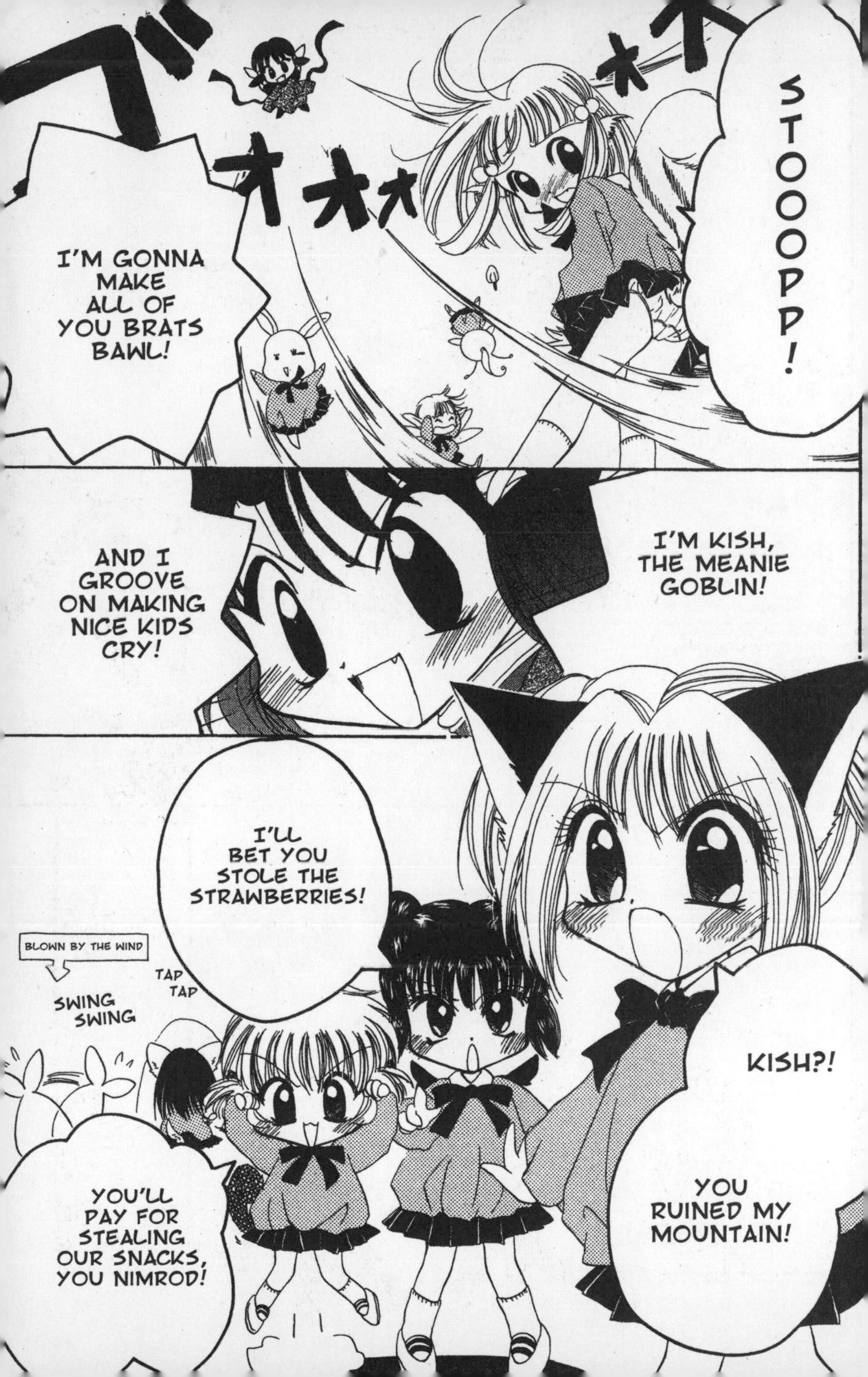
STOOOPP!
I'M GONNA MAKE ALL OF YOU BRATS BAWL!
I'M KISH, THE MEANIE GOBLIN!
AND I GROOVE ON MAKING NICE KIDS CRY!
KISH?!
YOU RUINED MY MOUNTAIN!
I'LL BET YOU STOLE THE STRAWBERRIES!
TAP TAP
BLOWN BY THE WIND
SWING SWING
YOU'LL PAY FOR STEALING OUR SNACKS, YOU NIMROD!

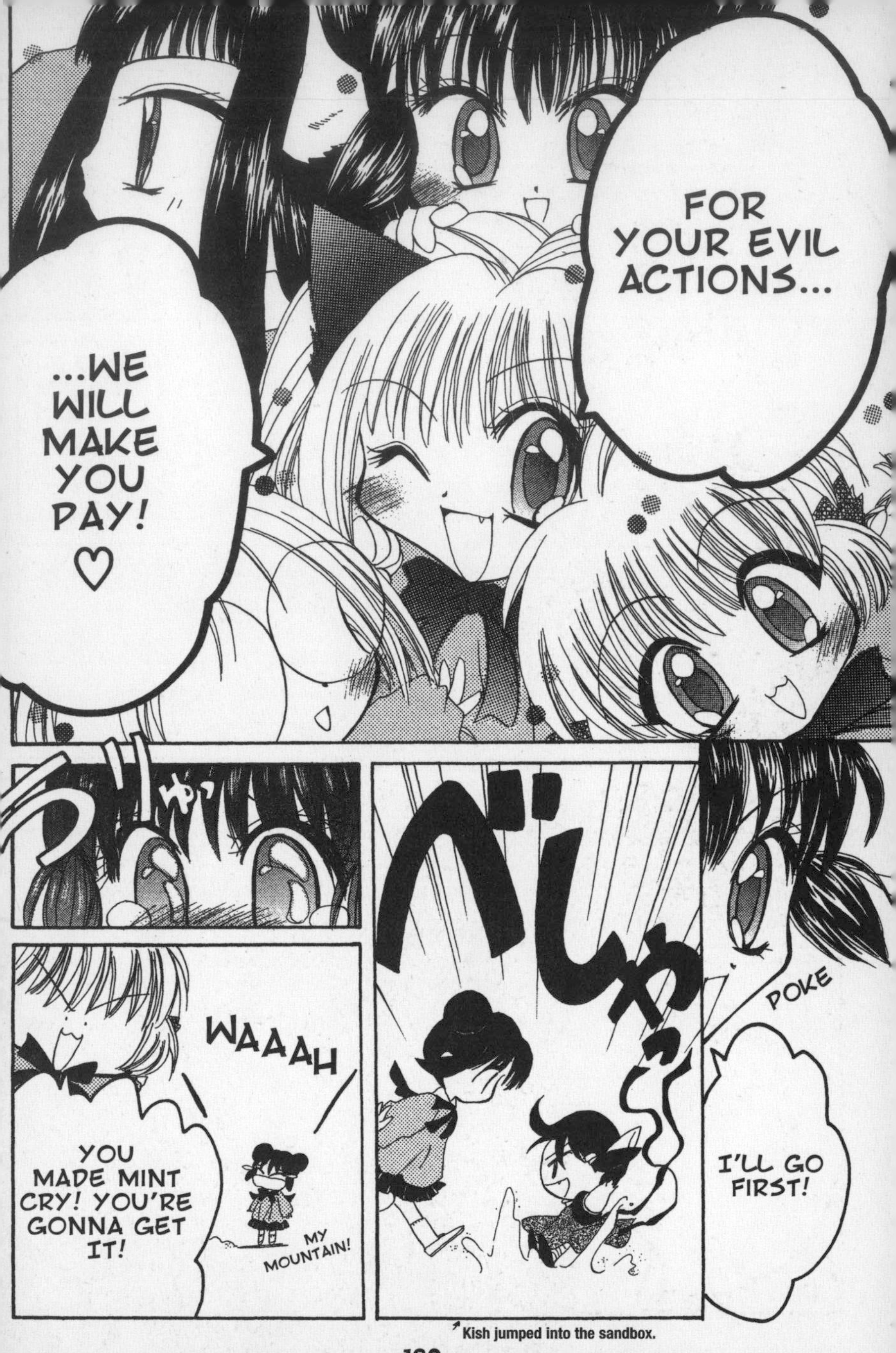
FOR YOUR EVIL ACTIONS...
...WE WILL MAKE YOU PAY! ♡
POKE
I'LL GO FIRST!
WAAAH
YOU MADE MINT CRY! YOU'RE GONNA GET IT!
MY MOUNTAIN!
Kish jumped into the sandbox.

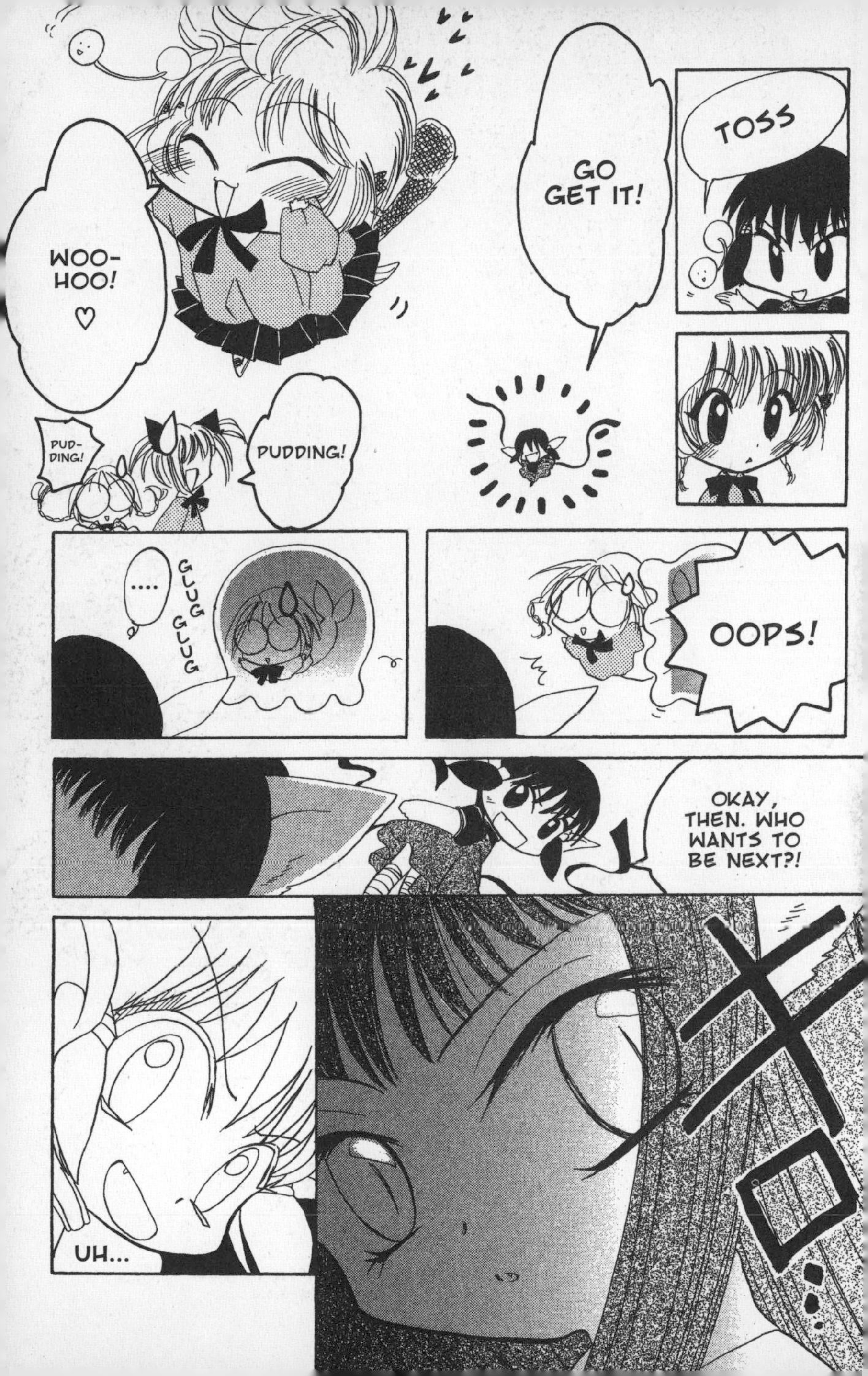

TOSS
GO GET IT!
WOO-HOO! ♡
PUDDING!
PUD-DING!
OOPS!
....
GLUG GLUG GLUG
OKAY, THEN. WHO WANTS TO BE NEXT?!
UH...

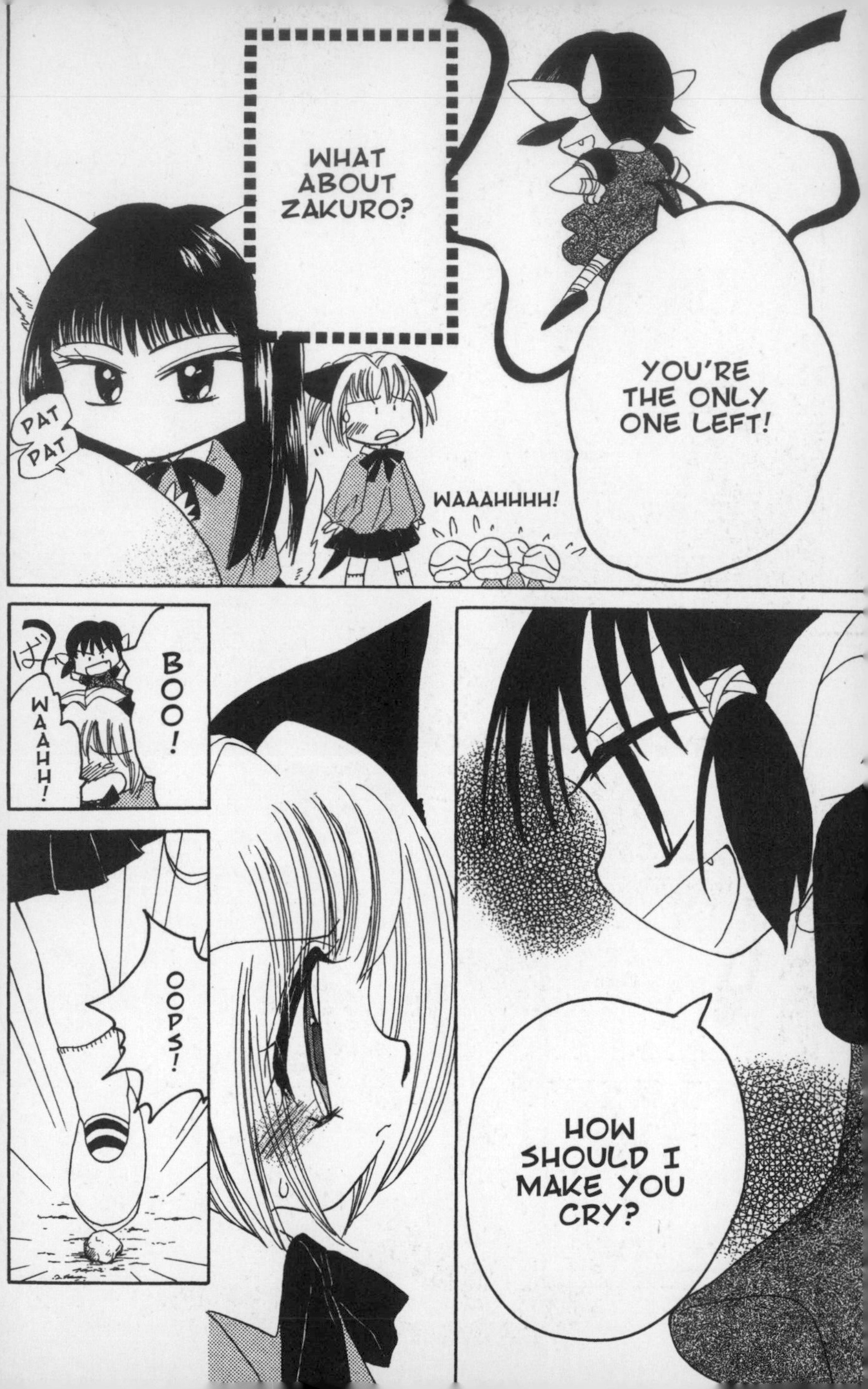
YOU'RE THE ONLY ONE LEFT!
WHAT ABOUT ZAKURO?
WAAAHHHH!
PAT PAT
HOW SHOULD I MAKE YOU CRY?
BOO!
WAAHH!
OOPS!

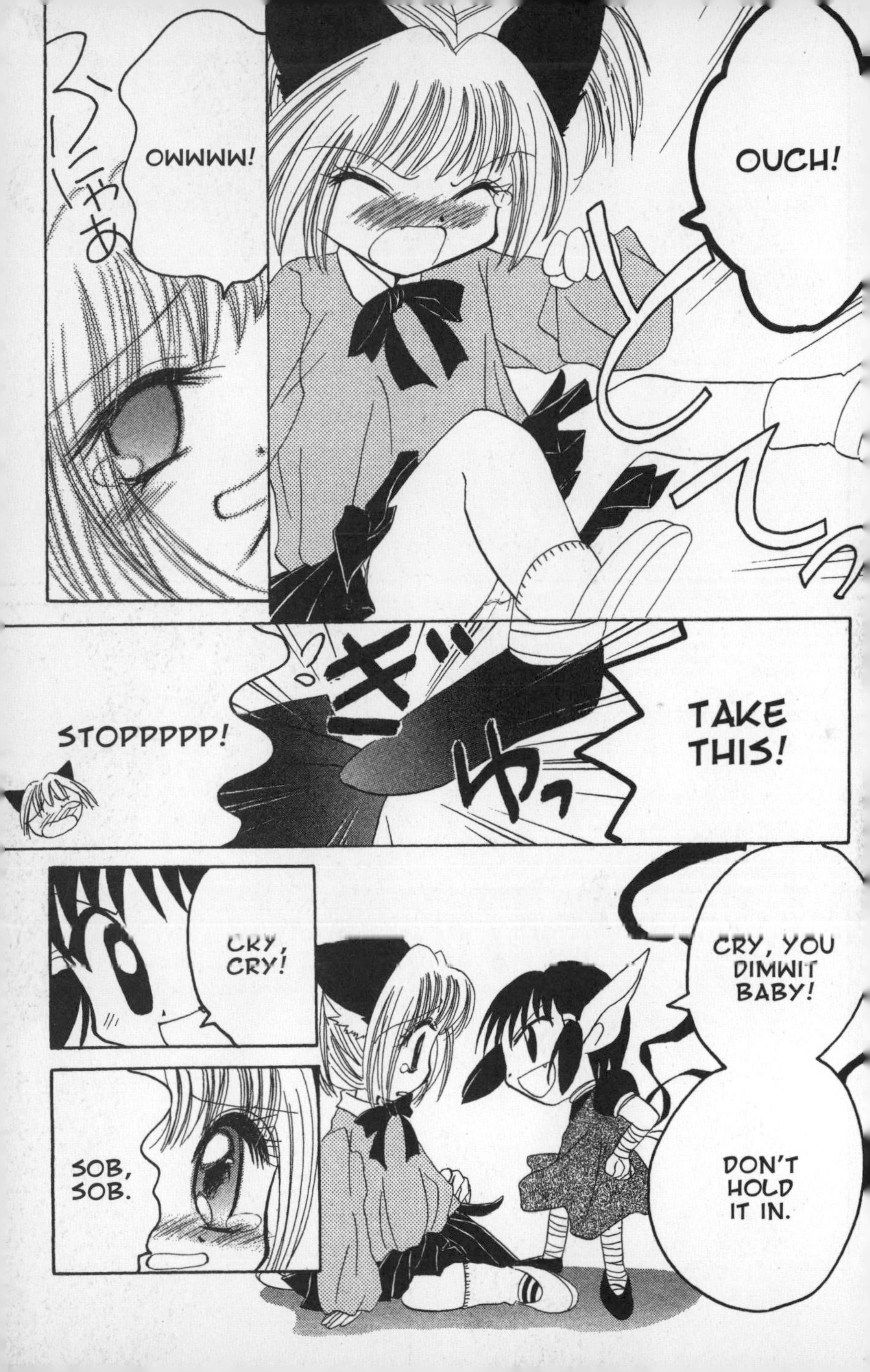
OUCH!
OWWWW!
TAKE THIS!
STOPPPPP!
CRY, YOU DIMWIT BABY!
DON'T HOLD IT IN.
CRY, CRY!
SOB, SOB.

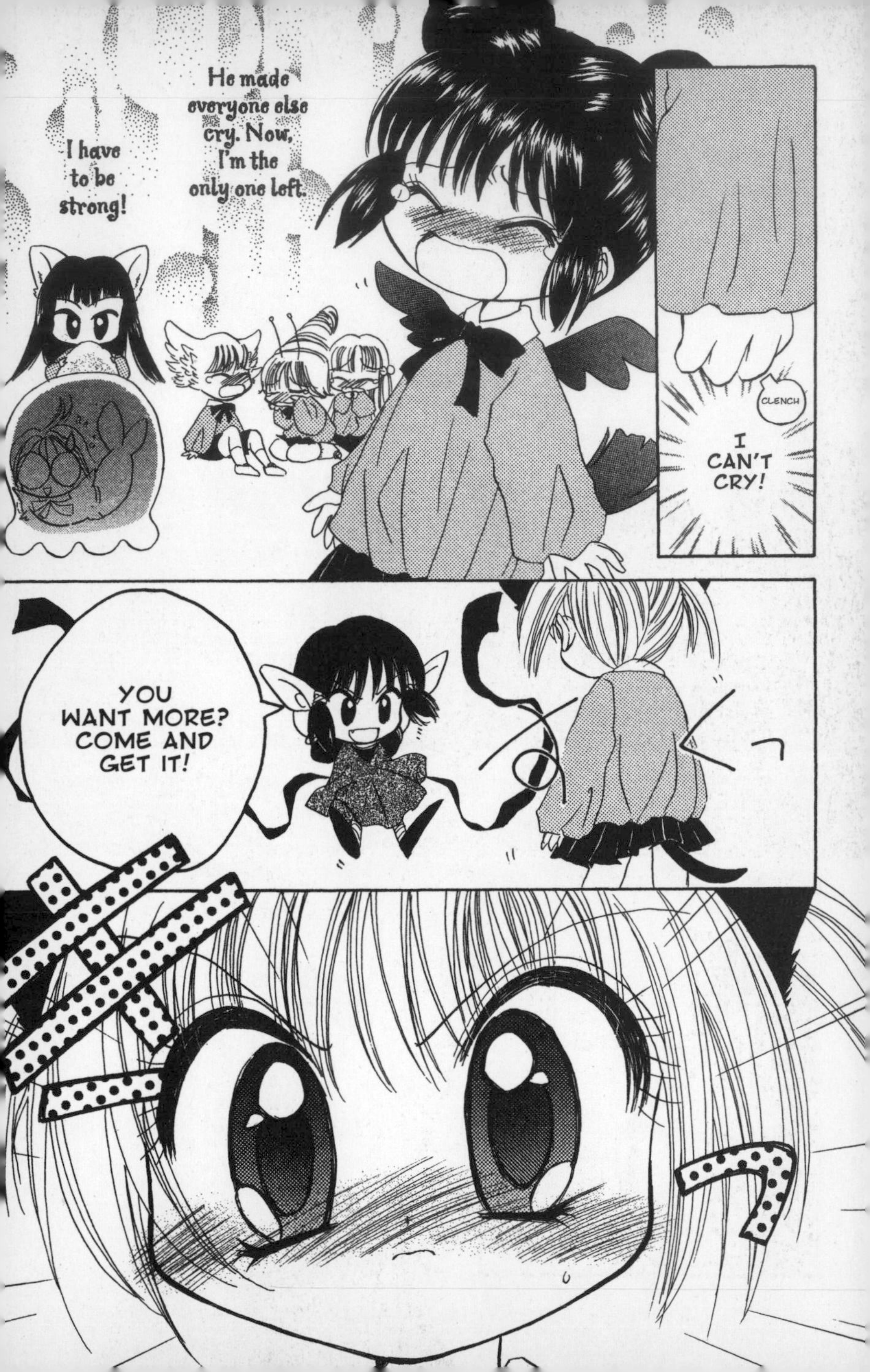
CLENCH
I CAN'T CRY!
He made everyone else cry. Now, I'm the only one left.
I have to be strong!
YOU WANT MORE? COME AND GET IT!

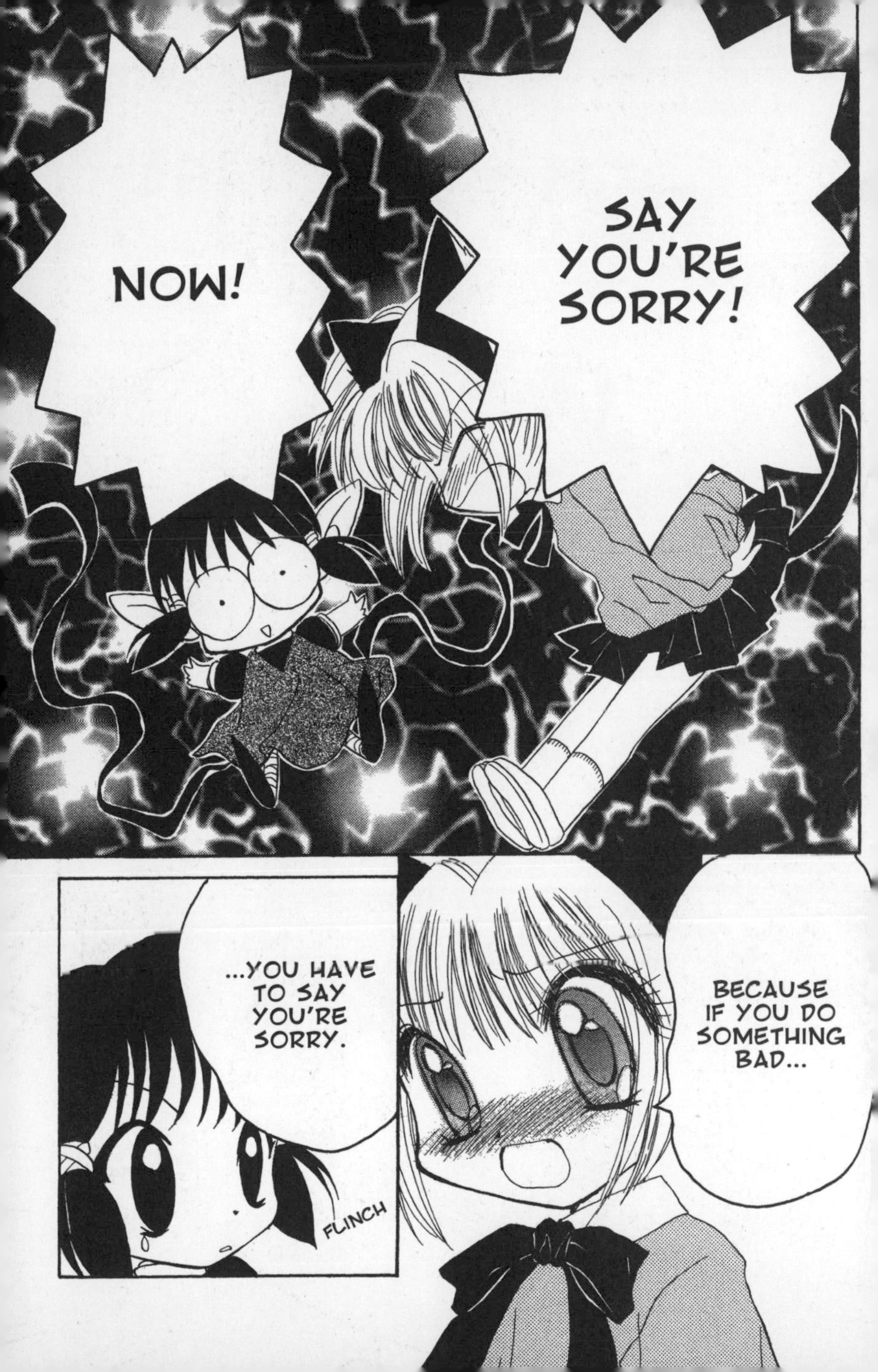
SAY YOU'RE SORRY!
NOW!
BECAUSE IF YOU DO SOMETHING BAD...
...YOU HAVE TO SAY YOU'RE SORRY.
FLINCH

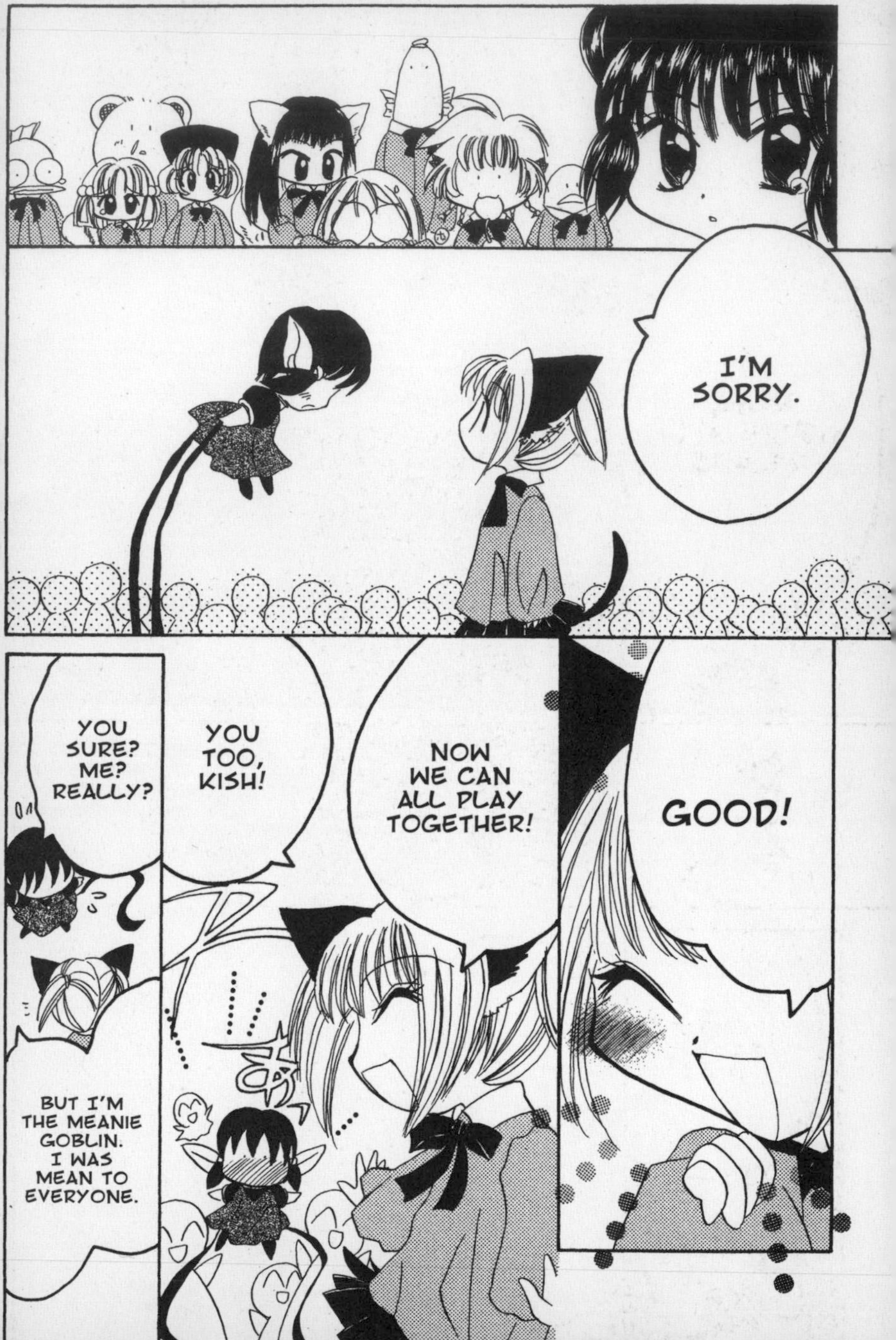
I'M SORRY.
GOOD!
NOW WE CAN ALL PLAY TOGETHER!
YOU TOO, KISH!
YOU SURE? ME? REALLY?
BUT I'M THE MEANIE GOBLIN. I WAS MEAN TO EVERYONE.

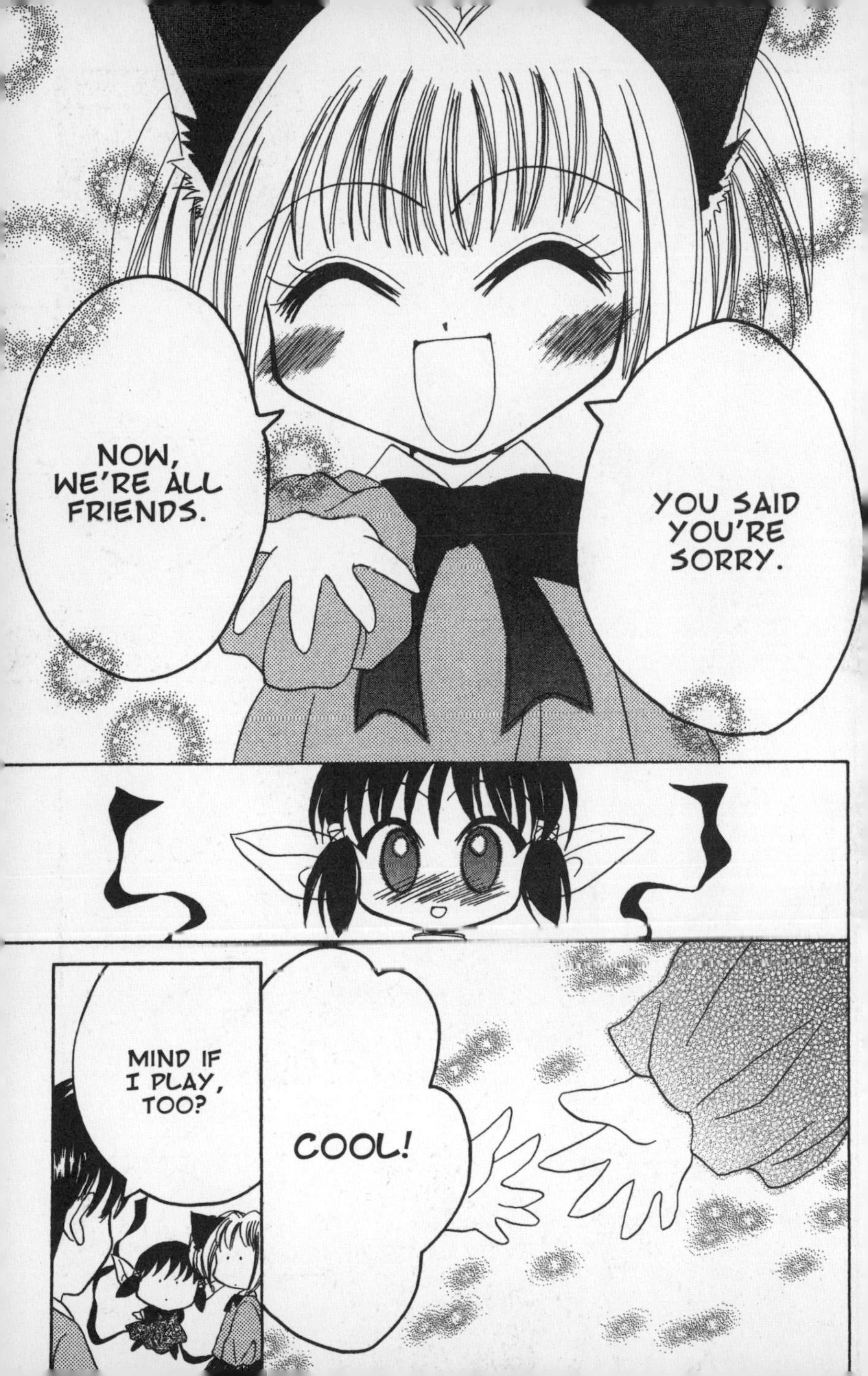
YOU SAID YOU'RE SORRY.
NOW, WE'RE ALL FRIENDS.
COOL!
MIND IF I PLAY, TOO?

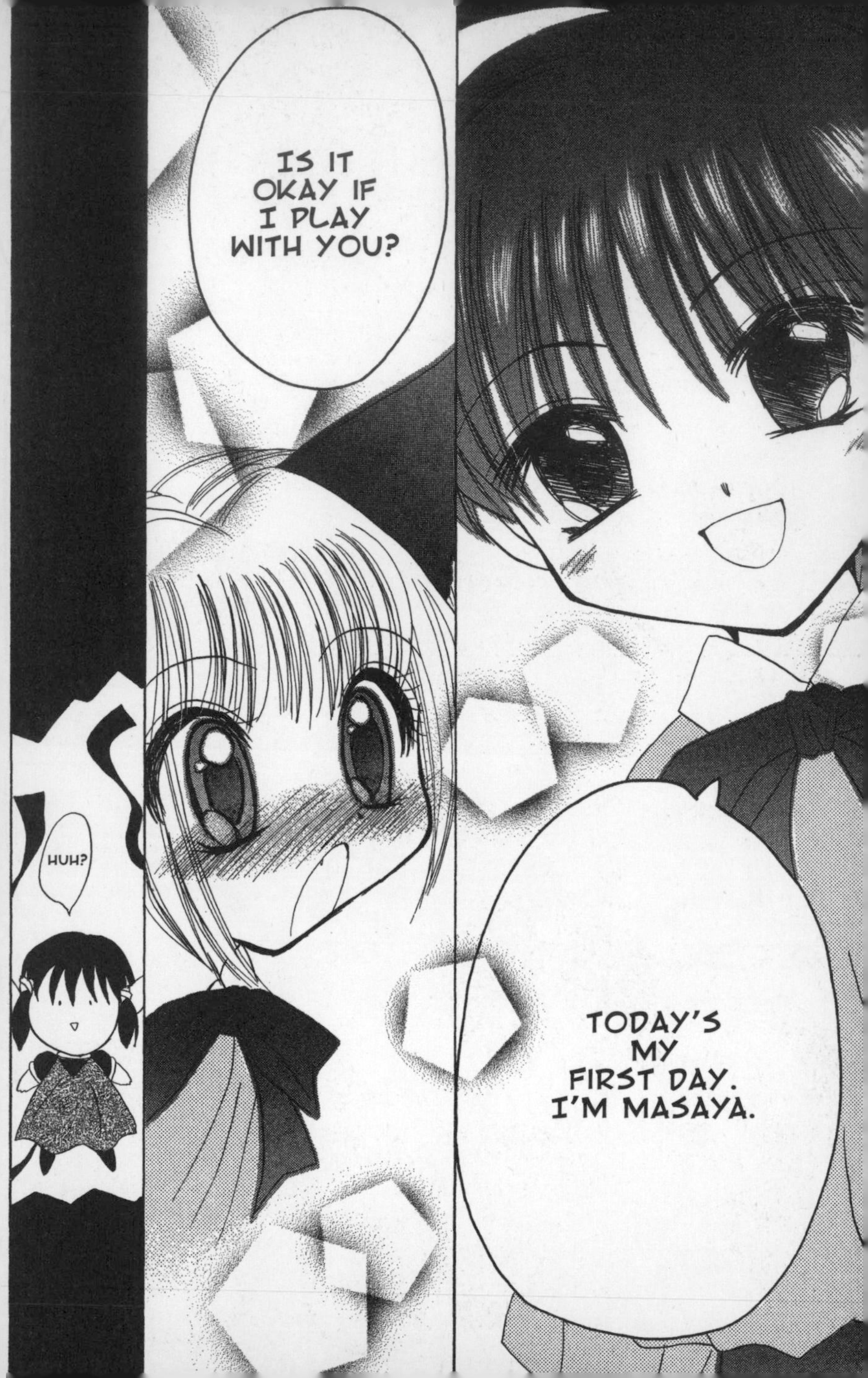
TODAY'S MY FIRST DAY. I'M MASAYA.
IS IT OKAY IF I PLAY WITH YOU?
HUH?

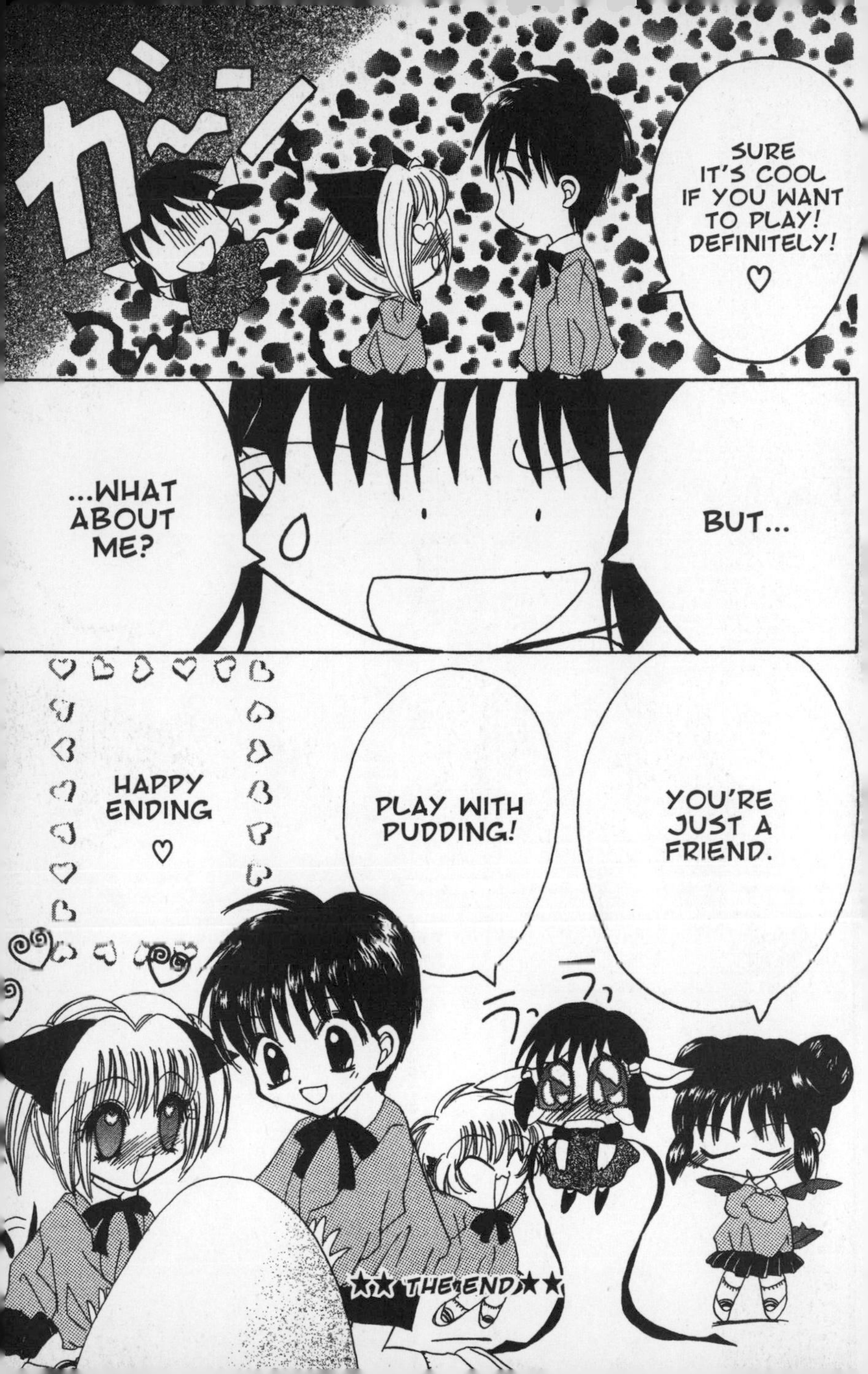
ガ～ン
SURE IT'S COOL IF YOU WANT TO PLAY! DEFINITELY! ♡
BUT...
...WHAT ABOUT ME?
YOU'RE JUST A FRIEND.
PLAY WITH PUDDING!
HAPPY ENDING ♡
★★ THE END ★★

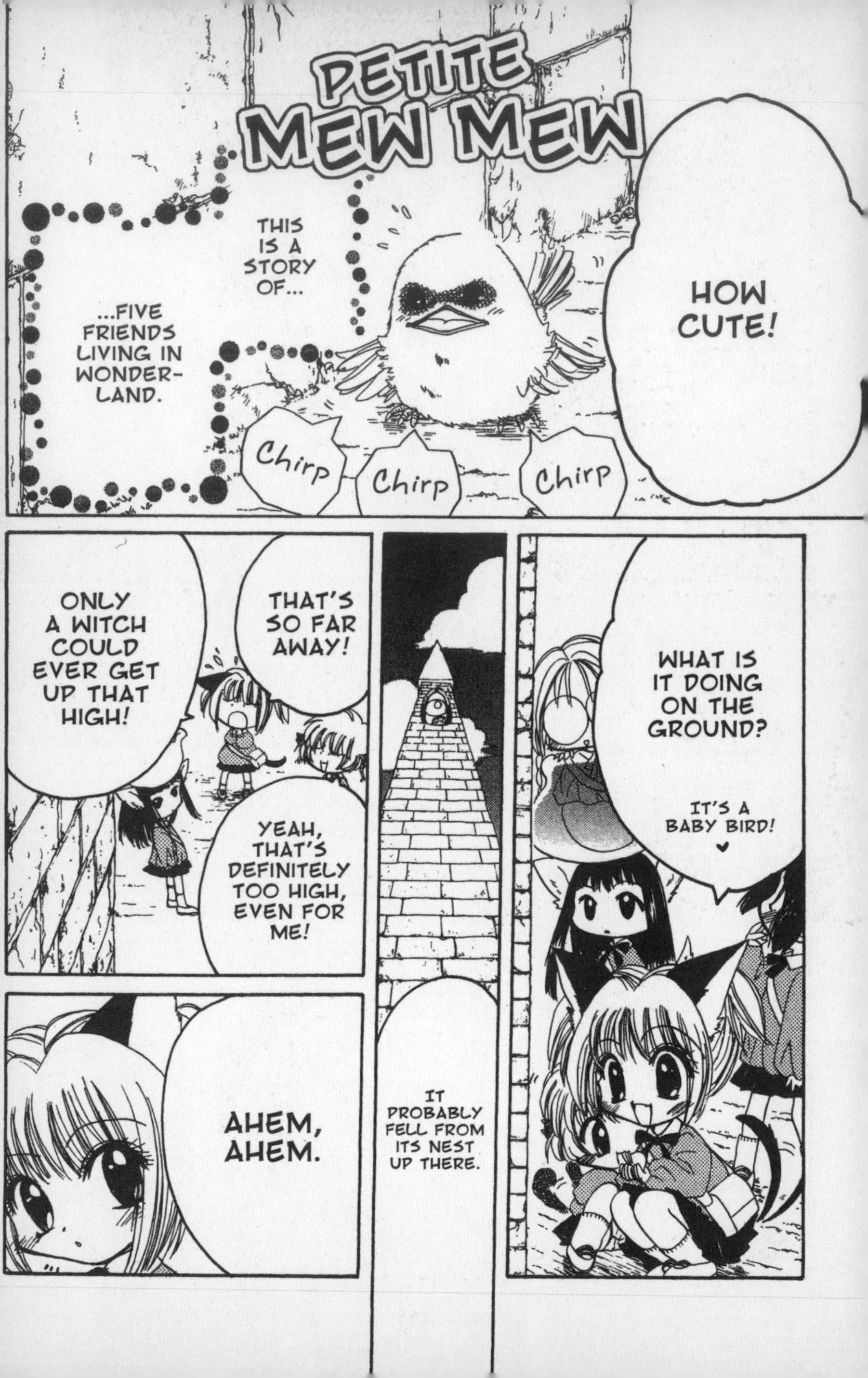
PETITE MEW MEW
HOW CUTE!
THIS IS A STORY OF...
...FIVE FRIENDS LIVING IN WONDERLAND.
Chirp
Chirp
Chirp
WHAT IS IT DOING ON THE GROUND?
IT'S A BABY BIRD! ♥
IT PROBABLY FELL FROM ITS NEST UP THERE.
THAT'S SO FAR AWAY!
ONLY A WITCH COULD EVER GET UP THAT HIGH!
YEAH, THAT'S DEFINITELY TOO HIGH, EVEN FOR ME!
AHEM, AHEM.

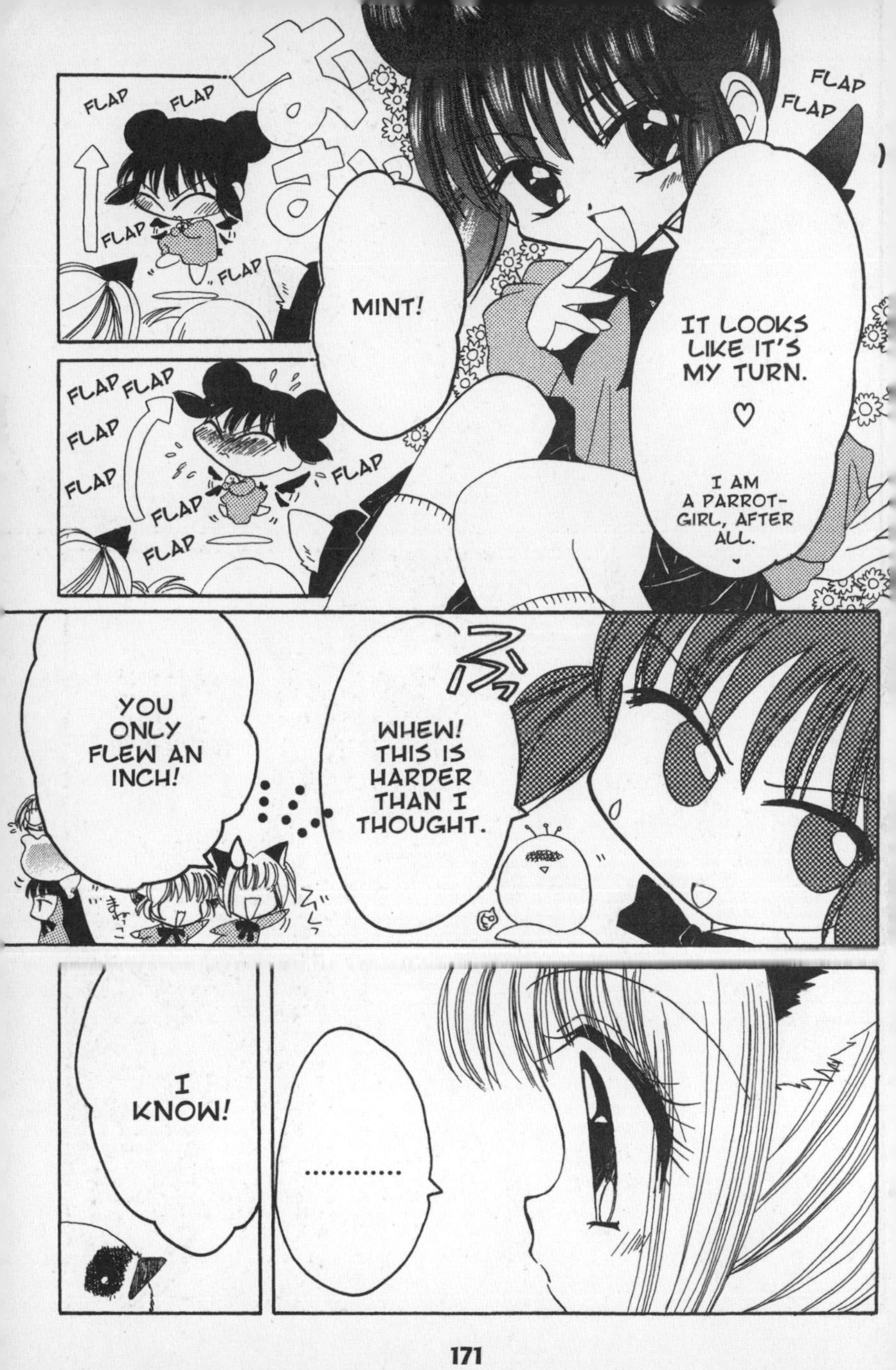
FLAP
FLAP
IT LOOKS LIKE IT'S MY TURN.
♡
I AM A PARROT-GIRL, AFTER ALL.
MINT!
FLAP
FLAP
FLAP
FLAP
FLAP FLAP
FLAP
FLAP
FLAP
FLAP
FLAP
WHEW! THIS IS HARDER THAN I THOUGHT.
YOU ONLY FLEW AN INCH!
....
I KNOW!

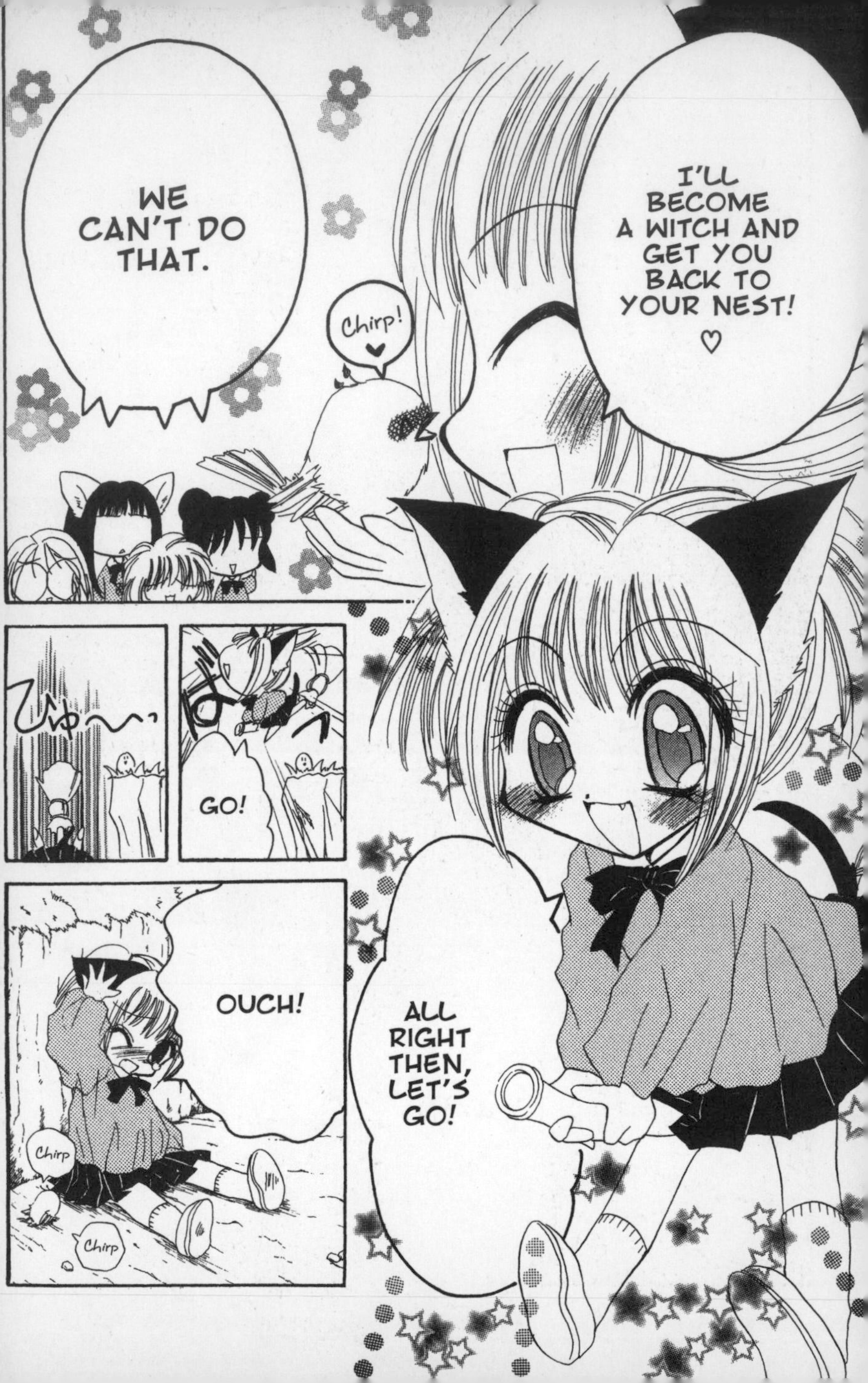
I'LL BECOME A WITCH AND GET YOU BACK TO YOUR NEST! ♡
Chirp!
WE CAN'T DO THAT.
ALL RIGHT THEN, LET'S GO!
GO!
ひゅ〜っ
OUCH!
Chirp
Chirp

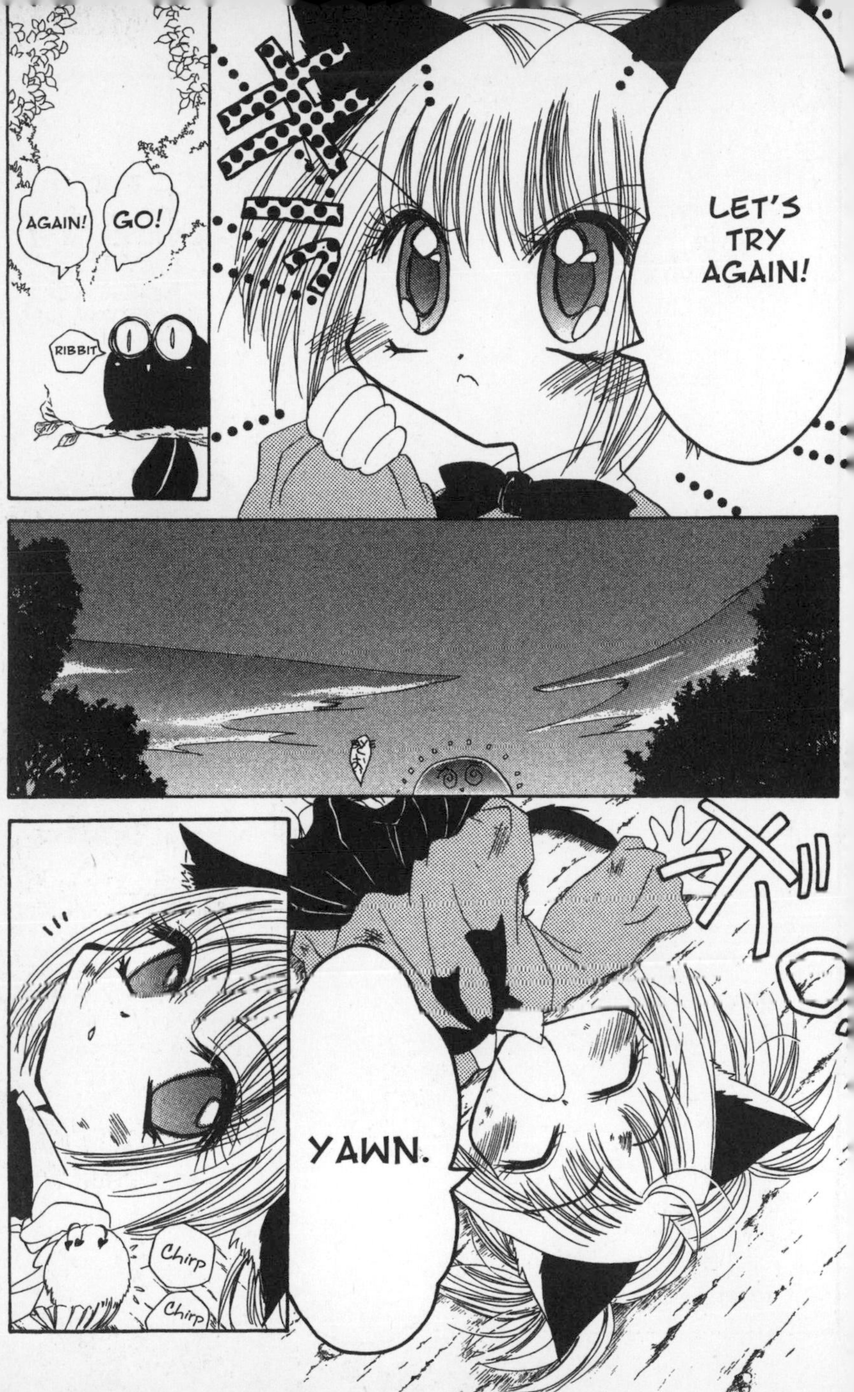
LET'S TRY AGAIN!
GO!
AGAIN!
RIBBIT
YAWN.
Chirp
Chirp

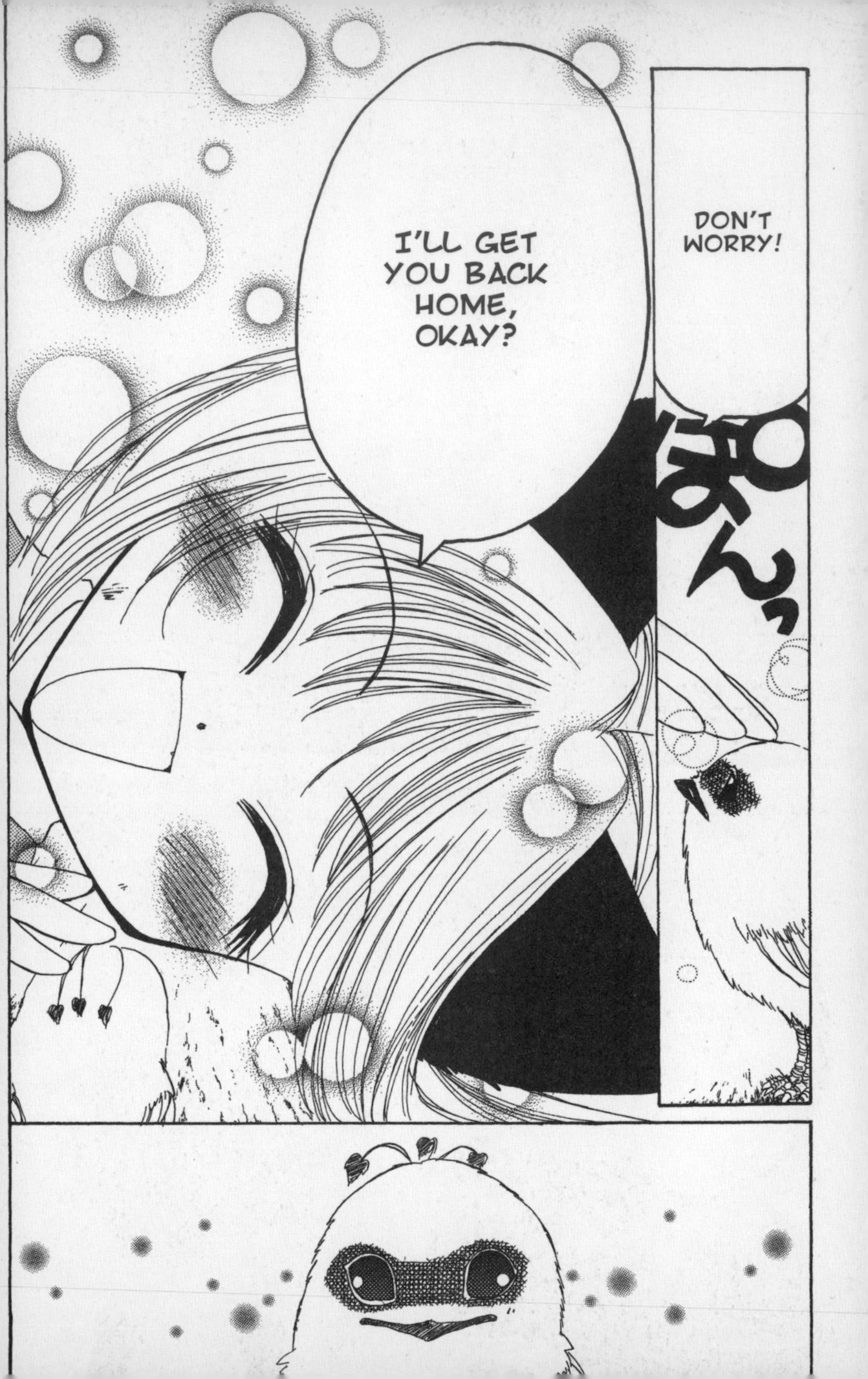
DON'T WORRY!
ぽんっ
I'LL GET YOU BACK HOME, OKAY?

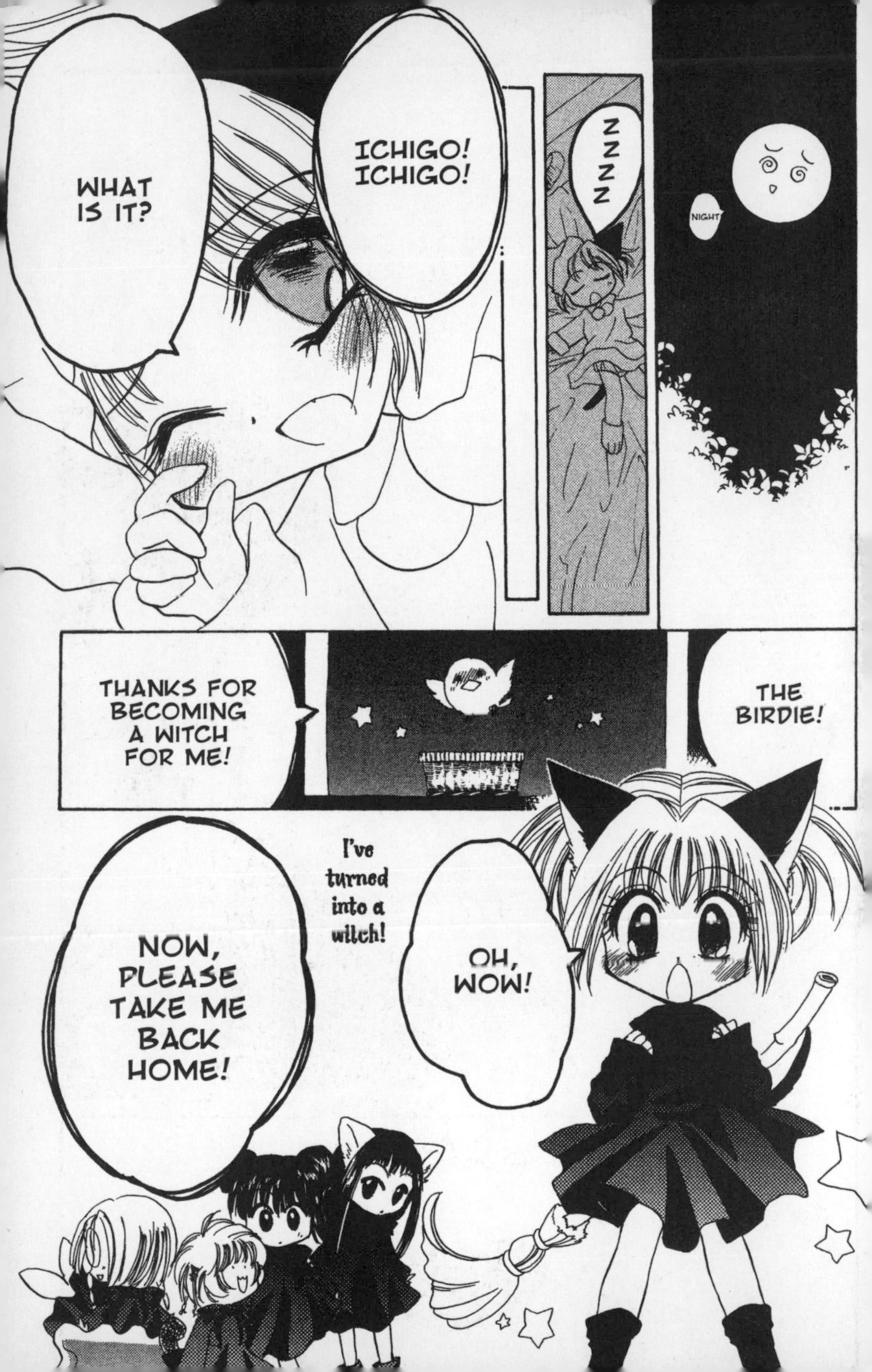
NIGHT
ZZZZ
ICHIGO! ICHIGO!
WHAT IS IT?
THE BIRDIE!
THANKS FOR BECOMING A WITCH FOR ME!
OH, WOW!
I've turned into a witch!
NOW, PLEASE TAKE ME BACK HOME!

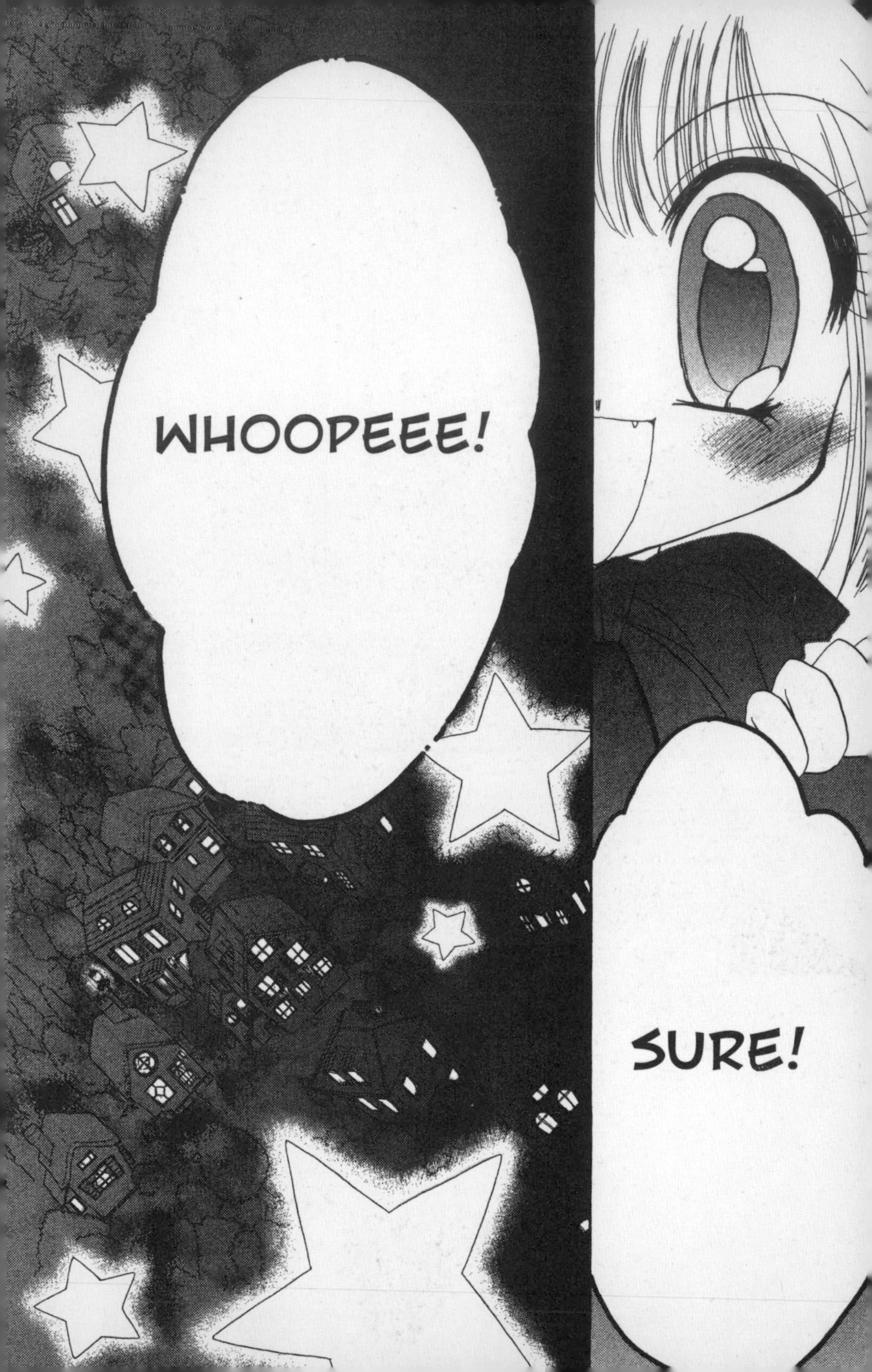
SURE!
WHOOPEEE!

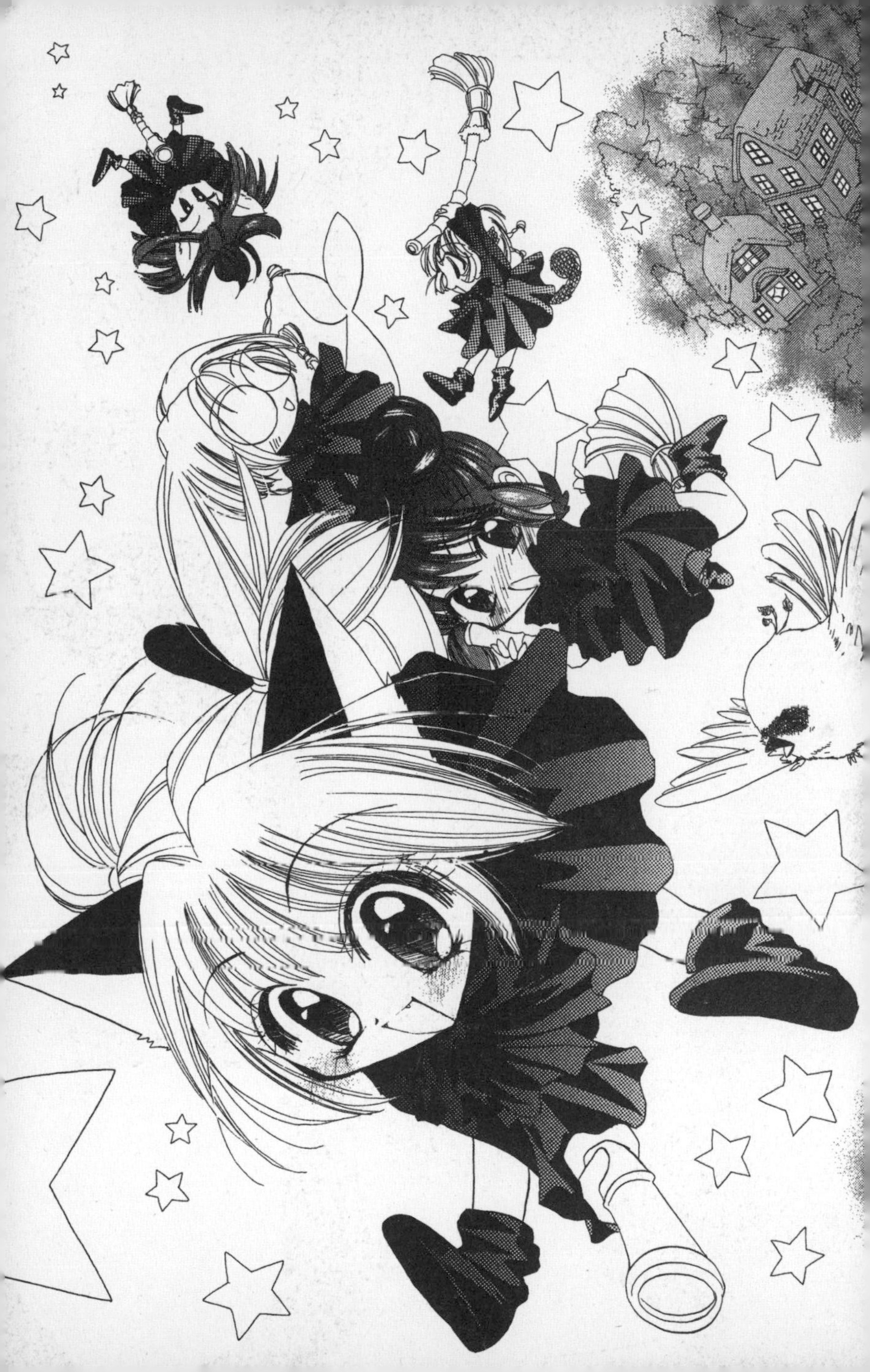

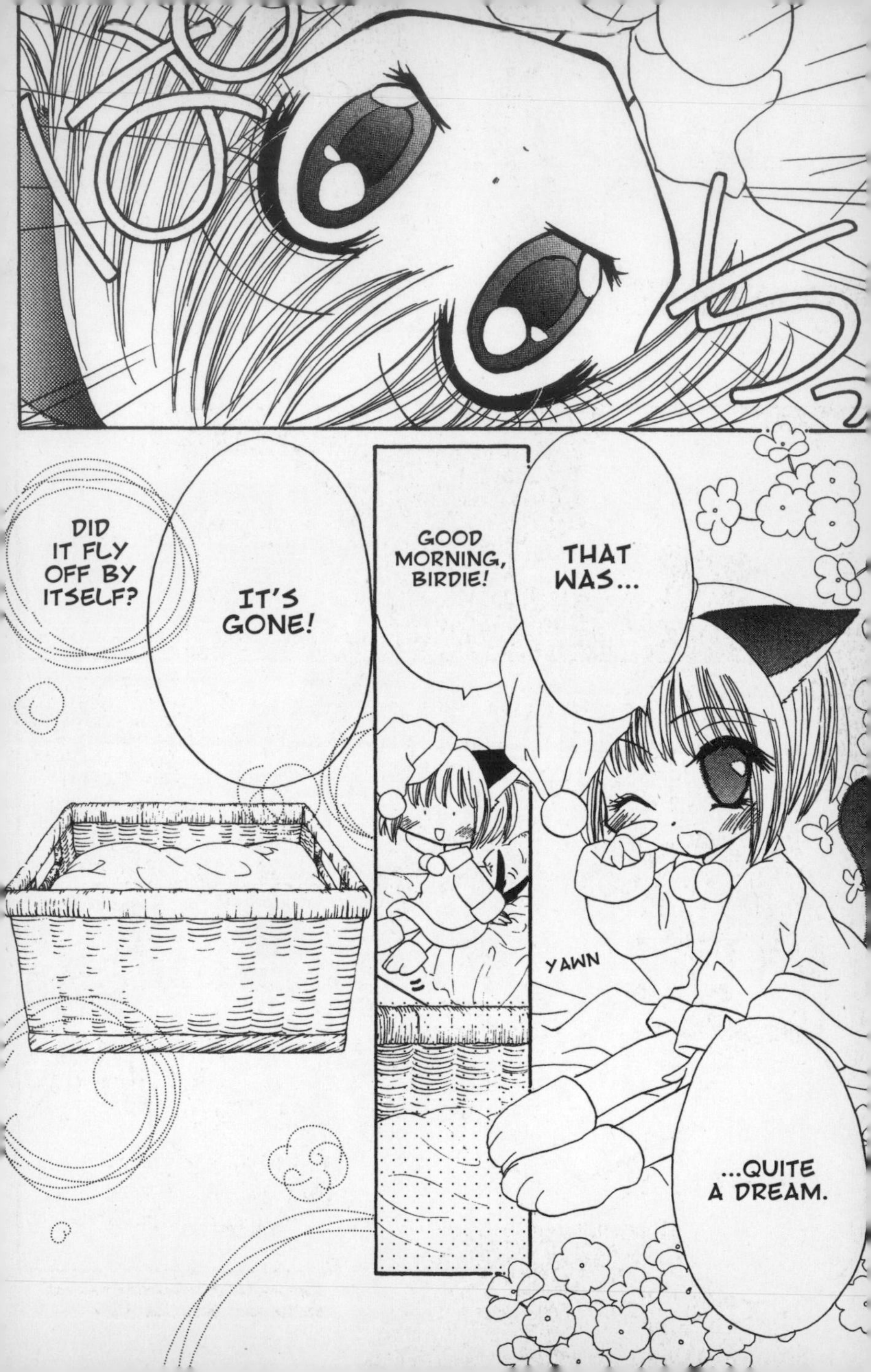
THAT WAS...
YAWN
...QUITE A DREAM.
GOOD MORNING, BIRDIE!
IT'S GONE!
DID IT FLY OFF BY ITSELF?

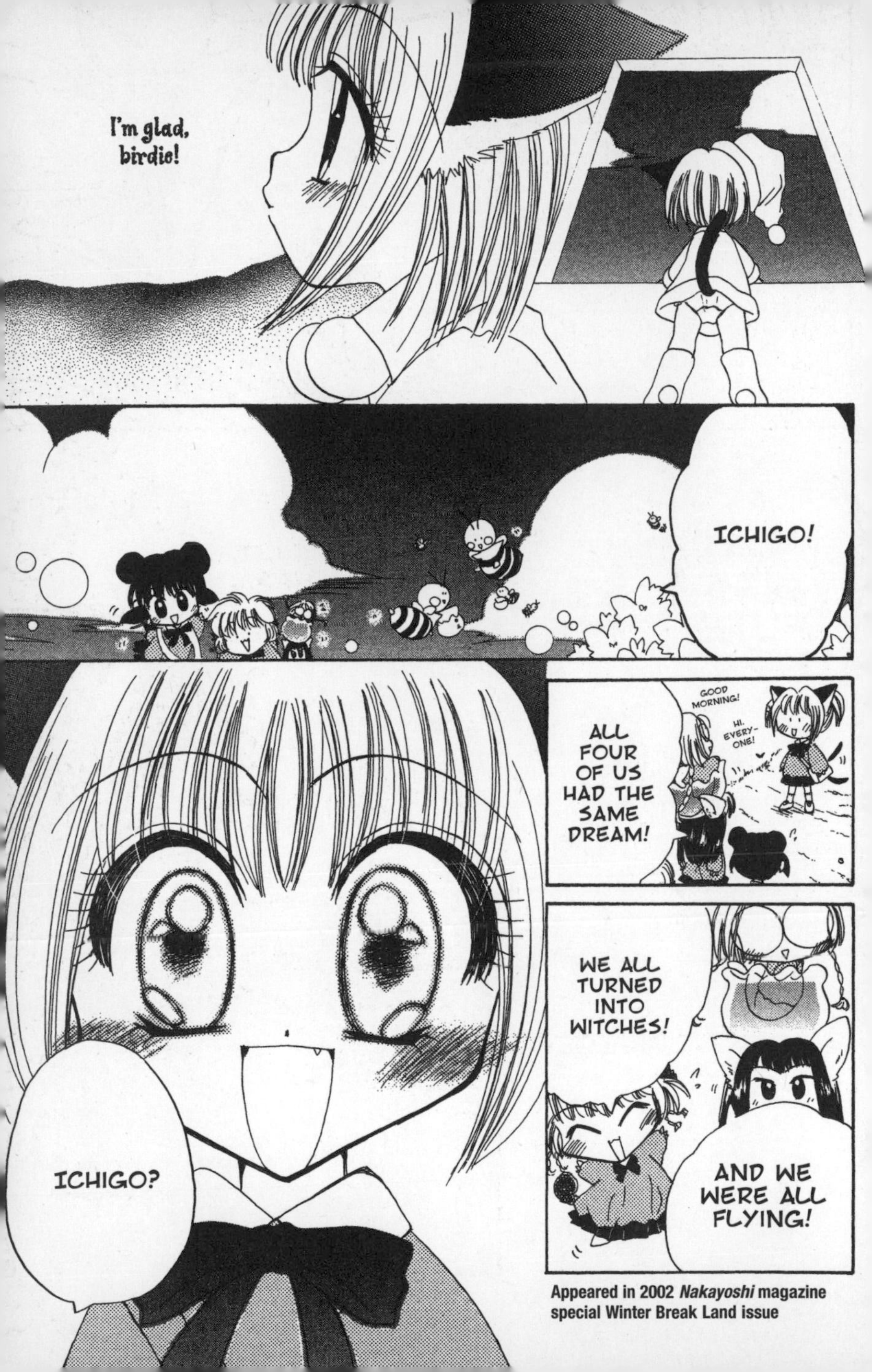
I'm glad, birdie!
ICHIGO!
GOOD MORNING!
HI, EVERY-ONE!
ALL FOUR OF US HAD THE SAME DREAM!
WE ALL TURNED INTO WITCHES!
AND WE WERE ALL FLYING!
ICHIGO?

Appeared in 2002 *Nakayoshi* magazine special Winter Break Land issue

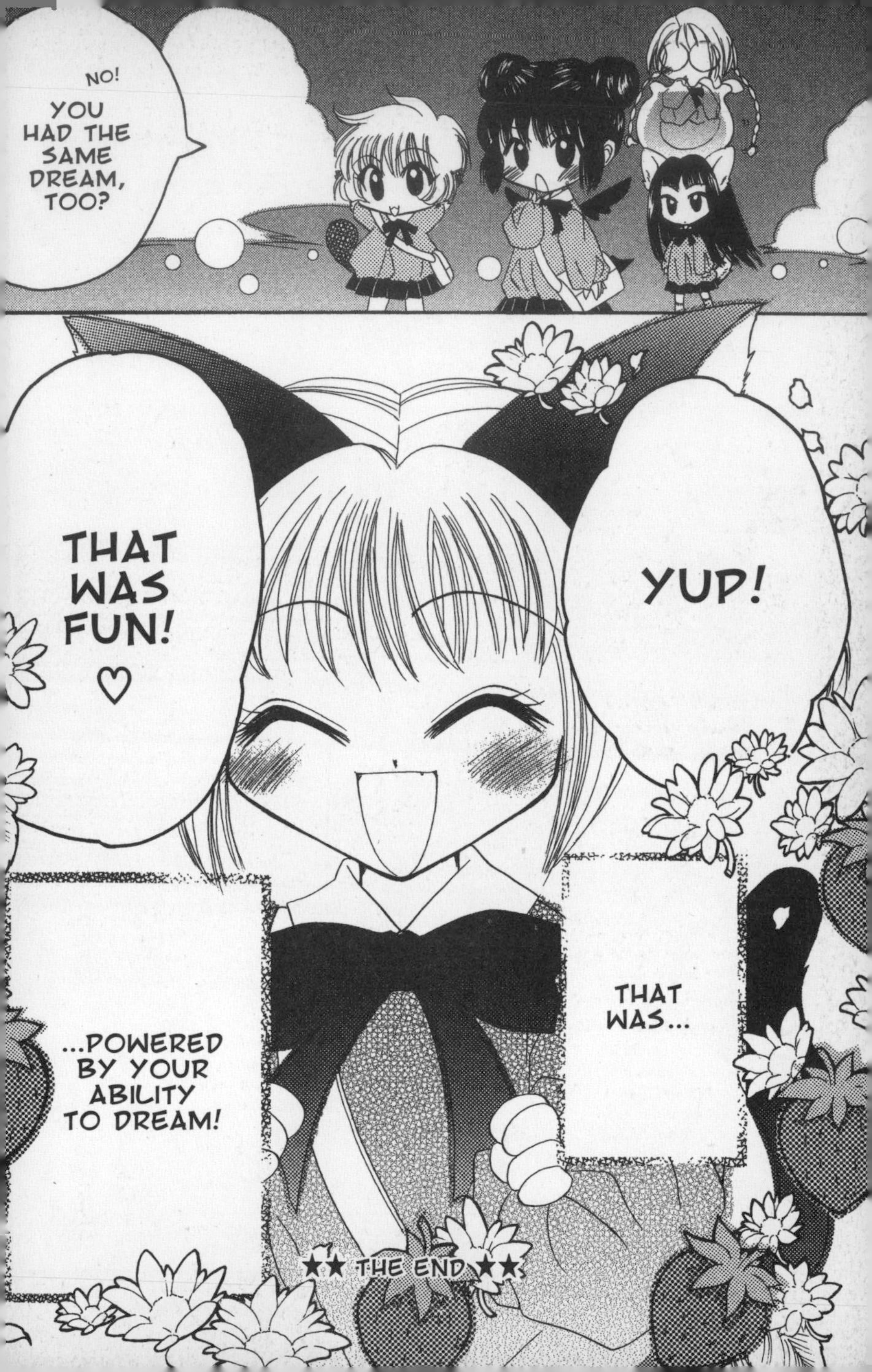
NO! YOU HAD THE SAME DREAM, TOO?
YUP!
THAT WAS FUN! ♡
THAT WAS...
...POWERED BY YOUR ABILITY TO DREAM!
★★ THE END ★★

Tokyo Mew Mew Special

In the role of Pudding Fong, Hisayo Mochizuki!! It's time to play Ukkiikii!!

In the role of Ichigo Momomiya Saki Nakajima meow. We're all doing our best meow! Blazing the way for everyone's future meow.

Got this from Aoyama.

Presenting Yumi Kakazu playing the role of Mint Aizawa. I'm studying imitations in the studio right now.

Wh...Wh...Wh...Whatcha' sayin'?! Sounds just like it, huh?

Presenting Kumi Sakuma playing the role of Lettuce Midorikawa. Lettuce wants some romance too by Sakuma!

Lettuce

Presenting Zakuro Fujiwara in the roles of Zakuro Fujiwara and Masha. Friends are sure nice to have!

In the role of Keiichiro Akasaka played by Hikaru Mitotsukawa.

I'll be your companion anytime!

Presenting Megumi Ogata in the role of Masaya Aoyama. "Because you're my cat..." Jingle it!! Ching ching!

In the role of Ryou Shirogane, Koichi Tohchika. Do you like money? Me? I have tons. Come play with me at Café Mew Mew. Now serving cold items. -Owner

In the role of Shintaro Momomiya (Dad), presents Katsuyuki Konishi.

"Sakura ♥ Whatcha' sayin'? ♥
"Shin-chan ♥ Whatcha' sayin'? ♥

In the role of Pie, Nobutoshi Kanna!! "You have a good spirit" "Next time your spirit..."

In the role of Tart— Kiyomi Arai. I go all out with practical jokes!! I love playing them!

"Let's metamorph together!!" Sakura Momomiya (mom) is Takako Honda.

SMOOCH

Daisuke Sakaguchi plays Kish! Ichigo's not paying attention to me, so I think I'll have to cheat here. Chimera Frog.

A SHORT NOTE TO OUR READERS FROM THE ANIME TOKYO MEW MEW REGULAR VOICE ACTORS. THANKS FOR YOUR SUPPORT!

Hello, it's me, Ikumi again.

Hola! It's been a while. Ikumi, here. At long last, Mew Mew is on its fifth volume! I'm really thrilled that all five Mew Mews have had their own cover now! This is only possible because you, the fans, have cheered the series on! Thank you!! I hope you keep supporting both the manga and the anime for a long time. (Although if this keeps going as well as it has been, I'm not sure what to do with the cover once it goes to the sixth volume...) While I was starting on the sixth page of this volume, there was a special project to have all the voice actors for Tokyo Mew Mew write out a comment for all the fans!! (See previous page.) We started on this before we got permission from the voice actors' agencies, so this ended up causing a little over a million headaches for many people. I'm really sorry! Please forgive me so we can all keep working together. Next time, I promise to get permission beforehand!

I wrote a little bonus manga about this on the last page. I hope you read this along with the bonus page!

Since we finally made it to Volume 5 of Tokyo Mew Mew...

You get a few more bonus pages!

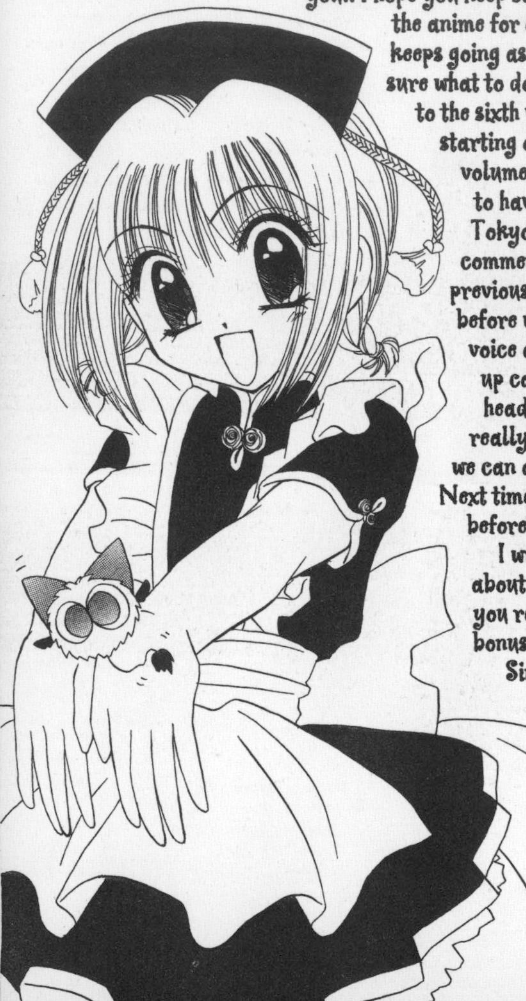

06-15-02

Mia Ikumi

Usagi no Tampopo

The rabbit's dandelion

That was the title of my favorite book when I was a kid. My elementary school library had a copy of it. I really enjoyed the artwork (back then of course, I was only looking at the pictures though). I don't remember the story, but whenever I was at a bookstore, I'd always look for that book in the children's section. (By the way, "Usagi no Tampopo" isn't the correct title of the book. For some reason, since I was in grade school, I always got the title wrong. Now I know I was wrong, but I still don't remember the real title... Maybe the picture on the right might remind someone of it.)

One day, I was at a bookstore with a friend, looking for this book. I was explaining to my friend about how much I used to love this book, so my bud said, "I want to read it," and bought the book for herself. I wanted a copy too, so I bought one for myself as well. For the first time in my life, I brought this book back home with me.

As I was looking over the book, I realized it was written in 1965. My edition was the 121st reprint! That's why the bookstore always had a copy in stock! I didn't know that this was such a popular bestseller!

Anyway, I finally read the book. I was totally touched. I loved the artwork in the book as a child. But as an adult, I was so moved by the story it made me cry.

I feel like the reason I couldn't forget the book and the reason why I didn't buy it for a long time was because it really made such an important impression in my memory. I was really amazed. If you ever come across this book, please read it. It will brighten your day. I hope my friend enjoyed it, too...

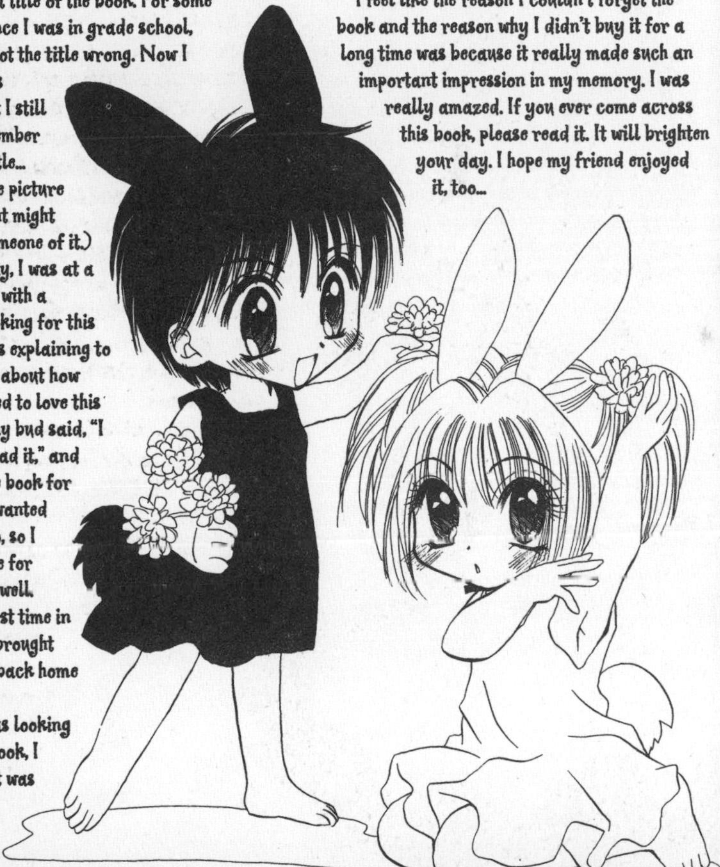

Afterward

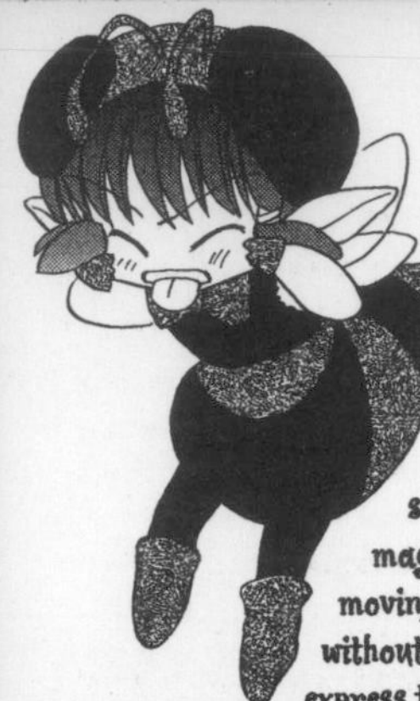

I'm amazed by the power of the human voice. The artwork comes alive, and becomes that much more impressive when it is given a corresponding voice. I was able to observe the recording of the pilot episode of the Tokyo Mew Mew anime. I was so moved. The next day, I was working on the manuscript, when a strange thing happened...

Suddenly, all my characters sounded just like the actors, and started to move around on their own!! It was like someone cast a magic spell... Well, okay, okay, so the artwork didn't exactly start moving around on its own. It's not as if the pen was moving around without my help, either (though this is kind of obvious...). I just wanted to express that it really made a difference. I can't really explain it well, but it's almost as if I could hear the characters saying their lines. (One of the voice actors asked me how it was different, and I couldn't explain to him, either). It's almost as if the characters were alive. As I would write the lines, I would think things like, "This person wouldn't talk like this." I would do the same thing with facial expressions and gestures, too. It's almost as if I wasn't coming up with the ideas, but just trying to depict what I heard and saw into artwork. It didn't make my work any easier, but I was really glad I had this experience. I'm really glad that, by working on Tokyo Mew Mew, I was able to experience this strange phenomenon.

Since this project has brought many wonderful memories to my life, I have to keep working hard! I'll always keep working harder and harder and harder. That's all I can say for now!

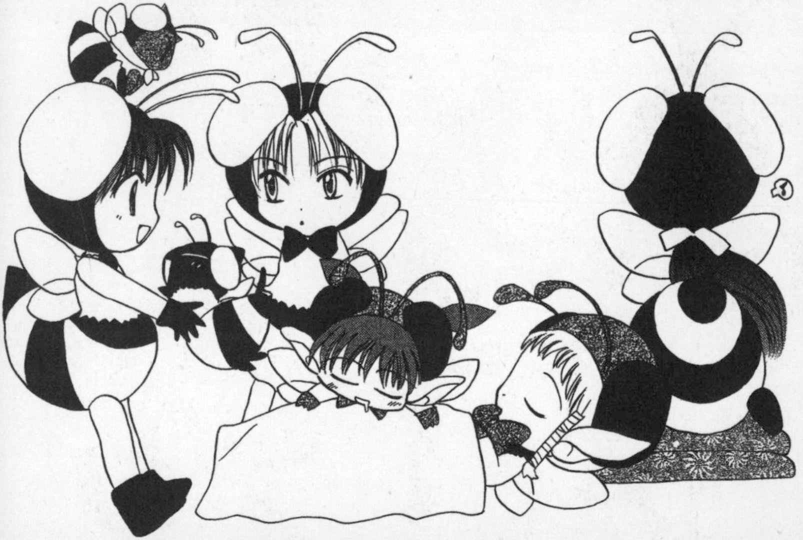

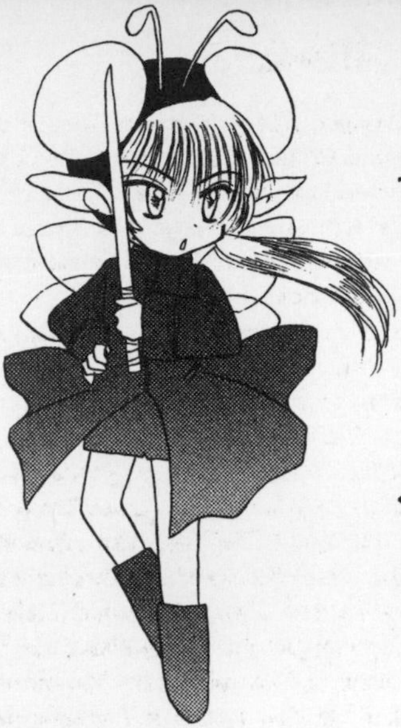

Finally...
To everyone who has helped me with this work...
To everyone involved with this project...
To everyone who has ever read this series...
I greatly appreciate your support!!

I will keep working hard!
I will become a stronger person!
And I will always keep going, no matter what!!

06-18-02
Mia Ikumi

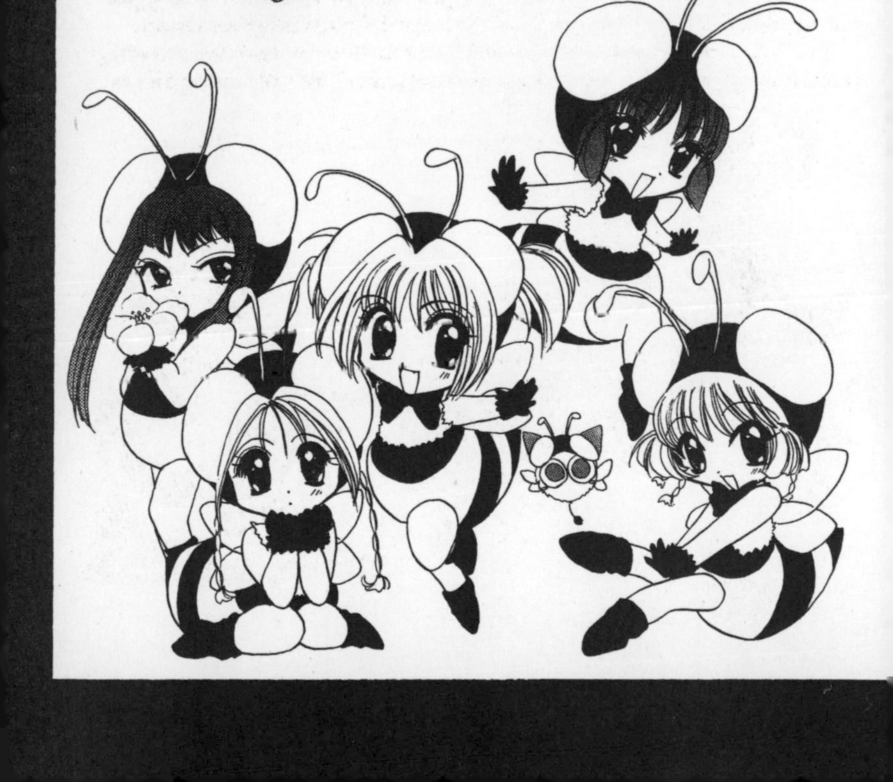

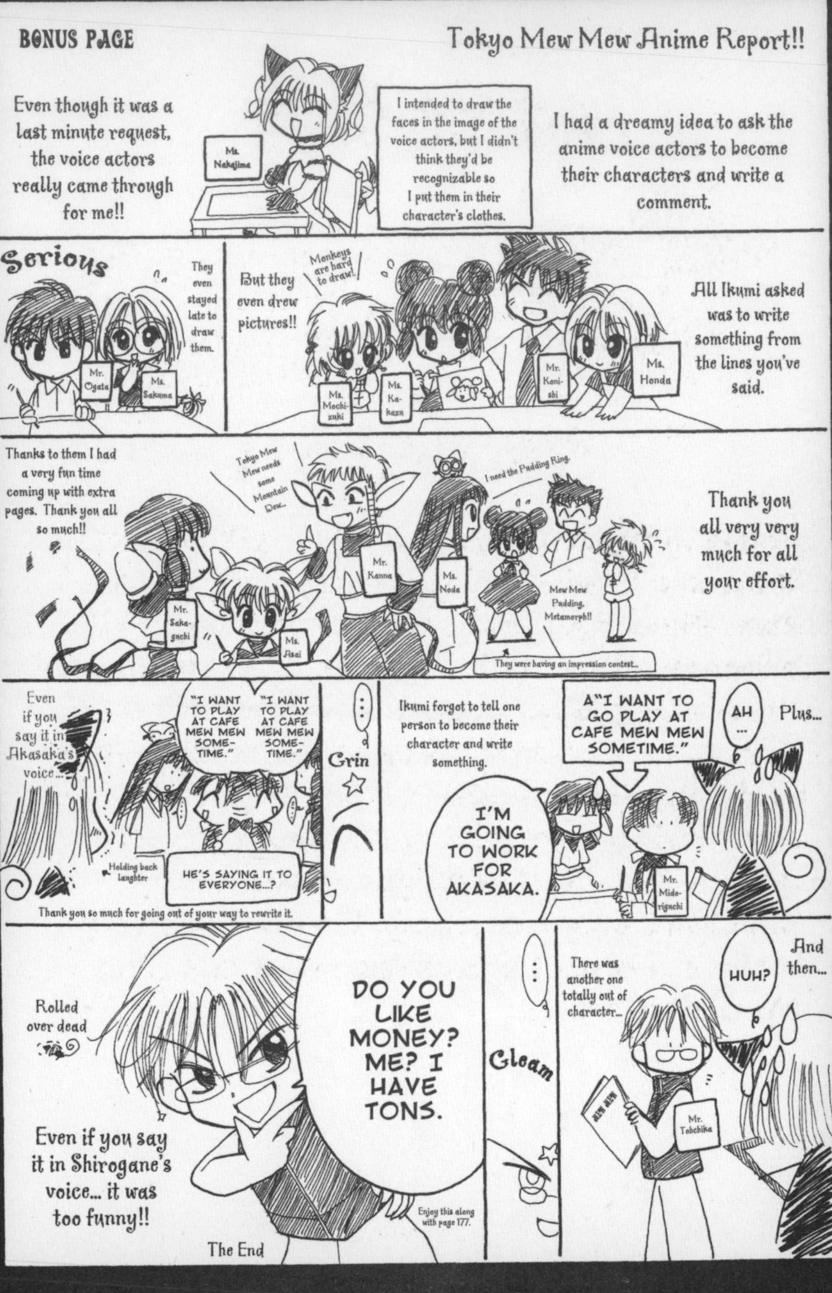
Tokyo Mew Mew Anime Report!!
BONUS PAGE
I had a dreamy idea to ask the anime voice actors to become their characters and write a comment.
I intended to draw the faces in the image of the voice actors, but I didn't think they'd be recognizable so I put them in their character's clothes.
Ms. Nakajima
Even though it was a last minute request, the voice actors really came through for me!!
All Ikumi asked was to write something from the lines you've said.
Ms. Honda
Mr. Konishi
Ms. Kakazu
Ms. Mochizuki
Monkeys are hard to draw!
But they even drew pictures!!
They even stayed late to draw them.
Ms. Sakuma
Mr. Ogata
Serious
Thank you all very very much for all your effort.
Mew Mew Pudding, Metamorph!!
I need the Pudding Ring.
Ms. Noda
Mr. Kanna
Tokyo Mew Mew needs some Mountain Dew...
Ms. Asai
Mr. Sakaguchi
Thanks to them I had a very fun time coming up with extra pages. Thank you all so much!!
They were having an impression contest...
Plus...
AH ...
A"I WANT TO GO PLAY AT CAFE MEW MEW SOMETIME."
Ikumi forgot to tell one person to become their character and write something.
I'M GOING TO WORK FOR AKASAKA.
Mr. Midoriguchi
...
Grin
"I WANT TO PLAY AT CAFE MEW MEW SOME-TIME."
"I WANT TO PLAY AT CAFE MEW MEW SOME-TIME."
Even if you say it in Akasaka's voice...
Holding back laughter
HE'S SAYING IT TO EVERYONE...?
Thank you so much for going out of your way to rewrite it.
And then...
HUH?
There was another one totally out of character...
Mr. Tohchika
...
Gleam
DO YOU LIKE MONEY? ME? I HAVE TONS.
Rolled over dead
Enjoy this along with page 177.
Even if you say it in Shirogane's voice... it was too funny!!
The End

COMING SOON...

VOLUME SIX

Those gorgeous, gutsy girls from Cafe Mew Mew are back--with a vengeance!! In Tokyo Mew Mew Volume 6, our headstrong heroines face their biggest challenges yet-- from Deep Blue, a dark and mysterious new force, to Kish and his creepy cronies, to a diabolical dome over all of Tokyo capable of destroying every living thing! With backstory galore, hilarious dialogue and a truly shocking surprise about Masaya, Ichigo's ultimate crush, this is the most exciting Mew Mew ever!!

Lizzie McGUiRE

CINE-MANGA™

TOKYOPOP®

EVERYONE'S FAVORITE TEENAGER NOW HAS HER OWN CINE-MANGA™!

GRAB YOUR FAVORITE SHOW AND GO!

TOKYOPOP

DISNEY'S
KIM POSSIBLE

©Disney

Disney's hottest animated series just got a
Cine-Manga™ makeover...

Available at your favorite book & comic stores now!

Watch it on
DISNEY CHANNEL
abc kids

Visit Kim every day at DisneyChannel.com

Y
YOUTH
AGE 7+

www.TOKYOPOP.com

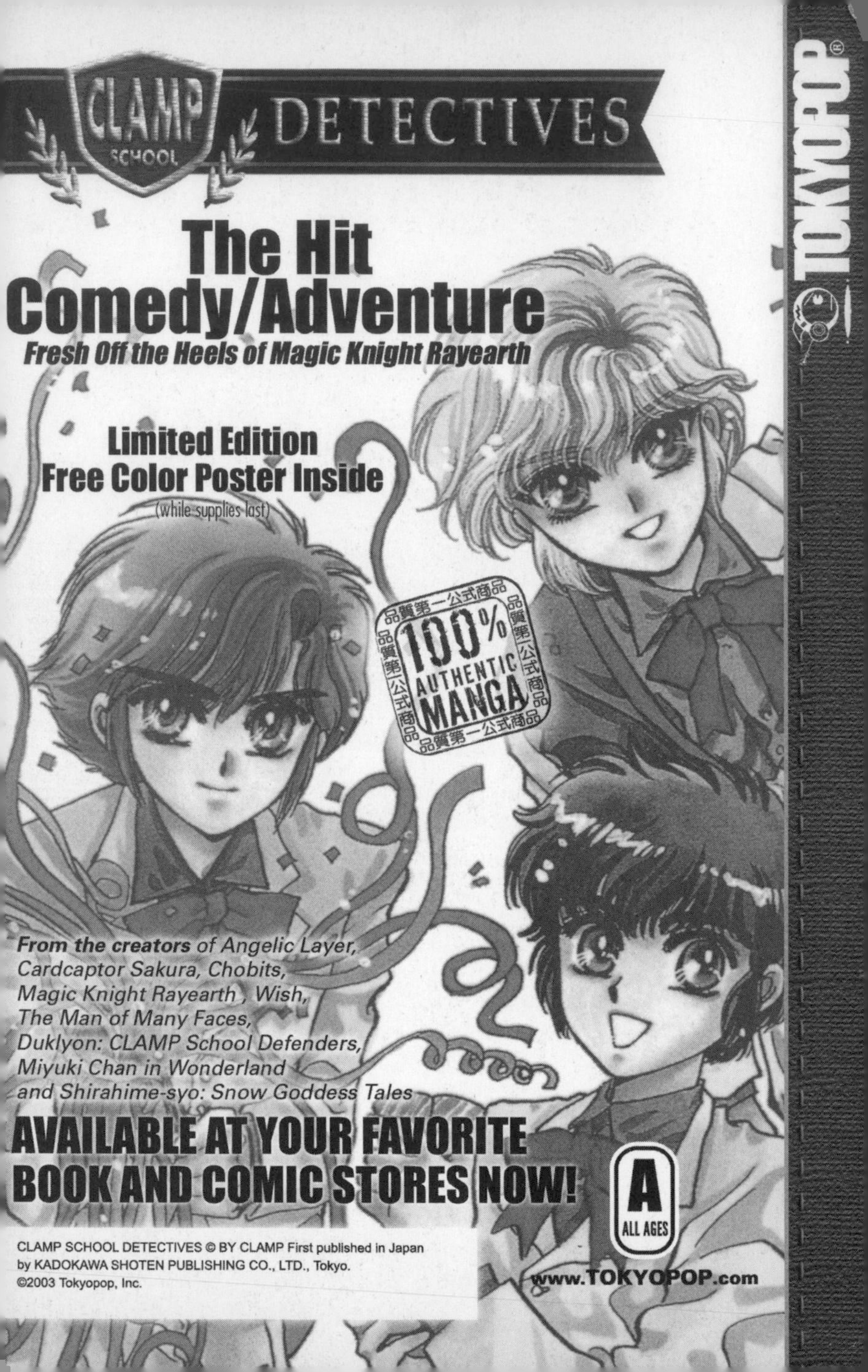
CLAMP SCHOOL DETECTIVES
The Hit Comedy/Adventure
Fresh Off the Heels of Magic Knight Rayearth
Limited Edition Free Color Poster Inside
(while supplies last)
品質第一公式商品
100% AUTHENTIC MANGA
From the creators of Angelic Layer, Cardcaptor Sakura, Chobits, Magic Knight Rayearth , Wish, The Man of Many Faces, Duklyon: CLAMP School Defenders, Miyuki Chan in Wonderland and Shirahime-syo: Snow Goddess Tales
AVAILABLE AT YOUR FAVORITE BOOK AND COMIC STORES NOW!
A ALL AGES
CLAMP SCHOOL DETECTIVES © BY CLAMP First published in Japan by KADOKAWA SHOTEN PUBLISHING CO., LTD., Tokyo.
©2003 Tokyopop, Inc.
www.TOKYOPOP.com
TOKYOPOP®
TOKYOPOP

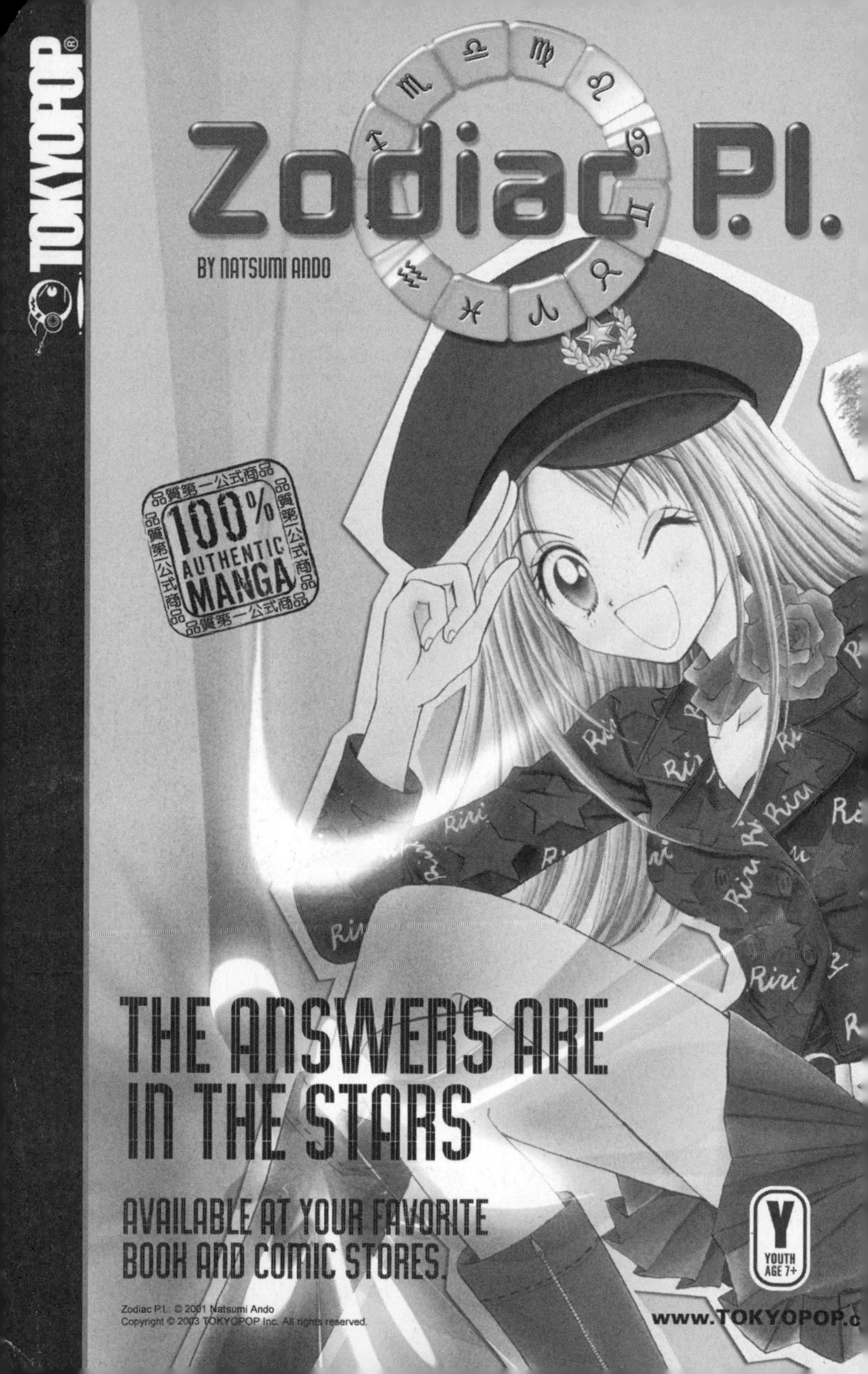
TOKYOPOP®
Zodiac P.I.
BY NATSUMI ANDO
品質第一公式商品
100% AUTHENTIC MANGA
THE ANSWERS ARE IN THE STARS
AVAILABLE AT YOUR FAVORITE BOOK AND COMIC STORES.
Y YOUTH AGE 7+
Zodiac P.I.: © 2001 Natsumi Ando
Copyright © 2003 TOKYOPOP Inc. All rights reserved.
www.TOKYOPOP.c

STOP!

This is the back of the book.
You wouldn't want to spoil a great ending!

This book is printed "manga-style," in the authentic Japanese right-to-left format. Since none of the artwork has been flipped or altered, readers get to experience the story just as the creator intended. You've been asking for it, so TOKYOPOP® delivered: authentic, hot-off-the-press, and far more fun!

DIRECTIONS

If this is your first time reading manga-style, here's a quick guide to help you understand how it works.

It's easy... just start in the top right panel and follow the numbers. Have fun, and look for more 100% authentic manga from TOKYOPOP®!